GILLINGHAM
THE MAKING OF A DORSET TOWN

'The Bridge at Gillingham', oil painting by John Constable (1776-1837), painted while staying in the town in 1823.
(Reproduced by courtesy of the Tate Gallery, London)

GILLINGHAM

the Making of a Dorset Town

JOHN PORTER

Best wishes to Mrs E. Pope,

John Porter

1.10.11

Gillingham Local History Society

First published in the United Kingdom in 2011 by Gillingham Local History Society, Gillingham Museum, Chantry Fields, Gillingham, Dorset SP8 4UA

Produced on behalf of the Society by the Hobnob Press, PO Box 1838, East Knoyle, Salisbury, SP3 6FA www.hobnobpress.co.uk

British Library Cataloguing in Publication Data
A catalogue record for this book is available from the British Library

ISBN 978-1-906978-13-6
Typeset in Minion Pro 12/16pt. Typesetting and origination by John Chandler
Printed and bound by CPI Group (UK) Ltd, Croydon, CR0 4YY

Jacket illustrations:
Front, see Fig. 36, page 139; Rear, see Colour plates 1 and 7

CONTENTS

(The colour plates will be found between pages 208 and 209)

FOREWORD

by Julian Richards

I N THESE DAYS of faceless developments, of High Streets that could, in the uniformity of their shops and facades, be almost anywhere, it is vitally important to celebrate differentness, what makes somewhere distinctive, the idea of 'a sense of place'. This is what this book does so well for Gillingham. It celebrates, in words and pictures, the making of a Dorset town from its earliest origins, through the 'quiet, pretty place' of 1906 to the town of today, massively expanded but still with an ancient heart. In doing this it celebrates those who shaped Gillingham's past, will intrigue those who live there today and will be a lasting legacy for those who are to come.

As an archaeologist I am familiar with Gillingham's origins. As an 'incomer' (having only been round for 25 years) I have seen massive change (some for the good) and can recognise in this book those things that are gone, but not forgotten. What has been such a pleasure has been to join up these two chronological extremes and explore, in the company of such a knowledgeable and enthusiastic historian, Gillingham's fascinating past.

It is fitting that this book is written by a Gillingham resident, under the banner of the Gillingham Local History Society (evidence if any were needed that a fascination with that 'sense of place' is alive and well in Britain today) and produced by a local press. Congratulations!

Julian Richards, Archaeologist
A hilltop town not far from Gillingham.
August 2011

PREFACE

FOR SEVERAL DECADES, the railway announcer has always been careful to remind us that the train departing from Waterloo is for 'Gillingham, Dorset'. The originator of this announcement might have had in mind that somewhere on the Dorset train were unsuspecting passengers who would really prefer to be travelling to Kent, and for whom the hard 'G' was an insufficient reminder that they were heading in the wrong direction.

The Dorset 'Gillingham' has always evoked mixed responses from its visitors. The reverse side of a Gillingham picture postcard sent from the Phoenix Hotel in 1906 reads 'Gillingham, is a nice, quiet, pretty place'. A writer on Dorset from around the same time could describe it as 'a bustling, thriving, rapidly improving place, with an increasing population and a future before it', adding that 'it is a remarkably healthy town, and the neighbourhood round about is picturesque to a high degree'. These sentiments were not shared by another writer of the same time, Sir Frederick Treves, who found the town uninteresting, and was dismayed by the many new red brick houses which had been springing up along its streets. Some seven decades later, Nikolaus Pevsner could be equally dismissive, affirming that 'for a small town, Gillingham is singularly devoid of architecture worth noticing', and that 'a perambulation need go no further than Queen Street, past the east wall of the churchyard'. It might seem surprising that Gillingham was never properly recognised as a town until very recent times, being for many decades the most populous parish of a rural district despite the numerous calls from its residents for official urban recognition.

The Gillingham story is more varied and interesting than its more dismissive observers might suggest. Before the arrival of the railway and the industries which followed in its wake, Gillingham had a long history as a royal manor and forest. Its well stocked deer park attracted the visits of medieval kings and queens, and for some decades in the thirteenth century the hunting lodge or palace of King's Court knew well the sounds of the hunting horn and of evenings spent in revelry. Venison from the forest graced the table of the Bishop of Salisbury, while its timbers were in demand for royal and religious houses as far away as Corfe Castle, Montacute, and Gloucester. In later centuries the countryside around Gillingham was divided up between the local gentry and their tenant farmers, the town itself becoming one of small traders, journeymen, and cottagers. This pattern of rural life might have continued for some several decades longer had it not been for the coming of the railway. In many places the arrival of the steam age produced some initial loud noises, sparks, and smoke, but otherwise did little to disrupt the gentle pace of life. In Gillingham, however, the railway had a more lasting impact, drastically changing the fortunes of the town and producing two generations of economic boom for those fortunate enough to take advantage of it. Little of this profit was seen by the many labourers who crowded into the town each morning to earn their living at the brick yard, the glue factory, or the many other trades and businesses, but Gillingham's industries were to define the character of the town well into the second half of the last century. It is only in the most recent decades that a new Gillingham has started to appear, and the older town has become less evident to its residents and visitors.

Given the many recent changes in the town, the start of the twenty-first century might seem to provide a good point to look back at how it came to be the town that it is. It was at the suggestion of Sam Woodcock, Chairman of the Gillingham Local History Society, that I began to write this book. It soon became a journey through

Gillingham's diverse past which involved meeting along the way many of the people who featured prominently in the Gillingham story, and a lot of wandering around the town to see the sites which they knew well, even if some of the buildings associated with these worthy townspeople are no more. From the outset it was decided that this should be the story of the town rather than of the smaller places which had been part of the parish or liberty in much earlier times. This meant excluding East and West Stour, Bourton, and Motcombe, although something is included about the latter in the earlier chapters, when it was part of the Forest of Gillingham. More is written about Milton on Stour, since its fortunes have always been closely linked with Gillingham, but these references are not intended to amount to a history of that village.

Building the narrative has meant regular trips to use the archives of the Dorset History Centre in Dorchester. Among the many records relating to Gillingham are the set of Gillingham manor court records, which with some gaps run in a sequence extending from the thirteenth century to 1934, perhaps the longest run of any manor court records in the country. However, the story would not be anything like as full without access to the many resources of the Gillingham Museum. The Museum's records, including transcriptions of early records and the collection of thousands of photographs, might be the envy of many larger towns. Throughout this project, the constant support and encouragement of the Museum, and of the Gillingham Local History Society, its committee, and members, has been vital to the book's completion.

I owe particular thanks to Sam Woodcock, Peter Crocker, and David Lloyd, who have spent many hours with me reading through early versions of chapters. The sharing of their collective understanding of the development of the town has proved invaluable. Others to whom I owe thanks for reading sections of the book, or making suggestions or information available, include Peter Barker,

Sam Braddick, Tony Coombes, Peter Cox, Mark Forrest, Bill Shreeves, and John Shephard. Further thanks are due to Andrew Jenkins and the governors of Gillingham School for making the school records available for study. Special thanks go to my wife, Margaret, for her long time spent reading my final versions, and her commitment to the finer points of grammar and punctuation. Any remaining errors, omissions, or oversights are entirely my own.

Acknowledgements are also due to the following for their permission to reproduce copyright material: to the Dorset History Centre for Figs. 16, 33, 35, 39, 61, and 102, and for colour plates 7, 10, 11, and 23; to Dorset County Council for Fig. 21; to the editors of the Proceedings of the Dorset Natural History and Archaeological Society for Figs. 12 and 14, which have been amended from the originals; to Peter Barker for Fig. 22; to the Governors of Gillingham School for Fig. 53; to the Salisbury and South Wiltshire Museum for Fig. 20; to David Lloyd for Fig. 115 and Plate 27; and to W.R. Lupton for Plate 18. Figures 3 and 18 are the work of Joan Haig. The many remaining historic views, some of which have not been published before, are from the collections of the Gillingham Museum, and include scenes which were contributed to the Museum by local families. I am especially grateful to Peter Crocker for his time spent in helping me to select the many older photographs. The remaining contemporary photographs are my own.

John Porter
May 2011

Dr. **John Porter** was a geography teacher before retiring to Dorset. He is a member of the Gillingham Local History Society and researches into the history of the Dorset area. He lectures for the WEA and is the author of *Discover Dorset: Towns*, published by Dovecote Press.

List of Text Figures and Colour Plates

List of Text Figures

List of Colour Plates

(between pages 208 and 209)

1

ORIGINS OF A DORSET TOWN

A NOTABLE FEATURE of the county map of Dorset is the bulge made by its far northern boundary where it meets the neighbouring counties of Somerset and Wiltshire. This northwards extension can almost give the impression of something added to the county as an afterthought, a rethinking of where the boundary with the neighbouring counties really ought to be. The shape can suggest an amendment to an original alignment which had been straighter, neater and tidier, but which ultimately had to be redrawn for reasons which are now lost. The bulge nevertheless coincides to some extent with the natural features of the countryside, since it takes in most of the upper courses of the River Stour and its tributaries, and is for the most part a low-lying area flanked by downs and low hills. Once enlarged by these headwaters, the Stour leaves the north of the county and continues its journey southwards, picking up further tributaries as it winds its way between the chalk hills of central Dorset towards the sea at Christchurch Harbour.

The three rivers

I N THIS NORTHERNMOST part of Dorset the Stour is joined by two main tributaries, the Shreen and the Lodden. The basin formed by the meeting of the these three rivers corresponds largely with the extent of the ancient parish of Gillingham and some of the villages closest to it. Until the nineteenth century the parish included East and West Stour, Milton, Motcombe, Bourton, and Enmore Green, an expanse of 15,886 acres or about 6,600 hectares. In much earlier centuries it may have been even larger (Fig. 1).

In and around Gillingham the three rivers cross the northern corner of the Vale of Blackmore, a mostly low-lying tract formed of Kimmeridge Clay, a stiff, wet clay notable in winter for its wet fields and muddy footpaths. In summer the surface dries after a few days of hot sun to a parched, cracked surface, but a day or two of heavy rain soon brings back the puddles. Names like Peacemarsh, Wyke Marsh, and Little Marsh, all now within Gillingham or close to it, recall that people once viewed these localities as places which never seemed to dry out. For many decades villagers could with justification complain about the depth of mud on the roads which prevented them from reaching the market at Shaftesbury. The potential of the three rivers to flood has meant that building development has largely avoided their flood plains, leaving the Stour and Shreen as green corridors through the more recently built housing areas. South of Gillingham the narrow channel of the Stour takes on a meandering, sinuous aspect as it wanders away from the town towards the villages of East and West Stour. Away from the streams the land rises to form higher ground, notably to the east of Gillingham where the breezy summit of Bowridge Hill affords fine views across the town and the village of Milton on Stour (Plate 1).

West of the town there is a more general rise in elevation as the clays of the Kimmeridge give way to the drier lands of the Corallian Beds, mostly of limestone but with some sands and clays, forming a plateau of low hills and ridges. Frequent copses and plantations break up the landscape of mainly pastoral fields bounded by thick hedges. Across its undulating surfaces, streams make deep incisions around Thorngrove and Langham. The western boundary of the old parish, part of it also forming the county boundary, is reached along the Corallian ridge above Cucklington, Buckhorn Weston, and Kington Magna – villages which seem to hang on to the side of the escarpment which affords striking views across the main part of the Blackmore Vale. Duncliffe Hill, south-east of the town, provides another high viewpoint from which a prospect of town and parish can be enjoyed as part of a longer view stretching to Alfred's Tower. Whitesheet Hill and the castle mound at Mere provide the viewing points from the north.

From these vantage points the town of centuries ago would have been difficult to distinguish among the many woods and copses, recognisable only from the position of its church tower. This was all to change once the brickworks and other industries came along and made Gillingham conspicuous as the workshop of north Dorset. Industrial growth turned it into the 'sprawling, uninteresting town with …many new red brick houses' observed in 1906 by Sir Frederick Treves in his *Highways and Byways of Dorset*. To Treves Gillingham was 'making haste to become an up-to-date town', but also finding things from its past which were 'hard to put away'. He was happy to dismiss Gillingham in three paragraphs, perhaps seeing it as a distinctly poor relative of its more scenic hilltop neighbour of Shaftesbury.[1] Since then further additions of housing and industries have confirmed Gillingham as being within, but not quite part of, the traditional image of rural Dorset; a growing space not easily missed when looked at from neighbouring viewpoints, but less well endowed than nearby towns with the sort of interest likely to attract the passing tourist.

For generations well into the twentieth century, town and surrounding countryside were closely entwined. Even when Victorian industries took over the town, its millers, blacksmiths, shoemakers, and solicitors alike looked for their livelihoods to the frequent appearance of farmer and labourer from Milton, East Stour, and Motcombe. The farmers in their turn looked to the grasses which turned the Blackmore Vale into a sea of green in summer, a place of which Thomas Hardy could write that 'the fields are never brown and the springs never dry.' Herds of dairy cattle produced milk to be turned into butter and cheese, a striking contrast to the flocks of sheep which populated the chalk downlands not far distant. The herds found their daily business among the mosaic of meadows and pastures

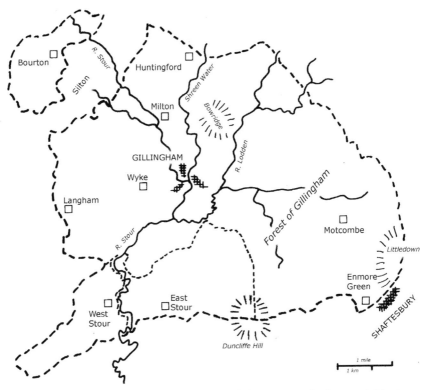

1 The historic parish of Gillingham, and the principal places within it. Bourton was a detached part of the parish. East and West Stour were within the parish but were never part of the medieval liberty of Gillingham. Silton was not part of the parish of Gillingham but may have been so in pre-Conquest times. Bourton, the Stours, and Silton are not dealt with in this book. Motcombe had become a separate parish by the nineteenth century. Enmore Green, now part of Shaftesbury, was originally within the Forest of Gillingham.

which were bounded by thick hawthorn and hazel hedges dotted with oaks and elms, sadly fewer today than even half a century ago.[2] To the farmer or dairyman watching the daily weather, observing the passage of the seasons, and concerned primarily with the birth and growth of animals and the price of milk, this landscape of hedges and fields might well have been there forever. Like the countryside, the streets of the town, with its houses, tradesmen, workshops, church, and inns, represented an unvarying fact of life.

Yet far from being fixed and unchangeable, the landscape around the meeting of the three rivers had been a product of centuries of change. The transformation of the oak woodlands into fields and farms had first begun in prehistoric times on the drier soils to the west of the Stour. The woodlands survived longest in the areas east of the Shreen which became the medieval forest, where the hand of crown administration could delay but not ultimately prevent the steady colonisation by farmers and cottagers. By the seventeenth century the landscape of fields and hedges was complete over most of the parish, the oak forests persisting only as scattered remnants or as isolated trees in hedges. Only in the north of the parish towards Mere were there tracts of open commons which resisted enclosure and cultivation until the nineteenth century. The town itself saw unexpected changes; a fire in 1694 swept away what was left of the medieval town, while the coming of the railway in 1859 brought with it even more far-reaching developments.

The first peoples

MAJOR STEPS IN the development of places can sometimes be revealed in unexpected ways. In 1912 excavations at Bay to produce a new swimming pool for the Grammar School revealed 10 feet below the surface a gravel bed with the remains of a structure of oak piles and beams. The nearby remains of occupation at the same depth included the skull of a red deer with signs of deliberate human damage, and flints with traces of human workmanship. The site was identified as a possible Neolithic dwelling dating from around 2,500 BC.[3] It may be giving a glimpse of the earliest known settled human occupation in the area, but we still have little idea of how widespread similar settlements may have been. In the Gillingham Museum is a Neolithic axe head, found during ploughing at Hunger Hill.

More striking evidence of early peoples in the area comes from excavation of a long burial mound at Slaughtergate or Longbury near the western end of Wavering Lane. This forms a prominent, elongated feature measured at 42 by 12 metres orientated east to west, and 2 metres high. It was opened in 1802 and 1855, when the remains of many human bodies were found. These were at first taken to be those of the Danes defeated and slaughtered at the nearby battle which is thought by some to give the place its name. A further excavation was carried out in 1951 by members of the Gillingham Local History Society. The site is now known to be a Neolithic long barrow, but possibly some of the skeletons may represent later, secondary burials. Barrows like this one are much more likely to be found on the chalk and limestone downs, but do occasionally occur at drier sites in lower areas. This one may be linked with the Neolithic enclosure of Whitesheet Hill overlooking Mere (Fig. 2).[4]

While sites and finds like these can be of some individual interest, they also reflect wider patterns of development and change. At this early period most settlement in Wessex was on the more open ground and drier soils of the chalk and limestone uplands, with areas like Cranborne Chase and the Mendips being intensively farmed. The clay vales, with their wet soils and dense oak forest, were less favoured, but settlement might occur on drier patches of ground. The Stour, which provided a corridor of penetration from Christchurch

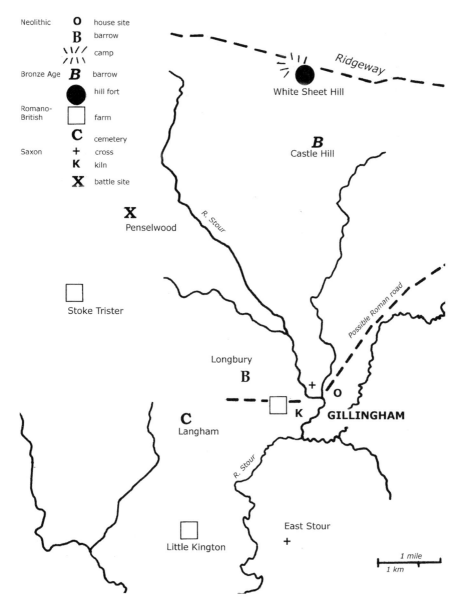

Neolithic — **O** house site
B barrow
\\\//// camp
/// \\\
Bronze Age **B** barrow
● hill fort
Romano-British — ☐ farm
C cemetery
Saxon — **+** cross
K kiln
X battle site

Ridgeway

\\\//
White Sheet Hill

B
Castle Hill

X
Penselwood

R. Stour

Possible Roman road

☐
Stoke Trister

Longbury
B

☐ +
K O
C GILLINGHAM
Langham

R. Stour

☐
Little Kington

East Stour
+

R. Stour

1 mile
1 km

2 The Gillingham area from prehistoric to Saxon times. The features on this map span many hundreds of years of history. The Roman road is a conjectural alignment only, and suggests a link between the Coldharbour site and the road from Bath to Badbury Rings

Harbour and the south coast through the forests towards the River Parrett and the Bristol Channel, was known to prehistoric traders, and some evidence of settlement might be expected along it. Some signs of early human presence around Gillingham are therefore not unlikely. At this time society was largely organised around the great causewayed enclosures or 'camps' which provided a ritual focus for the surrounding population. These had their origins around 4000 to 3000 BC, a time which saw a significant population growth and more sustained farming of large areas of Wessex. Each of these sites had its distinct 'territory' within which lay the many burial mounds or barrows with which it was linked. The Slaughtergate barrow is the only one to the south of the suggested territory of Whitesheet Hill, the others all lying on the chalklands to the north and east.[5]

There is little direct evidence in the immediate vicinity of Gillingham to remind us of the subsequent Bronze and earlier Iron Ages, a period of many hundreds of years which saw great technological and cultural change. However, much of the Dorset countryside not too far away, especially the chalkland areas of Wiltshire and eastern and central Dorset, was being heavily farmed. The growing body of archaeological work at places like Martins Down on Cranborne Chase has revealed a huge range of features including house sites, ditches, enclosures, field boundaries, barrows, and cemeteries. Closer to Gillingham, the chalk downland just to the north of Mere with its fertile light soils and abundant water supply from springs is known to be one of the most densely settled areas of prehistoric Europe. A group of round barrows dating from 2000 BC onwards has been identified on Long Hill, Mere, and there are many examples of small rectangular enclosures, field systems, and finds of domestic animal bones – all evidence of cultivation and stock farming. The east-west ridgeway across Mere Down was an important route for traders at this time, and from here there would have been ready access on to the Corallian ridge above Kington Magna, where substantial quantities of flints have been found dating from the Mesolithic to the Bronze Age (8500 to 850 BC).[6] Two miles north of Gillingham, recent cultivation of fields around Milton on Stour has been yielding up examples of worked flint tools from the same periods. As flint nodules do not naturally occur within the local geology, it can be suggested that they were brought into the area by settlers or traders from locations elsewhere. Recent excavations before the completion of the Waitrose site in Gillingham (below) has also produced examples of worked flints from Neolithic or Bronze times (4500 to 2500 BC). This variety of evidence points to a more intensive settlement of the area around Gillingham than might have been thought possible only a few years ago.

By the time of the late Iron Age on the eve of the Roman occupation, Wessex society had become organised into large tribal groups associated with the many hillforts of the region. The Gillingham area lay within the territory of the Durotriges, whose lands comprised the whole of Dorset, extending to the Wylye and Avon in Wiltshire and westwards to the Parrett in Somerset. The Durotriges were prolific hillfort builders, being responsible for more hillforts than any other tribal group in Iron Age Britain. The nearest hillforts to Gillingham were Cadbury Castle, Whitesheet Hill, Hod Hill, and Hambledon Hill. Ham Hill is a further probable site, but with much of the evidence of occupation quarried away long ago. Some forts like Hod Hill had many small round huts within the enclosure showing that they were intensively occupied, but also open spaces where people from the surrounding area may have come to find refuge in times of trouble. The Durotrigian countryside was a network of farms and villages, with people cultivating small rectangular fields and living in round, thatched huts, perhaps like the one recently reconstructed at Bradford Peverell in the south of Dorset.[7] Unfortunately, we can only speculate on what the Gillingham area was like at this time, and what use, if any, people made of the neighbouring hillforts.

The Romans

THE ROMAN CONQUEST of Britain began in AD 43, and it took several years before the Durotriges were finally subdued. Their stronghold of Hod Hill was itself fortified by the Romans for a time to prevent a revival of resistance. The final stand took place at South Cadbury in AD 60. Thereafter the military presence rapidly gave way to a civilian one. The Romanisation of the countryside took place only gradually, with Durotrigian farmers continuing to exist much as they had always done, living in their round thatched huts and cultivating their small fields. However during the centuries following the conquest, the population expanded rapidly and the countryside filled up with people. Everywhere across Dorset could be found Romano-British villas, farms, hamlets, and villages. There was more prosperity, with a wider range of crops being grown, and more refined types of pottery. In Dorset as elsewhere in Roman Britain, the population may have reached levels comparable to that of Tudor times, far greater than during the Durotrigian period.[8]

Towns and roads were important to economic and population growth, and to the adoption of a Romanised way of life. The Romano-British population of the north of Dorset, at some distance from the Roman roads and the towns of Ilchester and Dorchester, might therefore be expected to be sparse. However, in Gillingham Roman occupation debris from a site along Common Mead Lane had been known as early as 1869. A *Coldharbour* field name nearby, often associated with Roman sites and roads, also suggests a likely Roman presence. An investigation in 1951 produced second century Samian sherds, querns, and bones of domestic animals, suggesting a possible farm site. Further occupation material was found in 1974. By this time the imminent development of the site for housing made necessary a more thorough investigation.[9]

Excavation was subsequently carried out over a 6 hectare site on land now under the housing of Maple Way and adjoining residential roads. The enquiry showed the remains of several phases of building, including that of a large structure. The range of pottery, coins, and other artefacts indicated a building of agricultural use with occupation over a very long period. There was evidence of metal working although not of pottery making. A particularly striking find was a burial site with a skeleton at a little distance from the main building position, and partly covered by the remains of a modern building. Nearby pottery fragments showed the burial to be of Roman or post-Roman period date. All this was evidence for a Romano-British farm, but there were no tesserae (small tiles for mosaics) or indications of baths or other features to suggest a building of the status of a villa. The site appears to have been occupied during the Durotrigian period, possibly sometime between 50 BC and AD 50, and thereafter continuously from AD 75 into the fourth century. Unfortunately the very turn of events which initiated the excavation has ensured that the full significance of the Common Mead Lane site may now never be known.[10]   The *Coldharbour* name indicates that the farm or settlement would have been served by a local road or track linking it to a busier road, the nearest one being that between Badbury Rings and Bath. One suggested alignment for this is from Bay Farm south-westwards across Barnaby Mead, where Roman material has been found, and then north of the church towards Coldharbour, and Wyke.[11] The route would then follow Langham Lane in the direction of Ilchester.

The Gillingham farm site is not the only one to have been found in north Dorset in recent times. Following the discovery of the famous Hinton St Mary mosaic in 1963, other sites have come to light, each providing more evidence of the extent of Romano-British settlement. Investigation at Little Kington Farm, West Stour, in 1985 produced finds of Samian ware, pottery, tiles, and tesserae. The tiles suggested

3 Life inside a Roman house: detail from a display in the Gillingham Museum.

a possible hypocaust and mosaic flooring, features associated with a substantial building or villa. At Nyland in Kington Magna is another likely Roman site, possibly a small farm, dating from between the second and fourth centuries. Similar sites have been found at Stoke Trister and Wincanton.[12] Field walking in the Milton Down area near Milton on Stour has yielded a range of Roman coins, pins, roofing tiles, toilet implements, and brooches. These are of a type and value most likely to have been associated with persons of high social standing in Romano-British society, perhaps indicating that there was a farm or other building of some status in this area.[13] At all these sites the long period of continuous occupation suggests a stable countryside with an established society and prosperous farming well into the late Roman period (Fig. 3). It would not be surprising if other, similar sites in the Gillingham area came to light in the years ahead.

The Roman trackway from Coldharbour would have passed close to Langham. Here a very different sort of Roman find is recorded in the final edition (1868) of John Hutchins' history of the county. This reported the finding of a late Roman cemetery when limestone was being quarried, but neither the date of the discovery nor the exact location are known. Hutchins' account refers to unearthing a hundred skeletons, all regularly arranged, and all orientated east to west. An earlier edition of Hutchins had already pointed to similar burials in quarries at Marnhull and Todber, again laid in close ranks and with the heads of the second rank placed between the legs of the first, '... a clear proof of their having been regularly placed ... and not thrown in promiscuously'. Subsequent excavations at Marnhull produced even more late Roman burials; a skeleton from Todber is in the Gillingham Museum (Fig. 4). The east-west orientation of the bodies at Langham

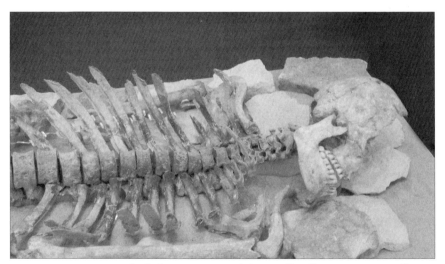

4 A Romano-British skeleton recovered from Allard's Quarry at Todber during an excavation conducted in 1967. The person reconstructed was around 40 years of age and showed some evidence of arthritis.

may show the gradual introduction of a Christian influence into a society which was still essentially pagan, with Christianity being one of several religions. It is also possible that some of these burials took place as late as the threshold of the Saxon conversion to Christianity, soon after which churchyards became the only acceptable place of burial.[14]

The Saxons

T HE FINAL DECADES of Roman rule in Wessex were characterised by the collapse of Romanised society and a reassertion of tribal rule. In Somerset, hillforts like South Cadbury were brought back into defensive use, suggesting a period of instability dominated by local warlords. It was not until the early seventh century that bands of Saxons first reached the north Dorset area. In 658 the Anglo-Saxon Chronicle tells us that the Saxons under Cenwalh won a great victory over the British at Penselwood, a few miles to the north of Gillingham. Penselwood is not far from the source of the Stour, and occupies a high, strategic point on the main watershed between the rivers flowing eastwards towards the Avon and those flowing west towards the Bristol Channel. This high belt of forested land, known later as 'Selwoodshire', had kept the Saxons out of the south-west of Britain for some years.[15]

We can assume that the Saxon occupation of the Gillingham area dates from around this time. The use they made of the British fields and farms is unlikely to be known, since we can only see the landscape of the Saxons from a later date when it had changed even further. At some time during these centuries a Saxon chief by the name of *Gylla* gave his name to a village or group of farms close to the meeting of the Stour, Shreen, and Lodden. Its name is not recorded until 1016, by which time it had become *Gillingaham*, the homestead or village (*ham*) of the followers (*ingas*) of Gylla. The spelling of the place name has seen some variations, *Gelingaham* or *Ingelingaham* being the version recorded in the Domesday Book.[16] The most likely place for the site of this settlement is around the area of the church, which appears to have occupied the same position since Saxon times. Here, between the meeting of the Stour and Shreen, on ground slightly above the river flood levels, people might have seen a cluster of huts or cottages. While this is recognisably the oldest part of the existing town, it has to be said that the detailed plan and layout of Gillingham remains shadowy until much later centuries.

Gylla's *ham* may have originally been one settlement among many in and around the Selwood area, but it eventually became the most important, giving its name to the 'hundred' or local administrative unit of Saxon times. Hundreds became formalised in the tenth century, their basis being the monthly meeting of men to dispense justice collectively, often relating to the pursuit of thieves and rounding up of stray cattle. The boundaries of hundreds continued to be used as a basis for local adminstration long after their main purpose had ceased, and were regularly shown on county maps up to the nineteenth century. These maps show that the Gillingham hundred, later renamed the Redlane hundred, extended southwards from Bourton as far as Stour Provost and Fifehead Magdalen. Within this area, Gillingham was by far the most important place mentioned in Domesday Book and the only one for which a church was recorded.

Gillingham was also taking shape in other ways. The settlement remained the property of the kings of Wessex and later of the English crown, and was never finally granted away from the monarchy until the seventeenth century. The establishment of Gillingham as a royal estate took place at a time when authorities and jurisdictions everywhere in Wessex were weakly defined. The shiring into Dorset, Wiltshire, and Somerset was barely recognisable, and royal estates were used as a way of extending monarchical control over areas with only nominal governance. It is noticeable that in Somerset most places which grew into early towns appear to have had a royal connection. Royal estates also provided convenient stopping-off points for courts which were largely itinerant, although there is no specific record of a Saxon king visiting Gillingham. The estate might have been expected to include a larger demesne farm where the king's bailiff would live, and which could be used as a royal lodging if needed. At a little later date, in February 1094, Archbishop Anselm is recorded as having met King William Rufus at *Ilingheham*, a meeting which may well have taken place at the royal manor.[17]

The vulnerability of the remoter parts of Wessex to outside assault, and the need for royal authority, was demonstrated in 878, when Alfred had to repulse a Danish incursion at Edington, in Wiltshire. Soon after this he embarked on a scheme of fortified towns for the kingdom, which included the creation of a new town at Shaftesbury, until then an isolated hilltop five miles east of Gillingham. Alongside the town he established the nunnery which was to become one of the wealthiest monasteries in the country. Both these foundations were to have consequences for Gillingham in the centuries to come. Over a century later the Danish threat came closer to Gillingham when the English had to fight off an assault by the Danish king Cnut, the Anglo-Saxon Chronicle telling us that 'Edmund … having taken possession of Wessex … soon after fought against the host at Penselwood, near Gillingham'.[18] Local tradition has it that the scene of the Danish defeat was Slaughtergate in Wyke, not far from the Longbury barrow, where some of the Danish dead are supposed to have been buried. However, *Slaughtergate* has been spelt down the centuries in different ways (eg *Slandergate*), making the correlation less likely.

The church also played a major role in the growth of Saxon Gillingham. The beginnings of Christianity in the area are marked by one of the least conspicuous of the church monuments. This is the base of a stone cross which rests on a window ledge towards the western end of the building. The fragment, of Portland stone, is an example of high quality Saxon carving, and had at various times been inserted in the former Victorian vicarage wall and used as a sun-dial in the garden of the earlier Tudor vicarage (Fig. 5). It is unlikely to have originated too far from the church, and most likely within the churchyard itself. A similar cross from East Stour is now in the British Museum. Its criss-cross interlace patterns are so like those of the Gillingham fragment that they may have both have come from the same hand or prepared template. There is a further Anglo-Saxon cross in the churchyard at Todber, but this is slightly later in date (10th to 11th century).[19]

5 The base of this stone cross can be found in St. Mary's church. It has a square-shaped socket hole which was intended to take the main part of the shaft, probably made of wood. The double-stranded interlaced work and cascading grape bunch pattern are examples of high quality Saxon carving.

All these examples of stone crosses speak of a well settled Saxon Christian community in and around the Gillingham area, perhaps as early as the eighth century. Worship may well have originated around these 'preaching crosses', with a permanent building coming later. A church was certainly in place by the time of Domesday Book (1086), where the church is shown in the possession of the abbey of St. Mary at Cranborne. This Benedictine abbey had itself been founded around 980, the church of Gillingham having been given to it by the Saxon named Hugh.

Soon afterwards William the Conqueror gave the Gillingham church to Shaftesbury Abbey in return for taking from the abbey a piece of land which it held at Kingston in Purbeck, and it was this land which the Conqueror used to build Corfe Castle. Gillingham then became a prebend of Shaftesbury Abbey, the abbey nominating a priest who would both serve the Gillingham parishioners and act as a chaplain in the abbey community.

Given the role of Gillingham as a hundredal and royal centre, its church would have served more than just the local community. Gillingham would have been a *minster* or 'mother' church with a wide territory or *parochia* extending across the entire hundred. Many of these churches are identifiable in Wessex by their 'minster' names, but there are others which were minsters despite not having this in their names. The importance of the church at Gillingham would have been enhanced by its location on the possible pre-existing Roman road through the town.[20] In later centuries several places within this early parish came to have churches of their own, but nevertheless remained part of the parish of Gillingham.

The royal and ecclesiastical importance of Gillingham has been underlined by archaeological work in recent years which has also shown something of the wider economic role of the Saxon settlement. In 1990-1 archaeological assessments were made in the area of Chantry Fields in relation to the proposed developments of the relief road (Le Neubourg Way) and the Waitrose supermarket (Fig. 6). The focus was a pattern of earthworks, the existence of which had been known for some time, and the subsequent excavations revealed these to be of a medieval site occupied at various times until the fourteenth century (see Chapter 2). However, the investigations also provided evidence of a much earlier phase of occupation in the form of fragments of stone and clay ovens used for grain drying. These were dated to the mid-Saxon period, around the seventh to early eighth centuries. There were also nearby quantities of iron slag, suggesting that the ovens may have been used for iron smelting.[21] The size and layout of the ovens indicates a use for the ovens that goes well beyond the needs of a farm or the small cluster of houses which at that time made up *Gylla's ham*, suggesting a wider commercial or manorial function. They may have been part of a wider trading system involving the importing of grain from elsewhere, using the local oak forests to provide the necessary fuel. Saxon occupation at Gillingham may have extended into other areas of the present town, recent archaeological evaluation suggesting the possibility of late Saxon occupation at Barnaby Mead on the opposite side of the town from Chantry Fields.[22] It may never be known what other Saxon remains lie beneath Gillingham's streets.

6 Archaeological excavations on Chantry Fields. Among the finds were the sites of clay ovens used between the seventh and early eighth centuries. The charcoal used came mainly from the oak of the surrounding forests; some of the samples recovered had a radiocarbon date of 640-680. The dominance of cereal grains among the carbonised seeds indicates that the most likely use of the ovens was for grain drying.

Domesday Book

W ITH THE NORMAN Conquest, Gillingham passed into a different system of landholding and government, one which depended more on written records and accounts, and has consequently left us more evidence of the condition of society and the nature of places. Domesday Book, the Conqueror's record of estates and their values, is for many places the earliest detailed indication of their size and status, or indeed of their existence. In Gillingham it is unable to give us a full picture of the state of the royal manor since its details are merged with those of the other royal estates at Dorchester and elsewhere, and cannot be recovered separately. However, we do learn that the group of estates as a whole was committed to providing enough food for the king and his household for one night, a common obligation on royal manors.[23]

Nevertheless there are details for those parts of Gillingham which had been granted away to other lords, and these are recorded individually. The largest was a separate manor held by the Norman Thurstan, son of Rolf, who also had manors in Gloucestershire, Somerset, and elsewhere, and may have been the standard-bearer at Hastings. His entry reads:

> Thurstan son of Rolf holds Gillingham from the King, and Bernard from him. Alwold held it before 1066. It paid tax for 3 ½ hides. Land for 4 ploughs. In lordship 2 ploughs; 8 slaves; 1 villager with 2 ploughs. Meadow 12 acres. The value was and is 60s.

His sub-tenant Bernard was probably Bernard Pancevault ('paunch face') who also held land from Thurstan in Somerset. Alwold was the Saxon thegn who had held the Gillingham manor at the time of

Edward the Confessor. The entry describes a sizeable estate valued for tax at 3 ½ hides, with arable lands for two plough teams worked by eight serfs or bondmen; the villager (or *villein*, of higher status than the serfs) worked two further ploughlands. The estate had maintained the same value that it had before the Conquest. Smaller estates were held by Edwin, Godric, Ulwin, and Edward the huntsman, described as *kings thegns*, probably meaning Saxons who had been allowed to retain their holdings in return for swearing fealty to the king or doing duties on the royal manor. These were valued for tax at a fraction of a hide, and each comprised half a ploughland (or land for three oxen in Edward's case). The recording of these separate estates shows some complexity of landholding on the Gillingham manor, while their identification with Saxon thegns indicates that they must have existed for many years before the Conquest. These smaller holdings are likely to be the forbears of freehold manors first recorded in the thirteenth century, including Madjeston, Wyke, and Langham.

Around Gillingham, the origins of several other villages, not part of the royal estate, are traceable through Domesday Book. Milton on Stour comprised two manors, one of which was held by the Norman, William de Falaise, and the other by the Saxon Gudmund, a king's thegn. William de Falaise also held Silton, a manor of eight hides. Wyndham, now a farm in Silton, was a manor of 2 hides. South of Gillingham the manor of *Stour* was held in two parts, recognisable as the later villages of East and West Stour. Kington Magna lay in three manors totalling 12 hides of taxable value, one of which was still in the hands of the king, while the others had been granted to Norman tenants. Buckhorn Weston and Fifehead Magdalen are other places recorded in Domesday Book which lay within the Gillingham hundred but no longer belonged to the king.

There are references in Domesday Book to the economic state of the countryside through the mentions of mills at Milton (two), Silton (three), East Stour (three), and Fifehead Magdalen. Mills could contribute significantly to the value of a manor. The mills at East Stour, which would have included the one at Stour Provost, contributed 30s out of the total manorial value of £10. The frequent mention of woods, estimated in *quarentens* or furlongs, is an indication of the still heavily forested nature of much of the countryside around the common fields which formed the agricultural holdings, but the sizes are not easy to interpret. For example, at Milton, the woods of William de Falaise are given as eight by two quarentens, but this may represent some estimate of the total amount of wood in his manor rather than some single woodland of a specific dimension.

While Gillingham may in total have been larger than some of its neighbouring settlements, it was not as large as other places soon to develop into towns. Stalbridge, a manor of the Bishop of Salisbury, had been valued in King Edward's time at 20 hides, and Sturminster Newton at 22 hides. Gillingham's bigger neighbour of Shaftesbury had paid geld or tax for 20 hides on the king's manor, which was only part of the town, the other part belonging to the abbess. At this time we can consider Gillingham to be little different from its neighbouring agricultural villages, a community of peasant farmers bound to the manor by obligations of labour and other services. It would be some centuries before it acquired some of the features which could identify it as a town.

2

GILLINGHAM AS A MEDIEVAL MANOR

E VERYWHERE IN ENGLAND the early Norman period brought new forms of government. The hundreds of Saxon times continued to be the formal units of administration, but became less important in real terms. Instead, power and government came to be increasingly centred on the manors or estates held by the king and his barons. We start to hear of the manor of Gillingham being described as a *liberty,* meaning that it was outside the normal jurisdiction of the county sheriff and subject instead to the direct authority of the king. The liberty remained the framework of administration in Gillingham throughout medieval times, eventually to be superseded by the parish, but it was still referred to on legal issues well into the nineteenth century. The eighteenth century historian, John Hutchins, used the liberty as the basis for organising his material on Gillingham in his monumental history of Dorset, and later editors continued to add more information to his existing structure. Gillingham is also sometimes described as a *peculiar,* an ecclesiastical equivalent of the liberty. The term often applied to places of royal status which were exempt from the normal jurisdiction of the bishop or archdeacon.[1]

Hutchins tells us that the Liberty of Gillingham lay in a number of divisions or *tithings*. The tithings were derived from the old Saxon hundred system, in which local communities were bound together for the maintenance of law and order. Each tithing was required to send its *tithingman*, an elected representative, to the manor court to present individuals who had offended against the customs of the manor. The largest of the Gillingham tithings was Gillingham Major, which was made up of the main settlement of Gillingham, including its extensive open fields, the greater part of the liberty east of the Shreen, and the smaller, outlying settlements of Bugley, Langham, and Huntingford (Fig. 7). The separate tithing of Gillingham Minor consisted entirely of the three freehold tenures of Wyke, Madjeston, and Ham, and had to send its own tithingman to the court. Bourton, Milton (which included Preston or Pierston), and Motcombe were the other tithings of the liberty. East and West Stour were never part of the liberty but were within the parish, while Silton was never part of the liberty or of the parish. One interesting consequence of this was that Bourton, although a tithing of Gillingham, was physically separated from it by the parish of Silton. It can be concluded that Silton may have belonged to the original hundred of Gillingham at one time, but by the Norman period, or even earlier, had become granted away and therefore severed from it, never becoming part of the liberty.

In addition to the tithing divisions, all the land east of the Shreen, extending to the Wiltshire boundary and almost as far as Shaftesbury, was from Norman times designated as the Forest of Gillingham. Although part of the liberty and manor, this area was subjected to additional laws and administration, and in the medieval centuries followed its own distinctive path of development. This included the development of Motcombe as a separate tithing, and eventually as a separate parish, within the Forest of Gillingham. The deer park and the royal lodge or palace of King's Court were other notable features of the medieval forest. The history and development of the Forest of Gillingham followed a separate but parallel path to that of the town, and is fully considered in Chapter 3.

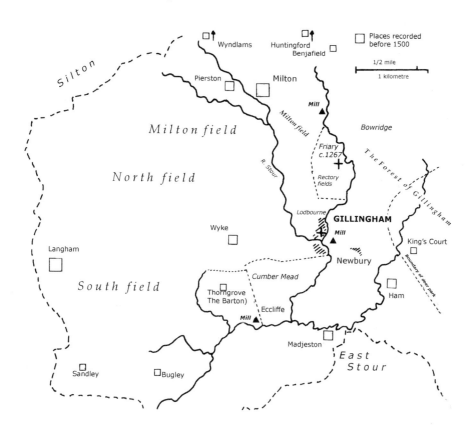

7 *Medieval Gillingham and surrounding parish, showing the common fields and places recorded before 1500. The boundaries of the common fields cannot be fixed with any certainty. Wyke, Madjeston, and Ham were freehold manors within the liberty of Gillingham.*

The manor, together with the forest, were from the thirteenth century regularly given by the king as a *jointure* (ie an income) to either the queen or the queen's mother. In 1261 Queen Eleanor of Castile, wife of Henry III, was granted 'the manor and town of Gillingham, with the hundred of the forest and other appurtenancies together with the advowsons of churches and all other benefices belonging thereto.' In 1299 Edward I granted Gillingham, amongst other lands, to his new wife Margaret, sister of the King of France. In 1318 Edward II gave it to his Queen, Isabella '... all of which the King granted … at the door of the church when he married her.' Henry VI (1422-61) settled it on his Queen Margaret of Anjou.[2] Later queens who possessed Gillingham included Katherine Howard, Catherine Parr, and James I's Anne of Denmark.

Shortly after Edward I came to the throne, he carried out an *Extent* or survey to determine the value of the Gillingham estate, by then in the hands of his mother, Queen Eleanor. This survey, of October 1274, gives a snapshot of the manor and its various sources of income.[3] The assessors noted first the 'well built' manor house or *berton* (barton), which would have been the home of the bailiff of the estate. The lands of the manor come next; firstly, the arable of 418 acres, which was used as a two-field system. Next were the areas of demesne meadow and pasture, used by the lord only for part of the year, and then opened to the tenants as a common pasture for the winter. There were four mills for the grinding of the tenants' corn. Further income came from the manor of Mere, whose tenants paid for using pasture within the manor of Gillingham.[4]

The survey then considered the manor's tenants. A small number were freeholders, holding their lands free of labour or feudal services. One named freeholder was Osbert Giffard, who held his three virgates of land by the rendering of a pair of iron spurs, a token gesture of feudal obligation. Most of the population of the manor were customary tenants or *sokemen,* a term rarely used in southern England, but meaning villeins of a higher status. They are described as 'holding divers tenements in divers ways', perhaps a reference to the shift away from the holding by labour services to the holding of tenures by rents and copy of court roll or copyhold. The survey also mentions some of the customary payments made by tenants, particularly *chirset* or church-scot, and *sheriff's aid*, which are described below. The value of newly-made *purprestures* or encroachments from the wasteland are also included, as were those of fines, heriots, pleas, and other dues deriving from the manorial court. There is a reference to the problems of collecting *tallage*, a tax which was levied from time to time at the king's will.

Some idea of the size of Gillingham at this time compared with other places not far away can be found through the records of the Lay Subsidy, a tax rendered in 1332. Only the better off freeholders and villeins paid the tax, and the number of exempted poor is unknown, but Gillingham had 63 taxpayers who paid £10 2s 8d. The two most heavily taxed dwellers paid 13s 2d and 10s 8d respectively, and several people paid only 2s or 3s, suggesting considerable differences in wealth. This compares with the larger centres of Sherborne (150 taxpayers) and Shaftesbury (109 taxpayers). Considerably smaller were Stalbridge (23), Silton (11), and Milton on Stour (10). At Milton the highest rated taxpayer was considerably wealthier than any of the other taxpayers.[5] Early fourteenth-century Gillingham therefore seems to have been a modest-sized agricultural manor of some importance to the surrounding villages. While it is convenient to refer to it in these pages as a town, since that is what it eventually became, it was notably smaller than Sherborne or Shaftesbury, which at this time were more recognisably urban in character.[6]

A manor customary and rent roll

T HE RIGHTS AND obligations of lord and tenants are explored more fully in the Manor Customary. The earliest known version of this is from the fourteenth century, and consists of a single, narrow, roll twelve feet in length. It was copied several times in later centuries. Well into the nineteenth century it could still be referred to on legal matters even though much of its everyday significance had by that time disappeared. This document may be unfamiliar to modern readers, but deals with matters which were commonplace to the tenants of medieval manors. Sections deal with the procedure for the surrender and regranting of copyhold tenements in the manor courts, and with the payment to the lord of the *heriot*, or gift paid to the lord by the tenant on taking up the tenement. This was required to be the tenant's best beast, excluding his horse or mare. There are references to the practice of *essoins*, the making of excuses for non-attendance at the manor courts; to the rights of *pannage*, or the grazing of pigs in the Forest of Gillingham; and to *brulocke*, the one brewing per year (at Christmas) which tenants were entitled to make free of toll. An important obligation was the requirement to use only the manorial mills for the grinding of corn, tenants being liable to punishment by fine if they took their corn elsewhere, for instance to a mill in a different manor which might be closer. An important manor official was the reeve, who was elected from amongst the tenants, and was answerable to the Queen's steward or bailiff. His tasks included organising the labour on the Queen's lands of the manor, keeping the accounts of the barton or demesne farm, making sure that the customs of the manor were observed by all the tenants, and collecting the rents and the fines imposed by the manor courts. In return he had perquisites which included the use of a horse and a cartload each of hay and wheat; he was also entitled to eat once annually in the barton at the Queen's table.[7]

On the reverse of the medieval version of the Customary is a list of the tenants of the manor, which presumably dates from around much the same time, around 1300. 220 people are listed as paying rent, some for tenements and virgates in the common fields, others for smaller pieces of land. There were 56 holders of virgates or parts of virgates, blocks of strips in the common field, usually of 30 to 40 acres. The holders of virgates were the better off farmers or villeins of the manor, and may also have included some of the craftsmen or tradesmen, and their rents can be assumed to include their houses. Their numbers correspond roughly with the number of eligible taxpayers of 1332. A further 115 people paid much smaller amounts for tenements, houses, and cottages without virgates or parts of virgates; these would be the larger, poorer section of the community who depended on the small pieces of ground around their cottages and the grazing of their animals on the common wastes and in the forest. Based on an average of four persons per household, this might indicate a population for the manor of around 700, which would include Bourton, Milton, and Motcombe, all part of the liberty. It must be emphasised that this can give only a very general indication of population size.

The rent roll of 1300 suggests a Gillingham medieval social pyramid. At the top were a small group of five free tenants, whose holdings were free of dues and services to the lord, apart from a nominal payment and attendance at the manorial courts. The wealthiest of these in terms of land was John of Mere. His three virgates, held by the rendering of a pair of spurs annually, might be identifiable with the holding of Osbert Gifford at the time of the 1274 Extent. John of Mere also held other lands in copyhold. He was a prominent inhabitant of Mere, and his name occurs in land transactions at this time in connection with Mere, Bourton, and Zeals. He also endowed the chantry in Mere church, and in 1330 was granted the castle at Mere, by then ruinous, together with its park and manor.[8] Another wealthy free tenant was John de Sandhull, who, together with his wife, Christina, held 80 acres in two tenements, as well as other, smaller pieces. 'Sandhull' is considered to be an early form of Sandley.[9] In 1332 he was wealthy enough to endow the chantry in St Mary's church in Gillingham, and also had land in Silton. In a royal manor like Gillingham, with no resident manorial lord, such people made up a 'village aristocracy', a knightly class with a material level well above that of the ordinary people.

Further down the social ladder were the many customary tenants or copyholders, so-called because their holdings were subject to the customs of the manor outlined above. Their lands were held by 'copy of court roll', meaning that their title to land was written on the records of the manor courts. The wealthier of these held a virgate in the common fields or a fraction (often a quarter) of a virgate, for which they paid a rent four times a year. A typical entry reads:

> Walter atte Moure [Walter at the Moor] holds a virgate of medium quality land according to custom aforesaid, and pays, yearly, 5 shillings at the four quarter-days; and for Church-scot 3½ pence or 3 hens and a cock to that value, for Sheriff's aid 7½ pence, for Peters penny ½ penny, and for Worksilver 22 pence at Michaelmas; and for an assart 1 penny at Michaelmas. He owes suit and service at the court.

Walter's land is described as 'medium quality', and his rent is half that of the higher quality land held by some of the other tenants.[10] Like all the holders of virgates and tenements, Walter pays in addition four customary dues. *Church scot* was payable by parishioners for the maintenance of the clergy; it was an ancient due established perhaps as early as 700, and was payable in money or in hens and cocks; in Gillingham a hen had a value of a penny and a cock half of that value. *Sheriff's aid* was paid towards the expenses of the sheriff in his administration of the county. In a royal liberty like Gillingham such impositions would be very much resented. *Peter's pence* was a tax levied for the maintenance of the cathedral church in Rome, and would have been equally unpopular. Walter's fourth due, *worksilver*, was one made by villeins who had once done customary work service but now paid for their land in rent. Its payment indicates that the manor was by now becoming an estate based on rented property rather than the rendering of labour services.[11] Another step in this direction was the permission in the Customary to tenants to 'freely demise their lands and tenements wholly or in part at rent' for a term extending to the lifetime of the tenant. This allowed tenants to sublet cottages and smaller pieces of land, and is reflected in the rent roll by tenants paying for more than one property. By the time of Charles I over three centuries later it is likely that the right to let had been extended for up to 99 years.[12]

Besides the rents paid for virgates and tenements, many tenants like Walter atte Moure paid further rents for assarts, enclosures taken out of the common lands and wastes. As population increased, the open fields became inadequate for the needs of the community, and tenants resorted to ploughing up woods and thickets beyond the limits of the virgate units. Assarts could be legally made under licence from the manor steward for a fine made in the manor court, but far more frequently they were unauthorised encroachments. At first, such encroachments might be pursued by heavy penalties, but eventually the queen and her stewards became content to accept fines and rents for the land so ploughed up; indeed such payments became recognised as an important source of Crown income. Many of the assarts appear to have been from the lands east of the Shreen subject to forest law, and the progress of assarting was an important contribution to the development of the forest (Chapter 3). Possession of assarts in the forest is indicated by the tenants being subject to 'suit and service at two courts', meaning the courts of the manor and also the additional courts which applied to the forest.

Some surnames appear several times in the rent roll, indicating households likely to be related to each other and forming strong family groups within the community. A family of some substance was the Hayms or Haimes, whose name appears also in other records. On the rent roll William Haym was a substantial villein who held a medium quality virgate as well as another tenement and various assarts. His son, Richard, held a further tenement, and further tenements were held by Simon, Michael, and John Haym. At the Extent of 1274, a William Haym had been a juror of the enquiry, and a Richard Haym had a large estate of 2½ virgates. In 1316 a William Haym gained the high office of Fee Forester of Gillingham Forest; and the John of

the rent roll may have been the John Haym who became Rector of
Sutton Waldron in 1326. The now disappeared Gillingham houses of
Haimes Place and East Haimes both bear the name. Although the
family tree linking these Hayms together can only be skeletal, there
can be no doubt that some villein families could nevertheless achieve
local positions of status and influence. In later centuries the Haimes
went on to become a prominent family in Shaftesbury .[13]

The manor courts

ALL HOLDERS OF tenements and virgates were obliged to give
'suit and service' to the courts of the manor, in other words
to attend them regularly. It was through these courts that
the workings of the manor were controlled and justice was dispensed,
with the tenants acting as the jury. This was based on the ancient
Saxon practice of each tithing being responsible for its own peace and
order. The rolls of the court provide a valuable record of conditions
on the manor, especially as they run continuously from 1291 to 1441
with only a few gaps and breaks, and the courts met several times a
year. During the period November 1296 to November 1297, the court
met ten times, at roughly four to six week intervals.[14] These meetings
are variously described as demesne courts, courts leet, or courts
barton, the latter name referring to the manor house or demesne farm
where the courts were held. The rolls record the business of the courts
in no particular order, but the content is roughly the same for each.
After the heading giving the date of the court, there is a list of *essoins*,
the means by which people excused themselves from attendance.
The cases follow and include pleas for debt and trespass, disputes
between tenants about land tenure, boundary disputes, or possession
of livestock (Fig. 8). At the court of 28 November 1296 we read of
John le Cheydnut's suit against one Walter le Pyres, who had evidently

come to one certain place within the Liberty of Gillingham called Holmershe and there seized one red ox [belonging to John] and unjustly drove the same ox from the said place to the park of Berton … the same John came and sought his ox peacefully, which he was not able to have …

However, this was not just a case of livestock stealing, as it might have first appeared. The ox had been taken by Walter with the authority of the constable or tithing-man in lieu of arrears of debt, and it was John who ended up being fined by the court. Sometimes tenants were sent away by the court and told to settle their dispute themselves, as in the case of

John de Mere and Johanna of Blakernestak who have had a day of reckoning come and confess themselves to be at one and the aforesaid Johanna is bound to the said John following the terms of their agreement I 4s 63/4d (sic) …

Often a 'love day' was assigned to the parties for this purpose, so that 'they may be at one before the next court.'

In other cases tenants were presented by the tithingman for breaking the customs of the manor. There were usually presentments for breaking the assize of bread and ale, mainly illegal brewing, and the same names often recur. On 26 March 1297 Robert Cole was presented for milling his corn at a different mill from that of the lord. Another common offence was allowing beasts to stray into the enclosure of the queen, which appears to have been a fenced-off pasture for the use of the demesne farm only. There are examples of disputes between tenants over fences, obstructions to the common way, and the diversion of water courses. We read of Richard Borgeys, who built on the land of Walter de Cruce, diverting the water course which formerly divided their properties, and taking over a piece of ground 18 by 6 feet. At the February court Roger de Swynheler was found to have raised a ditch to the damage of the royal highway, but he was allowed to keep it on condition that he pledged to maintain it.

A major function of the manor courts was to receive surrenders of copyhold lands and regrant them to others, as would happen when a tenant died or when one tenant agreed to sell land to another. The procedure for doing this was set out in detail in the Customary, so the references in the court rolls are brief. It was important to the new copyholder that this should be done properly, since the copy of the grant given to him was his only legal record of entitlement to his land. For example:

> William le Wyte surrenders into the hands of the lord king one parcel of land with a messuage which he held in Motcombe and which John Purdy receives and gives for having entry into the same 12d. Pledge Adam le Botine.

Other matters which came before the 1296-7 courts had a more criminal aspect. In December 1296 Thomas Brodmerton was hanged after burgling the house of Agnes Somerton and stealing linens and pelts; he had been apprehended following the raising of the 'hue and cry'. In March the tithingman of Gillingham was himself fined for failing to raise the hue and cry after thieves had entered the king's cattle shed at the barton and badly beaten one of the keepers. Giving lodging or sustenance to strangers or others of doubtful credentials always presented risks; in February 1297 a tenant was fined for 'harbouring certain merchants whom the town had prohibited'. The same court noted that 'Katharine Crawe, a felon, was harboured one night at the house of Mathilda de Bedales and another night at the house of Agnes Duddoc'; in this case it was once again the tithingman who was presented because he had failed to bring Crawe before the court. In another incident the suspicion of strangers may have been well justified:

8 A transcript of a Gillingham manor court roll of 1302-3. This page includes among other matters, an essoin (excuse for non-attendance), a fine paid for admission to a tenement, and an instance of trespass in the common fields.

Certain unknown robbers crossing through the middle of Gillingham on which the cry was raised by William, servant of John Cresselyn, because of suspicion, because they set off in flight and left behind one black hood price 2d, a shirt with belt 3d, a grey tunic 6d,a white collar 6d, 15 cloths of ribbed linen 15d, 3 pairs of new shoes 6d; having gone feloniously in search of them to house of Christine Paulyn in Silton, who can prove them to be her lawful chattels.

A later court roll from 1303 has the same mix of cases and business as the 1296 roll.[15] The roll records that the tithingman had to deal with the case of a troublesome dog:

that on Sunday next before Shrove Tuesday Richard Sweet's dog came in Henry de Bugley's croft, and there bit a lamb; and on Saturday morning next following the same dog came in another croft of the same Henry and there strangled another lamb, and he chased the said dog with hue and cry to Richard Sweet's house, who received the same dog back …

At this court there were fines paid for purprestures or encroachments, often of very small pieces of ground, but indicating the steady expansion of cultivated land at the expense of wastes and commons, such as

Walter of Wodeseynd …. Twelve pence for a perch and a half of purpresture opposite his door, paying rent one penny a year...

Geoffrey of Botine … four shillings that he may hold a perch called Schiremore for the whole term of five years paying yearly twenty shillings at Easter and Michaelmas …

The range of business of the courts was entirely that of an agricultural manor, with no references at this time to any of the features of a town, such as markets or visiting traders from outside the manor. While there are frequent references to pastures and animals, there are few to arable crops, suggesting that they played a lesser part in the economy, the common land consisting mainly of meadows and pastures. Although many places are mentioned in connection with the names of the tenants, such as 'John of Vynygge', a field name which occurs on a later map, the many changes to the names of fields and localities over the centuries make it difficult to trace where many of the places mentioned may have been. The manor of Gillingham had recognisable clusters of settlement at Gillingham itself, at Bourton, and at Milton, but the creation of assarts and encroachments meant that its many farms and cottages were by this time becoming dispersed over a much wider area.

The church

THE ONE PLACE which formed a focal point for the whole manor was the church of St Mary the Virgin. From the late eleventh century the church was held as a *prebend* of Shaftesbury Abbey, which meant that the abbey held the church and its lands in return for providing a priest or chaplain to minister to the population. In this way the abbey could provide for the needs of its tributary churches and outlying populations, while at the same time having a pool of priests available for larger abbey events. By the fourteenth century the prebend had become alienated to lay holders, and by Tudor times was held by Salisbury Cathedral, in whose hands it has remained until modern times. The prebend is sometimes described instead as a *rectory*, but this just seems to be an alternative name (Fig. 9).[16]

Possession of the rectory or prebend carried with it the valuable tithes on which the livelihood of the priest depended. In 1275 and

1276 Nicholas of Cranford, rector of Gillingham, found it necessary to petition the king in respect of the tithes of venison which he was accustomed to have from the Forest of Gillingham 'according to the apostolic instruction and exhortation' but which were no longer being paid to him. He also claimed tithes on the value of the hay, herbage, and pannage being sold from the forest; and further compensation for loss of tithes from the forest glade of Marley, which had been once used as arable land and therefore titheable, but was no longer used as such. The king ordered Guy of Taunton, the manor steward, to look into the matter, and especially to see if there might be a parcel of demesne land in the town which could be offered in exchange, but it is not known how the matter was resolved. In 1292 and 1341 the rectory and church were valued at £30.[17]

A monastic community appeared in Gillingham, but for how long is not known. We learn of this only because in December 1267 Henry III granted 12 oaks in Gillingham Forest to the Dominican

9 The Great Seal of Shaftesbury Abbey. The medieval church in Gillingham was tributary to the Abbey, which was the owner of lands and tithes in the parish.

friars to repair their friary. This is the only known reference to the Gillingham Dominicans or 'Blackfriars'. It gives no indication where their house might have been, but the 1624 Forest map marks a *Frayre* on land to the east of Peacemarsh and close to the west bank of the Shreen. The 1842 tithe map shows the surrounding fields with 'Friary' names, and there is a reference to a barton (farm) and barn. This evidence indicates a possible site in the present Highgrove and Claremont Avenue housing areas.[18]

Of more significance to Gillingham itself was the creation of the office of vicar in 1319, with William Clive of Motcombe as the first incumbent. The new priest was entitled to 'a house near the church of Gillingham, formerly belonging to the rector … the vicar of Gillingham should have the tithes of hay in the king's demesne meadows in the parish … the tithe of hay in all the vills of the parish, and all small tithes, and the tithes of churchscots, mortuaries, and the altarage.' The vicar was to provide all the books, vestments, ornaments, candles, and other lights needed at his own expense.[19] This followed the normal practice for the principal income from the tithes to go to the rector or prebend, the actual pastoral care being carried out by a vicar on a more lowly income. Nevertheless, the endowment of the vicarage is evidence of the advancing status of the church in Gillingham, consistent with a growing population and an increase in pastoral needs. Clive had a long incumbency which survived the Black Death, extending to 1361. From then until the time of Vicar Jesop in 1579 there were 17 vicars, the longest serving being Robert Symond (1386-1429).

The 1319 endowment also provided for houses for priests officiating in the chapels at Motcombe, East Stour, and West Stour. This is the earliest reference to places of worship at these villages, and is an indication that by this time the parish had become suitably populous to make separate chapels in its outlying parts worthwhile. East and West Stour were to remain as chapelries of Gillingham church for centuries to come, while Motcombe gradually developed as a separate parish, so that by the seventeenth century it was 'reputed as a chapel to the mother church of Gillingham two miles distant … [but had] … time out of mind, used all rights and customs belonging to a parish.' There was also a chapel at Milton, but in 1650 it was described as 'decayed and not used', and no further place of worship appeared in Milton until the nineteenth century.[20] For a time there was a chapel in the royal lodge at King's Court in the forest, but this went out of use when the lodge itself fell into ruin (Chapter 3).

The establishment of the vicarage took place at much the same time as the rebuilding of the church itself. Today the oldest part of the church is the chancel, the style of which dates from the Early Decorated period of 1270 to 1350. The chancel is the only surviving part of the wider rebuilding from this time, and is the oldest standing structure in the town (Plate 9). The church of the fourteenth century remained largely unaltered until 1838 apart from the raising of the tower in 1617, and is otherwise the building depicted in John Buckler's drawings from the earlier nineteenth century. As time went on, it gradually became too small to cope with the growing congregation, the majority of whom had to stand around the back and the sides. Even after the fourteenth century rebuild, the interior still retained the low arches and columns of Norman times.

A further significant development of the early fourteenth century was the establishment of a chantry chapel in the church. Chantries were a common feature of the period, being a space in the church set aside where masses could be sung for the soul of the donor of the chantry and his family. A chantry was often established by a knight or a wealthier townsperson or villager, who endowed it with land to maintain the chantry priest. The Gillingham chantry was known as 'The perpetual chantry at the altar of St. Katharine the Virgin, in the church of Gillingham.' This part of the church is still known as St Katharine's chapel. The donor was John of Sandhull or

10 Chantry Cottage is one of the few remaining thatched buildings close to the town centre. Before the Reformation it may have been the house lived in by the priest of St. Katherine's Chantry in Gillingham church. In later centuries Sherborne School held the manor courts for its Gillingham estate here.

Sandley, a freeholder of the manor. In 1330 he obtained a royal licence to alienate 2 messuages, 54 acres of land, 4 acres of meadow, and pasture for 6 oxen in Gillingham and Milton on Stour to a chaplain to celebrate divine service daily in St Mary's church for himself, John de Wyke and their ancestors and successors. A royal dedication was also included, in this case to the soul of Margaret, Edward I's second queen and widow (d.1318).[21] The land given for the maintenance of the priest in Gillingham was that later known as Chantry Fields, which prior to the endowment appears to have been a suburb of the town with houses (below). The endowment was considerably added to in 1399 by Sir John Bettesthorn of Chaddenwych (Charnage).[22] Documents of the eighteenth century show that the cottage now known as Chantry Cottage on the south side of Chantry Bridge was then known as the Chantry House, and is therefore likely to have originated as the house of the chantry priest (Fig. 10).

Town and fields

T HE LAYOUT AND appearance of the Gillingham described in its manorial documents can only be conjectural, as there is very little map evidence before 1820 and the rebuilding after the fires of 1694 and 1742 may have modified the earlier layout. The one structure which is known to have remained fixed in position throughout all these centuries is the parish church, which has always occupied the highest point of the medieval settlement above the terraces of the Stour and Shreen. Around the church lay the burial ground and glebe land, which initially extended across the entire space from St. Mary's Place to the Shreen, including the vicarage and its grounds. Other features which have persisted through the centuries are the two open spaces to the north and south, presumed to have been used as market areas (Fig.11). The former, St. Martin's Square, is named after a defunct chapel which once occupied it, and the name occurs frequently in the parish registers from the sixteenth century. The southern open space, always known as the 'Square', may once have been larger, the name Back Lane (now South Street) perhaps indicating some degree of infill of an originally larger square. The name Church Gate occurs in Tudor registers and must refer to access to the church from one of these squares. Since Gillingham never became a borough or is known to have had burgesses, there are no burgage plots to indicate the layout of the medieval settlement. However, on the west side of St. Martin's Square a number of small plots, possibly medieval, still face on to the square. On the opposite side extending up Queen Street, medieval house plots may have extended down to the River Shreen, but are now barely recognisable through later amalgamation and redevelopment.

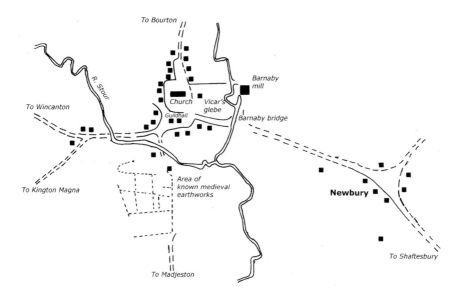

11 A possible layout of Gillingham around 1200-1350. The church and its glebe formed the central part of the town, with housing plots to the north and south, extending across the Stour into the 'Chantry' area. The depiction of buildings here is largely schematic.

From The Square, fords or bridges gave access across the Stour and Shreen to the surrounding fields and outlying parts of the parish. Northwards, a route lay across Peacemarsh towards Milton and Mere. Westwards, the route crossed the Shreen and then divided, one road going towards Bruton and Wincanton, the other across the Common Mead in the direction of Kington Magna and Sherborne. Southwards, the road lay towards East Stour. This route has now wholly vanished; it lay directly south from Chantry Bridge across the old common lands to reach East Stour by way of Witch Lane, one of several old routes around Gillingham erased by post-medieval change.[23]

All this suggests a village or small town which lay north of the Stour and west of the Shreen, but early Gillingham seems to have been more extensive. In 1275 and again in 1296 and frequently thereafter, we read of the name Newbury, meaning 'new manor house'. The name suggests a settlement of some size, and has always referred to the higher ground between the Shreen and the Lodden still known as Newbury today.[24] The map of the Forest of 1624 shows that by then Newbury was a populous locality of small tenements and cottages clustered around the lower end of Hardings Lane, a name which appears several times in the Tudor parish registers. Newbury lay within the Forest boundary, close to the town but not entirely part of it, almost a 'suburb' of medieval Gillingham. Newbury may have arisen as a 'planned' settlement, similar to many other new towns and planned urban areas which were coming into being around this time, or alternatively could represent piecemeal reclamation of waste land along the roadway through the Forest towards Shaftesbury.

It is to the south of the Stour that the most striking evidence has been found of the more widespread extent of medieval Gillingham. In the 1990s the town underwent several new developments, notably the construction of the relief road (Le Neubourg Way) and the Waitrose supermarket, later followed by an extension to its car park. These developments presented archaeological opportunities which otherwise would probably not have occurred, and resulted in a series of excavations undertaken between 1991 and 1999 (Fig. 12). These works indicated that, far from having always been the meadow and pasture fields of recent times, the area south of the Stour close to the relief road had been well used for settlement at different periods between Saxon times and the fourteenth century. The evidence for a Saxon grain drying establishment has already been described above (Chapter 1). On a further adjoining site close to the supermarket building, excavation revealed evidence of ditches, platforms for buildings, and enclosures consistent with settlement and agriculture, perhaps of a small farm complex, dating from between the twelfth and fourteenth centuries, when the site was abandoned.[25] A third site, the supermarket car park extension, had yet more to reveal. Here was found evidence of a large, substantial building, with features and remains suggesting that it could only have belonged to a person of some quality and wealth. A notable feature was the external garderobe, in itself a sign of a house belonging to someone of status. Types of glassware suggest that the occupier was someone who could afford the services of a physician. Demolition and abandonment appear to have taken place during the fourteenth century, with perhaps the stone being used at a later date for building elsewhere.[26]

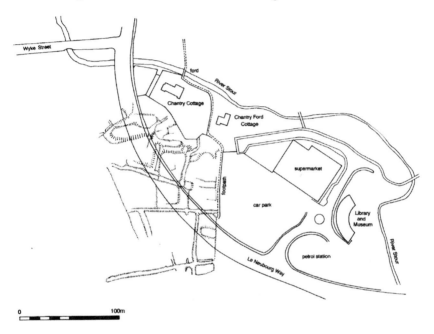

12 Chantry Fields, excavated in the 1990s at the time of the building of the by-pass and supermarket. The medieval earthworks, shown by the hatched lines, had suggested the existence of a former substantial settlement. Some of the excavation work can be seen in Figure 6.

Each of these investigations is only a snapshot of a wider picture, but taken together would seem to indicate that medieval Gillingham was larger and more extensive than is first apparent. The spread on to land south of the Stour might reflect sustained population growth around the town before the early fourteenth century. The sites all lie on land given by John de Sandhull to the church around 1330 for the maintenance of his chantry, described above. The size and quality of the stone house is in keeping with the wealth and influence of this personage. The chantry endowment might be seen as a possible reason for the eventual disappearance of the buildings, leading to the settlement reverting to pasture and meadow. However, not too many years ahead lay the Black Death, an equally if not more, valid cause of depopulation and abandonment in Gillingham, as many of its inhabitants were soon to discover.

A building of importance to all the inhabitants of the manor was the *Berthona* or Barton. This was the demesne farm, which also seems to have had a park or enclosure within which the queen's beasts were held. The Barton was also used for the holding of the manor courts, which are frequently referred to in the Customary as the 'courts barton'. It was in existence in 1274 and grew in importance during the fourteenth century, replacing the royal palace at King's Court in the Forest as the administrative centre for the manor and forest. The Barton, known in later centuries as the 'Queen's Farm' was at Thorngrove, adjoining Common Mead Lane (Figs. 13, 14). In 1608-9 it was described as part of the 'capital messuage or site of the manor', and the Tithe Map of 1841 still shows the 'barton' or 'burton' field names. In 1993 a ground survey at Thorngrove, now a care home and garden centre, revealed ditches and banks outlining a moated site of some 100m each way, large enough to enclose the manor house of medieval times.[27]

Substantial areas around the town belonged to the church, and were never part of the manor. The endowment of the prebend or rectory of the church comprised a large tract north of the town and west of the Shreen, still known in 1841 as 'The Rectory', and now occupied by Claremont Avenue and Gyllas Way area housing. It was this area that was also the site of the short-lived Dominican friary referred to earlier.

A large part of the manor to the west of the town comprised the common fields. The 1274 Extent describes the common fields as 418

Thorngrove or the Queen's House

13 Thorngrove in Victorian times

Thorngrove is a name first recorded in the thirteenth century, from which time it was the site of the *barton* or Queen's House. It was from here that the medieval manor of Gillingham was administered and the manorial courts held. The site occupies a strategic, elevated position, and traces of a possible moated site have been discovered here. In the nineteenth century the mansion was much rebuilt. Early in the twentieth century it was the home of Sir Harold Pelly, and subsequently became a billet for American soldiers, a children's home, and a care home.

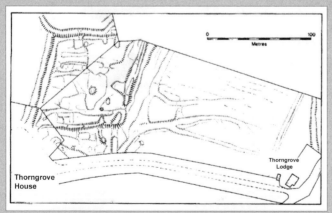

14 Ground survey plan of Thorngrove. The results suggested a possible moated site (left).

acres, farmed on a two-field system of which 'a moiety ought to be sown each year and the other moiety lies fallow, and then is common pasture of the men of the manor.' The detail given in the Elizabethan version of the Customary names adds up to a much smaller area of 82 acres and the fields are named as the North and South fields:

> And it is to be known, that whensoever the North field is common for all men accustomed, then may the same south field be aered (eared, ploughed) and sown; and whensoever this said South field is common, then the North field may be aered and sown.[28]

The location and extent of the two fields can only be known generally from the handful of identifiable field names, but the North Field seems to have been generally to the north of Langhams Lane stretching towards Longbury and Woodhouse Cross, bordering upon the common fields of Milton. The South Field lay south of this, extending towards Bugley.[29]

The 1274 Extent records 53 acres of demesne meadow, and also the pastures of Holmersh and Thorngrove. These belonged to the king in summer, but could be used by the tenants of the manor for pasturage in winter. The Elizabethan Customary similarly records these lands, in more detail. Between them they amounted to the lands later known as the Common Mead, an area shared by all the tenants of the manor, and particularly important to the poorer tenants with little land of their own who depended heavily on the common meadows for the pasturage of their animals. The name is still preserved in Common Mead Lane, from which the common grasslands extended southwards towards the Stour (Plate 2). It was the last area of common land in Gillingham to be enclosed (in 1812).

All tenants were obliged to have their corn ground at one of the manorial mills, of which there four. In 1274 one of these had been destroyed by floods, but all four are listed and named in the c1300 rent roll. These were the mills at Bourton, Prouet's farm, Barnaby's Mill (Gillingham), and Eccliffe Mill (Plate 3). The second named can only be Purn's Mill, which has also been known subsequently as Redlinge Mill and Parham's Mill.

Outlying farms and hamlets

OUTSIDE THE TOWN or main settlement of Gillingham lay a growing number of outlying farms or smaller settlements. Some of these had originated as early grants of land by the king, perhaps even before the time of Domesday Book (Chapter 1). The largest of these settlements was at Langham. Aerial photographs from the 1940s show the remains of enclosures and house sites close to Higher Langham Farm, suggesting that there may have been a small village or hamlet. The site is close to the large cemetery site mentioned in Chapter 1. The name first appears in records in 1156, but Langham was almost certainly one of the Gillingham estates mentioned but not named in Domesday Book, most likely that of Thurstan son of Rolf. In 1251 the estate passed to Osbert Gyfford and by 1318 was in the hands of the wealthy landholder, John of Mere, who was still holding it by a quarter of a knight's fee in 1347.[30] The two Langham farms are all that remains of the once larger settlement.

Other outlying settlements were Wyke, Madjeston, and Ham. Together these made up the 'free' tithing of Gillingham Minor, each place developing as a separate manor outside the manor of Gillingham. They could well be the three estates of the king's thegns in 1086, the privilege of sending their own tithingman to the hundred being a reward for service to the king. Wyke, often written *Weeke*, is first recorded in 1244, the name meaning 'dairy farm'. The original location and early history of Wyke is obscured by the later building

15 Madjeston, one of three settlements making up the 'free tithing' of Gillingham, in which lands were held free of manorial obligations.

of Wyke Hall and the surrounding park, and it is possible that neither the hall nor the older cottages of the Lydfords Lane area may represent the initial site. A Walter of Wyke was a juror at the 1275 Extent, and in 1328 Richard of Wyke held 2 messuages and 35 acres (about a virgate) of the king in chief. The oldest forms of Madjeston are *Malgereston* (1205) and *Magerston* (1256), which means 'farm belonging to Malger' (Fig. 15). In 1316 the manor was found to be held by a knight's fee, and in the fifteenth and sixteenth centuries was in the hands of the Servington family.[31] On the north side of Madjeston Bridge the later tithe map marks a 'Madjeston Green', and this may be a clue to the site of this now much shrunken medieval village.

The location of early Ham is far less certain. In 1158 lands at Ham were given to the priory at Montacute, but otherwise little about early Ham seems to be known, Hutchins referring to it as an ancient manor and describing its origins as obscure. The 1624 Forest map shows 'The Mannor of Ham' as two farms along the edge of the broad common way making up the Shaftesbury Road, an area known more properly as Ham Common. The name means 'enclosure or river meadow', suggesting a possible different location for the settlement. The Dorset topographer, Thomas Gerard, described the river Stour as passing between Bugley and Ham, indicating yet another possible location.

Other places which gradually appear in the medieval records are Huntingford, Sandley, and Bugley. Huntingford, first recorded in 1258, means 'hunter's ford'. It lies on the boundary of the Forest of Gillingham, and so the association with hunting is clear. Sandley appears on the rent roll of c1300 (Walter of Sandhull) and appears again in connection with John of Sandhull and the chantry endowment (c1330). Bugley is another early settlement, with several tenants on the rent roll being described as 'of Bugley'.[32] Other settlements and farms possibly in existence by this time include Culvers Farm, Benjafields, and Kingsmead.[33] The last named is no longer to be found.

Gillingham's origins as a royal manor tied to its adjoining forest meant that it was slow to share in the gradual acquisition of urban status which characterised some neighbouring places of similar size. It never acquired borough status nor was officially granted the holding of fairs or markets, although its status as a royal manor may have meant that a charter to hold markets was not essential. The existence of the two squares indicates that markets were sometimes held, but it is not known why there should be two squares nor how they were used. North of the town the open space of Lodbourne Green was used for fairs regularly in later centuries. Otherwise the population would have had to do their buying and selling at the neighbouring markets in Mere, Wincanton, Hindon, and particularly at Shaftesbury. In this respect the role of Shaftesbury Abbey may have been significant. The Abbey was a major landowner in north Dorset and the owner of successful markets less than five miles from Gillingham; and as the patron of the town's church it was in a strong position to influence developments in Gillingham and to suppress any competition which might arise from its lesser neighbour. Gillingham's quest for urban status was to re-emerge as an issue much later in its history.

3

THE MEDIEVAL FOREST OF
GILLINGHAM

I N 1300 A group of twenty jurors of the forest courts, chosen
by the Fee Forester of Gillingham Forest and his two verderers,
made a *perambulation* of the forest to establish its extent and its
boundaries. The perambulation was ordered by Edward I to determine
how far his rights extended and which places were or were not subject
to the royal forest courts. As with many royal surveys of the time, a
principal motive was to maximise the fees and incomes due to the
crown, for example by looking into uncollected fines, or rights being
exercised for which no legal entitlement could be produced. There is
an earlier account of a perambulation in the time of Henry III which
was found inside the *Book of Cerne*, an ancient collection of Latin
gospels thought to have belonged to Cerne Abbey. A similar exercise
was carried out in 1568 at the behest of Elizabeth I. Although some
different boundary marks are used in these surveys, the boundaries
established were for all intents and purposes identical, and are the
ones shown on the map of the Forest.[1]

Although the names of many of the landmarks described in
the perambulation are no longer used, the forest boundary itself can
be readily traced. Beginning at Barnaby's Bridge on the Shreen, now

the Town Bridge, the forest boundary followed the Shreen (or 'Mere Water') to Huntingford, where it then turned east to join the county boundary between Dorset and Wiltshire. This took the boundary past Pimperleaze and Cowridge to Kingsettle, where the forest met the lands of the Abbess of Wilton; the forest boundary then ran southwards, where it met the lands of the Abbess of Shaftesbury (the 'Abbess of St. Edward') at the foot of the hill on which the town of Shaftesbury stands. From here the boundary ran westwards to the top of Duncliffe Hill. Turning north, the boundary followed the Fernbrook (or 'water of Sete') into the Lodden, and hence to its confluence with the Stour. From here it once again turned north to Barnaby's Bridge.[2]

The potential for forest creation had been the main reason for the establishment of a royal manor at Gillingham. In medieval England great areas of woodland and wastes covering a substantial part of the kingdom were set aside by decree as royal forest. In these areas the customary rights of the inhabitants were severely restricted, and the forest law was directed entirely towards protecting the wild beasts, so that they might be found in abundance for the king's

16 A sketch of a huntsman and hounds chasing a hare. From a document in the Dorset History Centre.

hunting (Fig. 16). Such tracts were not only areas of trees and woods, but could also include moors, heaths, and wetlands. The creation of forests accelerated in Norman times until the declaration of new ones was eventually prohibited by Magna Carta. In these areas the Forest Law did not supersede the Common Law, but supplemented it by creating new offences, particularly in relation to wild beasts and the vegetation which formed their habitats. In the early Norman period the law was especially harsh and oppressive.

The Forest of Gillingham was one of several forests across Dorset and Somerset which in early times had been part of a greater forest of 'Selwoodshire', a large tract which had straddled the watersheds between the Avon, Parrett, and Stour. Thomas Gerard, the seventeenth-century topographer, described Gillingham as 'heretofore part of Selwood forest, only distinguished by names'.[3] Other forests in the region in early medieval times were the Forest of Selwood proper, which lay between Penselwood and Frome; the Forest of Blackmore, which had once covered the whole of the Blackmore Vale; the Grovelly Forest, north-west of Wilton; and the even greater Cranborne Chase, which in itself covered a quarter of Dorset. Around Gillingham, the attention of the Saxon kings would have been attracted by the extensive tract of heavy clay mostly east of the Stour and Shreen, with its oak forest cover and abundance of beasts of the chase. In the reign of Henry II the zealous Chief Forester, Alan de Nevill, succeeded in extending the boundaries of Gillingham Forest southwards, so that it included Stour Provost, Todber, and Marnhull, almost reaching Sturminster Newton. In 1217 the Forest was cut back to the boundaries noted above, but for some time afterwards this did not prevent the queen's tenants from claiming rights of pasturage in Stour Provost, on the grounds that it had once been part of the Forest of Gillingham.[4]

The forest was within the liberty of Gillingham and a part of the manor, but with something of a separate status and administration.

Its extent and general features are to be seen on a map produced several centuries later, in 1624, at the time of disafforestation (Plate 7 and Chapter 5). This *Plott of the whole extent of the Forrest of Gillingham* was drawn when much of the forest had been enclosed, but many of the features of its earlier period are still to be found on the map. The Tudor traveller, John Leland, had estimated the forest as 'four miles in length, and a mile or thereaboute in breadth', but in modern miles it is considerably larger. The greater part lay on the damp, undulating surfaces of the Kimmeridge Clay, where the oak woodland was at its most dense, but towards the east the forest rose on to the higher, drier grounds of the Greensand around Kingsettle. In time, royal activity became limited to the central areas of the forest and the area around the royal palace at King's Court, while the outer parts of the Forest, especially around Motcombe, Enmore Green, and Ham, were gradually subjected to *assarting* (woodland clearances for farming) and settlement by the tenants of Gillingham manor and other neighbouring manors.[5]

Gillingham was clearly popular with twelfth century monarchs. This was a time when the court was itinerant, often on the move between towns and manors, stopping to hear petitions, dispense royal justice, or deal with matters of state. A comfortable lodge or palace, in the middle of fine hunting grounds, provided kings with a welcome break from frequent journeying. The venues chosen had to be large enough to accommodate additional members of the royal family, together with the entourage of ministers and servants. Henry I visited Gillingham in 1132, and his charter to Lincoln Cathedral from here bears the words 'Witness the King at Gillingham'. The frequent visits of Henry II are recorded in the Pipe Rolls. The Sheriff of Dorset and Somerset's account for 1155 refers to the cost of livery for the king's house at Gillingham, suggesting that the servants were uniformed, as might befit a royal household. Gillingham and its Forest were especially popular with John, who also had lodges in Dorset at Corfe,

Cranborne, and Bere. He visited it every year between 1204 and 1214, sometimes three times a year. The Pipe Roll for 1204 has items 'for the expenses of the King hunting at Gillingham, and for a feast to the poor at the King's first entrance into Gillingham, and for necessary expenses made by Ralph, the park keeper, and his associates, with the king's hawks, horses, and his pages ... £7 3s 6d.'[6] In 1213 he stayed for the entire period from 15 March to 8 July, and again from 10 July to 8 August. His interest in Gillingham was continued by his son Henry III, who expended considerable effort and funds in improving the royal house. During these visits protracted feasting and entertainment could be expected, as evidenced in the many orders to provide meat and drink for the king's table.[7]

The king and his party might be present for only a few days or weeks per year, but for the rest of the year the forest had to be managed as any other estate. Responsibility for this lay with the Chief or Fee Forester, an office which was granted to a person of some status and was hereditary. The Fee Forester's official reward for the post was a virgate of land in the manor, but in his position it was not difficult to add various perquisites which he could regard as his rights. A check on such irregularities was provided by the courts of the itinerant Justices of the Forest, who enquired into the maintenance of the forest laws and the extent to which forest officers might be abusing their privileges. In the twelfth century the office was held by the Nevills, who often tried to restrict the privileges of the men of Gillingham in the Forest to their own benefit. In 1246-7 the court for the Dorset forests found that John Joce, the Fee Forester of Gillingham, besides claiming the allotted virgate, also claimed common pasture in the forest for his animals without limit, as well as *husbote* and *heybote* (timber for the repair of houses and fences). When a later John Joce died in 1311, it was found that the entitlements of the Forester had notably increased, for he held a capital messuage (large house), 3 virgates of land, 4 acres of meadow, the rents of 4 tenants, rights to windfall wood, rights of pasture for his swine and cattle, and 'the left shoulder of every deer taken in the forest and park.' By this date the office had been held by the Joces for at least four generations. The Joce family found itself in dispute with the dowager Queen Margaret, the outcome of which was that in 1316 the office passed to the Haym or Hame family, who held it until 1401.[8]

Subordinate to the Fee Forester were wardens responsible for particular areas of the forest, the day-to-day work being done by lesser foresters or keepers. Forest laws were imposed through a system of courts, the highest of which was the Forest Eyre held by the itinerant forest justices, but this would only deal with the more major cases. Most forest law was dispensed through *attachment* courts which dealt with all offences against the *vert* (green wood) and *venison* (deer and other game), and usually punished offenders by fines. Such courts could be attended and scrutinised by the *verderers* appointed by the sheriff. In 1236 such a commission of verderers and twelve knights was appointed to view and report on the condition of the vert and venison.[9] Another court held regularly was the *swanimote*, to arrange the pasturage of pigs on the king's acorns (*pannage*) and the fees to be paid by forest tenants for the privilege. The law required the attachment court to be held every six weeks and the swanimote three times a year. It is likely that in practice the attachment and swanimote courts were held together as one session.

The forest laws were at their most severe between the time of Cnut and Henry III. At this time the penalties were graduated according to the social position of the offender; a freeman was fined 10s if he harried a deer, whereas a villein could lose his life for the same offence. The Forest Charter of Henry III in 1217 moderated the harshness of the laws, so that no man could lose his life for taking venison, heavy fines being substituted. However, one restriction consistently applied was the expediation or *lawing* or *hambling* of dogs, which meant cutting off the front claws of the dog's forefeet so that they could not harry the deer. In 1250 it was ordered that the hambling of dogs in the Forest by the men of Gillingham should be postponed until after Michaelmas, presumably on account of the unnecessary hardship this was causing to the local inhabitants.[10]

Park and Palace

WITH TIME THE Forest of Gillingham became divided into separate areas so that its game and timber reserves could be properly managed (Fig. 17). The most important of these divisions was the deer park, which occupied some 760 acres enclosed within a perimeter fence of a ditch and bank. Deer parks were a frequent feature of the medieval landscape in forests and chases; they provided an area where the deer could be bred and looked after, safe from the depredations of thieves and poachers. High banks and a ditch ensured that the deer park was separate from the rest of the forest, access being only through clearly marked gates and stiles, the height of the bank being enhanced with stakes or pales. While some hunting might take place within the park perimeter, the deer could be released into the surrounding forest for a more protracted chase. Gaps or 'deer leaps' in the boundary allowed the deer free ingress and exit. Maintenance of the ditches, banks, and gates was considered by medieval lords as of considerable importance, often being achieved only at some cost, particularly with the constant renewal of the palings.

There is no known date for the creation of a park at Gillingham, the earliest reference being in 1204 to a park keeper who was responsible for the king's feast, and for supplying pages, hawks, and horses. The outline of the park enclosure is well preserved in the existing pattern of field boundaries, mostly east of the Lodden and occupying much of the countryside between Gillingham and Motcombe. Preservation of

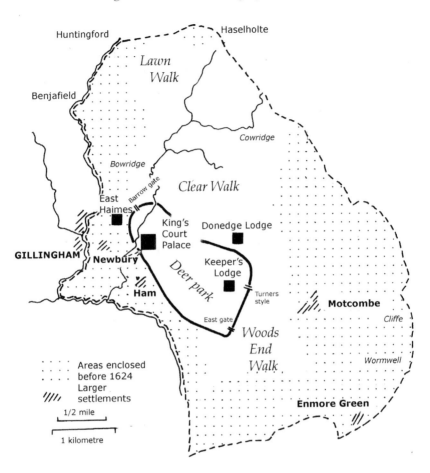

17 The Forest of Gillingham in medieval times and later. The Forest at this time included the whole of Motcombe and extended to Enmore Green at the foot of the hill on which Shaftesbury stands. The enclosed areas are those shown on the 'plott' of 1624.

the actual bank itself is more limited. There is a short length of bank about 2 feet high and 20 feet wide not far from Woodwater Farm near the old Barrow Gate on the northern side of the park, but the best preserved section is a length of some 1½ miles on the eastern side of the park between Donedge Lodge Farm and Waterloo Farm (Plate 4). There were entrances to the park at Barrow Gate, at the King's Court palace to the south (West Gate), and at Turners Style and an East Gate on the eastern boundary. Outside the park other large parts of the forest were divided into 'walks' or areas of woodland grazings. These were the Lawn Walk and Clear Walk, both north of the park, and the Woods End Walk, to the east towards Motcombe (Plate 5). These were the areas most drawn upon when timbers were needed, and the 1624 map or 'plott' of the forest marks them as being still heavily wooded. A royal enclosure or pasture frequently mentioned in records is Merley or Marley, but the location of this is now lost. The same map also marks a 'keeper's lodge' and another structure, possibly also a keeper's house, within the park. There was a further lodge, Donedge Lodge, outside the park boundary. Initially the walks would have covered a bigger area, but assarting and encroachment around the edges of the forest steadily reduced them to the extent shown in 1624.[11]

The most important structure and feature of the park was the royal palace or lodge, used principally for the pleasure of the king during his visits. The site has always been known as 'King's Court' and is so marked on the 1624 map. This was a quite separate location from the barton or 'queen's house' of the manor, which became more significant once the use of the King's Court palace declined. The earliest reference to the 'king's house' is of 1155, and the present-day site of the former residence suggests little of its previous significance. All that can be seen today is a rectangular outline measuring some 90 by 50 metres, surrounded by a bank up to 15 metres wide and a metre high. Outside the bank is a ditch, up to 18 metres wide and over a metre deep, which has a further bank on its southern and western sides (Fig. 18). These are the remains of a former moat. The entrance was in the south-western corner, over a bridge across the moat to a gate-tower on the inner bank. The reconstruction suggests that within this area there was an inner enclosure which contained the house itself and the other principal buildings. Other buildings, perhaps those used in connection with the park and forest, occupied the space between the inner enclosure and the outer boundary.[12]

18 A reconstruction in Gillingham Museum of the royal hunting lodge at King's Court, about 1250. The outlines of the boundaries and the entrance are still to be seen. The principal building was the Great Hall, used frequently by John and Henry III to entertain their guests.

The appearance and layout of the house itself can only be conjectural, even though there is some specific detail in relation to the building alterations. The high costs of building and alterations (£349 spent by John, and perhaps another £500 by Henry III), suggests that the main buildings were built of stone, most likely of Greensand, which would have been brought from some distance. The principal building on the site was the Great Hall. This may have been a typical aisled hall of the period, with the king's table at one end and a central fireplace with a hole in the roof to let out the smoke. Beyond the king's end of the hall there would have been the private apartments. Another of John's lodges at Clarendon, near Salisbury, followed this layout. However, John's halls at Corfe and Cranborne, built around the same time, were first floor halls entered by a flight of steps, with an undercroft or cellar below for storage of wine and provisions, and it is possible that King's Court may have been of this type. The building eventually contained chambers for both king and queen, and a chapel. In 1239 a chaplain was appointed 'for the king's chapel at Gillingham' at a salary of 50s per year.[13]

The development of King's Court can be followed through the various references to building works and alterations which occur in the royal records. In 1199 John ordered three lime kilns to be built, clearly expecting to carry out major building work, and in 1209 he held a feast to celebrate the completion of extensions to his house at Gillingham.[14] In 1228 it was ordered that £8 should be spent on repairing the king's houses at Gillingham, Powerstock, and Feckenham (Gloucestershire), and in 1233 the king's houses in Gillingham were to be roofed and repaired. Further repairs were needed in 1237 following recent storm damage. In 1244 a 'privy wardrobe' for the king's use was to be made between the king's and the queen's chambers. In 1250 the king's carpenter was to take 50 oaks from the forest for the king's works, one of many references to the use of oak trees for building repairs.[15]

Around 1250 Henry III embarked on an ambitious programme of renovation and building at King's Court, particularly with reference to the chapel and royal chambers. In October 1249 he ordered the rebuilding of the old chapel which was threatening to fall down, and in January of the following year 40 oaks were needed for the king's chapel. In July another order was made

> to furnish the king's chapel as begun; in the king's chamber under chapel ie on the long side facing the king's chamber, to make a fireplace and by it on the east side a window with a column in the

middle, and on the other side in the corner a privy chamber; in the chapel above, to make 6 windows with columns in the middle; to lengthen the queen's chamber by 15 bays and to make a chapel of 9 bays for queen; under addition to make a fireplace for the court; at the east end of king's hall to make a chamber 40ft long and 22 ft wide across the north end with fireplace and privy chamber; to amend and repair other defects as necessary.[16]

The detail and scale of the alterations give some idea of the sort of building in which a member of a royal or noble household might expect to live, even if only periodically, and suggests that the king was expecting to spend considerable time at Gillingham. By 1251 much of the work had been carried out, but it was still unfinished. Further works were put in hand in 1253, when the king's bailiff at Gillingham was ordered to enclose the house with a ditch, with a bridge leading towards the gateway. There were other detailed orders concerning a new wardrobe, an almonry house, new windows and wainscoting in both the king and queen's chapel and chambers, completion of a new kitchen, and accommodation for the king's son, Edward, the chaplains, and even for the porter. The windows of the king's chapel were to have images of the Virgin Mary, Edward the Confessor, and St. Eustace; those in the queen's chapel were to have Edward the Martyr and Edward the Confessor. The reference to Edward the Martyr was clearly intended to relate to the abbey at Shaftesbury. In 1261 the king's eating arrangements were revised, with an order for 'a certain bench between the king's hall and the kitchen, to arrange the king's dinner on.'[17]

However splendid these alterations might have been, the king was overreaching himself financially. In April 1253 it was ordered that revenues from Gillingham, Bridport, and Somerton should be used to pay for the king's works at Gillingham, and in June one William of Monte Sorrello was ordered to take charge of the works, perhaps suggesting that they were not going well. In May 1255 Henry had no money to pay the workmen, and the Abbot of Pershore was ordered to pay them out of the income from corn from Gillingham. The following month some of the woods were ordered to be sold to pay the king's debts. In November 1256 the Sheriff of Somerset was ordered to pay 30 gold marks to the king's workmen as part of the king's debt, the remainder to be paid by the next month. The wainscoting of the chapels and the work on the kitchen bench was not completed until 1268, when the Pipe Roll records an entry for £4 18s for the work.[18]

From the reign of Edward I, much less is recorded about King's Court. Edward was staying there in April 1278, but there is no record of further royal visits. By this time the court was becoming less itinerant and more settled around London, and the need for a network of royal lodges and palaces had diminished. In 1369 Edward III ordered that it should be demolished, and in 1399 stones from it were being used to repair one of the other lodges in the forest.[19] Much later, in the reign of George III, some stones were used in the making of the Gillingham to Shaftesbury road.

Pasturage, deer, and oak trees

WHILE LOCAL PEOPLE might find the forest laws oppressive, one benefit they could enjoy was that of rights of pasturage within the forest. As the forest was part of the common lands of the liberty of Gillingham, all holders of land within the liberty were entitled to common rights within it, subject to the rights of the king. This was of considerable importance to the poorer tenants, who had little land in the common fields and came to depend heavily upon their grazing rights in the forest. From time to time enquiries or inquisitions were held to establish the rights of the tenants, sometimes following attempts to restrict them by the foresters or stewards. In 1278 such an enquiry was held following complaints by the tenants against Guy of Taunton, the queen mother's bailiff, that he was denying them their rights. The enquiry found that the men of Gillingham 'were wont to common within the forest of Gillingham with all their animals, except, pigs, sheep, and goats, everywhere except in the region of Marleghe and the park, but by what warrant or from what time the jurors know not.' This right was shared by the inhabitants of Milton, Pierston, Wyndlam, Majeston, and Wyke, and by the tenants of the prior of Montacute at Ham. The right also extended to the men of Mere 'on the north side of the park', an arrangement perhaps reflecting a once indeterminate boundary between the commons of Gillingham and those of Mere.[20]

Despite the existence of the park fence, tenants somehow still managed to find ways into the park to graze animals there, for in 1228 the grazing rights of the Gillingham men within the forest were confirmed, provided that they stayed outside the deer leap and did not enter the park. The problem clearly persisted, for the following year any livestock found in the park were ordered to be removed and used for fattening for the royal larder. Sustained grazing by livestock of both tenants and crown alike could have damaging impacts for the forest, leading to deterioration in the quality of the grazings, and also restricting the growth of the trees, reducing the cover for the deer. In 1251 the king's oxen and other beasts were ordered to be fed outside the bounds of the forest because of the damage they were doing to the herbage. A further order instructed them to be grazed in and around the town instead, directing the men of Gillingham to find their pastures elsewhere, a requirement which no doubt caused them some hardship.[21]

A particularly important right, limited by manorial custom, was that of *pannage*, the right to browse pigs on the acorns of the forest oaks. The Customary prescribed that between Michaelamas (September 29) and St Martin's day (November 11), the time of greatest mast or acorn fall, all tenants were allowed free pannage for one pig aged one year or more, but other pigs had to be paid for at the rate of 2d per yearling pig and 1d for other pigs. This was to safeguard the pannage for the swine of the lord's demesne farm. Pigs of the tenants were allowed *agistment* (ie grazing but not on the pannage), but any other pigs found to have been in the forest for more than a day and a night were to be forfeited to the crown.[22]

While the Norman kings initially saw the forest as a royal retreat and hunting ground, it gradually became more important to them as an economic resource, especially in relation to its supplies of deer and timber. These could be used not only to repair and maintain the hunting lodge and to supply the table on royal visits, but also to supply the needs of royal palaces and building enterprises elsewhere. Gifts of deer and oak trees could also be used to reward loyalty and support or to settle disputes, the forest thus becoming a political and social asset as well as an economic one. The supplying of deer and oak trees from the forest can be followed through the many orders and instructions referred to in the calendared references to the Close Rolls and Liberate Rolls for the middle decades of the thirteenth century (Fig. 19). For example, in July 1241 the king's huntsman was directed to take 20 bucks from the forest for salting and keeping; in November 1244 30 does and 5 hinds were required for the king's larder at Westminster, no doubt in preparation for Christmas. November 1256 saw instructions for 24 deer for Christmas, with a further 40 needed in July 1257 and 24 in August of 1258.[23] Gifts of deer to nobles and ecclesiastics in 1258 included 5 carcasses each to the Bishop of Salisbury, the Bishop of London, and the Abbess of Shaftesbury.[24]

The Close and Liberate Rolls similarly record the stripping of the forest for its oak trees. Between 1234 and 1297 these rolls record the use of over 900 oak trees for use in the various castles, palaces, and religious houses around Gillingham and north Dorset, but also further afield. Many other oaks were taken for purposes unspecified. In many cases it has been possible to trace the particular buildings for which the oaks were used, although hardly any of these structures now remain.[25] King's Court itself was one of the biggest users of oak trees for building and repairs. Over the period 210 oak trees are recorded as being used specifically for these works, for example, the work on the chapel. Other oaks were used for the 'king's works' without the site being specified, as in November 1251 when

> John of Venois, seneschal of the forest, is directed to cause those in charge of the king's works at Gillingham to be supplied with 80 logs, viz. 40 from the park at Gillingham and 40 from the woods outside to enable the said works to be proceeded with.'

Many of the references specify that the oaks should be taken from beyond the park, in order to safeguard the timbers within the forest itself. There are also references to oaks needed for the manor barton and for a fishpond.

Many oak timbers were used to supply other royal manors and buildings around the south of England. The largest single user of the Gillingham oaks was Corfe Castle, which used 264 trees over the thirteenth century. Sherborne Castle was another stronghold in the hands of the king at this time, and was extensively rebuilt by John and Henry III. In the 1250s the latter ordered timbers from Gillingham Forest to repair the roof and the domestic quarters. East of Salisbury was the hunting lodge at Clarendon, transformed into a palace by Henry II and Henry III, but long disappeared. It was the residence from which Henry II issued his *Assizes and Constitutions of Clarendon*, a major codification of English medieval law in the 1160s (Fig. 20). Gillingham's contribution to this structure, almost a century later in 1244, was to supply 10 logs and 40,000 shingles or wooden tiles for the repairs of its roof, and a further 10,000 shingles were required two

The figures alongside the bars represents the number of miles from Gillingham 'as the crow flies'.

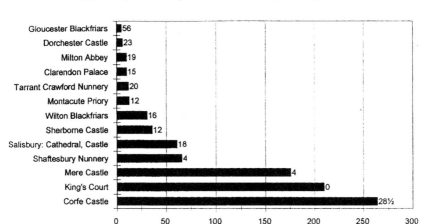

19 The wide range of destinations for Gillingham's oak trees shows their importance to Dorset's royal and religious houses, as well as to other major buildings elsewhere.

years later. Another royal building which used Gillingham oaks was the castle at Dorchester, later demolished to become the site of the Dorchester prison.

Gifts to religious houses were an important instrument of policy for medieval kings. Besides demonstrating spiritual commitment and helping to secure salvation for the royal family, gifts could be carefully controlled to ensure political loyalty amongst the powerful and wealthy ecclesiastical interests. Not surprisingly, the nearby and important Abbess of Shaftesbury was favoured with gifts of timber for the nunnery. John gave the Abbess Marie, who was his great aunt, the right to collect two loads of brushwood daily from the forest; but Henry III had little regard for a successor, Agnes de Ferrers, and she had to fight for this right against the obstructive steward of the manor. Gifts of oak trees are recorded to the nunnery at Tarrant Crawford, the priory at Montacute, the friary at Wilton, the abbey at Milton Abbas, and Salisbury Cathedral. The furthest distance travelled by Gillingham oaks was to the Dominican Friary

20 *The royal palace at Clarendon, near Salisbury. Timbers from Gillingham Forest were used extensively for repairs to the roofs during the thirteenth century.*

at Gloucester, a journey of 70 miles, recorded in 1257. This building is still in existence, the roof timbers of the south range having been dated by dendrochronology to a felling period of between 1230 and 1269. This is close to the 1256-7 orders for the Gillingham oaks, making it possible that the roof still contains some timbers which once came from Gillingham Forest.[26]

Other oaks found their way as gifts into the houses and strongholds of secular lords. John de Lacy, Earl of Lincoln and Constable of Chester, was a trusted follower of Henry III, who in 1233

and 1234 gave him oaks for his manor at Kingston, now Kingston
Lacy. The building in which they were used was a predecessor of
the much more illustrious manor house of Restoration times, and
may have been a first floor hall house similar to that built at Corfe
some decades later. Richard of Cornwall, the king's brother, was also
favoured with gifts of oaks for building the castle at Mere. The castle,
newly built in 1253 with six towers, a gatehouse, hall, chapel, and
dungeon, was an imposing and dominating feature of the landscape
overlooking Gillingham and the Blackmore Vale. In that year Richard
had 60 oaks for use in the building of the castle, and had over 170
trees altogether over the period of the mid-thirteenth century. These
fortifications never seem to have been called upon in time of anger;
the castle was ruinous by the fifteenth century, and today only its
mound survives.[27]

Besides the use of mature trees for major building works, a
multitude of smaller trees and underwood must have found their way
into the many humbler uses which were vital to sustain the economy
of the manor and its tenants – houses and outbuildings, charcoal,
firewood, thatching spars, hurdles, and many other uses. There is
little in the records about these functions, and their value to the local
population is easily overlooked. The occasional reference to wood
needed for 'charcoal for horse-shoes' or the making of 'channels in
the fish pond' is a reminder of the wider contribution of the resources
of the forest to the local economy.

The varied uses and destinations of the Gillingham oaks
indicates that it may be misleading to think of the manor and Forest
of Gillingham as no more than an isolated royal outpost, visited
occasionally by kings for hunting, and otherwise of little significance.
Instead it can be seen as part of a wider system of trade and movements
of goods which linked the many royal estates, religious houses, and
households of the nobility in and around Wessex.

Assarts and forest settlements

W HILE INITIALLY THE entire Forest of Gillingham would have been used for hunting, the effective area used for deer grazings and the chase was steadily reduced over the medieval centuries. The manor rent roll of c1300 records many tenants paying for assarts or enclosures which they held in addition to their virgates in the common fields, while other entries relate solely to assarts, most probably in the forest. Many of these holders of assarts are recorded as owing 'suit and service to two courts', one of which must have been the court of the barton, and the other the attachment court of the forest. Within the rent roll, and also in the manor court rolls, we come across tenants who are described as being of Kingsettle, Haselholte, Woodsend, or other places which are identifiable as being within the forest. All this indicates that the forest was becoming well inhabited by this time, with new fields and cottages gradually being carved out of the oak woodlands. Initially the forest officials might have tried to resist these clearances, but it soon became the practice that assarts were acceptable as long as a fine was paid in the courts and a rent thereafter, and that the king's (or queen's) rights were not infringed. By the fourteenth century, when royal interest in hunting was declining, fines for new enclosures were becoming an important source of royal revenue.

The detailed progress of new clearances and settlement is unrecorded, and its extent is only apparent from the *plott* of 1624 (Plate 7). This shows that large areas of the forest were covered with fields and hedges, all interspersed with farms and groups of cottages. Most of the farmland and settlement was around the outer edges of the forest, amounting to a partial disafforestation of these areas centuries before it ceased to be forest in law. This left the inner parts clear of settlement for the deer park and the three forest 'walks' as the effective royal demesne. On the western side enclosures had colonised Bowridge Hill and much of Ham Common, suggesting that the initial clearances had come from Gillingham itself; on the south side enclosures stretched towards Duncliffe Hill and to the foot of Shaftesbury at Enmore Green, perhaps carried out by people from East Stour, Stour Provost, or from the town of Shaftesbury (Plate 6). All these enclosures must have taken place long before their first appearance in maps and records.

It was on the eastern side of the forest that enclosure and settlement was most evident. By 1624 a large tract of settled countryside stretched north from Enmore Green through Kingsettle and Motcombe towards Knapp Hill, much of it on the hillier but drier areas of Greensand. The name *Kyngesettl* first appears in 1268, and means 'king's seat', perhaps referring to a hunting lodge of the medieval forest. In c1300 rents were paid by Walter son of Istin of Kingsettle, Edith the wife of Istin, and by Simon Kingsettle, all of whom had virgate lands in Gillingham. Another old name which first appears in the fourteenth century is Wormwell, later Coward's Shute, between Shaftesbury and Motcombe. Cliff or Cliff House in Motcombe may be the place of origin of William Clive, who was Gillingham's first vicar and is thought to have come from Motcombe.[28]

The most important consequence of the settlement of the eastern part of the forest was the rise of Motcombe as a separate village. The name, first recorded in 1244, means 'valley where meetings are held', and may have been the site of the meetings for the courts of attachment and swanimote, or even for the hundred of Gillingham during Saxon times. By the fourteenth century Motcombe was populous enough to have a chapel, since the endowment of Gillingham church in 1319 also included ' a house at Motcombe for the priest officiating in that chapel.' [29] The earliest part of the village was around the chapel, but soon came to include many dispersed clusters of cottages elsewhere.

Although within the forest, Motcombe was recognised as a separate tithing with its own tithing-man, and later could be considered 'distinct in all parochial affairs', with its own parish officers and responsible for its own highways and relief of its poor.

4

BLACK DEATH TO
REFORMATION

T HE LATE THIRTEENTH and early fourteenth centuries, the
period of Edward I's survey, and of the rent roll and manor
court rolls described in preceding chapters, represented a
high point in the history of medieval Gillingham and its population.
Around 1300 population size was probably the highest it had been
for many centuries, and the lands of the manor were being farmed as
intensively as at any time previously. It is also likely that the population
was becoming too large for the land needed to support it. Many of the
tenants held only a fraction of a virgate, perhaps only ten acres, while
others were holders of tenements with hardly any land at all, dependent
entirely upon the grazings on the common wastes and in the forest.
The spread of enclosures and settlements in Gillingham Forest can be
seen as a response to the hardship caused by the shortage of readily
cultivable land, encouraging tenants to move on to the more difficult
wet clays of the oak forests. Not far from Gillingham, the farmers of the
chalk valleys and downlands around Mere responded to the problem of
land shortage by expanding up on to the thinner soils of the hillsides
and turning them into cultivable terraces or lynchets.[1]

For just about everywhere in England, the years 1315-22 brought
about a major crisis. The summer weather of 1315 was unusually bad,

producing disastrous harvests and famine. The price of wheat across the south of England rose to as much as three times its usual value. In the many manors of the Bishop of Winchester, some not too far from Gillingham, the number of heriots paid in manor courts for new admissions to land increased sharply, indicating a marked rise in the death rate. Poor harvests and destructive plagues among cattle and sheep continued through the 1320s. There was a dramatic decline in agricultural yields, and the abandonment of arable lands for grass. Faced with a shortfall of income, lords readily encouraged villeins to abandon their labour services and pay money rents instead. On the Dorset lands of Glastonbury Abbey at Sturminster Newton and Buckland Newton, yields of corn declined, marginal demesne lands were leased out, and the commutation of labour services for rent greatly increased. Much less is known about what was happening in Gillingham at this time, but it is unlikely to have escaped the hardships and drastic changes that were engulfing manors not far distant.[2]

The depression of the early 1300s was a prelude to the greater catastrophe to come. In July 1348 a ship arriving at the port of Melcombe Regis, now part of Weymouth, brought with it an outbreak of bubonic plague. From here the Black Death began to spread rapidly through the country, and Dorset, being the county first affected, was one of the hardest hit. The plague spread throughout Dorset during the summer and was in Somerset through the autumn and into 1349. The severity of the onslaught can be gathered from episcopal registers of the diocese of Salisbury, which show that half of the incumbents of its Dorset parishes died during this period. The plague raged particularly over the winter, and may have been at its most virulent in the chalkland parishes in the south and centre of the county, where villages were compact and nucleated, and people lived close to each other. The plague was to return in 1361, but on a smaller scale than previously, with fewer fatalities. The vicar of Gillingham, William Clive, was fortunate to escape the first onslaught, but died in 1361, and may therefore have perished with the second attack.[3]

The fate of his parishioners can be revealed from the pattern of entries in the court rolls of the time. In a normal year, a population the size of Gillingham, around 300 tenants in the early 1300s, might have been expected to produce around eight to ten new admissions to copyholds each year as tenants died and holdings were surrendered to the manor before being regranted. Instead, 166 tenants are recorded as dying between the courts held on 14 October 1348 and 24 February 1349, amounting to more than half the population over a space of five months. When the plague returned in 1361, there were 44 deaths between June and December. The virulence of the infection over the winter, and the speed of its spread, suggests that it was a mix of bubonic, pneumonic, and septicemic plagues, rather than just the bubonic variety which tends to be most active during the summer and spreads more slowly. Across Dorset, and no doubt everywhere around Gillingham, houses and farms were abandoned, lands went untilled for the want of labourers, and people starved for lack of food. Around Gillingham, the hamlet at Langham may have been a casualty of the period (Fig. 21). The setback to social and economic life was huge, and it is likely that the population did not regain its former size until Tudor times, or even later.[4]

Despite the hardships and disasters, society continued to function normally in many ways. The many deaths did not bring about the collapse of family structures or traditional inheritance patterns, since in most cases a close relative was able to be admitted to the property at the next court. The Gillingham manor courts continued to meet regularly throughout both the 1348-9 and 1361 epidemics. In 1348-9 much of the normal business was suspended, the courts meeting only to record the deaths of tenants and to regrant lands; but in 1361, in the midst of further pestilence, the courts continued with their normal work of fining tenants who brewed without a licence, or trespassed with their livestock on to the fields of others. A key factor

21 An aerial view of Higher Langham from 1947. Langham Lane runs across the top of this view. The outlines of the sites of former buildings adjoining Higher Langham Farm can be seen. This was once one of the larger outlying medieval settlements of Gillingham. Its shrinkage might have begun as early as the fourteenth century, at the time of the Black Death.

in the continuity of society through the first epidemic may have been the survival of the manor bailiff, John Haym, and of another principal tenant, John Bagge, who were able to stand pledges for other tenants and maintain the normal process of property transfers. In the longer term, the plague may have hastened the end of villeinage or labour services in Gillingham, a process which was already well advanced by 1300. It is notable that there are fewer uses of the term *villein* in the court rolls after this time. Some families may actually have benefited from these events, which enabled them to move from a state of near landlessness to one of substantial copyholder over a period of months.[5]

During the years following the Black Death, the shrunken population was no doubt reminded many times by its priests of the vulnerability of life on earth and the importance of focusing one's thoughts on the life hereafter. Some evidence of this comes from the fields around Milton on Stour. Here field walking in recent years has unearthed examples of *ampullae*, the small flasks containing holy water brought back from pilgrimages. The returning pilgrims wore the ampullae around their necks, and it is believed that on reaching home the holy water was sprinkled on the ground at a special service, and the ampulla itself was buried in the hope of producing a bountiful crop. The existence of ampullae in Milton's fields makes it almost certain that at some time Milton people had been on pilgrimage. The most likely period for this was between the fourteenth and sixteenth centuries, when pilgrimage mania was at its height. One particular ampulla from Milton has even more significance, since its specific design indicates that it could have come only from Bromholm Priory in Norfolk, a principal shrine of medieval England (Fig. 22).

22 *Some ampullae or containers of holy water, found in a field at Milton on Stour. The distinctive hearth shape means that they could have come only from Bromholm Priory in Norfolk. Whoever dropped or buried the ampullae had most likely been on pilgrimage from Milton to Bromholm.*

Notwithstanding the general hardships of the time, there were clearly people prepared to add to them the specific hazards of the long pilgrim's road.[6]

The account of John Nyman

A GENERATION AFTER the Black Death, a snapshot of the normal functioning of village life is given in the 'account' of John Nyman, who lived at Motcombe towards the end of the fourteenth century. His account is a list of his expenditure over the year 1378-9. It is not known who John Nyman was, or for what purpose his account was written, but the fact of the account being written at all suggests that he may have had an official post for which written accounts were needed. The mention of a bow and its strings could suggest that he was a forest keeper. The account is written on the reverse of a court roll of a much earlier date. Above the start of the text is a sketch of a huntsman and his dog chasing a hare, perhaps a self-portrait of Nyman himself, and on one side of the text the writer has doodled away at a further sketch (Fig. 16). The inclusion of the place names of *Northay* and (Elena atte) *Clyve* (or Cliff) help us to locate his home to the North Haye area east of the village. We learn that he had a 'croft called Northaye, over against [his] father's house', and close to this the 1624 map marks the field called *Newmans*. In 1327 a Roger le Nieuman had paid 2s 6d in Lay Subsidy, but no Newman is mentioned in the later 1332 assessment.[7]

The account begins in September 1378 by stating that he then owns 34 sheep, including 16 two-year olds, and a *veverhogg*, presumably a type of ram. He also has a part share in a bullock. He records a visit to Shaftesbury market where he sells birds to the value of 10d, then spends the money on the items he needs. His biggest outlay is on beans to sow (4d), but he also buys peppercorns and strings for his bow. Spiritual needs are not overlooked, for he spends 1d on an oblation, most likely for a forbear, and another 1d on a donation. Around early December he sells a horse and nine lambs, and is given two hedges to ditch and trim in return for keeping all the trimmings to his own use. He afterwards sells the hedges and also 15 pounds of wool. During the spring he hires or leases a croft from Elena Atte Clyve for a year starting at Pentecost. In June he makes another trip to Shaftesbury market, where he buys a lamb and makes other purchases, which include red ochre for marking his sheep, tar soap, and more strings for his bow.

By this time the beans which he had sown earlier have finished growing; he notes the yield and the 'turnover', perhaps the surplus ones he can sell. Next comes the haymaking time. He leases the haymaking from a meadow belonging to Elena atte Clyve; his share of the half-day's haymaking is 2½ stacks of hay, all of which he sells to others, but notes that he has still not had the 11d for the half-stack which he sold to Richard Coppedok. Then follows a trip to Hindon market in October, where he buys six sheep. After this some things go badly. One sheep is bitten by a dog, owner unknown; another sheep is bitten by Ralph Palmer's dog; and two lambs die of murrain. The sheep lost amount to 4s in value. The final paragraph is an agreement to lease to William Holme *a certain croft called Fryte*, from that time, which was the Feast of Ss Simon and Jude, 28 October, until Pentecost the following year. Once again, Elena Clyve is part of the picture, since 'he will not trim the hedges without [her] permission.'

The document gives just a fleeting glimpse of the life of a small farmer towards the end of the fourteenth century. In it we notice the elements of the farming scene with the references to sheep, meadows, and vegetables, and the enclosed nature of the land in this part of the forest through the references to hedge trimming. We notice also the agreements between farmers for short-term leasing of land, which were clearly commonplace. By this date the role of the forest as a royal hunting ground was long past, and its value to the crown was increasingly as a source of income from its rents and fines. In the meantime the attachment courts of the forest went about their usual business of collecting fines for making encroachments and felling timbers. The queen's rights were carefully guarded, with the rights of tenants to erect boundary stones being challenged and then only allowed provided that 'it should be of no prejudice to the queen'.[8]

From manor to country town

T HE HISTORY OF Gillingham during the fifteenth century is far more shadowy than during the preceding two centuries. There are none of the manorial surveys with their long lists of tenants and their holdings which provided much of the basis for understanding what Gillingham was like during the earlier period, and there are few court rolls beyond the early parts of the century. In these court rolls few new place-names appear, suggesting that there was little creation of new farms or fields at this time, not surprising for a population still recovering from the calamities of the fourteenth century.[9] One important court roll reference is to a *Gildeaule* in 1441, and further references to a 'guildhall' appear in the sixteenth century, suggesting a market hall or similar structure, and the existence of a gild or body of craftsmen or traders making use of it. An earlier reference to a *Richard atte yeldhouse* in 1356 may be to the same building. Although Gillingham was never granted a charter for markets or fairs, these references indicate some level of market trading, even if no official recognition is known.[10]

One interesting document which relates to Gillingham's status at this time is the so-called 'Charter of Gillingham'. This document, reproduced in full in the later editions of Hutchins, is dated 1563 but is a reaffirmation of a much earlier grant of rights from 1453. The

23 Sir John Betteshorn of Chaddenwick (Charnage) near Mere was an owner of lands in Mere, Gillingham, and neighbouring villages. His brass is in Mere church.

original grant gave the people of Gillingham the privilege of going to all fairs and markets in England to sell their produce without paying the usual duties and tolls, to be exempt from serving on juries of assizes and sessions, and other privileges and benefits. The need to reaffirm the grant in the sixteenth century suggests that it may have been considered to have been of some value. A further affirmation dates from 1610. Much later again, in 1766, a manorial jury proposed that the charter should be revived. One view of the charter is that the rights within it are merely 'derivative', being granted to Henry the Sixth's Queen Margaret of Anjou for all her manors, but having no specific validity for Gillingham and therefore conferring no legally recognised benefits. Its existence, and subsequent reappearance down the centuries, may also suggest an expectation of the inhabitants of Gillingham that, in the absence of a borough charter, the place ought to have some sort of official recognition as a town. This quest for urban recognition was to recur frequently well into modern times.[11]

The later medieval period produced further chantry endowments in Gillingham. The St. Katharine's chapel endowment was considerably added to in 1399 by Sir John Bettesthorn, who may have been a successor to the Sandley estate. He was the wealthy owner of the manor at Charnage, near Mere, and already had a chantry chapel in Mere church, with three chaplains (Fig. 23). A few days before he died he gave a further 80 acres of (arable) land with five acres of meadow in Gillingham and in Milton. After his death it was found that besides 3½ virgates in Gillingham he also had lands and rents in Kington Magna, Buckhorn Weston, and Milton, as well as a half share of the profits of the courts and market in Shaftesbury.[12]

There is also the likelihood that a second chantry foundation existed in Gillingham at around this time. Although no medieval record of it exists, the chantry dissolution records of 1553 refer to a chapel which had belonged to the Fraternity of Jesus in Gillingham. Such fraternities or gilds were common in medieval towns, and represented a coming together of townspersons or craftsmen to pray together, maintain a lighted candle at a church altar, administer charity, attend burials of their fellows, endow a chantry to commemorate a prominent townsperson, or some similar activity. The Gillingham fraternity had its own priest and lands in Motcombe, and also at Bishopstone and Homington in Wiltshire near Salisbury. Nothing is known of its specific activities or meeting places, but its existence coincides with that of a *Martynschapell*, which may have stood close to the church in St Martin's Square. Hutchins refers to 'a toft [small dwelling] in Gillingham parish, where St. Martin's chapel once stood,' (1586) but gives no further information about the chapel, or of the origins of the St. Martin name. The existence of a fraternity in Gillingham, involving a drawing together of common interests, indicates some degree of urban consciousness and organisation among the more important inhabitants.[13]

Free School and Reformation

A FURTHER SIGNIFICANT development in the history of Gillingham as a town came in the early years of the sixteenth century. Between 1516 and 1530 a group of eight Gillingham copyholders came together and gave lands to form a trust. Its stated purpose was:

> that out of the issues and profits thereof, there might be perpetually maintained within the said town a schoolmaster, for instruction of youth in good literature, for the better discharge of their duty to God, the King and the Commonwealth.

In this way there came into being the Free School, which was one of the first schools in Dorset to be established which was not a church or abbey foundation (p.98). It has existed continuously as a school in different forms from that time to the present day. The founders were John Grice, John Ludwell, William Brown, Richard Small, John Crouch, John Cave, William Somes, and William Henton. They were subsequently known as the *feoffees* of the school, meaning trustees. Nothing much is known about any of them, except that some of their names appear in the Lay Subsidy returns of 1525 and 1545. The amounts paid by them in tax suggest that they were of substantial enough means to be taxed, but were not the wealthiest inhabitants of the town.[14]

Until that time there had been limited opportunities for schooling in and around Gillingham. The vicar or the chantry priests might have expected to help out with some learning, but more formal schooling would have been obtainable only from the abbey schools at Shaftesbury and Sherborne.[15] The Free School foundation shows the willingness of a group of townspeople to commit income and resources to the education of the sons of their own class, the future gentlemen and property owners of the town. In so doing they were taking on a role traditionally carried out by the church, but which the church was unable to fill.

The details of the endowment, with its lands and houses, were recorded at the time of a dispute which engulfed the trustees some seventy years later (Chapter 5). Various tenements and parcels of land are noted. Although some of the individual field names are now lost, others can be located with some certainty, since throughout this period the lands remained in the possession of the feoffees. The earliest grant is that of Richard Small (1516), who gave 'a cottage on the south side of the cross with one shop, lately in the tenure of Thomas Dirdoe'.[16] The cross referred to is mentioned in other records, and was most likely a market cross, although it could have been the Saxon cross now located on the nave wall inside the church, but at that time still in the church grounds. The 'cottage' is undoubtedly the site in the High Street next to the Phoenix used by the school from its origins in 1516 until the foundation of the grammar school in 1876. The site is now marked by a commemorative plaque, and the existence of the School on this site suggests that the market square was by this time becoming partially infilled with buildings.

The lands from John Grice and John Ludwell (1529) included *Haimes Place* and various other parcels in Newbury, one of which was the large field north of Newbury on which the grammar school later came to be built. William Brown (1528) gave a cottage near the guildhall and a cottage in Newbury, with some other cottages and enclosures at *Smithmead* and *Haddesham*. His other grants were at *Woollands* south of Newbury, and these are shown on the 1624 map. Some of the other grants by the feoffees were at Bourton; and also at Motcombe, including cottages near the church. A similar list of feoffees' property is found in the manor survey of 1608 (Chapter 5).[17]

The feoffees' foundation document had another important provision which went well beyond the establishment of a school. This was that '... the church of Gillingham be better repaired, poor people there relieved, prisoners refreshed, and highways, causeways, and bridges thereabouts, kept and maintained.' Until this time local administration had been in the hands of the manor, which had regulated matters such as obstructions to the highways, repairs to bridges, and pursuit of minor felonies through the manor courts. The acquisition of these functions by the feoffees shows the emergence of a local group important enough to not only found a school for the benefit of the sons of its own class, but also to take control of those matters essential to the promotion of its own trading and commercial interests. Eventually the parish vestry would regain the duties relating to the church, the roads, and the poor, but the feoffees would continue to be involved in local administration well into the nineteenth century.

The Reformation of Henry VIII had little direct impact on Gillingham compared with its larger neighbour of Shaftesbury, where the loss and destruction of the abbey changed the face of the town in a major way. In Gillingham the changes were those which developed from the later dissolution of the chantries by Edward VI. The Protestant monarchy regarded the chantries as idolatrous and superstitious places, and used the opportunity to seize their properties and assets, preferring to endow new schools whose loyalty to the crown would not be in question. The value of the lands of St Katherine's chantry in Gillingham was clearly recognised by its last priest, Galfryd or Jeffrey Gyll, who in the 1540s was regularly taking rents from lessees for its lands. Among the several leases recorded then or just later was one in 1541 to Thomas Nichols for seven acres in Cumbermead, one in 1552 to John Henbury for six acres of meadow and pasture on the south side of the Stour, and one to Robert Dirdo in 1541 of two closes containing three acres on the west side of the Chantry House.[18] The house referred to here was most likely the chantry priest's own home, and later maps show that the house known as Chantry House was the present Chantry Cottage opposite Chantry Bridge. The recording of these leases shows that the church, like any other holder of land, regarded its properties as an asset in the local land market.

In 1549 the St Katharine chantry lands, and those of the Fraternity, were appropriated to the Crown. Jeffrey Gyll was retired with a pension of £5 per year. The lands of the St Katharine chantry were given by the Crown as part of the endowment of Sherborne School, and those adjoining the town have since been known as Chantry Fields. At the time of the grant to Sherborne School the chantry lands were in 21 parcels, several of them in the adjoining Cumbermead. The new owners revived ancient manorial rights, and began to hold manor courts in the old chantry house for its tenants. The lands of the Fraternity in Motcombe and Wiltshire were granted in 1558 to lay owners.[19] A consequence of the changes regarding school and chantry was that both the feoffees and the trustees of Sherborne School were to be significant landowners around the town in the centuries to come.

5

1579 TO 1680: THE
GILLINGHAM OF JOHN JESOP
AND EDWARD DAVENANT

T HE LARGE TOMB monument in St. Mary's church hidden
behind the organ and in a state of some disrepair is that of
John Jesop, vicar of Gillingham between 1579 and 1625.
He is depicted lying on his back and holding a prayer book, and lies
alongside his brother Thomas, who had died ten years earlier (p.167).
Thomas had been the town physician, and the two men, in different
ways, had been responsible for the care of the sick and the poor over
their lifetimes. At the other end of the church, high above the nave, is
a tablet to Jesop's successor, Edward Davenant, unreadable from the
floor, and in Latin. This very different man, often quite retiring and
esteemed for his intellectual and academic qualities, ministered to the
town through the turbulent years of the early seventeenth century and
the Civil War. Between them, the two vicars looked after the town's
pastoral needs for a little over an entire century.

The population under the care of Jesop and Davenant was
spread well beyond the town, the parish at this time still including
Motcombe, Milton, and Bourton. The size of this population is not
easy to estimate. In 1545 around 120 dwellers paid the Lay Subsidy

(tax) in the whole parish, but it is not known how many more were exempt from payment. A survey of the manor of Gillingham in 1608 recorded 118 households and tenements; this total would have included the town and some nearer parts of the forest, but would have excluded smaller numbers of people living in the lesser manors of Ham, Madjeston, Wyke, and the Chantry. There were a further 80 named tenants in Motcombe and 39 in Bourton. At roughly four persons per household, this might suggest a Gillingham population of around five hundred.[1] The Hearth Tax assessment of 1662-3 lists 122 names in Gillingham, with further numbers in Milton, Motcombe, and Bourton, but again the number of exemptions is not known.[2]

Although we do not know the exact number of people, there are indications that the population was steadily increasing for much of the period, gradually returning to the levels of before the Black Death. For the early seventeenth century, the parish registers record some 50 baptisms per year compared with 30 to 40 burials, suggesting a growing population. Later in the century the number of baptisms was similar, but the number of burials had risen, suggesting a slowing down in the overall rate of growth. However, there were many fluctuations from year to year, some years producing an extremely large number of deaths, as in 1570 when there were 60 burials, and 1597, when there were an enormous 88. The cause of these high fatalities is not recorded, but outbreaks of smallpox are the most likely reason. In the parish registers we are much more likely to read about the mishaps and unfortunate ends of particular individuals than about any general causes of mortality. One such unfortunate was John Cave, who fell into the well at Thorngrove in 1574, and broke his neck; another was John Perrott, a stonemason who was killed trying to repair the chimney at John Belman's house in 1587; and poor Sarah Butt, who was murdered and left to die in a ditch in 1638. One who left Gillingham never to return was John Peverill, who in 1598 was riding towards London with his neighbour John Spencer, when he was attacked near Maidenhead. He nevertheless had the privilege of a burial in St. Paul's churchyard in London.³

Manor and town

T
HE MANOR OF Gillingham as recorded in the survey of 1608 shows some changes since the survey of the thirteenth century (Chapter 2), but is recognisably similar in other ways. The 116 named copyholders occupied between them 2,120 acres of land, but it has to be remembered that the size of the acre may have differed from

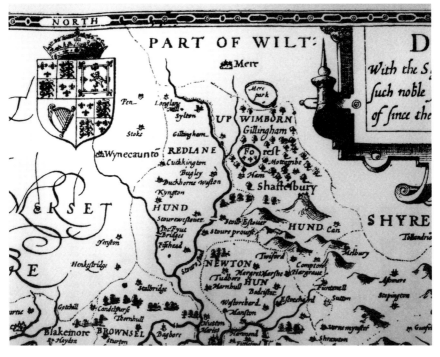

24 An extract from Speed's map of Dorset of 1610. Gillingham, at the junction of the Stour and Shreen, is shown as less important than Shaftesbury, Wincanton, and Mere. Gillingham Forest is depicted as a distinct area, more wooded than the neighbouring countryside.

that of the present day. Most tenants held some land in the common fields, of which five are named. These were the North Field, South Field, Woodhouse Field, Stockfield, and Madgeston Field. It is likely that the five fields represent the remaining parts of the greater North and South fields of medieval times, which had by this time become reduced in size and fragmented by enclosure. Other land was held in enclosed meadows and pastures. No fewer than thirty tenants held land in the Cumbermead or Common Mead, all of them holding both enclosed meadows and common grazing rights.[4]

In April 1588 there was an attempt by some leading townspeople and copyholders to enclose the remaining common fields. The leaders, named as Henry Nicolls, Thomas Dirdoe, John Allen, Robert Cave, and John Willes, claimed to be acting on behalf of the majority of copyholders, and were awarded a commission by the Court of Exchequer, so that the lands 'be measured and allotted unto the farmers, tenants, and freeholders, to every one of them severally a due and just proportion thereof, according to the quantity and value of their several interests of the soil, common, and other profits.' However, two other copyholders, Edward Sheppard and Nicholas Histock, affirmed before the manor court that 'the greatest part of the said copyholders did utterly dislike and disagree from any such enclosure.' They were no doubt speaking for the many poorer people with little land in the common fields, but highly dependent on their common grazings and other common rights, which they would no longer have after enclosure; their small allotment would be of little value by comparison with what they had lost. As a result of their objections, the Court of Exchequer ordered that any enclosures already made should be laid open.[5]

A few days later a new commission was set up to enquire into the enclosure of the *Comb Mead* or *Cumbermead* (i.e.Common Mead*)*. A different set of commissioners was appointed, and in this case it was directed that during the enquiry any enclosures so far made should remain standing. This proposal may have proceeded no further, since in 1608 much of the Commonmead still lay open, and remained open for a further two centuries.[6]

During the reign of James I the tenure of the copyholders became more secure. Until then, many of the fines paid by the tenants on admittance to their properties appear to have been *uncertain*, meaning not fully paid at the time of admittance, or still not fully paid. The copyholders paid the Crown the sum of £500 to have their fines made certain, possibly as a consequence of a royal enquiry into payments it considered to be owing. This was a considerable sum, but in the long term it gave the copyholders security of tenure, comparable with that of leaseholders and freeholders. This was confirmed by decree in 1610-11.[7]

The largest holding on the manor at the time of the 1608 survey was that of the Queen's own farm at Thorngrove. This comprised 362 acres held by William Blacker, who also held the manors of Ham and of Pierston. The farm had land in each of the five common fields, including 120 acres in the South Field and 104 acres in Woodhouse Field. Other land was in enclosures in the Cumbermead, and in other pastures which were near or adjoining the farmhouse and its outbuildings. Another large holding was that of Edward Lord Stourton, a local aristocrat and Fee Forester of Gillingham Forest, whose brother-in-law, Francis Tresham, is more widely known for his involvement in the Gunpowder Plot. Stourton had 210 acres, all in the hands of thirteen tenants of his own. Morgan Cave had 109 acres at Bugley and a further 60 acres at Shearstocks in the forest. Thomas Dirdoe, who held the manor of Milton, had 115 acres, and was also a freeholder in Gillingham manor with further lands and properties. Thomas Jesop and the feoffees of the Free School held in trust for the school 51 acres, some of which was in Newbury and the rest at Sandley and in the common fields. Nine houses and cottages are recorded as belonging to the feoffees, including two houses near the Guildhall, a cottage by the church, and two other cottages adjoining the church yard.

Only a dozen or so copyholders held much more than 40 acres, the majority of tenants having much smaller holdings. Thirty-two tenants had less than five acres of land each, some holdings consisting entirely of small pieces in the common fields. A further 18 tenants had cottages with no land at all. Some of these tenants with small parcels may have been the tradespeople of the town who were able to make a living from other means, but many others, those with only a few acres, must have depended heavily upon the common grazings and pannage in the forest and the other open lands of the manor for eking out a basic existence.

The town inhabited by these copyholders of divers means had barely started to resemble the Gillingham of today. The various references in the manor documents and parish registers to the Free School and other feoffee's properties, the Guildhall, and St. Martin's Square, suggest a focus of activity in and around the church and its nearby streets. A seating plan for the church dating from 1615 shows that the main body of the building had a north and south aisle, but there were also smaller aisles called the Wyke, St. James, and Morrowmass aisles. There are 128 names on the seating spaces allocation.[8] The royal arms overlooking the wooden screen dates from this time (Plate 8). Opposite the church John Jesop built a new vicarage, John and his brother Thomas carving their names on the wainscoting and on the ceiling. The vicarage later underwent various alterations and extensions, but remained there until it was replaced in 1883 by the vicarage which is now Rawson Court.

Northwards from St. Martin's Square, the names Lodbourne and Peacemarsh start to appear frequently in the manor and parish records after 1550. It seems that at this time the population was gradually expanding on to these areas of then open land, which over the following centuries became entirely enclosed apart from remnants such as Lodbourne Green. *Wivering Lane* first appears as a place name in 1610. Another name frequently appearing in the parish registers at this time is 'Porage Hill' or 'Poridge Hill', the old name for Bowridge Hill. The name refers to the rising ground east of the Shreen and Bay Bridge, and it is likely that many of the cottages and farms extending up Bay Lane from the bridge and on to the hilltop had their origins at this time. There was then no through way across the Forest to West Knoyle, Bay Lane merely bending round the edge of the old park towards Donedge Lodge. On the Shreen itself stood *Releishe* or Redlynch Mill, originally the mill for Milton, and later known as Purns Mill or Parham's Mill.

Not far off Bay Lane lay the now vanished mansion of East Haimes, one of the largest buildings shown on the plan or 'Plott' produced in 1624 at the time of disafforestation. This was clearly a house of some importance, being one of the perquisites of the office of Fee Forester, and is always referred to in the grants as a 'capital messuage'. In 1615 Edward Lord Stourton leased it to Thomas Jesop, the vicar's brother, along with the office which by now had become largely honorary, but Thomas was unable to enjoy it much since he died a few months later. In the 1630s the house was in the hands of Richard and Rachel Perne. It is last recorded in 1700. Its site, not far from Windyridge Farm, is no longer visible.[9]

West and south of the town square across the Stour, the land which had once belonged to the medieval St. Katharine chantry was now in the hands of Sherborne School, which had been given the land by Edward VI. Along with the property, the school acquired the rights to hold its own manor courts, and continued to do this well into the eighteenth century, the courts meeting in the Chantry House, the present-day Chantry Cottage. The Sherborne School property was known henceforth as the Chantry Fields. It may be from this time that the direct route across the Chantry Fields towards East Stour came to an end, the route subsequently being via Newbury and Oldlands Lane, which later became New Road. Along Oldlands Lane lay Madjeston, which had always been a separate manor from Gillingham. In 1655 this sizeable estate had eight dwellings, 160 acres of arable land, 60 acres of meadow, and a further 100 acres of pasture, as well as common pasture for cattle in Gillingham, which probably refers to rights in the forest.[10] West of the town beyond the Queen's Farm lay the manor of Wyke, which during the sixteenth century belonged to the Crespyn family, and later passed to the Frekes of Hannington in Wiltshire. The earliest parts of Wyke Hall may date from this time, and include the minstrel gallery and fireplace dated 1611, making it Gillingham's oldest building other than the church. The oldest cottages in Wyke are those around Lydford's Lane, possibly the site of the village at this time.

The town east of the Shreen and the Barnaby (Town) Bridge is shown on the forest map or 'Plott' of 1624. Much of this is too small to be seen on the version shown in this book (Plate 7), but can be reconstructed from close scrutiny of the detail on the map itself. From the town, off the bottom side of the map, a road crosses the bridge into Newbury, and to the left, on the north side of the road, is a depiction of Barnaby's Mill, faded but still to be seen. In 1608 the mill had been in the hands of Thomas Dirdoe, who paid the Crown a rent of 24s for a corn mill and a malt mill. Further along the north side of Newbury is the large *School Land* enclosure which belonged to the feoffees and later became the site of the Grammar School. Beyond here the road widens out to form the junction with Hardings Lane, where several cottages are shown. Hardings Lane is one of the locations regularly mentioned in the parish registers. On the south side of the road up the slope from the bridge are a number of cottages, leading towards a larger house belonging to William Hame, occupying the site of the later Newbury House. Just after this house Oldlands Lane cuts off southwards towards Madjeston, passing through a large enclosure called *Woollande,* which much later became part of the brickfields site. Beyond the Oldlands Lane junction Newbury has become the Shaftesbury road, crossing the Lodden at *Colehaies* Bridge. Beyond the Lodden bridge the land to the south of the Shaftesbury road is the manor of Ham, now in the hands of William Blacker. On the north side the site of King's Court and the old park boundary comes into view, shown as closely hedged, with access through a *West Gate.* From here the Shaftesbury road follows a broad belt of common land, bounded by cottages and enclosed fields, the consequences of earlier settlement and enclosure from the forest.

By the time of the Jesops, much of the governance of the town had passed into the hands of the feoffees of the Free School, as related in the previous chapter. Besides the running of the school, the feoffees had responsibility for the relief of the poor and the maintenance of roads and bridges. In 1598 a major dispute erupted between the town and the feoffees. Richard Estmonde, John Butler, and other tenants of the manor brought a suit in Chancery against Thomas Dirdoe, Edward Lawrence, James Frampton, Robert Allen, John Hayward, and William Barter, on the grounds that the these people had been converting the trust property to their own use. As a consequence an Order in Chancery was made which amounted to a reform of the feoffees' constitution. In future the trust property was to be administered by twelve trustees. When the number had decreased to eight it should be restored to twelve by the manor court meeting with the vicar and the constables. Procedures were established for the receipt of rents and the payment of the schoolmaster, and that 'the rest of the rents and profits of the said lands, all reasonable and necessary charges being first deducted, to be employed yearly to the reparation of causeways, highways, bridges, and the rearing and bringing up of poor orphans, and other charitable and necessary uses mentioned in the said decree.' The Chancery decree thus confirmed that the feoffees would be a major governing body in the town for some time to come.[11]

The Free School

The Free School, founded in 1516, was in the hands of its trustees or feofees, who also had responsibilities for the poor and for the bridges of Gillingham. In 1598, following a dispute in the Court of Chancery, the constitution of the feofees was reformed. Behind the later facade looking on to the High Street are the features of the much older building known to Thomas Dirdoe, Edward Hyde, and Robert Frampton (Fig. 25).

26

25 (above) A recent view from the High Street. The pedestrian on the far side has just passed the building which once housed the Free School, identifiable by the circular 'heritage' plaque on the wall.

Edward Hyde (1609-1674) is thought to be the most distinguished scholar to emerge from the school at Gillingham. He was born at Dinton in Wiltshire, and attended the school sometime around 1620 or shortly before. At the age of 13 he passed on to Oxford, to emerge many years later as the Earl of Clarendon (Fig. 26), Lord High Chancellor of England to Charles II.

Disafforestation, enclosure, and riots

WHILE THE TOWN itself was growing in population and importance, the Forest of Gillingham was in a state of some stagnation and even decay. The courts of the forest continued to function as they had done for centuries, raising fines from tenants for building new hedges and enclosures, felling timbers, or grazing livestock outside the permitted areas. A 1600 copy of the standing orders of the *swanimote* or 'wood' court shows how the forest was meant to be administered, but it can be supposed that many of its requirements had long fallen into abeyance, since by this time around half of the forest had already been enclosed.[12] In 1559 Sir John Zouche was appointed keeper of the forest, and he set about trying to reassert the rights of the Crown. In 1574 the tenants of the manor made a series of complaints against Zouche, alleging that he had claimed the boundaries of the forest to be greater than what they were; cut down the hedges of tenants whose lands adjoined the forest; that he had enclosed ground at Duncliffe Hill, preventing the tenants from taking their lawful pannage; unjustly fined tenants in the woodcourts; and prevented them from clipping the trees for deadwood. However, the Court of the Exchequer found in favour of Zouche, ordering the complainants to pay a hundred marks.[13]

Although the Zouche dispute represented a temporary victory for the Crown over the tenants, the influence of the Crown in the forest was on the wane. It came at a time when the Crown was looking at ways of relinquishing the upkeep of its forests and parks, and profitably disposing of them to raise cash for the costs of government and wars. The maintenance of many of the royal parks was by this time becoming a particular burden to the Crown. In 1585 a royal report pointed to the scarcity of timber in all the royal woods south of the

Trent, so that insufficient wood could be found for the navy. A major cause was seen to be the number of pales used for maintaining the deer fences in the royal parks. In some parks, including Gillingham, it recommended that in future quickset hedges should be used instead of pales; and that other parks, now too expensive to maintain, should be disposed of.[14]

The disposal of Gillingham Forest and its park, when it eventually came, involved the town in one of the most serious outbreaks of popular discontent in England to erupt in the years before the Civil War. The background to this was the increasing impoverishment of the governments of James I and Charles I. Denied money in taxation because of their conflicts with Parliament over many years, they increasingly turned to their manors, estates, and forests as sources of revenue. Disafforestation and the leasing of forest lands was seen as a way of raising ready cash. In July 1625, soon after his accession, Charles I granted a lease of the forest and park of Gillingham to Sir James Fullerton, his former tutor, for forty-one years, and the lessee was to disafforest, enclose, and improve the land. Shortly afterwards Fullerton was granted the Crown stewardship of the manor and forest. The leasing may well have been anticipated before 1625, as the previous year the large, detailed plan or 'plott' of the forest had been drawn up, indicating the areas previously enclosed and the open grounds remaining (Plate 7). This showed that while large parts of the forest were already enclosed, especially around Motcombe, Ham, and Enmore Green, large open areas remained within the park and the nearby 'walks'.[15]

Fullerton at once began the task of enclosing the land, appointing Commissioners to negotiate with the tenants the amount of land each should receive as compensation for loss of common rights. The allotments were to be at the rate of one acre for every ten acres of enclosed land held within the forest. Further allocations were made for the poor of Motcombe, for cottagers within the forest, and for the feoffees of Gillingham. A total of 505 acres were allotted by the Commission. At a meeting with all the tenants, Fullerton was able to present the proposals as being to the tenants' advantage, so that each in turn signed their acceptance of their new allotments. It is likely that at first the tenants failed to grasp the full meaning of the new proposals, each signing because he saw that everyone else was doing so, and 'that he might not be singular'. Following the meeting, during the winter of 1626-7, Fullerton quickly set about destroying the deer, felling the trees, and laying out new enclosures.

By this time many of the tenants were having second thoughts as they realised that what they were gaining in allotment ground by no means compensated for what they were losing in common rights. The growing discontent was sufficient for a second Commission to meet in March 1627, to which the tenants outlined their grievances. There was particular dissatisfaction with the amount of land each tenant was to receive in lieu of their grazing rights, the distances that some allotments lay from the homes of tenants, and the poor arrangements for access to the new lands, which would have involved tenants trespassing on the rights of others. Another complaint, which was to prove a major problem in the years ahead, was the closing off of existing roads, and the narrowing of others. As a consequence, a further Commission met in August, to which were invited

> any tenant of Gillingham or Motcombe... that can complain of inconvenient laying of his allotment, or of the passage or strengthening of any highways, watering places, or any other cause of complaint by the Inclosure of the Forest of Gillingham: let him repair to His Majesty's Commissioners at the Lion in Shaston upon Tuesday the one and twentieth day of August 1627 by ten of the clock that day, and then and there make good his complaint, and some remedy may be given.

The Commissioners took seriously the complaints of the tenants, and produced a revised scheme of enclosure which met some of their grievances. Some 43 amendments were made. For example, it was instructed that highways from Shaftesbury to Gillingham and Mere through the Lawn enclosures (north of Motcombe) should be 100 feet wide, and that four acres of ground at Bowridge Hill should remain open. Lox Lane, Colestreet Lane, and Ham Common were other areas which were to remain unenclosed. But their recommendations were brushed aside by Fullerton, who continued with his original plan. His action so enraged the tenants that early in 1628 a group of a hundred of them 'all of them armed and most of them disguised, in a riotous and rebellious manner', began to tear down the hedges, fill in the ditches, and prevent Fullerton's workmen from enclosing further ground. In May 1628 a company of soldiers sent to suppress the revolt instead sided with the tenants. Disturbances continued throughout 1628, with the rioters burning new plants intended for the enclosed grounds, and killing the deer. Further troops were sent in November to dislodge the rebels, but they were too well entrenched, proclaiming 'Here we were born, and here we stay', and it took until February 1629, by which time even further troops had been sent, before resistance was overcome.

The identities of the rioters and the roles they adopted give some indication of the reasons for their protracted success. Far from being a rabble of impoverished malcontents, they included some of the most prominent figures in the manor and town. One was John Phillips, a tanner of some standing; another was one Alford, who came to be known as the 'Captain'; Morgan Cave, who farmed at Bugley and Shearstocks, who was named the 'Lieutenant'; and other substantial tradesmen and farmers. The military titles accorded to some of the rebels suggest some sort of disciplined organisation. Another figure of some importance was Henry Hoskins, who is considered by some to be an outsider who also masterminded comparable revolts which took place around the same time in Wiltshire and the Forest of Dean. One view of the Gillingham disturbances is that they were part of a wider series of organised revolts in the Wessex countryside, linked through the supposed leadership of 'Lady Skimmington', a figure whose existence has never been proven. Another view is that there was little connection between the Gillingham riots and those which erupted elsewhere, and that Hoskins himself was of only local importance.[16]

At the end of 1629 some eighty rioters were taken to London to be fined and censured before the Court of Star Chamber. The fines, however, were light, perhaps as an incentive to good future behaviour and in recognition that the rioters were poor men quite unable to pay fines. The opposition to the enclosures by no means ceased with the arrests and sentences, and intermittent rioting continued during the next twenty years. In the summer of 1643 the people of Mere and Gillingham assembled in groups of up to 300 armed with muskets and other weaponry to destroy the enclosures and show their contempt for the Earl of Elgin, now the lord of the manor and owner of much of the forest. In 1651 during the Commonwealth, the Council of State ordered a troop of horse to Gillingham to crush further riots. It is interesting to note that despite all the rioting and disturbances, the manor courts continued to function normally, and there is no mention in the court rolls of the profound events of these years.

The rioters were mostly artisans, or non-agricultural workers following trades and crafts, rather than farmers, yeomen, or husbandmen. Of 74 convicted rioters from Gillingham in 1632, 45 followed skilled trades, the largest group being cloth weavers. Only 21 were husbandmen or yeomen. These men characteristically lived in small cottages with little land, often as subtenants of copyholders. They depended heavily on their common rights in the forest to augment their incomes. Not surprisingly they had the most to lose from enclosures which would destroy these rights and give them little or nothing in return.[17]

It is likely that the enclosure scheme for the forest was soon completed, but a small part around White Hill remained open until after 1809. One unsought for consequence of enclosure was the narrowing of roads, which meant that the tracks of carts and wagons were concentrated together, churning up the roads in winter into impassable tracts of mud. This made it difficult for farmers to reach the market at Shaftesbury, leading the town's traders to complain that their trade had suffered because of the enclosures of Gillingham Forest. One innkeeper of the town affirmed that the roads were now 'deep and dangerous for travellers with their cattle in the winter by reason of the enclosures of the late forest of Gillingham' and that the market of Shaftesbury was in consequence 'much impaired ...for now that the west country men cannot come to the said market to vent the commodities which the hill country men bring to the said market.' However overstated the problem may have been, it is clear that the enclosures made travel through the old forest more difficult.[18]

The disafforestation riots marked virtually the end of both the forest and the manor of Gillingham as a fief of the Crown, and the true end of the medieval period of its history. In 1632 the Forest and Manor of Gillingham were granted to Thomas, Lord Bruce, Baron of Kinross and Earl of Elgin. For the next two centuries following the disafforestation, Gillingham and its former forest were to belong to their landed proprietors and gentleman farmers. But the change meant little for the living and working conditions of the majority of its inhabitants.

Gillingham and the Civil War

N OT TOO MANY years after the enclosure of the forest, the loyalties of Gillingham people were to be strained once again, this time by the coming of the Civil War. Gillingham's past history as a royal manor ensured that royalist sympathies were likely to be strong, and this was clearly the case with the wealthier and more educated people. The vicar, Edward Davenant, had strong royalist leanings, as had his curate, Samuel Forward, so that the royalist cause would have been proclaimed from the pulpit. Another staunch royalist was Robert Frampton, the headmaster of the Free School, which at that time was described as being 'full of the sons of royalist gentlemen.' These people, the intellectual and spiritual leaders of the community, were clearly in a strong position to influence the sympathies of the townspeople as a whole. Of the positions of some of the leading gentry and farmers rather less is known, but it could be expected that the Dirdoe family of Milton, who had acquired the manor of Milton in 1554, would also be royalist sympathisers even if not actively engaged. Another royalist was George Kirke of Charing Cross in London, who held lands in Lawn in 1646. His lands were sequestered by Parliament in 1648, but after the Restoration they were returned and he became Groom of the Bedchamber and Keeper of Whitehall Palace to Charles II.

In Gillingham there was little direct involvement with the conflict until 1644. From September and through the winter the Parliamentary general, Sir William Waller, was in the Shaftesbury area, oppressing the local population by raising money to pay his foreign mercenaries. He had various exchanges and skirmishes with the royalist leader, Lord Goring, who was at Bruton. The church at Gillingham was ransacked and the vicarage was plundered, the vicar's valuable library being confiscated. Davenant was deprived of some of his living, losing the income from the chapels in the parish. The living was given to Thomas Andrews, who had been organist at Warminster. In 1657 John Pannel was ministering in the church. A number of estates in Gillingham and Motcombe considered to belong to royalists were sequestered (ie confiscated) by Parliament at this time.[19]

Some Gillingham people became even more directly involved in the conflict in 1645, when groups of ordinary townspeople and villagers around Dorset came together to form a militia known as the Clubmen. This organisation arose through local people becoming increasingly outraged at having their crops and livestock regularly plundered by the passing companies of soldiers of both sides. Similar groups of Clubmen arose in other counties including Worcestershire, Herefordshire, and Wiltshire. They declared themselves neutral and wore white cockades, carrying banners on which was sometimes displayed 'If you offer to plunder or take our cattle, rest assured we will battle.' Despite their proclaimed neutrality, the parliamentary leaders were convinced that they were really royalists. On 2 August 1645 a force of Clubmen fortified Castle Hill in Shaftesbury, before being overcome by the parliamentarian Colonel Charles Fleetwood. Among the ringleaders taken was Samuel Forward, curate to the vicar of Gillingham, who may well have been accompanied to the gathering by others of his congregation. Two days later Oliver Cromwell, marching from Sherborne, encountered a force of Clubmen on Duncliffe Hill, but after a meeting at which the Clubmen put their grievances, they dispersed. Cromwell then turned south to confront another force of Clubmen who were dug in on Hambledon Hill. Among them were Robert Frampton, the master of Gillingham School, and his four brothers. The brothers were all wounded but Frampton himself escaped.[20]

This brought an end to the Clubmen episode in north Dorset. After the fall of Sherborne Castle to Cromwell, parliamentary troops were quartered all round the area. The Gillingham parish registers record:

2 April 1645 a soldier of the king, killed at Wyke

and

The first day of December (1645) Ambrose Lillie, upon denial of his horse, was shot to death by a parliament soldier at his house and was buried the third day of December.

Restoration and after

A FTER 1660 GILLINGHAM entered a more settled period, in contrast to the troubles and disturbances of the previous generation. The vicar, Edward Davenant, was restored to his living, and continued to minister in the parish for a further twenty years, to be succeeded in 1680 by Thomas Ward. The liberty of Gillingham was now considered to comprise the tithings of Gillingham town, Milton, Motcombe, and Bourton, the medieval 'free tithing' having been absorbed into the town tithing. An order of Commonwealth times instructed the separation of Motcombe from Gillingham, and from this time Motcombe came to be regarded as no longer part of Gillingham, although still part of the parish, and with its tithes still payable to Gillingham church.

Some idea of the general level of living of the population at this time can be found in the Hearth Tax returns for 1662-3. This was a tax based on the number of hearths in the homes of each householder, and so indicates a general scale of wealth and material well-being. In Gillingham, of the 122 householders recorded, two had thirteen hearths; of these one was the vicarage, built some decades earlier by John Jesop. The other larger houses shown on the return at this time could have been Wyke Hall, East Haimes, or maybe Newbury House, but it is not possible to specifically identify these on the returns. Some 50 occupiers had houses with between three and five hearths, while at the lower end of the scale 71 occupiers had only one or two hearths. It is probable that the return is not complete, and may omit people who were judged too poor to pay any tax at all. In Milton tithing Dorothy Dirdoe had a house of eight hearths, presumably The Old

House, which the Dirdoe family are known to have lived in at this time. In Motcombe a house belonging to Sir Edward Nicholas had 25 hearths. He was one of Charles II's principal Secretaries of State, and since 1660 lord of the manor of Gillingham. Henry Whitaker's house of 11 hearths would have been Payne's Place at the foot of the hill leading to Shaftesbury. As in Gillingham, the majority of the houses were cottages with only one or two hearths.[21]

An interesting aspect of Gillingham's relationship with Shaftesbury was renewed at this time. In the medieval period Shaftesbury, dominated by its Abbey, had been by far the more important place of the two, with Gillingham little more than a village by comparison. Of great importance to Shaftesbury was the right to draw water from wells in Enmore Green, at the foot of the hill on which the town stands, but outside the borough and within the forest and manor of Gillingham (Plate 6). In return for this privilege, the townspeople of Shaftesbury were obliged to perform a ceremonial dance for the Gillingham people, as described in this document from 1527:

> The Sunday next after Holy Rood day in May every year, every parish within the borough of Shaston shall come down that same day into Enmore Green, at one of the clock in the afternoon, with their minstrels and mirth of game, and in the same green of Enmore, from one of the clock till two of the clock ... they shall dance ...

In this ritual the Mayor of Shaston was to give as homage to the Queen's bailiff the best of local produce: a penny loaf, a gallon of ale, a calf's head, and a pair of gloves. These gifts were accompanied by the *byzant*, a decorated staff which people danced around. After accepting the gifts, the Queen's official then handed back the byzant to the Shaftesbury people. If the Mayor was unable to render this homage, then the bailiff had the right to refuse the water to Shaftesbury. In 1663

Sir Edward Nicholas renewed the agreement with Shaftesbury, with a change of date to the Monday before Ascension Day, when it would not interfere with Divine Service. After the ceremony the Mayor and townspeople spent the rest of the day in revels and festivities. During the eighteenth century it became customary for the parts of lord and steward of the manor to be enacted by people in costume, and the ceremony became more elaborate, the byzant being adorned with plate, lace, and jewels. The byzant ceremony was last performed in 1830, by which time it had become too elaborate and expensive, but there have been some revivals of it in recent years.[22]

Prominent people and families

FROM 1579 TO 1625 life in the town was dominated by the Jesop brothers, John and Thomas. Both were highly educated people whose presence in the town suggests the emergence of a professional, middle class element within the population. Thomas, the town physician, acquired in 1615 the house of East Haimes along with the office of Fee Forester, but he died a few months later, ten years before his brother.[23] Both men are strikingly depicted in the large tomb monument in the church, with inscriptions which testify to the esteem in which they were held in the town (Fig. 27). They would often work together for the general well-being of the townspeople. The parish registers show that in Lent, when the population was not allowed to eat meat, Thomas would issue a licence endorsed by John exempting invalids from this rule, for instance in 1594 to

> Elizabeth Trenchard ... through infirmative and sickness of her body to us appearing, cannot eat fish without harm or danger of her health and body ...[we] licence the said Elizabeth Trenchard to eat flesh limited by the statute during this time of Lent only.

The Brothers Jesop

The monument to John and Thomas Jesop is the oldest and the largest memorial in Gillingham church. The brothers were the sons of John Jesop, Rector of Chickerell and Upwey near Weymouth.

Thomas Jesop (d.1615), the further figure, was the town physician. He was a Master of Arts, Doctor of Medicine and former scholar of Merton College, Oxford, and also a county Justice of the Peace. His memorial panel, now disappeared, read 'Father to brothers; friend to the honest; benefactor to the poor.'

27

John Jesop (d.1625), the nearer figure, was the town's vicar from 1579. John, the vicar and builder of the vicarage, was a Master of Arts, Bachelor of Divinity and Fellow of All Souls College, Oxford. He was also a prebendary of Salisbury Cathedral and had another living at Upwey. He is thought to have been the builder of the Tudor vicarage. His memorial describes him as a 'man of every highest virtue and known among his peers for his generosity'.

Jesop the vicar was succeeded by Edward Davenant, another highly educated man but different from Jesop in many respects. He was born in London, the nephew of the Bishop of Salisbury, and educated at Queen's College, Cambridge. Besides the vicarage of Gillingham, his ecclesiastical offices came to include prebendaries at Chute and Chisenbury, the archdeaconry of Berkshire, and the treasury of Sarum. He was an intellectual and retiring figure, perhaps more at home with his books and studies than the day to day issues of parish life. He was known to other intellectual figures of the day, notably Archbishop Usher, whom he helped with the compilation of his biblical chronology by calculating all the eclipses which had happened since the creation. He was acquainted with the antiquary and biographer, John Aubrey, who included the vicar in his 'Brief Lives' pen pictures of contemporary figures. We learn from Aubrey that Sir Christopher Wren considered Davenant to be the best mathematician of his time.[24] His memorial plaque in the church, in Latin and too high to be read from below, tells us that he 'very wisely put theology before all the rest of his studies … embraced in his mind the whole world of the arts and sciences, devoting many more hours to them than most men.'

Aubrey depicts Davenant as a spare figure of middling height, troubled with gout in spite of temperate habits, and rarely venturing further than the church. He left many of the day to day details of life to his wife, and the running of the church to his curates. In the winter evenings he would teach mathematics to his four daughters and six sons. As related above, this peaceable churchman lived through the troubled times of the Civil War and the Commonwealth. He was not looked upon favourably by Cromwell's troops, who plundered the vicarage and stole his library of rare books. He was deprived of much of his living, which was not restored to him until the time of the Restoration. His last two decades were less eventful, and in his will he included £100 to enhance the salary of the master of the Free School.

Another towering figure from Civil War times onwards was Robert Frampton (Fig. 28). He was born at Pimperne, educated at the Free School in Blandford, and studied at Oxford. On his return to Dorset, he quickly took up the royalist cause and played a part in resisting Cromwell's troops at Hambledon Hill in 1645. In 1648 he became master of the Free School in Gillingham, where he was soon befriended by Dr. Davenant. Once more his undisguised royalist sympathies brought him into confrontations with parliamentarians, notably one John Gage, with whom he had several encounters ending in blows and scuffles. Around this time Frampton was persuaded by Davenant to be ordained, no easy decision since the Church of England itself was out of favour with the new parliamentary order. His first sermon in Gillingham church, to a congregation which included Puritan officials, predictably included references to the deposition of the anointed king. This outspokenness alarmed his friends, and soon afterwards Frampton was persuaded to take a less public position, becoming domestic chaplain to the Earl of Elgin, who had bought the manor of Gillingham from the Crown. The later, longer part of Frampton's career lies outside Gillingham, leading him to become Bishop of Gloucester in 1680. He became heavily involved in the religious and political intrigues at the time of James II, and was deprived of his see in 1689 when he refused to take the oath of allegiance to William III. Robert Frampton died in 1707.[25]

One of the most frequently occurring family names in the records of this period is that of Dirdoe, often spelt in other ways, such as Dyrdoo or Dirdo. The earliest mention is in 1514, when William and Robert Dirdoe, gentlemen, held a cottage and a close of land in Milton. A Thomas Dirdoe is recorded in connection with lands granted to the Free School in the reign of Henry VIII. The family fortunes had considerably advanced by 1553-4 when Robert Dirdoe, son of the previous Robert, bought the manor of Milton from Sir John Leigh for £6 11s 6d. He had a son, William, who died in 1582, by which

Robert Frampton

28

Robert Frampton (1622-1707) was an outspoken royalist, who was present at a skirmish with parliamentary troops, and then became headmaster of the Free School in 1648. Shortly afterwards he became embroiled in a series of confrontations with John Gage, a Parliamentary Quartermaster, described as 'a man of resolution in an engagement, but of less personal valour than would support a single quarrel.' At their first encounter blows were exchanged 'which Mr. Frampton repaid with interest.' Their second confrontation took place in a room at the Phoenix Inn, where Frampton 'turned his [Gage's] heels higher than his head and beat him out of doors' using his schoolmaster's cane. Gage's third attempt to even up with his adversary was a plot to kidnap him by night to a place where he could be dealt with, but this was soon thwarted by Frampton, who drove his adversaries away and almost into the River Stour.

time the value of the manor had risen to £11. Several Dirdoes feature in Chancery suits concerning property in and around Gillingham at this time. Both a Thomas and a Christopher Dirdoe were involved in the Chancery suit concerning the Free School in 1598. In 1601 the manor of Milton was in the hands of Christopher Dirdoe. In 1608 both Thomas and Christopher Dirdoe were freeholders of the manor of Gillingham, while Thomas also held Barnaby's Mill and was one of the principal copyholders. In the 1615 church seating plan there occurs both the wife of Thomas Dirdoe, and also a Thomas Dirdoe the younger. A quoin stone on one of the outbuildings to the Old House at Milton records the marriage of Edward Dirdoe in 1640 (Fig. 29). The Dirdoe family were Catholics, and occur on the list of those who did not take the oath of Protestation in 1641. In 1650 Parliament held an enquiry into ecclesiastical property, revealing that Christopher Dirdoe held the ancient free chapel at Milton, the chapel then being in a decayed state and not used. In 1678 Dorothy, wife of Christopher Dirdoe, bequeathed to the church a flagon, which is still part of the church property. While the relationships between these family members may not be fully known, it is clear that this Milton gentry family played a significant role in Gillingham affairs at this time.[26]

A number of Gillingham families from this period are remembered for their overseas connections. Edward Rawson of Milton, born in 1615, married Rachel, daughter of Richard Perne of East Haimes, their daughter Rachel being baptised

29 The cornerstone of an outbuilding at the Old House in Milton, recalling the marriage of Edward Dirdoe in 1640. The stone may possibly have been removed from the house during rebuilding.

30 Howard Taft (1857-1930) was President of the United States from 1909 to 1913. Among his ancestors were the Rawson family, who emigrated from Gillingham to Massachusetts in the seventeenth century.

in Gillingham church in 1636. Shortly afterwards, the parents emigrated to Newbury, Massachusetts, leaving the daughter in Gillingham. Beginning as a settler and farmer, Edward Rawson had a distinguished public life which took him into the colonial administration and then into the House of Deputies of the Massachusetts Bay Colony. In 1652 he was elected Secretary to the Colony, a post which he held for 36 years. A major achievement during this time was his rewriting of the Laws and Liberties of the Colony. The Rawsons had eleven children, their son William having twenty children himself, so there may be a large number of their descendants in America today. A later family marriage linked the Rawsons to the American political dynasty of the Tafts, which produced both a president and senator of the United States (Fig. 30). Today in Gillingham the care home of Rawson Court, formerly the rectory, is a reminder of this family which distinguished itself on the far side of the Atlantic.[27]

Edward Rawson's marriage linked his family to the Pernes, who lived at East Haimes and were also owners of the Milton mill, which became known as Purn's Mill. Rachel's father, Richard Perne, had acquired the house of East Haimes and the Fee Forestership in

1615. He died in 1636, his wife, formerly Rachel Greene, remaining in the house until her death in 1656. The property then passed to her son Richard, who made over the rights to a brother-in-law, John Tyse. In 1673 the lease passed to Mary Goddard. East Haimes may have disappeared soon after this time. Another of the family was John Perne, who in 1662 had a house in Milton valued at eight hearths, one of three similarly large houses in Milton at the time, and thought by some to be a forerunner of Milton Lodge.

Richard Perne's marriage had linked the Pernes to another nearby family who became emigrants, the Greenes of Bowridge Hill. This family claimed a descent from King David of Scotland, and were also linked by marriage to the family of Archbishop Grindal, the church leader of Elizabethan times. John Greene of Gillingham, uncle of Edward Rawson's bride Rachel, had been a surgeon at Salisbury before emigrating to Salem, Massachusetts, eventually living at Rhode Island. A much later descendant, Nathaniel Greene, was a prominent commander in the revolutionary war against Britain.

To the west of Gillingham the Pile family appear to have acquired the manor of Wyke sometime in the late sixteenth or early seventeenth centuries. In 1645 William Pile bequeathed all his lands and farm at Wyke to a cousin, Gabriel Pile. In 1651 Gabriel Pile was found to be living at Milton with a 'farm at Wyke'. He died two years later, and in 1662 Thomas Pile transferred the property to his relations, the Frekes, who had the estate until 1807. By 1662 the estate had become a capital messuage, mansion house, and farm, with 340 acres of land. It seems likely, therefore, that Wyke Hall may have been built by Gabriel Pile in the 1650s. Much of the striking carved panelling in the house appears to date from this period. A will and inventory of George Freke, who died in 1686, mentions only a few rooms, far fewer than might be expected for a mansion, but it is possible that he occupied only a few rooms in the house.[28]

Another Catholic family were the Gildons, who lived at Kingsettle, Motcombe, paying tax for a house of ten hearths in 1662-3. Charles Gildon was born in 1663 and went to the Free School before moving to Douai to train for the Catholic priesthood. Hutchins tells us that 'having greatly injured his fortune by thoughtlessness and dissipation' he turned to writing works on spiritual and philosophical themes, as well as some dramas, but seems to have been largely unsuccessful. A contemporary writer describes him as a person of 'great literature, but a mean genius; who having attempted several kinds of writing, never gained much reputation in any.' Charles Gildon died in 1723 or 1724, perhaps less successful and certainly less remembered than some of his contemporaries in the town.[29]

6

1680 TO 1820: POPULATION, LAND, AND LIVELIHOODS

O N JUNE 19 1694 a fire broke out in the middle of Gillingham at around three in the afternoon. Within three hours it had consumed 40 houses together with their outbuildings, with damage to the value of £3,900. Fifty-four families were made homeless by the fire. Other than a brief reference in the minute books of the overseers of the poor, little else of the fire is known. The fire clearly merited a national appeal, since a village near Hertford is known to have contributed 1s 2d in relief, and there may have been other contributions from elsewhere which have not been recorded. The Shreen Water may have prevented the fire from spreading across to Newbury. The fire, devastating as it may have been, was not the only fire to have affected the town; another in 1742 destroyed six houses.[1] The 1694 fire, and subsequent events, may provide a reason why Gillingham has few buildings around its old town centre dating from earlier than 1800. Other Dorset towns were ravaged by numerous fires around this time, for instance Beaminster, which had fires in 1644, 1684, 1781, and 1786. In many towns the closely packed nature of houses, and the widespread use of thatch for roofing, made the rapid spread and devastation of fire inevitable.

At the time of the 1694 fire the tithing of Gillingham may have had a population of around 600-700, a figure loosely based on the 122 payers of the Hearth Tax recorded in 1663. Milton and Motcombe tithings at this time had a further 86 taxpayers, perhaps suggesting a population of around 400 or so for both of these places.[2] For the remainder of the seventeenth century and much of the eighteenth century the population size may have increased slowly or changed little. The number of burials recorded in the parish registers fluctuated considerably from year to year but averaged around 30 to 40 interments annually for much of the eighteenth century. However, baptisms showed a more general trend to increase in the middle and late parts of the century, indicating an overall population growth in the later decades, which continued into the early nineteenth century. These estimates take no account of movements of people into or out of the parish. These may have been considerable, since in the late eighteenth century we hear of cottages being erected to be sold to incomers, and the vestry found it necessary to tick off the overseers of the poor for issuing too many settlement certificates to visitors.[3]

The first definitive statement of Gillingham's population is the 1801 census, when 1,873 people were recorded for Gillingham, a figure which included Milton. Motcombe had a further 917. East and West Stour, although within the parish, were not part of the old Liberty of Gillingham and were recorded separately. The 1801 census caught the town at a time of rapid growth, for by 1811 the population figure had risen to 1,992, a six per cent increase, and by 1821 it stood at 2,246, a further increase of almost thirteen per cent.

Within the wider pattern of population change there were frequent fluctuations from year to year. The most extreme variations were the result of smallpox outbreaks, which were a major cause of mortality everywhere in Georgian England, accounting for about ten per cent of all deaths. In Gillingham the vicar occasionally noted 'smallpox' in the burial register, as in 1711 and 1715. Nineteen of the thirty-one burials between 26 October 1710 and 26 April 1711 were smallpox victims, marked with 'SP' by the vicar. The records of the overseers also indicate when money was spent on expenses arising from the outbreaks, such as relief for victims. Otherwise the virulence of the infection is indicated by the very high levels of deaths in any given year. In 1729 there were 55 burials, in 1740 45, and in 1767 112. Deaths from smallpox often peaked in winter and spring; in 1767 the outbreak claimed 82 of the 112 burials between March and July, reaching its peak in May, when there were four burials on the first of May and again on the tenth.[4]

The parish registers also suggest something of the pattern of marriages and childbearing of the time. Between April and December 1735 eight marriages were recorded in Gillingham church. Of these, seven couples produced children which were baptised in the church in subsequent years. Five of the couples had five or more children, but several were lost in infancy. Edward and Sarah Henbury, married hurriedly on 21 December 1735, had twins Edward and Sarah the following month, but lost both in little more than a year. Their two subsequent children were also named Edward and Sarah. Thomas and Grace Hill, married in September 1736, had son Thomas in March 1737 but he was buried in December 1740; a second Thomas was buried in 1742; a third Thomas was born in 1745. Altogether the wife bore six children, of which three died in infancy. While the registers from the earlier part of the century show that most couples stayed in the parish to have children, those from the later decades have a different pattern. These show that surprisingly few baptisms are traceable to couples married at this time, indicating that most couples married in the parish church did not stay in the parish long enough to have their children baptised there, moving away to other parishes.[5]

Landowners and tenants

B Y THE EIGHTEENTH century the pattern of landholding in and around Gillingham had markedly changed from how it had been in medieval and Tudor times. In this earlier period most people had been copyhold tenants of the royal manor or liberty, working the common fields of the manor and dependent on the pasturage and pannage of the common wastes and the royal forest. However, the changes of the Tudor and Stuart periods, involving disafforestation, enclosure, and the alienation of the manor from the Crown, had produced a new rural society dominated by gentry and well-off farmers. The modest manorial copyholders of Tudor times had given way to substantial men who could justifiably write 'Mr' before their names or maybe even 'Esq' afterwards. Many could trace their prosperity back to their Tudor forbears; others had acquired it through marriage, or by careful purchase of fields or entire estates on the land market. Some lived elsewhere than Gillingham, leasing their estates or parts of them to farmers who could more fittingly describe themselves as 'yeomen', while a few other smaller farmers could proudly affirm that they owned their own farms. At the lower end of the social scale were a large number of people occupying very small pieces of land, often only a few acres, followed by the 'husbandmen' or labourers of little or no property.

Something of this pattern of landowner and tenant can be seen in the Land Tax returns from 1780 onwards. In Gillingham from 1781, excluding Milton, Motcombe, and Bourton, the assessed amount of £328 was divided between 101 landowners. Of these, just 10 owners of land were responsible for paying 54% of the tax.[6] The largest single tax payment was of £35, paid for Wyke Hall and its estate by Thomas Freke of Hannington, near Swindon in Wiltshire. However soon after this time his estate seems to have become divided, since in 1786 the Freke estate had four occupiers paying between them only £8 13 9. Another large payer was the Reverend John Fullerton, who as absentee rector had the glebe lands known as 'The Rectory' on the Peacemarsh side of the town, for which he paid £31 10s. He also owned a number of smaller tenements for which he paid a further £12 10s.[7]

The largest landowner around Gillingham in terms of property and land tax was Sir Francis Sykes of Ackworth Park in Yorkshire, who was lord of Gillingham manor. Sykes had been an administrator in India, and became Member of Parliament for the borough of Shaftesbury. As lord of Gillingham manor, Sykes had inherited much of the property of the old forest in Gillingham and Motcombe. A map of 1767 shows his land in detail, an estate of several farms and many small hedged pastures (Fig. 31). When it was sold in 1821 it comprised 2,212 acres, mostly within a consolidated ring-fenced block. The largest farm was Woodwater (338 acres), the other principal

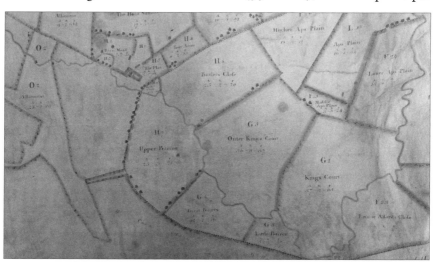

31 Extract from the estate map of Sir Francis Sykes. Sykes was lord of the manor and the largest landowner. Much of his property lay in the old forest areas. This extract shows the old park pale and the 'Kings Court' fields. The buildings on the upper left are those of Woodwater Farm.

farms being Woods End, Park House, Donedge Lodge, Coppelridge, Larkinglass, and Wolfridge. There were several smaller pieces of ground and many cottages, some in Gillingham and Motcombe, others around the countryside. The land tax was £106 19s 8d.[8]

A larger number of owners had smaller estates rated at under £10 each, but very few of the farms are named. William Read paid £9 8s for his estate at Langham and three other holdings. On his death in 1798 his estates amounted to 344 acres in Langham and Bugley. His monument in Gillingham church records his bequests to the parish, including money for the distribution of bread on St. Thomas's day, and weekly sums to the poor, excluding 'those who misbehave or become immoral.' At the other end of the land tax scale, the far greater number of landowners were small owners contributing no more than a few shillings each in tax. Most landowners leased their properties to occupiers, of whom the number in 1781 is difficult to calculate from the returns, but there were some forty owner-occupiers, mostly of smaller properties. Many of these may have been the townspeople, who had small pieces of land but gained most of their living from other livelihoods.[9]

Motcombe, which by this time had become separate in most respects from Gillingham, had a similar landowning pattern to its larger neighbour. Outside the Sykes estate, there was a wide spread of estate sizes and values, including many lower valued properties. At Milton, land was largely in the hands of a few large landowners and there were few small owners. Earlier in the century much of Milton had been in the hands of the Dirdoe family, whose rise has been described in an earlier chapter. The family fortunes advanced further when Henry Dirdoe (1647-1724) married Dorothy White, the daughter of a Sherborne merchant, who brought to the family a marriage settlement of £1,500. They had five sons and ten daughters.

However, the Dirdoe dynastic fortunes were to have an unexpected end. Henry outlived all of his sons, all of whom died young or were unmarried, so that on his death the estate was left to his wife and then to his daughters, and subsequently became divided. The estate then included the mansion house at Milton, known as the Old House, with its outhouses, dower house, fishponds, garden, and orchards (Plate 24). This passed to the Parham family, and eventually to the Matthews family. Henry had also owned the manor of Kington Magna, and lands at Kington Magna, Gillingham, Buckhorn Weston, East and West Stour, Nyland, and Motcombe. Three of the daughters are remembered in the 18-foot high memorial in

32 The 18-feet high monument to Frances Dirdoe in Gillingham church. Frances and two of her sisters, Rebecca and Rachel, are depicted as the 'Three Graces' of Greek mythology, the daughters of Zeus and handmaids of Venus who personified grace, beauty, and charm. Frances died at the age of 34 'in years scarce past her bloom, but in body wasted with a lingering disease.' The epitaph would have reminded people that life could be short for both rich and poor.

Gillingham church (Fig. 32). The family left a charity chargeable on Milton Farm, to be distributed to the poor on St. Thomas' day, later used for the assistance of apprentices. Since 1981 this charity has been joined with the Read charity.[10]

In 1781 the largest landowner at Milton was Albinus Martin of Pierston (1732-90), who paid £24 9s out of the total tax of £62. His estate, advertised for sale by auction in 1801, was a good example of a prospering country estate, being described as '607 acres of rich feeding land and water meadow, all within a ring-fence … the river Stour abounds with trout, running through the centre of the premises.' Its rents were valued at £970. In 1781 the name of Matthews appears several times in the Milton land tax records, ushering in a family which in time was to acquire much of Milton and also contribute hugely to the future growth of Gillingham. In 1802 John Matthews (1764-1820) paid tax for his own land and was also the lessee of substantial land from George Whitchurch and Joseph Long. He is thought to have acquired Milton Lodge, which he then rebuilt. The Sly family, who have a monument in Gillingham church, were landowners and farmers in Milton at around this time.[11]

Silton, with a population of only 341 in 1801, was even more in the hands of a single gentlemen landowner. In 1781 Humphrey Sturt paid almost half of the land tax of £77. He was of the wealthy Sturt family who owned the mansion and park of Moor Crichel and had built Horton Tower earlier in the century. Sturt, described as a man of 'inviolable integrity and a good heart', was a patron of both the arts and agricultural improvement, and has been described as representing well the characteristics and qualities of the Dorset landed gentry of his time. In 1791 his Silton estate was offered for sale as 1,270 acres, 'the property of a man of fashion.'[12]

Other landed families of substance in and around Gillingham are more difficult to trace. A monument in Gillingham church records several members of the Helmes family, one of whom died in Nevis in the West Indies. Families in Antigua, not far from Nevis, are known to have had this name. The Gillingham Helmes are associated with the large properties of Newbury House and Thorngrove, but nothing more is known of any overseas estates they may have had.[13]

The eighteenth century saw a long-running dispute over land and property concerning the lands belonging to the Trustees of Sherborne School (Plate 10). The School had first been endowed

33 A schedule of some of the lands belonging to Sherborne School. The schedule was produced because ownership of these parcels was disputed with the Frekes of Wyke Hall, giving rise to a law suit that extended over many years.

with these lands after the dissolution of the St. Katharine's Chantry in 1549. Following this event the school revived ancient manorial rights attaching to these lands and began to hold manor courts in the Chantry House, the present-day Chantry Cottage. The minutes of the court and the numerous surrenders and admissions indicate that manor courts were held until at least the middle of the eighteenth century. The school also continued the leasing of its lands, a practice continued from the days of chantry ownership (Chapter 5), the school records containing many copies of leases between the sixteenth and early nineteenth centuries. One such lease related to 19½ acres of land in the north and south fields of Gillingham. The school had leased the land to Hugh Wyndham in 1666, but by the 1720s these lands were claimed by the Freke family of Wyke Hall and were in the tenure of a number of people, so that the School rights were disputed (Fig. 33). This land lay in parcels scattered around the common fields, and it is likely that the fragmentation of the holding had contributed to the situation. Francis Fisher, acting for the school, attempted to reclaim its land, which led to the dispute going to the court of Chancery between 1724 and 1727. John Toogood, a governor of the school, continued the work of Fisher in the 1770s, with the result that the lands and rents were successfully recovered.[14]

Farming and enclosure

AGRICULTURAL COMMENTATORS OF the time were in no doubt about the sources of wealth of the Gillingham landowners. William Stevenson, in his report on the agriculture of Dorset in 1815, pointed to the high value of the pastures in the Vale of Blackmore, which could be rented at between 30s and 60s per acre. This was comparable with the £2 to £3 which could be had for the rich water meadows around Wareham, and notably more than the 18s to 24s for arable chalklands. The prime pastures in this 'vale of little dairies' were the meadowlands along the Stour, in particular demand for hay for the overwintering of dairy cattle, and of sheep or 'hogs' which would be returned on to the higher grounds of the chalklands after Ladyday. The Vale lands were everywhere heavily stocked over the winter, and there was a general shortage of cowhouses, so that cattle had to be kept outside, leading to foot damage. Meadows might be expected to yield half a ton of hay per acre, the better meadows along the streams perhaps producing up to a ton per acre, enough to keep one ox in hay for twelve weeks. A rule of thumb was that an acre and a quarter of Blackmore Vale pastures would support a fully grown ox.[15]

The Devonshire type of cow was becoming increasingly popular, considered to be well adapted to the low, sheltered pastures of the Vale, a good beast being worth £12, more than in other parts of the county. The cream and milk they produced was made into butter and cheese; the skimmed milk into inferior cheese, salted and sold in the London and Portsmouth markets. Beef was sent to the markets at Salisbury, Shaftesbury, Sturminster, and Stalbridge, and also sold to contractors for sale in Poole and Portsmouth. By the early nineteenth century, pastures were dominant everywhere, suggesting a shift away from the more mixed husbandry recorded in the probate inventories of a century earlier. Stevenson estimated that no more than ten per cent of the land of the Vale was arable, but this may have been an overstatement since in 1821 a quarter of the Sykes estate was under arable fields.[16] But away from the Stour on the drier slopes of the Corallian west of Gillingham the proportion of arable may have been higher; the estates of the late William Read at Langham and Bugley, sold by auction in 1798, had around half their acreage under arable.[17]

On the Sherborne School lands, leases determinable on three lives were the normal tenure. The lessee paid an entry fine and an annual rent, and the lease held good as long as one of the three entered names was still alive. A small number of short leases of a few years are recorded, but with severe penalties for ploughing up the pastures. On the Sykes estate farms, tenancies were from year to year, although some cottage leases were determinable on lives while a few were held under fines certain. In this respect Stevenson suggests that the Vale was behind the rest of Dorset, where fee simple, or freehold ownership, was more common. On the Sherborne lands some families occupied their tenements for many decades, with the lease being renewed through the generations. For example, a close of pasture of two acres and a further 14 acres of land in Milton leased from Sherborne School by John Butt in 1550 remained in the Butt family until at least 1730, the lease having been renewed five times in the intervening period. Another lease of six acres south of the Stour in 1552 to the Henbury family was in their possession until 1689 and can be traced further through other families well into the eighteenth century, the last recorded lease of this piece of land being to John Tinney in 1744.[18]

In the areas of the old forest, and in other parts of the parish away from the common fields, owners and occupiers alike had been able for centuries to gradually build up consolidated estates and holdings. This was not the case in the areas closer to the town, where much of the common field still remained unenclosed and where holdings were highly fragmented. A survey and map of the Sherborne School lands, made in 1733 at the time of the dispute discussed above, reveals that apart from one large field on the boundary with Silton and a few smaller closes near to the Chantry house, the rest of the estate lay in tiny parcels scattered across the common fields (Plate 10). Many of these were strip-like parcels of no more than an acre or so; some were described as 'bounded out' or 'set out', perhaps indicating imminent hedging or fencing; others still remained as 'lanchards' or unenclosed strips. Altogether the school owned 134 acres in Gillingham and Milton dispersed across the fields in 76 parcels or fields. In the Cumber Mead or Common Mead occupiers had created several encroachments, clearly distinguished on the map. It can only be assumed that the lands of other landowners were similarly fragmented and dispersed. The survey appears to glimpse the Gillingham common fields at a time of their gradual, otherwise unrecorded consolidation and enclosure, but still with extensive unenclosed tracts of open field. A further survey of the Sherborne School lands in 1780 records only 64 acres in twenty parcels, indicating that some lands may have been disposed of in the meantime.[19]

By the eighteenth century the waste lands of the manor survived only as small areas or as verges along the common waysides. In Gillingham the largest was the Common Mead and Smith Mead, some 130 acres mostly south of Common Mead Lane. Ham Common amounted to 41 acres spread out along both sides of the Shaftesbury Road, while Peacemarsh Common had 43 acres similarly spread along the road to Mere. There were smaller patches at Wyke Marsh, Coldharbour, and Lodbourne Green. In Milton there were common wastes at Little Marsh, where the Mere road divided from the Bourton road. The largest tracts of commons in Milton were at Mapperton Hill and White Hill, which was of 90 acres. These areas were used jointly with the commoners of Mere, which had about 200 acres of wastes at each of the two sites.[20] By 1770 the population of Gillingham was rapidly rising, and throughout the 1770s the manor court rolls record numerous instances of encroachments on the wastes, including the erection of cottages. Between 1777 and 1798 there were 58 presentments for encroachments on the commons, and a further 25 for the erection of cottages and other buildings. It is more difficult to know how many of these were 'repeat' presentments following removal orders which had not been complied with, or how many encroachments were followed later by the erection of a structure on the same ground. However there can be no doubt that encroachments on the commons by squatters were coming to be seen as a major problem.[21] Many of these encroachments were of small pieces of land and of laneside verges, which until that time had been wide enough for the movement and grazing of cattle. The result was a significant narrowing of the trackways and reduction in the true areas of common land. The pattern is well seen along the south side of Ham Common, along Peacemarsh, and at Little Marsh and Wyke Marsh, where there were numerous cottages standing in small plots.

In December 1776 a meeting was held which ordered that recent encroachments should be thrown open, and no further encroachments were to be allowed. Application was to be made to Parliament for an enclosure bill, in which allotments would be awarded to those with rights of common, and encroachments already made were to be incorporated into the enclosure scheme. The expenses of the scheme were to be raised by subscription, and the reverse of the note lists the subscribers, all of whom were the principal landowners of the parish. In June 1777 William England, a Shaftesbury surveyor, produced a map showing the location of the various wastes of the manor (Fig.

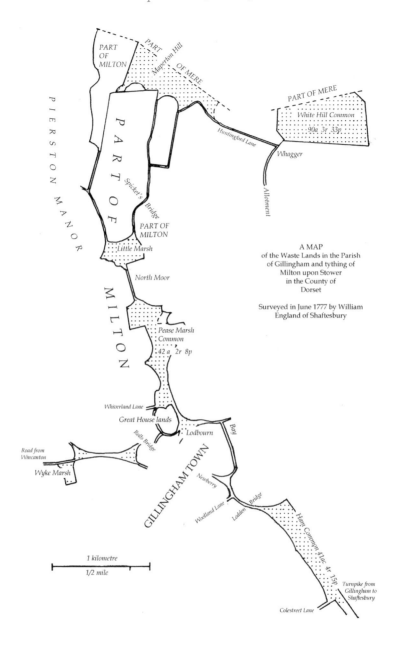

34 *The waste lands of the manor of Gillingham, from a map of 1777. Mapperton Hill and White Hill were part of a wider area of common land which extended into Mere, and were used jointly by the inhabitants of both parishes.*

34).[22] Nothing much seems to have followed, since in July 1781 a letter was written to Sir Francis Sykes, lord of the manor, from landowners and occupiers, although no signatories are included on the copy. The letter noted the many encroachments lately made by the poor, not only erecting new cottages but making enclosures for gardens and orchards, which had since been sold to people outside the parish. This in turn had encouraged families from outside to come and settle, thus increasing the demands on the poor rates. There was a further request to prevent further encroachments and to apply for a bill of enclosure.[23] A further proposal for enclosing the commons is not dated, and may be later or earlier than the above. This included matters such as the establishment of trustees, the raising of expenses, and the outcome for existing encroachments. Mere, which had commons bordering on Gillingham, was also to be invited to join the scheme.[24]

Enclosure of the remaining commons was finally achieved by an Act of 1809. No scheme or map of enclosure has been found, although a map of the whole of the parish dated 1820 may possibly relate to the enclosures. The Mapperton Hill and White Hill enclosures were carried out jointly with enclosures in the parish of Mere. It was another few years before enclosure was finally achieved, the references to 'allotments' on the later tithe map (1841) indicating the grounds enclosed. The enclosure was highly unpopular with farmers and commoners who had depended on the wastes for grazing their livestock, and in March 1810 this discontent came to a head. The Salisbury and Winchester Journal reported that:

> The inclosures of Milton and Mere Commons have excited much discontent. On Saturday se'enight nearly three hundred men from Gillingham and parts adjacent met on Maperton Hill and Pier'swood and destroyed a long line of the new defences. A troop of horse from Dorchester barracks is now quartered in the neighbourhood, and several ringleaders of the rioters have been taken into custody.

A number of people were tried at Salisbury in August, and were bound over for future good behaviour; several seem to have been people who had been using the commons illegally rather than farmers with a legal right to their use.[25]

Rather more is known about the enclosure scheme for the Common or Cumber Mead and Smith Mead. A plan shows that 130 acres were enclosed, divided into 23 allotments (Fig. 35). The largest of these, 16 acres, was awarded to J. Kneller of Thorngrove; another of 12 acres went to the Trustees of Sherborne School, as recompense for the former encroachments described above. The accounts survive for the wages paid to the labourers for the banking, ditching, and hedging of the Common Mead enclosure: quickthorn plants were paid for at the rate of 2s for every hundred planted, and among the many items

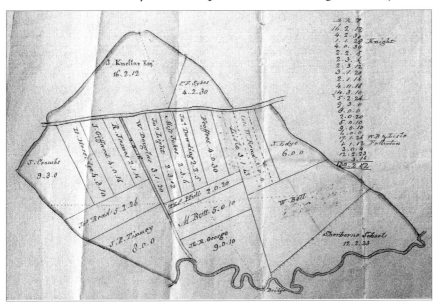

35 The scheme of enclosure for the Common Mead and Smith Mead, carried out around 1812. Common Mead Lane runs from left to right across the upper part of the plan. The lane extending southwards to the river today gives access to the Sewage Works.

in the daily wages book are £1 16s 'paid to Thomas Light for a small oak gate … and setting up between Home and Bottom Jubilee'.[26]

Industries, trades, and the Silk Mill

I N ANY DORSET village or town with a population of more than around five hundred, it was to be expected that the community at this time would be largely self-sufficient in all its material needs. In Puddletown, which was smaller than Gillingham, a survey of the village made by the vicar in 1724 revealed 28 different occupations, and there were as many people employed in trades as in agriculture.[27] While there is no similarly methodical survey for Gillingham until 1823, a look through the many wills and inventories of the town for the period reveals a similarly wide range of livelihoods. In the wills, shopkeepers, blacksmiths, and wheelwrights are notably prominent; but close behind are shoemakers, milliners, tailors, saddlers, and surgeons. The tallow chandler, stonemason, and tin plate worker are also to be found among the occupations given, filling out the picture of a town which expected to provide for its services from amongst its own people.[28]

Other references in wills are to an architect and an attorney, suggesting the existence of a professional middle class in the town. This would have included William Tinney, a major landowner in the town, sometime owner of Purns Mill, and an original partner in the silk mill venture. He was the solicitor who aided John Hume in his Exchequer case (Chapter 7) and was also active in the Gillingham church consistory courts dealing with legacy disputes. He could be an example of the many 'eighteenth century lawyers [who] throve on copyhold and tithe disputes', often 'leading the winners to mere paper victories and the losers to ruin'.[29]

At this time there were three corn mills in and around the town. In Gillingham itself was the town mill or Barnaby's Mill, by the bridge over the Shreen; in 1751 this belonged to Stephen Hannam. Further upstream was Purns Mill, owned by Richard Perne in 1687 and by John Card in 1751. By the 1820s it belonged to Matthew Parham, who had purchased it from the Tinney family (Plate 14). Downstream from the town was Eccliffe Mill, recorded in 1751 as belonging to John Toogood, but it is not known if it was working at this time.

The most frequent reference in documents to occupations other than farming or husbandry is to cloth making. Gillingham was reckoned as one of nine cloth-making towns in Dorset in the early eighteenth century. There is mention in wills of linen weavers or 'linmen'. The growing of flax and the manufacture of linen was becoming increasingly widespread in parts of Somerset and Dorset at this time. Although centred on the area around Chard and Crewkerne, the industry was also present in west and north Dorset, with the growing of flax being particularly suited to the damper soils. The industry was especially well developed at Silton, where the growing of flax is recorded as early as the fourteenth century. After harvesting the flax plants were tied in bundles and laid out to be bleached by the sun, to be then rotted in water. The family then undertook the processes of combing, spinning, and weaving. The products included bed ticking, a strong twill fabric with a narrow blue band; dowlas, a plain, coarse, linen cloth; and linsey woolsey, a rough cloth with a linen warp and woollen weft, used for working clothes and dairy maids' aprons.[30]

In the Gillingham parish registers there are references to linen weavers in the 1650s, and they are often mentioned in court rolls, leases, and wills whenever occupations are given. A directory of 1783 lists Amos Heal and T. Mitchell as manufacturers of ticking in Gillingham, and another of 1793 includes Isaac Maggs as a tick manufacturer at Silton.[31] The manufacturers employed many people in their homes as outworkers, so that the total number employed in the trade in some way was considerable. The industry had a particular appeal to cottagers and smaller farmers for whom it provided an additional means of livelihood in the winter. Where space could be found for a loom, other members of the family could be employed in spinning or dyeing. An essential outbuilding was the 'bucking house', where the yarn was washed.

Probate inventories from the late seventeenth century give us some striking references to this 'cottage industry'. Thomas Lane, who died in 1678, had a bleachyard with 630 lb of yarn, and a bucking house with two furnaces. He also had stocks of flax, with further flax belonging to him being spun elsewhere, and a weaving shop with two looms. The total value of his inventory, which would have included his stocks of materials, was £296 16s. Jeremiah Gatehouse of Motcombe (d.1684) had stocks of flax and yarn, and also had a bucking house and a loomshop, and his assets amounted to £241 14s.[32]

These references give little indication of the extent of the industry in Gillingham or how it was organised. A key figure in the area in the 1670s must have been Thomas Barnes. He was buried at Gillingham on 19 September 1682, a week after his inventory was made, but he may have lived at Motcombe, Milton, or possibly Bourton, where a Richard Barnes died in 1694. His huge stocks of linens, woollen fabrics, and other textiles and dress materials make up an inventory many pages long, and were worth £235. Barnes appears to have been a clothier and dealer, a key figure in the trade, and we might expect that his business involved organising the work of the weavers and spinners around the district, travelling around the cottages and farms and arranging for the collection and movement of materials and finished fabrics. Another leading manufacturer was William Boulting of Silton, who in 1767 retired and transferred his business to his son, another William. His extensive trade network included debtors as far away as Devon, Cornwall, Somerset, Hereford, and London.[33]

One step towards the wider development of industry in Gillingham came around 1769 with the opening of the silk mill. The silk industry in England dates from the early seventeenth century and expanded under the influence of Flemish immigrants and Huguenot craftsmen in London. In 1740 the silk industry had arrived in Sherborne, and by the 1770s the original workings at Westbury Mill had been considerably rebuilt and enlarged. The success of the Sherborne venture may have encouraged Stephen Hannam, the owner of Barnaby's corn mill, to expand into the business of a silk throwster. He entered into a partnership with the lawyer William Tinney, the Bruton clothier Joseph Whitehead, and with John Daniel of Yeovil. The partners undertook to build a silk mill on a site adjoining the corn mill and to invest in the necessary water wheels and machinery. In 1776 this partnership was dissolved and Stephen Hannam found a new partner for his business.[34]

The silk was largely sourced from Italy, but it is also recorded that local people were encouraged to breed silk worms and hand in the cocoons to the mill for spinning. The worms lived on the leaves of mulberry trees, and until recently these trees were to be found in gardens around the town. It may be relevant that William Willmott of the Sherborne mill had frequent trouble with outside suppliers, and also with his water supply, and that in the original Gillingham partnership it was agreed that, in event of a water shortage, the needs of the silk mill should take priority over the corn mill.

From the 1780s much of the labour for the mill was provided by girl apprentices, who were indentured from London workhouses by Catherine Hannam to 'learn the art and mystery of a silk throwster.' Several of these indentures have survived: a typical group of eleven is that from the parish of St. Leonard's in Shoreditch, dated between 1781 and 1784. The children varied in age from 9 to 15 years, the indenture binding them to serve the mill until the age of 21 or marriage. Some indentures from other parishes were to the age of 18; one obliged the mistress to provide 'double apparel of all sorts, good, and new … one suit for holydays and another for working days.' Besides Shoreditch, children were recruited from the parishes of St. Marylebone, St. Mary

The Gillingham Silk Mill

36 Above: The town mills, at the time of the Hannams, as depicted by Henry Moule around 1835. Left: washing and drying block, with dormitory above. Centre: silk mill. Right: corn (grist) mill. Opposite page: The mills at around 1900, showing the rebuilt corn mill. The new mill manager's house is just off the right of the picture. By this time the silk business had come to an end.

The Gillingham silk mill was built by Stephen Hannam in 1769, and remained in the Hannam family throughout its working life. After his death in 1780 the business was for a short time in the hands of his wife, Catherine, before passing to their son, Josiah, who managed it until 1828. It then passed to his son Samuel Hannam (d.1840) and to Samuel's brother Josiah in 1840. Josiah subsequently entered into a partnership with a nephew, Thomas Thompson. By this time the family had also acquired the adjoining corn or grist mill. On Josiah's death in 1874 the company was acquired by his nephew, Samuel Hannam Stephens, until its closure in 1895.

The business of the Hannams was as silk throwsters, that is 'one who prepares raw silk for the weaver by cleansing it and twisting it', the word 'throw' meaning to twist into thread. The preparation of the material up this point involved some fourteen distinct operations. The manufacture was heavily dependent on female labour. Some of the items of machinery used in the manufacture of silken thread are to be found in the Gillingham Museum.

A sketch and later photographs show the Hannam silk mill as a three-storey building with further lights in the roof, directly adjoining the corn mill. The wheel for both mills was at the north end of the mill buildings and was transmitted under the floor of the grist mill store by wooden drive shafts. Next to the mill, facing east towards the river, was an additional double-storey building; the lower part was used for washing, drying, and working rooms, while the upstairs served as the dormitory for the apprentices. To the east of both mills was the mill manager's house (Figs. 36, 37).

The dormitory building was later used by the printer, T.H. Brickell. The main mill range, derelict for some years, remained one of Gillingham's most distinctive buildings until its destruction by fire in 1982. The mill water wheel can still be seen in a field by Waterloo Mill, Silton (Plate 15).

Another firm in the local area engaged in silk manufacture was that of Charles Jupe and Son, who worked at Hinkes' Mill further up the Shreen Water, in Mere. They had other mills in Mere, Crockerton, and Warminster, and employed a thousand people.

le Bow, and St. Botolph without Aldersgate. On arrival in Gillingham the apprentices were accommodated in the mill's dormitory building. By the early nineteenth century around 160 persons may have been employed in the business. Outside the mill around the town and countryside, cottagers were engaged at home in winding the skeins of silk on bobbins, ready for twisting. A wagon was kept to carry the silk and bobbins from the cottages to the mill for spinning into yarn.[35]

37 An item of silk winding machinery to be found in the Gillingham Museum

There were a number of small early brickworks in Gillingham and its nearby area, using the underlying Kimmeridge Clays. The 1608 manor rental mentions a 'Brickmore acre lying in the common field' and there was a brickworks at Long Cross during the eighteenth century. The brickworks at Kings Court was in existence in 1825 and flourished until the 1860s (Chapter 8). Another site was further along the road at Parkhouse Farm. A further early nineteenth century brickworks may lie beneath the Lidl store in Newbury.[36]

By the mid-eighteenth century there was a malthouse in Queen Street behind the house now known as The Barton. A 1747 fire insurance policy refers to this house and also to an adjoining thatched malthouse, with utensils and stock, all in the hands of Edward Cox. The later tithe map of 1841 shows a long premises extending to the rear of the house, and a maltster named in the trade directories of the 1840s can be linked with this address.[37]

We have to wait until Pigot's directory of 1823 for a more overall look at trades and occupations in Gillingham in the early nineteenth century. It stated the population of the whole parish as 2,246, 'great numbers of which are employed in spinning silk, and in the manufacture of tick and dowlas.' Besides the industries described above, there are references to carpenters and joiners, coopers, wheelwrights, as well as to a sadler, maltster, woolstapler, and butter factor, all occupations associated with an agricultural town. We also find references to providers of more personal and domestic needs, including bakers, butchers, milliners, surgeons, and tailors.[38] While it is unlikely that this directory is at all comprehensive, it suggests the growing range of services in the town at this time.

Housing

T HE EIGHTEENTH CENTURY saw the beginnings of a wider rebuilding of houses in and around Gillingham, particularly among the better off of the population. In the town itself there are few examples of homes from this century because of the widespread extent of later rebuilding, and houses from this time are more common in the countryside and villages. The simpler buildings are mostly constructed in uncoursed rubble, only the few larger examples having coursed walls or ashlar dressings around windows and doors. Many of these houses now have tiled or slate roofs, but thatch was once much more widespread. Frontages have small casement windows and sometimes have central doorways, a simple concession to the Georgian fashion. Hipped roofs were fashionable for larger buildings. There is little brick in houses of this time, but sometimes it occurs in chimney stacks and garden walls; it is likely that the bricks produced by the small local brickworks were not of sufficient quality for house walling, but adequate for other uses.

Probate inventories from the earlier part of the period, up to 1740, give us a glimpse of what homes might have looked like inside, and what they contained. These inventories, valuing the contents of the home, were made shortly after a person died, usually by groups of three or four neighbours or local men, and are usually found attached to the will of the deceased. The inventory of William Blacker of Gillingham, who died in 1677, records that he had a small dwelling with just a hall, kitchen, a chamber over the kitchen, and another chamber over the passage. The use of the word 'hall', with no chambers over it, suggests a main room which was open to the roof, making his house not too different in layout from houses of medieval times.

Thomas Nason (or Nation, died 1680) had a more substantial farmhouse with a hall, kitchen, and parlour downstairs, and five chambers upstairs. John Ellis (d.1666) is described as a yeoman, and his house had a hall, chamber, brewhouse, and buttery, the house having been rated at four hearths in 1663. The farmhouse of Edward Carrant (d. 1681) was quite substantial, having a parlour, hall, closet, kitchen, buttery, brewhouse, and dairy house, with four chambers and a cockloft above. Christopher Green (d.1721) had a parlour, parlour chamber, hall, hall chamber, another chamber, kitchen chamber, garret, and kitchen; outside were a dairy house and barn. All these were houses built to a comfortable standard, with more chambers or personal rooms, and probably had more stone in their structure than their predecessors.[39]

The inventories itemise the contents of each room, and often list the stocks of farm produce and the farmer's livestock. John Ellis had stocks of cheeses, bags of malt, and sides of bacon. Outside the valuers found 6 acres of corn still growing, a rick of wheat, four bushels of peas, 2 heifers, and 2 colts. The livestock of Edward Haym of Motcombe (d.1689) was 4 oxen, 7 heifers, 16 pigs, 21 cows, a bull, a calf, 11 'weaning' calves, 7 horses, 64 sheep, and 104 geese and poultry. Christopher Green had ricks of wheats and oats, stocks of barley and peas, as well as 12 cows, 12 young beasts, a yoke of steers, a fat pig, and 120 sheep. Such detail gives a glimpse into the diversity of domestic and farming life in and around Gillingham at this time.[40]

Markets, fairs, and roads

ITTLE IS KNOWN about the holding of markets in Gillingham in earlier centuries, but in 1823 Pigot's Directory was able to record a small market on Friday. There is no indication of where in the town this might have been held, but the Square is the most likely venue. Two fairs were held annually, one on Trinity Monday and the other on the 12th September, for horses, bullocks, and sheep.[41] These were held on Lodbourne Green, then larger than it is now, much of the space having been built over in recent times.

For much of this period the growth of business and trade was limited by the poor condition of the roads. In medieval and Tudor times the roads had largely been broad trackways across the open commons and between the blocks of the common fields. Given the wet nature of much of the ground, wide tracks were essential for the regular movement of livestock if the ways were not to be trampled into seas of mud. Some of these tracks are shown on the 1624 map. By the eighteenth century enclosure and encroachments had steadily reduced the width of many roads, turning them into impassable muddy tracks as the ground was churned up by the increasing concentration of hooves. The problem was particularly acute around Motcombe, often making it difficult for the farmers to reach the market at Shaftesbury (Chapter 5).

An Act of 1555 required the annual appointment of an overseer or surveyor of the highways for each parish. Like the overseers of the poor, he was empowered to raise a local rate for highway maintenance, and to present his accounts to the vestry. A further Act of 1563 required each householder to work under the supervision of the overseer for six days each year. This obligation, although widely evaded, remained the basis of road maintenance for the next three centuries. In practice, overseers often found it easier to use the highway rates to pay labourers for the work done. A highway overseer's account of 1791 records the expenditure of William Bell in paying for road repairs. This consisted mostly of quarrying stone from the quarry at Slait near Silton. The stone was then 'beaten' and 'thrown' on to the roads, presumably to fill up the many potholes and produce a firmer surface. Another source of roadmaking material was gravel from White Hill. The labourers were paid 5d or 6d per load. The many locations where roads were repaired included Ham Common, Back Lane (South Street), Langhams Lane, Pothooks Lane, Jukes Lane, and Wyke Lane.[42]

Turnpiking eventually produced some improvements on the main roads, and is more fully discussed in Chapter 8. In the meantime the continuing bad state of roads produced complaints from outside the parish. In 1811 a Mr T.Phillips of Charnedge (Charnage) Farm near Mere complained to the surveyors of the road leading from Sly's Lane towards Benjafields farm 'being much out of repairs', and gave notice that he would prefer an indictment at the ensuing Shaftesbury Quarter Sessions. He may have had land in the Benjafields neighbourhood, and like many other farmers and landowners found the poor state of roads a limitation to the development of land improvement and better husbandry.[43]

7

1680 TO 1820: MANOR,

CHURCH, AND PARISH

To A MODERN generation accustomed to well-marked lines of responsibilities and accountabilities in local government, the workings of parish administration in Georgian times can seem anything but clear. Manors and vestries, haywards and overseers, churchwardens and constables, all seem to jostle with each other in their endeavours to impose order, while the focus of authority shifts around between rectory, vestry, manor house, and poor house, the decision-making itself rarely straying too far from the local inn. Upstarts against the system could find themselves before a manor court, a justice of the peace, or even a church court, depending on the nature of the offence. On and around this stage, the lead actors fulfilling the various parish duties are few in number but appear frequently, wearing different hats to suit the changing roles.

In Gillingham local administration had acquired several layers over the centuries. The Saxon system of liberty and tithings had become the royal manor of medieval times, modified to embrace the distinctive laws and systems of the forest. In Tudor times a new authority had emerged in the school feoffees, who besides looking after the Free School were also given responsibility for the roads, bridges, and the poor. By the eighteenth century most powers had been taken into the hands of the parish vestry, a group of leading townspeople which appointed the churchwardens, overseers of the poor, and highway surveyors, and so-called because they usually met in the vestry of the church. The parish itself was one of the largest in the county, in 1801 containing 15,886 acres, and including Motcombe, Milton, Bourton, East Stour, and West Stour. The system administering this large area was to last mostly unaltered well into the nineteenth century, and only finally disappeared with the arrival of new local government in 1894.[1]

Law and order; fire and water

LAW AND ORDER was maintained by the constables, elected to serve annually by the manor Court Leet, as in Elizabethan and medieval times. One means they could use to enforce authority was the stocks, which were in use as late as 1841, when the manor court ordered that they should be repaired (Fig. 38). Another feature intended to promote order was the town pound, where the haywards kept cattle which had broken through hedges and strayed. The pound was at Wyke by Pound Lane, and there was also one at Motcombe, but references in the manor court rolls suggest that trespassing cattle continued to be a common nuisance.

Less easily ignored was the 'lock-up', built by the vestry for the use of the constables around 1750. The lock-up was built in the yard behind the Free School on land belonging to the school feoffees, and conveniently sited only a few yards from the Phoenix and Red Lion public houses, from which any disorder might be expected to originate (Plate 12). This tiny but forbidding building, accessed only by a single heavy door, was also known as the 'Blind House' on account of its lack of windows. It remained in use until the police station was built in 1890, reminding us of a time when disorder was dealt with in a more summary way than is often the case today.[2]

38 A modern depiction of the use of the stocks. They are assumed to have been placed somewhere near the Square or the church. The upper part of the stocks can be seen in the Museum.

Offences more serious than simple disorder or drunkenness were heard before the magistrate at Shaftesbury or Sherborne. Punishments for theft could be harsh, even if no violence was involved. In 1764 Thomas Francis, a labourer, stole two fowls from an outhouse, and tried unsuccessfully to sell them. When he failed, he flung the fowls into the mill pond, and was apprehended. His punishment was to be publicly whipped in Sherborne market place the following Saturday. Thefts of farm produce and livestock were considered major offences; in 1818 a five guineas reward was offered for apprehension of the thief of quantities of hay stolen from fields at Wyke Street and Chantry.[3]

Another innovation by the vestry was a recognition of the need to deal promptly with fires, which had inflicted considerable damage on the town in previous generations. A consequence of this was the purchase of the first fire engine in 1790. This was housed in a room under the Free School and remained in service until 1836, when a a new horse-drawn fire engine was purchased (Plate 13). The churchwardens accounts have several references to the fire engine, including '1793: a quart of oil for the fire engine 1s 8d ……. Paid David Phripp for plastering the engine house 1s 8d'.[4]

As the town population increased, water supply became a growing problem. Until this time water had been obtainable only from shallow wells or the river, but by the eighteenth century this was becoming inadequate for the needs of the town. The solution was the sinking of the town's first deep well at the corner of St. Martin's Street opposite the church. This went down 100 feet through the Kimmeridge Clay into the underlying limestone, ensuring a supply of water which would rise under its own pressure to within a few feet of the surface. The cost of the well was met by the vicar, William Douglas, and the event is marked by a stone tablet. The site is still known as Spring Corner.[5]

The manor courts

T HE WORKINGS OF the later Gillingham manor courts are well documented in the 45 bound volumes of proceedings which cover the entire period from 1700 to 1934 apart from the years 1705 to 1725. Despite the shrinkage in their role and significance since medieval and Tudor times, the courts still met approximately once a month, a few meetings being spread over two days. Over one year between 1 September 1780 and 8 September 1781 there were 15 days when the court met. On six of these days only the officers attended and no specific business is recorded. Between 1745 and 1750 the officers appear to have been most noticeable by their absence. Hutchins tells us that 'the court was held anciently in a house

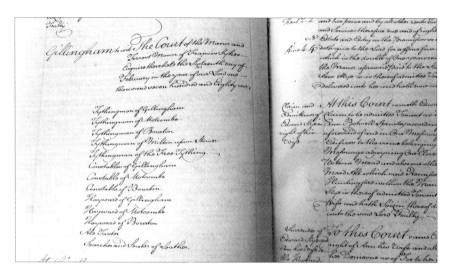

39 An extract from the manor court book of 1781, listing the officers of the manor. Many of the entries in the books refer to the transactions of land and property between tenants.

near the church acres, near the Red Lion inn which being damaged by fire, they are now held at the Phoenix inn.'[6] On most court days, the business was entirely about surrenders and admittances to copyhold lands (Fig. 39). Many areas of the parish that were still copyhold lands of the manor of Gillingham, and required the surrender of land and the payment of a fine before a new copyholder could be admitted to the property. Many of these entries relate to family farms and record the passage of land from one descendant to another over generations. The details of each transaction are carefully written into the court book, and it is the recording of these that fills most of the pages in the volumes.

The most important meetings, with business extending beyond copyhold transactions, were those of the court leet for the liberty of Gillingham. This court, concerned with civil affairs and minor offences, had been the main instrument of medieval administration, but by now its role was diminished and limited to petty misdemeanours around the town and the common lands. Until 1751 the court leet met twice annually, but thereafter met only once at the beginning of October. Its first task was the appointment of the officers of the manor: these were the tithingmen of each of the five tithings of the manor, the constables and haywards of Gillingham, Motcombe, and Bourton, and the ale taster and 'searcher and sealer of leather' for Gillingham. The appointment of the last named may indicate the existence of a leather or tanning trade in the town. This was followed by the swearing in of the jury of 15 people which would hear the presentments of offences to the court.

The constables and some of the tithingmen appear to have been mostly drawn from some of the smaller landowners and better-off tenant farmers or owner occupiers. These people are readily identifiable from the payments of substantial sums of land tax for their holdings. In 1780 the three names considered for constables were all occupiers or tenant farmers for which £8 or more of land tax was paid. The tithingman appointed for Milton was Edward Sly, who both owned and occupied lands in Gillingham and Milton and had other tenants of his own; his memorial tablet is to be found in Gillingham church. John Harris was another constable who occupied land in both places and whose name appears on a church tablet. The jurors on the other hand were often lesser men, frequently owner occupiers paying only a few shillings in land tax, but nevertheless with land of their own, and considered worthy and independent enough for their views and concerns to be taken seriously. Edward Card, a smallholder with other land and tenants, was jury foreman and had also been an overseer of the poor. Thomas Godwin was a juror in 1780 and 1781, and considered but not chosen as a constable in 1781; he was also an overseer of the poor in 1778. He occupied land worth £1 5s 6d in land tax, and another tenement worth 4s. He, too, has a memorial tablet in Gillingham church.

The many presentments, although dealing with minor matters in themselves, between them cast valuable light on life and work in

Gillingham. The 'offenders' presented could be farmers, tradesmen, or householders, but were just as likely to be landowners, the school feoffees, the vicar, or the lord of the manor. In October 1733 the lord of the manor was presented for not repairing the Town Hall and the Cross. The following October these had still not been repaired, and there were further complaints about the Town Hall in 1737. There is now no trace of either Town Hall or Cross, which may have disappeared soon after this time.

In 1766 the jury of the court leet attempted a revival of the 'Charter of Gillingham', first granted to the town in the reign of Henry VI, and confirmed by Elizabeth I (Chapter 4). It is difficult to see what commercial benefits this conferred, but the attraction may have been the exemption from serving on juries of assizes and quarter sessions. The jury further complained that the records of the manor ought to be kept in the chest as 'anciently according to the custom of the manor' and that the bailiff of the liberty of Gillingham ought to inspect the weights and measures throughout the liberty according to ancient custom.' Given the volume of court rolls and books which had accumulated by this time, it is hard to see the ancient chest still being fit for its purpose.

There were frequent complaints about the upkeep of the town's bridges, which were the responsibility of the school's feoffees (Figs. 40, 41). The state of Barnaby's Bridge (the Town Bridge) often made it difficult to get from one side of the town to the other. In 1780 King's Court bridge was in a bad state, and immediate repairs were ordered. In 1797 complaints referred to Milton Bridge, Spickett's Bridge at Milton, and Barnaby Bridge. Presentments about the condition of the bridges diminished somewhat with the building of the 'County Bridges' after 1800, but complaints about the minor bridges continued well into the next century. Many presentments related to obstructions on the roads or common ways, the digging of ditches, and encroachments on the wastes. In 1768 John Read was fined 20s for enclosing a piece of waste ground adjoining the highway

Gillingham's Town Bridge

The bridge across the Shreen between the main part of the town and Newbury was always known in earlier centuries as Barnaby's Bridge. In 1742 the jury heard that 'the footway at both ends of Barnaby's bridge is now so worn that in times of high water

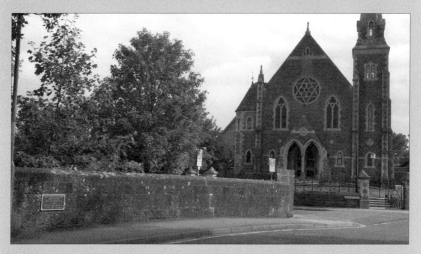

40

foot passengers cannot well pass the road', and the feofees were ordered to repair under penalty of 40s. Clearly little was done, for in April 1745 the feofees were again ordered by the court to repair the bridge. The problem was resolved only with the building of a new stone bridge of two arches in 1800; this is the bridge shown in Constable's well known painting.

41

in Wyke Street, William Tinney was fined 20s for an encroachment in Colestreet Lane, and William Dunn the same amount for erecting a workshop near Coldharbour. In 1771 Robert Turner had dug a ditch in Danrams Lane which is 'a great annoyance to people walking the footway from Tomlins Lane to Gillingham Town'. At the same court a ditch which had been dug along the way from Tomlins Pond to the Barking Gate and thence to the Great House was ordered to be dug up within three months. A serious obstruction, considered worthy of a penalty of £5, was that in 1784 of 'Joseph Long Esq, for digging up the soil in the highway from Woodward's [Woodhouse] Cross to Bainly Bottom and digging a quarry which is dangerous for people to pass the road and not thrown up according to the last presentment.' In 1797 the vicar, the Rev. Mr. Douglas, was fined 10s for having the vault of a water closet open adjoining the highway; this can only refer to the rear of the vicarage property opposite the church.

References to the misuse of manorial property include failures to repair the pounds at Gillingham and Enmore Green, and to fence the wells at Enmore Green. Some inhabitants had removed stiles, probably because they were in the way of livestock movements. Haywards were often admonished for their failure to remove trespassing cattle.

From a few presentments a year, the number mushroomed to 64 in 1797 and 68 in 1798. There seems to have been a surge in the building of hayricks, and particularly of dunghills, on the common waste; some of the latter must refer to rubbish heaps on verges and odd scraps of land. However many of the items were repeated presentments from previous years, indicating that no action had been taken by offenders. This can only reflect the increasing ineffectiveness of the manor courts in enforcing the fines it imposed, and also hastened the need for enclosure of the remaining commons.

To judge from the composition of its juries and officers, by the end of the eighteenth century the remaining functions of the manor courts had become the preserve of the better-off tenant farming community rather than of the wider society of labourers, journeymen, and townspeople. The wealthiest landowners, some of whom lived elsewhere, probably saw little relevance in the institution and could hardly be expected to be constrained by juries consisting of cottagers and smallholders; the labouring poor in their turn were unlikely to raise complaints against their betters, to whom they owed rents and who paid their wages. The accumulation of hayricks and dunghills is perhaps therefore unsurprising, as is the breaking of pound locks and knocking down of stiles; and all can be seen as a wider scepticism of the role and usefulness of manorial authority.

Church, churchwardens, and dissent

THE CHURCH KNOWN to John Jesop and Edward Davenant in Tudor and Stuart times remained largely unaltered well into the nineteenth century. The building as depicted in drawings by the artist John Buckler in the early 1800s had a small nave in which a growing population struggled to find space to sit or stand (Fig. 42). The inadequacy of the church for the congregation was one of the reasons for the later enlargement and rebuilding (Chapter 8). Within the church, seating space was jealously guarded, with pews belonging only to the better-off families who could afford to rent and maintain them. In 1744 a dispute arose over the occupation of a pew towards the south side of the singing gallery. The seat was said to belong to a house in the north-west corner of the churchyard; but others claimed that it belonged to a house in the south-west corner of the churchyard known as the 'mansion house of Mr. Thomas Alford.' One statement on the issue was clear that:

> Not an old man or woman to be found in the parish that can remember any person else but the inhabitants solely of the house in the north

west corner of the churchyard ever claiming or possessing a seat in the said pew… to the recollection of those old people, some of whom are upwards of 84 years old.'

On a slip of paper we learn that 'William Harrison (one of the parties) was bolted out of the pew by Mr Joseph Hawkins', on 13 June and 20 June 20, but the year is not given.[7] The dispute was not resolved until 1802, when we read that it was agreed by all the parties that

> the occupiers of the two houses in the church yard belong to Mr Phripp and Mr Harrison, whose family occupy the first seat in the aisle called Madgiston aisle, 2 persons of each family, some of each in either side.

The landowning gentry had no such difficulties in finding space. In 1735 Thomas Freke of Wyke Hall complained that 'although possessed of considerable estate' he had no convenient seat or pew, and that at his own cost he was willing to erect a pew suitable for himself and his family. William Newton, the vicar, found the family an old seat or pew that was 'useless and unnecessary', although until that time the seat had been occupied by the vicar's own family and servants. Freke was allowed the necessary faculty to allow him to erect a new pew in place of the old 'on the north side of the great chancel fronting the west end, six feet long and the same wide'. There was evidently another convenient seat for Newton's family and servants.[8]

The congregation of this time was ministered to by a succession of incumbents, some distinguished in learning, others in wealth and plurality. John Craig, vicar briefly in 1696, was described by Hutchins as an 'inoffensive, virtuous man, master of a good Latin style, and excellent mathematician, and esteemed by Sir Isaac Newton.' William Newton (vicar 1696-1744) published several theological essays and sermons as well as a history of Maidstone, where he was born.

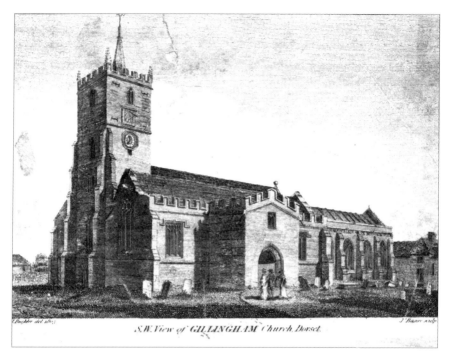

42 John Buckler (1770-1851) was an artist and occasional architect who made many drawings and engravings of cathedrals, churches and other historic buildings. Shortly before 1800 he was commissioned by Richard Colt Hoare of Stourhead to produce ten volumes of drawings of churches and buildings in Wiltshire. He made drawings of Gillingham church in 1805 and 1829. They depict the church with the medieval chancel still seen today, but with a battlemented nave and porch, the tower extending into the nave, and a spire on the tower. In the 1805 picture, shown here, the forbear of the later Vicarage School Room is to be seen.

He provided Hutchins with much of the information he needed for his account of Gillingham. John Perne (1744-70), who came from Cambridge, also held the prebend of Chute and Chisenbury in Wiltshire; his son Andrew was curate in 1770 but died soon afterwards. John Hume (1770-83) spent much of his time tracking down unpaid tithes as described below, but had for several years as a curate Richard Purdy, who also ministered at Motcombe. Dr Purdy (d.1808) published theological books, and a volume of his lectures was published after he died. Edward Emily (1783-92) was a wealthy pluralist who held several offices and livings around Salisbury, but left a considerable sum to Harnham Hospital. William Douglas (1792-1819) held several distinguished offices, including Archdeacon of Salisbury, Canon and Precentor of Salisbury Cathedral and Canon of Westminster Abbey. Hume, Emily, and Douglas all numbered the prebend of Coombe and Harnham near Salisbury among their livings.[9]

These learned and well-endowed clerics may have had less of a spiritual impact on the townspeople than they would have desired. Much of the time they were absent, their work being carried out by curates. On the occasions when they were to be found in church their congregations may have gained little insight from their sermons, and were known to exclaim 'What a famous scholar our minister is, his learning is so great that we do not understand the half of what he says.'[10]

While the church might not have altered much over this time, the same cannot be said for the vicarage house. The house of the Jesops was a substantial enough structure, but was steadily altered to reflect the more refined tastes of its later occupiers. William Newton in 1733 obtained a faculty to take down and rebuild parts of the old house, which had become dilapidated; and John Perne built a long picture gallery, afterwards divided into two rooms, with a kitchen and servants' hall beneath, on the side opposite to the churchyard. Even more alterations and additions followed from archdeacon Douglas, possibly in expectation of a visit from the Prince of Wales, which never materialised. He added a 'justice' room (possibly a drawing room), a waiting room, a bathroom with a heating copper, a brew house, and a coach house. Outdoors the additions amounted to a larder house, house of office (latrine), coal shed, cold bathroom with dressing room, dairy, and milk house with cow stable. By the 1800s the vicarage may have come to resemble a country manor rather than a priest's house. The layout of these various structures is no longer known, but something of them may be glimpsed in Buckler's drawing of the church of 1805, where a double-storey building can be seen in the position of the later schoolroom.[11]

By 1815 a Sunday School had been established in the town, its expenses being paid by subscriptions from the clergy and the more prominent trading and business people. Notable among these were the Hannams and other Quaker families, who were keen to run the school along 'Lancastrian' school lines, with its emphasis on education for the poorer classes.[12] In its fifth annual report of 1820, the school had 62 boys and 107 girls in four classes; and in the previous year 202 reward books had been given out, exclusive of bibles and prayer books given by the vicar. However, while the school had gained many new pupils during the year, no fewer than 37 had been dismissed for irregular attendance. The lack of commitment was particularly noticeable among the boys. The report exhorted subscribers and parents to greater efforts to ensure attendance, and concluded with a comparison between levels of education and those of criminality. In the accounts, the greatest single expense had been the cost of bonnets for the girls; the other main expenses were for cleaning and heating. It is not known where the school was held, but a building with a sizeable room was clearly needed.[13]

The churchwardens at this time exerted considerable powers not only in the church but also within the town itself. Besides the management of worship and church affairs, they had the responsibility of scrutinising the accounts of the constables, the overseers of the poor and highways, and other officers. Two churchwardens were elected each Easter to serve for a year, their positions being confirmed at the next 'visitation' by the Official of the Peculiar. There are many instances where the pair served for more than one year. It was common, but not invariable, for the churchwardens to follow their year of office by serving for the following year as sidespersons. The churchwardens were always chosen from the more prominent landowners, farmers, or townspeople, often holders of other parish offices. In 1780 the churchwardens were Robert Phripp and William Butt, and the sidespersons William Godwin and John Jukes.[14] All were substantial payers of land tax, with Phripp and Jukes also serving as tithingmen to the manor.

In 1758 the elected churchwardens were George Godwin and William Edwards. They were also to serve for the next year, Godwin having previously served in 1753-5. Their account shows an income of £26 from the church rate in Gillingham, £3 from the church rate in Bourton, and £12 from the balance of the previous year. The wardens rendered separate accounts for outgoings, Godwin's being much the longer, perhaps because he was the minister's warden. The outgoings included regular items such as salaries to the clerk and sexton, bread and wine for the sacraments, oil for the clock and chimes, and the washing of surplices and plate. There was an item of 1s for 'taking care of the black cloth', probably the pall used to cover coffins. Other items related to repairs and maintenance, including glazing. A salary of 10s was paid to the 'dog whipper', which may refer to the removal of dogs during church services; the whipper also had a new coat from the wardens' account. A regular, costly item paid out by both wardens was for the destruction of vermin, which in 1758 amounted to 25s 8d. Both wardens noted the payments of 'Green's money', a charity which was distributed on Good Friday and St. Thomas' day.[15]

The churchwardens also made occasional payments as they saw fit, for instance to persons passing through the parish, usually those with a pass from their place of origin. In 1758 6d was given to two women travelling with a pass, and the same amount to two sailors. Payments in some other years include money for beer for workmen after the repair of bells; beer for the ringers on Coronation Day in 1763, and for food and beer for the poor on Confirmation Day at Shaston in 1785.[16]

Churchwardens were also responsible for the orderly conduct of people in church, but this did not prevent things from sometimes getting out of hand, In 1737, a section of the congregation which always sat in the gallery claimed the right to sing anthems and psalms as and when they thought fit, not just when the vicar or the service required it. They refused to discontinue this when so requested by vicar Newton, who then took legal proceedings against the offenders in the Quarter Sessions. The persons involved were found guilty of a 'high misdemeanour' and were told to abide by the vicar's rulings. They were bound over to keep the peace, and only nominal fines were imposed. A number of conditions were made, which included the right of the parish clerk to announce the hymns and anthems; and the limiting of the gallery to members of the congregation with approved credentials.[17]

Churches at this time were subjected to periodic ecclesiastical visitations, the purpose of which was to enquire into matters such as attendance at services, the condition of the church buildings, the conduct of parishioners, and the evidence for dissent and nonconformity. These visitations were usually carried out by the archdeacon, but as Gillingham parish was a royal peculiar, the visitation was carried out by a church official known as the Master Clerk and Register of the Peculiar. The visitations book survives for the period 1733-89, and indicates that the Clerk attended annually for each of these years. However, for the most part the book records little other than confirmation of the appointments of churchwardens and sidespersons for both Gillingham and Motcombe.[18] There are some references to repairs needed, and one or two notes relating to the immoral conduct of parishioners such as:

> John Tinney & Jane Ham cohabiting in state of incontinence, the said Jane having several base born children of the said John.

The visitation records also reveal the holding of 'consistory' courts in the church building by the clerk of the peculiar. Such courts could be held to determine disputes in matters such as tithe payments or probate cases. One such probate or 'legacy' case which survives in detail is from 1740. The will of the late William Cox was in dispute between Mary Cox, a named legatee, and another William Cox, who claimed to be the executor. Another named legatee was Jane Lush, who pursued a separate action against Cox. Between July 1740 and January 1741 the court met fourteen times, but each time judgement had to be delayed or deferred, mostly because of the non-appearance of William Cox or his proctor. On one occasion the court itself could not be held because of a fall of snow which prevented the clerk travelling from Salisbury. On several occasions Cox was pronounced 'contumacious' for ignoring the court, and was twice excommunicated. The principal beneficiaries seem to have been the legal representatives, for by December the legal costs had amounted to £8 for Cox v. Cox and another £7 5s for Cox v. Lush.[19]

By the early nineteenth century the established church was starting to notice the influence of Methodism in the town. In nearby Shaftesbury, Methodist passions had been inflamed as early as the 1750s by the powerful preacher, John Haime (Fig. 43), and the town received a number of visits from John Wesley. In Gillingham the Wesleyan doctrine was introduced through John Cave, a Gillingham man who had worked in Wales but returned to his home town to preach the message. Cave preached at out-of-doors meetings and tried to stimulate religious discussion locally. He recounts that one meeting produced so much dissension that the Riot Act had to be read, 'and from that time persecution commenced against me throughout the whole town, and the Minister every Sunday railed against the Methodists.' Cave felt so persecuted that he left the town. 'After this I removed and came back to Wales; but have often wondered why the Lord suffered me to go to Gillingham to experience so much trouble.[20] Nevertheless, the Methodist presence continued to grow. A Methodist chapel was opened at Shorts Green in Motcombe in 1774.

Gillingham's early Methodists

John Haime (1709-84), a button-mould maker of Shaftesbury, did much to energise Methodism in north Dorset. He was a founder of chapels in Shaftesbury and Motcombe, and it was from Motcombe that Methodism established a permanent presence in Gillingham.

John Cave, born in Gillingham, was a glover and excise officer and had worked in Talgarth in Wales. On his return to Gillingham he wrote an *Epistle to the Inhabitants of Gillingham* and became a preacher, but met so much opposition that he eventually left the town.

Henry Broadway (1742-1829) was a Motcombe farmer who gave the Methodists a

43 John Haime

permanent presence in Gillingham. In 1792 he sought a licence for 'his house situate in St. Martin's Street, Gillingham.' Out of this grew the first Methodist chapel, built a few years after his death (Chapter 8). His group also sought licences for places of worship in Milton and Bourton.

44 The memorial plaque of Henry Broadway

One of its trustees, Henry Broadway, later moved to Gillingham. After a disagreement with the vicar over a pew in the parish church he decided to build his own church (Fig. 44). Dissenters were allowed to hold meetings in buildings as long as they registered the use with the authorities, and so in 1792 Broadway sought such a licence for his house in St. Martin's Street. Broadway himself became a local preacher for thirty years, and is remembered as a man with strong passions and feelings, but also someone with a great regard for the poor. He had married Mary Carpenter, reputed to be a religious woman who 'frequently held public prayer meetings at five o'clock in the morning.' He later provided the money for the Wesleyan chapel built in 1836.[21]

There were also Quaker families in the town, notably the Neaves and Hannams. They were active in public life, but there may have been other Quaker families who were less well known. These families regularly represented the Gillingham Quakers at the Meeting House in Shaftesbury, where meetings were held monthly. After 1804 the Shaftesbury group joined with other Quaker communities, so that the Gillingham people had to travel instead to meetings at Marnhull, Sherborne, Bridport, and sometimes Wincanton.[22]

The tithe dispute

T HE PERIOD SAW a protracted dispute between church and tenant farmers relating to the tithes payable to Gillingham church. The traditional rendering to his church by the husbandman of a tenth of his produce had by the eighteenth century become a source of resentment for both parishioner and priest. While the husbandman toiling in the fields might resent the priest benefiting from the fruits of his labours, the priest in turn might have little else to support him and could be dependent for his very existence on this fraction of the produce of the soil. This was particularly the case in parishes where the glebe land of the vicar was small, and where the priest had no other lands or independent means of support.

In Gillingham the church had substantial landed property dating back to the Norman Conquest, but most of it was held by absentee rectors and was not available to the vicar who performed the actual parish ministry. The vicar's glebe, the land which could be used by the vicar to grow crops or rent out to others, was limited to an area around the church now forming the church grounds and vicarage site extending as far as the Shreen. However, the vicar was entitled across the whole of the parish, including Motcombe, Milton, and Bourton, to the 'small tithe' due from cattle, sheep, pigs, dairy produce, and fruit. Such tithes could be particularly valuable in an area dominated by pastoral farming, but to have a comfortable clerical living in Gillingham required more than just income from tithes. Perhaps not surprisingly, by the seventeenth century Gillingham's vicars had become more substantial men with several livings and landed property elsewhere. These clerics would be liable to see the annual assessment and exaction of tithes as a nuisance, a time-consuming chore likely to interfere with their more scholarly or leisure pursuits. Perhaps this was why in the 1660s Edward Davenant 'wearied by the storms of the 1650s' when he had lost much of his living, and 'wishing nothing more than to enjoy the remainder of [his] days in peace and love' with his parishioners, had concluded an agreement with the farmers of Motcombe. Instead of tithes in kind they should pay instead a composition or 'modus', valued at a shilling in the pound, of rent.[23]

Such agreements in place of tithes in kind were a common arrangement and often produced a satisfactory outcome for both priest and farmer, freeing both from the controversial issue of annually assessing the value of the produce for tithe payment. In Dorset, however, moduses were often relatively low compared with other parts of the country. As the value of land and rents increased through the eighteenth century, earlier moduses began to look like poor value for the clergy. The rise in the value of the Blackmore Vale grasslands particularly showed up the diminishing value of the 'small' tithe. Davenant's successors appear to have been content to leave things as they were, but later incumbents began to look for ways of recovering the tithes or revising the low moduses. John Perne, vicar from 1744 to 1770, considered securing a better deal from Motcombe, but was persuaded to pursue it no further.

However, his successor, John Hume (1770-83), took up the challenge wholeheartedly, devoting most of his ministry to recovering the lost tithes. He spent many hours riding round the farms of his parishioners, carefully calculating the value of their produce and the amounts he considered due to him. In these rural rides 'John Jukes' single house cow was as important to Hume as John Mills' unusually large herd of twenty cows.' A glimpse of his earnestness comes from the consistory court of 1773, when Robert Herridge was presented for non-payment of tithes, but he may have been one among several tithe cases brought by the vicar. In 1776 Hume was able to present one East Stour family with a bill of £85 5s for the preceding five years.[24]

In November 1775 Hume brought his claim to the Court of Exchequer. The basis of his case, presented by his solicitors, William Tinney and Walter Whitaker, was that Davenant's agreement was only a temporary composition, and that the farms now represented far greater wealth than previously. The Motcombe tithe payers, for their part, claimed that the payment was well established by a century of usage, and that the farms were living on the margins of subsistence. The plaintiff claimed to see a land overflowing with agricultural produce, with 'divers milch cows from which they respectively had many calves and great quantities of milk'. By contrast the defendants painted a picture of the direst poverty, one farmer pointing to his two chickens which had produced between them only twenty-five eggs. Hume's case was successful; the small tithes of Motcombe once again had to be paid in kind, or the farmers had to accept a composition more favourable to the vicar.[25]

Hume's successor, Edward Emily, although a wealthy man and a pluralist, was no less aware of his financial rights and continued the fight with the tithe payers; but he was less fortunate and ended up in a poorer position than he expected, having to accept a lower composition than Hume had achieved. In the meantime tithes remained a source of contention for landowners, clergy and farmers alike; it was to be almost another seventy years before the payment of all tithes of kind in Gillingham was finally superseded by a fixed payment and ceased to be a major issue.

45 The novelist Henry Fielding lived for part of his early life at East Stour, where his tutor was Mr. Oliver, the curate of Motcombe, then still in the parish of Gillingham. Oliver is widely believed to be the model for Fielding's Mr Trulliber in Joseph Andrews, *the coarse and fat pig-rearing parson more interested in his food and drink than in the condition of his parishioners.*

The Free School and education

A MEMORIAL STONE on the south side of the chancel in the parish church marks the last resting place of a scholar of the Free School who died in 1702. The inscription is very faded and not all readable, but with the help of the entries in the parish registers it can be determined that this relates to Samuel, the son of John and Martha Ash, and that his age was 15. This is one of the few references that exist to an individual member of the school at this time.

The site occupied by the Free School in the High Street adjoining the Phoenix is thought to have remained the same since the school's foundation in 1516, described in an earlier chapter. Hutchins described it as a 'large old building near the church with a mean house for the master', and this may have been the school known to Samuel Ash (p.98). By the early nineteenth century the headmaster was living in a separate, more spacious house on the opposite side of the road on the corner with Queen Street, and it is likely that at this time the school expanded to accommodate more pupils. Both these buildings are fully described in Chapter 8.

Since its foundation, the school was in the hands of its trustees or feoffees, whose powers and responsibilities had been laid out in the Chancery decree of 1598. The feoffees were to be twelve in number, and when the number had decreased to eight it had to be restored to twelve at a meeting of the manor court. Every tithing of the parish in which there was trust property had to be represented by one or more feofees. From the rents of the feoffees' properties, the sum of 20 marks yearly (around £13) was used for 'the finding and maintenance of a schoolmaster … to teach the children of the parishioners *gratis*', the master to be appointed by the feofees. The remainder of the rent income was to be used to repair the causeways, highways, and bridges, and to the bringing up of poor orphans. By the eighteenth century some of these other functions had passed to officials appointed by the vestry, but the feoffees still remained responsible for bridges as well as the governance of the school.[26]

The feoffees annual meeting, at which the accounts were approved, was always on Whit Tuesday and was announced by the ringing of the church bell, for which the sexton charged one shilling. The meeting was always preceded by a dinner at the Phoenix, which was charged to the accounts. A feoffees record of 1810 supplies some names of feoffees, records the procedure for appointing new ones, and lists the property owned by the school. The appointment of new feoffees was carried out in the manor court; the existing feoffees surrendered their trust and were then reappointed along with new ones, bringing their number to twelve.[27]

The school owned various properties around the town and the neighbouring fields, its land deriving from the original grants of the sixteenth century (Chapter 4) and subsequent additions. In 1769 Jane Fathers leased from the feoffees a cottage 'on the west part of the schoolhouse and yard', which would seem to refer to a building in the yard behind the school. In the same year there was a lease of school property in Bourton to William Child. In 1799 the feoffees granted two leases to property in Back Lane (now South Street) to James King and Hugh Herridge, both linen weavers. In 1819 the School received rents from 35 properties.

Little can be known of the schooling itself at this time, although something might be learned from an advertisement in the *Sherborne Mercury* by John Prince, curate to vicar William Newton, who had started a rival school in 1737. He intended to give a 'constant and diligent attendance upon it …. Young gentlemen may be taught the Latin and Greek languages after an approved method, and also Writing and Arithmetic … Here are convenient places for boarders at a reasonable rate.' By implication, this was the sort of education offered at the Free School – an education based on classics and literary studies for the sons of the local gentry.[28]

The schoolmaster at the time of John Prince's rival bid was William Young, who was in the school until at least 1746. He was succeeded as master by William Alner (1749-58), Francis Nation (1759-63), and Robert Phripp (1764-89). By 1800 the post was held by Hugh Hansford, who had the school house and garden and a salary of £40 a year, out of which he had to provide his own teaching materials. He remained headmaster until 1838.[29]

A rather different education seems to have been had by the children of Stephen Hannam, the Quaker owner of the silk mill.

In the Dorset History Centre are the exercise books of George and Josiah Hannam for 1772. The schooling they received was most likely at home in the Mill House, which still stands, and consisted entirely of preparation for the world of commerce. The handwriting practise included repetitious copying of homilies well grounded in the Quaker work ethic, such as 'Diligence ought to be encouraged and commended', or 'Attempt not too hastily nor pursue too eagerly'. Long sections of the books include the copying out of accounts, orders, and bills, mostly to do with the cloth trade, sometimes using contrived names, but often including surnames of local families such as the Cards or Hansfords. Between the leaves can be found carefully pasted printed sheets explaining how to do division or multiplication, and the worked examples often extend to many digits. Schoolwork for the Hannam children also extended after hours, and included 'Questions for exercise at leisure hours', of which this is an example:

'I am dispatched on a commission from London to Edinburgh distant by computation say 350 miles and my route is settled at 22 miles a day; you, 4 days after, are sent after me with fresh orders, and are to travel 32 miles day; whereabout on the road shall I be overtaken by you ?'

The answer is evidently 68 2/5 miles on this side of Edinburgh.[30]

Overseers and the poor

THE 1516 FOUNDATION of the Free School had specifically given the feofees the duty that 'poor people may be relieved', while the 1598 Chancery decree specified their duty for the 'rearing and bringing up of poor orphans.' The 1597 and 1601 Poor Law Acts ordered the annual election of overseers of the poor, to be answerable to the parish vestry and Justices of the Peace. The overseers were empowered to raise the revenue needed for relief by charging local poor rates. These officers were elected around Eastertime, were fined if they refused to serve, and received no payment for the work. The overseer had to submit his accounts to the vestry at the end of the year and was only allowed expenses approved at that meeting. The office was expected to be performed by rotation, with the officer serving only for one year. The office was onerous but was usually judged to be a local honour; it was normally the role of the tenant farmer who had some means of support during the year, rather than the impecunious labourer or cottager.

An important measure for the overseer to understand and implement was the Act of Settlement of 1662. This defined the ways in which a poor person could claim to be settled or have residence within a parish. Since all poor people in a parish were a charge on its poor rates and the community, it was important that persons not able to claim settlement should be made to promptly move out of the parish and not receive poor relief. Among the Gillingham records is a long memorandum of questions and answers from 1765 on all aspects of the operation of the poor laws, obviously intended to help the overseer interpret his task.[31]

In Gillingham, a large parish, two or three overseers were elected at Easter each year. Their accounts were carefully recorded in books, of which two survive covering the periods 1687-1739 and 1740-77. From 1687 to around 1735 the accounts follow a common format. The account for each year opens with the names of the overseers and of the churchwardens. There then follows a calculation of the poor rate to be levied on each property in the parish, the amount paid by each property being then listed. The next section is a list of people in receipt of regular monthly payments. These were all people whose need for regular relief had been agreed by the vestry and churchwardens. This in turn is followed by the list of additional disbursements made to parishioners for specific items of relief as their need arose. The account concludes with a summary of income and expenditure for the year, signed by members of the vestry.[32]

For the year 1725-6 the overseers were Edward Hixon, Edward Henbury, and John Sly, and the churchwardens were James Musgrave and John Butt. There were no new names on the list of 193 ratepayers from previous years. Sixty persons were in receipt of regular payment. Since the previous year three had died, two had ceased to need payment, and there were three new cases. During the year, 232 payments were made for additional or occasional relief. Many of these were of only small amounts of around 3s or 4s. Most payments were in relation to clothing, house rents, and sickness. The amount spent on regular payments was £190, and a further £129 was disbursed in the occasional payments. These outlays were fairly typical of Gillingham relief payments of the early eighteenth century.

In 1729-30 the expenditure was markedly higher because this was a year when smallpox was flourishing. An unusually large number of payments (93) were for sickness, and there were also 20 payments towards burials. Some particular items connected with the smallpox outbreak included:

> House room and burials (among two families) and the purchase of hartshorn, frankincense, ale, small beer and sack, cheese, butter, and beans   £8 12 3

and

> Benjamin Sanger after his recovery from smallpox and promising not to become chargeable on the parish anymore   10s

and

Mary Harris for inspecting into the people supposed to have smallpox 3s

An ongoing concern of overseers was to see that poor incomers did not become a burden on the poor rates, and if necessary, arrange their removal to the parish in which they were legally settled. In 1729-30 expenditure included items of 5s 6d and 8s 6d on removing a family from the parish and returning them to their home parish; carrying a vagrant woman and child out of the county and victuals for them; and carrying another woman out of the county 'as likely to become chargeable'. A system of passes allowed poor wayfarers to pass through the parish without challenge from the overseers, such as (1716):

Mary Williams, who had a pass and was big with child.   1s.

The settlement in the parish of unmarried, pregnant women was especially scrutinised, since the child would become eligible for poor relief.

Of particular interest are the many different reasons given for the occasional payments, since they throw light on the wide-ranging duties and concerns of overseers. These included costs of burials, clothing, house rents, house repairs, apprenticeships, food, and fuel. The overseers were also responsible for the costs of court appearances and custody for paupers; there are many references to transportation costs to 'bridewell', meaning the county gaols at Dorchester or Sherborne. Costs for 1699 included:

Carrying John Ramson to prison   £1 12 6
Carrying John Ramson's son to Bridewell   5s
Apprehending Richard Sheppard and for his guard to Shaston 14s

Another task for which the parish and overseers were responsible was the arrangement of apprenticeships for the sons of paupers. An indenture was drawn up binding the boy to a master, and it was the task of the overseer to make the payment to the master and ensure that the indenture was signed by the Justice of the Peace. The master or the justices might live in another parish, so that the task could involve frequent journeys. And so we read (1733):

> For six pair of blank indentures, for filling them in and getting the signatures of justices to binding poor children apprentices 35s

In 1735 there were 21 indentures to be signed. The parish also had to pay the master for the clothing of apprentices, as in 1732:

> Paid Thomas Freke Esq and Mr John Barnes for clothing the apprentices who were put to them by the overseers and the churchwardens 30s

The overseer was expected to temper mercy for the needy with the knowledge that the ratepayers at the vestry meetings would demand an explanation of his expenditure. Comparison of the figures from year to year between the 1680s and 1730s might suggest the constancy of some elements, such as the number of people on regular relief, but there was a more general rise in the number of payments for occasional relief. By the 1730s the vestry had evidently become convinced that a more cost-effective solution to the problem of the permanently poor in the parish was the building of a workhouse. By accommodating all the poor on a single site, many of the incidental claims for items such as rents or house repairs could be eliminated and the task of running the house could be farmed out to the contractor prepared to undertake the task for the lowest cost.

In 1735 the overseer's accounts record a parish meeting about buying a workhouse, and the same account records £1 12s 6d spent on 'repair materials for the repair of Lodbourne house'; there were also articles of sale drawn up between its owner and the parish. This is the forbear of the building which still stands on Bay Road, and the account suggests that it must have had a previous existence before it became the workhouse (Fig. 46). There was a grant of £100 towards its purchase from the will of a Mrs Alford. In 1736 £48 was paid towards the purchase, and the following year a final payment of £164 was made.

46 Gillingham's parish workhouse. The house was acquired by the overseers in the 1730s and much rebuilt in 1761. It became less useful after 1835 when the new Union Workhouse at Shaftesbury was opened, and was eventually sold. In 1871 it was called Spring Gardens and had five occupiers, mostly farm labourers.

The accounts record regular maintenance to the workhouse, but in 1761 work of a more far-reaching nature is recorded. This involved considerable sums spent on bricks, tiles, stones, windows, and digging foundations, producing a bill for the parish of £194 14s 11d.

This could only have meant a complete rebuilding of the structure, no doubt in response to the need for a bigger house from the increased number of paupers. It is this house, which is still seen today, in more recen times having been divided into cottages.

Of the running of the workhouse little more is known, presumably because it was in the hands of a contractor, and continued to operate until 1834. The overseers' accounts from this time for the most part record only the items of additional relief of the variety described above. In 1750 there is a page of sharp reminders to the overseers, which includes unauthorised spending of money on liquor, and the making of payments over 2s or of apparel without vestry approval. Churchwardens and overseers were not to give certificates of settlement to persons or families outside the parish, or to bind poor children as apprentices without vestry approval; all these were ways in which the burden of poor relief could be increased. A final reminder was that the only doctor or apothecary to be engaged on behalf of paupers was Dr. Tatum of Mere; perhaps because his costs were below those of others.[33]

The charities

A NUMBER OF charities were in existence around this time, and were able to provide a further, if occasional, source of relief for some of the poor. The oldest charity was that of the school feofees, which each February was obliged to distribute the surplus of its funds to the 'second poor of the parish on the alphabetical list', but the meaning of this is not explained. In 1826 £66 4s 6d was so distributed.

Frances Dirdoe, who died in 1733, left a charity of £5 a year, chargeable on the Dirdoe farm at Milton, to be distributed to the poor on St. Thomas' Day. It was originally dispensed in small amounts to any who required it, but this sometimes led to disorderly behaviour with 'the poor collecting in riotous mobs to the number of 500 or 600'. It was altered around 1815 to be used for the assistance of apprentices and to help young boys to buy tools, and continued until 1982 when it was combined with Read's Charity.

Green's Charity also involved payments to the poor on St. Thomas's Day and Good Friday, and is recorded in the Churchwardens' accounts, but otherwise little about it is known.

The charity of William Read, who died in 1798, was widely used. Read was a wealthy farmer with land and farms at Langham and Bugley, but he died at the young age of 44. His memorial in Gillingham church recalls his many acts of benevolence and details his bequest to the poor. This was £20 to be distributed in bread a year after his decease; and £4000 to be invested to produce £20 annually,

> ... to be distributed in Bread on St. Thomas's Day; the remainder in sums of five shillings weekly to such Poor Men and Women of the age of Sixty Years and upwards as appear deserving this bounty.

A proviso was added that

> ... those who misbehave, or become immoral, are at any time removable at the discretion of the Trustees.

In 1835 800 loaves at 4½ d each were given away, some larger families receiving as many as four loaves.[34] Read's charity, like the other charities, remained a source of relief for poorer people for decades to come.

8

THE GILLINGHAM OF JOHN
FISHER AND HENRY DEANE

Fisher and Constable

IN JULY 1820 Archdeacon John Fisher, then not long installed as
Vicar of Gillingham, received a visit at his Salisbury home from
his friend, the young artist John Constable. The two had met
several years earlier through Fisher's uncle, Dr John Fisher, who later
became Bishop of Salisbury. The younger Fisher (b.1788) had been
ordained by his uncle in 1811 and appointed to Salisbury Cathedral
Deanery. In 1813 he became vicar of Osmington, and in 1817 was
installed as Archdeacon of Berkshire. In 1819 he was appointed Vicar
of Gillingham, a valuable appointment worth £1,000 a year, but for
some time he continued to live either at Osmington or Salisbury.
Nevertheless Fisher took the opportunity to travel around and show
his friend his new living. During this visit Constable made several
sketches of a cart with the bridge at Eccliffe, and another sketch of
Common Mead Lane. In August 1823 Constable made another
visit to Fisher, this time staying at the vicarage in Gillingham, and
was able to do more sketching and painting. Fisher was a source of
encouragement to Constable as an artist, and bought several of his
works. The two men corresponded regularly, and their letters contain

their reflections about life and conditions in Gillingham at the time.[1] A map of 1820 shows the town and parish at the time of Constable's visits (Plate 11).

During his 1823 visit Constable especially came to enjoy Parhams or Purns Mill in Milton. This scene itself was not to endure, the mill being lost to fire in 1825 (Plate 14). Fisher had no choice but to write to Constable about the demise of his favourite location and its replacement by something far less appealing to the artist:

> The news is that Matthew Parham's (alias Perne's) mill is burnt to the ground and exists only on your canvas. A huge misshapen, new, bright, brick, modern, improved, patent monster is starting up in its stead.

Constable's scenes of Gillingham

John Constable (1776-1837) visited Gillingham in 1820, when he made four drawings of scenes around the town. In August 1823 he returned for a further stay, completing two oil paintings. A further three paintings of Gillingham scenes were made in his London and Brighton studios between 1824 and 1827. Copies of all of Constable's Gillingham scenes can be seen in the town Museum. Although the Museum has no originals, it is the only place where all the Gillingham items can be found together. An *Entrance to Gillingham* sketch of 1820 depicts the town viewed from a point not far along Common Mead Lane. The same view cannot be seen today as the road has become more built-up, but the house now called Folly's End is clearly recognisable. An interesting feature, now no longer there, is the spire on the church tower. *The Bridge at Gillingham* (frontispiece) is the scene best known to local people, and is the only completed oil painting of Gillingham made by the artist whilst he was actually staying in the town in 1823. His favourite location was outside the town at Purn's Mill or Parham's Mill near Milton. He made an oil sketch and three paintings of this location, which he valued highly for its picturesque qualities. One of these was exhibited at the Royal Academy and is especially acclaimed in the art world. This painting is now in the Tate gallery.

To which Constable responded in some despair:

> I am vexed at the fate of the poor old mill. There will soon be an end
> to the picturesque in the kingdom…

Constable was profoundly struck by the picturesque nature
of the landscape around Gillingham, and this is reflected in his
correspondence with Fisher, and also when he wrote home to his wife
during his second trip. After his 1820 visit Constable wrote to Fisher:
'You are always in luck in the beautiful places you come to - and I
have often said such are my delight. The mill at Gillingham (Purns
Mill) was beautifully situated'. In 1823 he wrote to his wife 'This is
a melancholy place - but it is beautiful, full of little bridges, rivulets,
mills and cottages - and the most beautiful trees and verdure I ever
saw.' In another letter he mentions that the '…mill at the bottom of
the garden is now rattling away and makes me think of old times
at Flatford." But he was aware of the impoverishment which was
the down side of this rural idyll: 'The poor people are dirty, and to
approach one of the cottages is almost insufferable. Fisher has done a
great deal of good, especially in the medical way. This sad place is out
of the world entirely'.

Fisher shared Constable's enthusiasm for the Gillingham
countryside and his love of painting, and was himself a purchaser of a
work by the artist. In one of his letters he says:

> The more I see of this country the more and more I delight in it. It is
> genuine home scenery. The greens are most vivid and the foliage in
> the greatest luxuriance. It has the true flat Claude horizon broken
> occasionally by a distant hill.

But as the spiritual mentor of the town he knew also of the
poverty of its inhabitants and went on to add: 'I see and hear nothing

47 A watercolour by Henry Moule showing lower Common Mead Lane and
Wyke Street. The cottage on the right later disappeared to make way for the
mansion of the Chantry. The picture suggests that thatched roofs may have
been common throughout the town at this time.

here but old women, sick children and quakers' hats'. The comments
might have referred to the large amount of time the archdeacon was
spending visiting the sick and to the number of dissenters who by
now were forming a conspicuous group separate from his flock.

Constable was not the only artist to record the town in colours
at this time. Between 1825 and 1829 the Reverend Henry Moule
lived in the town as a curate of John Fisher. He subsequently became
vicar of Fordington, but his eldest son, Henry Joseph Moule (1825-
1904), appears to have returned to Gillingham in or around 1835,
and painted a number of watercolours of the town. His scenes include
the vicarage, Common Mead Lane, Eccliffe, Chantry Bridge, and the
interior of the church (Figs. 47, 48). On the title page of the album
containing the prints is written:

48 *The Vicarage and its garden at the time of John Fisher: a watercolour by Henry Moule. This was the Vicarage built by John Jesop in Tudor times, but from its style clearly much rebuilt by later vicars. It was superseded by the vicarage of 1883, now Rawson Court.*

Gillingham, Dorset.
Her charm around the enchantress, memory throws.

It is tempting to think that the very young Moule may have known Constable through his father's association with Fisher, and may have been encouraged by the great master to take up painting. Moule's depiction of Gillingham from Common Mead Lane uses the same subject as the Constable sketch, but the master sketched from a viewpoint further up the lane. Photographic reprints of the Moule paintings are held in the Gillingham Museum.

Gillingham and the world outside

FISHER'S TOWN OF old and sick people, not to mention its more thriving tradespeople and labourers, were slowly coming to know more of the world outside as the road links to and from the town began to improve. Until the eighteenth century both of the nearest coaching routes lay outside the town. A southerly route along the 'Sherborne Causeway' between Shaftesbury and Sherborne, the modern A30, could be joined at East Stour and provided the main way to Salisbury, London, and Exeter. North of Gillingham another turnpike route to Salisbury and London via Hindon passed over White Sheet Hill, accessible through Mere. These routes could be reached from the town only by minor roads which were often impassable in wet weather; similarly all post or news from outside places or of great national events, were subject to the same slow pace of travel. West of the town the countryside was well linked together by lanes and tracks, but to the east the areas of the old forest were more poorly served, with the lanes towards Motcombe and West Knoyle being far from direct.

Improvements came gradually with the turnpiking of roads through the town (Fig. 49). These roads were administered by trusts which maintained them by charging for passage through gates set up at regular distances. The first of Gillingham's turnpike roads was the section of the Sherborne Causeway which crosses the southern edge of the parish between Shaftesbury and East Stour. This was one of the roads improved by the Shaftesbury and Sherborne Trust, first set up in 1753 to maintain the Donhead to Sherborne section of the 'Great Western Post Road' between London and Exeter. A turnpike gate and tollhouse were built at the junction with Lox Lane.[2]

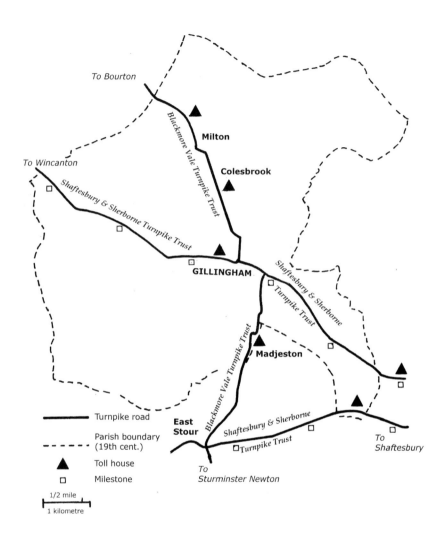

49 Turnpike roads in the Gillingham area. The boards showing the tolls payable at the Colesbrook and Madjeston toll houses are to be seen in the Gillingham Museum.

The Trust also provided for turnpiking from the 'Angel Inn (Shaftesbury) … and thence to and through Gillingham to the index post at the foot of Saltern's Hill in Penselwood', where it met the Somerset boundary and the road from Mere to Wincanton.

This road, the present B3081, had been turnpiked by 1777; in 1791 it was recorded that 195 loads of stone were spread on the turnpike at Ham Common and Newbury. A cottage popularly known as the Old Toll House stands on the hill towards Wyke, but has no external features to indicates its use as a toll house. In 1838 the toll house at Latchmere Pond was moved a mile westwards to its present position at the Motcombe junction. The name 'turnpike' relates to the iron gates which would have been swung across the road to prevent the passage of traffic until the toll had been paid. The trust also erected milestones, two of which can be seen by the New Road junction in Newbury and by Milestone Way in Wyke.[3]

John Constable used this road for the last stage of his 1823 visit to Gillingham, with Fisher meeting him at Salisbury so that they were in the town by the evening. He reported to his wife on the journey from London via Salisbury and Shaftesbury:

> I had not at all a disagreeable ride though it rained now and then and did not look very tempting - the difference in price between outside and in is fourteen shillings which is not a trifle. It cost me nothing on the road and at six I was sitting down with Fisher at dinner.[4]

In 1831 the Blackmore Vale Turnpike Trust, which already maintained the road from Sturminster Newton through Stalbridge to Holton, obtained a fresh Act of Parliament to improve several roads in the district, including the one

> from Walton Elm … in the parish of Marnhull … to pass through the several parishes or places of Marnhull, Todber, Stower Provost, Stower East, and Gillingham, to join the present road leading from thence to Bath …

THE PUBLIC

Are respectfully informed, that on the 9th of April, next,

A NEW LIGHT

Coach,

CALLED THE

SOMERSET,

Will leave the *Mermaid Inn*, YEOVIL, every TUESDAY, THURS-DAY, and SATURDAY Morning, at half past seven o'clock; call at the *Angel Inn*, SHERBORNE; *Greyhound*, WINCANTON; *Red Lion*, BOUR-TON; *Phœnix*, GILLINGHAM; *Red Lion*, SHAFTESBURY; and arrive at the *Black Horse*, SALISBURY, at three o'clock; whence Passengers and Parcels will be forwarded by the old Salisbury Coach to LONDON; and return from thence every MONDAY, WEDNESDAY and FRIDAY Morning by the same route, immediately on the arrival of the LONDON Coach.

The Proprietors beg leave to assure the public, this conveyance will be put on in the truest sense for their accomodation; Fares will be low; and luggage carried at Van price.

Passengers and Parcels booked for their Coach at the *Bell* and *Crown*, Holborn; *New White Horse Cellar;* and *Gloucester Coffee House,* Piccadilly, LONDON.

Performed by   HENRY WHITMASH
                        NICHOLAS BROWN
                        JOSEPH BROWN.

GILLINGHAM, *March 29th,* 1822.

GILLINGHAM; PRINTED BY E. NEAVE.

50 A poster from 1822 advertising the 'Somerset' coach. John Constable used this coach on his trip to Gillingham in 1823.

The promoters of the scheme included several Gillingham people, notably William Read Bell, Ambrose Heal, Edward Hannam, Josiah

Hannam, Thomas Matthews, and Edward Neave. All were prominent owners of land or businesses in or around the town which were likely to benefit from the improved state of the roads. The Act relates to the road from East Stour through Madjeston and the town towards Milton, Stourhead, and Frome, and indicates that the section north of the town towards Bourton might already have been turnpiked by this time.[5] The Trust had tollhouses at Madjeston and Colesbrook, of which the former has now disappeared. In the Gillingham Museum is the Colesbrook tollhouse signboard displaying the charges.

The turnpiking of the main roads into and out of the town led to some improvement in the town's coaching and carrier services. The *Somerset* coach, introduced in 1822, called at the Phoenix three times weekly on its way from Yeovil to Shaftesbury and Salisbury, from where passengers could take the London coach (Fig. 50). By 1830 the *Somerset* had given way to a through London coach called the *Hope* which ran on the same days. Pigot's 1830 Directory also records the appearance of the *Wellington*, which called at the Red Lion on three days a week on its way to Frome and Bath; the return journey on three other days was to Shaftesbury, Blandford, Wimborne, and Poole. The *Wellington* service is traceable through the directories of the period into the 1850s, only finally disappearing with the coming of the Somerset and Dorset Railway and its service to Bath via Templecombe. In 1830 there were regular weekly carrier services to Wincanton, Bristol, and Poole, and also a London service with 'days uncertain'. In 1852 the places served by carriers were Shaftesbury, Salisbury, Poole, and Wincanton.[6]

These coaching and carrier services could all be joined at the Phoenix and Red Lion inns, which for a time became busier hostelries. However, Gillingham lay too far off the main routes to be a considered a 'coaching town'. By comparison, nearby Hindon in 1830 saw the arrival and departure of 24 coaches each week, double the number of Gillingham. Hindon was on one of the main coaching routes from London to the south-west, and had two coaches to London daily, as well as services to Taunton, Barnstaple, Honiton, and Exeter.[7] Gillingham's postal services at this time were run by the school headmaster from his house opposite Spring Corner. In 1851 letters arrived from London and the west of England at 9 am, and from Salisbury at 5 pm; despatch times to London, via Wincanton, were 5 pm, and to Salisbury at 9 am. These timings continued until the coming of the railway at the end of the decade.

A labouring population

THE GILLINGHAM VISITED by John Constable had been rapidly increasing in population. In 1821 the wider parish, which included Milton, Motcombe, and East and West Stour, had a population of 4,924, a thousand more than two decades earlier, in an area of 15,886 acres, one of the largest parishes in Dorset. Gillingham itself, which in 1821 was considered to include Milton, had a population of 2,246 in 1821. This was to continue to grow steadily over the next two decades to 2,760 in 1841 and 2,806 in 1851. Although the rate of growth between 1841 and 1851 was slower than in previous decades, by 1851 the population of the town had increased by half since the start of the century.

For this burgeoning population, life could be shorter than might be expected today. Of the 674 burials recorded in the parish registers between 1824 and 1837, 209 or 31% were of children under 10, the majority of these being under two years. At the other end of the age range, only ten per cent of the population of 1841 were older than 60, very few reached 80, and there were more women than men in the higher age groups. There were more teenage boys than girls, but more girls than men in their twenties.

In 1841 59 heads of households in Gillingham and Milton

gave their occupation as farmers. The outputs from their fields and pastures depended not just on the efforts from their own work and animals but also from the exertions of the 300 or so labourers and their families spread around the parish. The labourers in turn expected to have many mouths to feed, no less than a quarter of the population in 1841 being under the age of ten. Many households had five or six children, and it was common to find labouring families with several infants dependent on one worker's wage, sometimes also supporting an elderly relative. There were particular concentrations of labourers in the many cottages around Wavering Lane, Peacemarsh, and Ham. In 1841 boys as young as 10 are listed as agricultural labourers, and girls as 'female servants', but it is likely that some were younger than the ages recorded.Many girls and younger women also found work in the silk mill.

A typical labouring family of 1841 might be that of 40-year old James Sanger, who lived on Peacemarsh near the corner with Wavering Lane with his wife of 41. Two of his sons, aged 14 and 10, were also labourers, while the daughter of 12 years was a silk throwster. There were four other children of 7, 5, and 3 years, and of 6 months. Stephen Stone, another Peacemarsh labourer, had a household of nine, with no other occupations recorded but his own. John Stuart of Ham had no wife and kept his four children and 70-year old relative on his labourer's wage.

By the 1840s the land worked by the many labourers and their families was largely in the hands of a number of wealthier proprietors and their tenant farmers, a pattern which had become well established during the previous century, as related in Chapter 6. Earl Grosvenor, as Marquis of Westminster and lord of the manor of Gillingham, was now only one of several large landowners in the parish. Another large estate was the Crown properties administered by the Commission of His Majesty's Woods and Forests, which had land in the north and east of the parish. Around and within the town itself there was a more

Jane Deane's portraits

Jane Deane, the first wife of the vicar Henry Deane, painted several portraits of local people in or around 1847. Seen here are **Elizabeth Lloyd** (right), a dairymaid, daughter of George and Jane Lloyd; **Jacob Stacey** (below left), a shoemaker; and **Daniel Cave** (below right), a schoolmaster and sexton of Gillingham church.

51

52 Landowners in the main part of the town, as shown on the Tithe Map of 1841. A comparatively small number of proprietors were owners of many of the plots. The church and the mill (Josiah Hannam) were major landowners.

F	Feofees of the Free School	12	William Green
1	Thomas Tapp	13	John Jupe
2	Robert George	14	Robert Phripp
3	Sarah Dunn	15 `	William Phripp
4	Nathaniel Read	16	Robert Phripp
5-6	Edward Neave	17-18	Mrs Le Hardy
7	John Read	19-21	John Coombs
8	Mary Herridge	22	John Herridge
9	Ann Lawrence	23	Samuel Harris
10	Charles Sparrow	24	William Hall
11	George Edwards	25	Hugh Hansford

complex pattern of property ownership and tenure, with some land in the hands of neighbouring farmers and other fields and plots owned and rented by the more successful business people of the town (Fig. 52). There were also numerous owner-occupiers of shops and smaller pieces of ground. Some owner-occupiers might also be occupiers of other property elsewhere, while other occupiers might rent various plots without owning any of them. This highly varied situation is traceable firstly to the period of the royal manor centuries earlier, when copyholds were readily transferable and could be sublet, and also to the later breaking up of the remaining crown lands following disafforestation. In this way Gillingham can be contrasted with other towns or villages such as Stalbridge, where most of the land remained in the hands of a single squire or wealthy proprietor. It was also a situation which made small properties accessible for commercial opportunities and business developments in the decades ahead.

Winds of change

THE TOWN MINISTERED to by Archdeacon Fisher is that shown on Plate 11. Although most of the town still lay to the west of the Shreen, he would have regularly crossed over the new bridge to Newbury, which still lay separate from the main town. The streets and most of the buildings seen by Fisher would have been instantly recognisable by the vicars of a century earlier. As had happened for many decades, decisions about town and parish were still taken in vestry and feofees meetings dominated by the same small group of people. Half a century earlier these would have been mainly landowners, but by the 1820s more of the principal business interests of the town were evident in these groups.

Around the town in the late 1820s clouds of rural discontent were beginning to gather. The period after the Napoleonic Wars was one of considerable hardship for labourers and poorer tenants, characterised by long hours of work, bad conditions, and appallingly low wages. Dorset and Wiltshire labourers were the poorest in England, being paid eight shillings a week. Already in 1815 15 per cent of the total population of Dorset were receiving parish relief. Landowners and farmers frequently cited the high costs of the payment of tithes as a reason for not being able to pay higher wages. In the late 1820s bad weather and poor harvests made the situation still worse, as Fisher wrote to Constable:

> Summer has set in with its usual severity. The rains have swollen the rivers and swamped all our Dorsetshire meadows. The uncut hay is all muddled … and every paddock is spoilt with what they call, technically, "cows-heels". This is the third consecutive year that this has happened and in consequence all my Gillingham farmers are ruined, and seven of them are now breaking stones on the road.

Throughout the autumn of 1830 the storm of the 'Captain Swing' riots swept across the south of England, bringing with it a wave of machine-breaking and arson attacks. In November 1830 a pitched battle occurred near Tisbury between 400 labourers and a troop of yeomanry sent to disperse them. In Dorset the disturbances mostly affected the chalk areas of the county, but also spilled over into the Vale of Blackmore around Buckland Newton and Stoke Wake. When the rector of Stour Provost found the rectory surrounded by thirty to forty men, he shouted 'I am used to rows and not afraid of them', and defied them to do their worst. At Stalbridge in December 1830 the curate claimed that rioters were destroying threshing machines and asked for a detachment of cavalry to be quartered in the village, but there is no evidence that any actual damage was done.[8]

With the rumblings of discontent so close, and perhaps fearful of a repeat of the enclosure disturbances of 1810, the Gillingham landowners met to consider the situation on the 2nd December. The meeting was led by William Read Bell, the attorney, and was attended by 37 landowners and occupiers. The outcome was an agreement that the labouring population should be paid at a higher rate 'so as to render them … independent of parochial support'. A standard wage rate of 9s per week was agreed, and a plea was made for a reduction in tithes and rents so that the tenant farmers could afford the increase in wages. This appears to have been enough to defuse any problems, and there is no record of further discontent. By January 1831 the Dorset disturbances were over. 'The few temporary improvements in wages were quickly lost, and the Dorset farm-labourers were soon in as desperate a condition as before'.[9]

Two years later a further attempt to relieve the plight of the Gillingham labourers came with the setting up of the Gillingham Labourers' Friends Society, which had its first meeting in February 1833, again chaired by William R. Bell. The Society had as its aim the 'improvement of the condition of the labourers of this parish, and the promotion of habits of industry among them.' A committee of landowners and farmers was set up and resolved to rent lands in order to sublet them to members who had paid a subscription. This was set at 5s a year, the maximum allocation to any labourer being an acre, 'the cultivation to be carried on by spade husbandry only, with no more than half of the allotment to be under potatoes'.[10]

The agricultural riots of the 1830s, and the fear by the authorities that worse might come, ushered in a major national change to the poor laws. In 1834 the Poor Law Amendment Act abolished the old system based on overseers and parish workhouses and set up a new one based on unions of parishes run by boards of elected guardians. Henceforth all relief was to be provided indoors in new 'union workhouses' to be established for all the parishes in the union. In Gillingham poor relief had been provided for many years through a mix of outdoor relief and the indoor provision of the workhouse in

Bay Road (Chapter 7), and there was also a workhouse at Motcombe. Gillingham parish now found itself within the Shaftesbury Poor Law Union along with eighteen other north Dorset parishes.

The guardians of the union had their first meeting in October 1835. The Gillingham representatives were William R. Bell and Thomas Matthews. A sub-committee was set up to look into the future of the Gillingham and Motcombe workhouses, and this reported to the next meeting. The Gillingham workhouse in particular was found to be in a poor state of repair, and neither house would be large enough to take the 250 paupers for whom space was needed. It was recommended that, rather than spend money on the old workhouses, a site for a new one should be found. A loan of £4000 was obtained from the Exchequer and a site was bought at Alcester in the St. James parish of Shaftesbury.[11]

While the new workhouse was being built the guardians continued with the existing practices of outdoor relief and the use of the Motcombe and Gillingham workhouses to capacity. In February 1836 the Gillingham house had 15 children and 19 adults, mostly aged, and there was room for another 20 double bedsteads. At Motcombe there were 4 children and 12 adults, with room for 48 single beds. To make the best use of both premises, it was resolved to move all the male inmates to Motcombe and all the females to Gillingham, a move which brought about the inevitable breakup of entire families. The minutes of the Shaftesbury Union indicate that this was a time of hardship and severity for the unfortunate occupiers of these houses, particularly as husbands and wives were now forced to be apart. But there were also some positive aspects, such as the quest to find meaningful work for inmates, money spent on the upkeep of the houses, and the purchases of food and clothes. One case linking tragedy and hope could be that of 'a young man who had both legs amputated as a result of frost is recommended for two wooden legs and crutches and gets them.' A conclusion could be that 'however hard in principle the treatment of paupers may have been they were in practice looked after in this district conscientiously'.[12]

The new Shaftesbury workhouse opened in 1839. In 1842 the Gillingham workhouse was still in the hands of the parish officers, but it was subsequently sold and divided into cottages.

For those unwilling to consider the workhouse as the inevitable outcome of their poverty, there was the option or possibility of emigration. As an alternative to continuing to support the paupers through the poor rate, the Vestry took seriously the option of making payments to people to allow them to emigrate. In May 1847 the Vestry agreed to give £120 towards the emigration expenses of poor persons settled in the parish, to be paid out of the poor rates. In February 1848 another £40 was agreed on, but a further £100 requested in December was 'not acted upon'. In January 1849 another £100 was agreed.[13]

Changes also came to one of the town's longest-established institutions, the Free School. In 1835 the feoffees decided that the number of boys elected to the main school was to be limited to 25, but younger fee-paying boys of 6-8 were to be taught in a separate 'reading school' in a room adjoining. At first 20 boys were admitted to the reading school, with a further 10 the following year. It was required that all boys should attend Sunday School and Church both Sunday mornings and afternoons: 'Those who do not consent to do this will be removed from the School and others elected in their room.' In 1836 a Royal Commission appointed to enquire into charities visited the school and noted that:

> There is a school containing two rooms, one above, and one below, in which two schoolmasters teach separately. They are appointed by the feoffees and receive a salary one of £50 and the other of £10.

The salary of the schoolmaster was actually based upon the number of boys on the roll, since in June 1833 Hugh Hansford received a half-year salary of £30 for thirty boys, but his December salary was only £26, the number of boys having fallen.

The school at this time owned considerable property around the town, all of which, apart from the school and school house, was rented out, producing in 1834 an income of £204 9s 0d (Fig. 53). Many of the properties had belonged to the feoffees from the time of the original endowments, but they also included allotments from the 1809 Enclosure Award in Common Mead, Peacemarsh, and elsewhere; there were also three cottages recently rebuilt in the west Back Lane, with 'a yard, in common,' at a cost of £250. Robert Goldsborough of the Phoenix next door rented a small room in the schoolyard which he used as an additional bar. Much of the feoffees' minute book consists of listings of payments and expenses, including repairs to properties, land taxes, rents for properties which the feoffees leased, and maintenance of some of the town's bridges, for which the feoffees were still responsible.[14]

In 1838 Hugh Hansford retired, and was succeeded as headmaster and postmaster by James Read, with James Sheppard as under master (p.295). The feoffees determined that the number of free scholars should be limited to 65, and that the school should be wholly under their scrutiny, so that they 'will at all times convenient to themselves visit the school and examine the boys in such manner as they shall judge right.' In 1855 Read and Sheppard exchanged posts so that Read became the under master; throughout this time he also continued as the town's postmaster.[15]

In the 1830s and 1840s another school in the town was that of Daniel Cave, who had an 'Academy' in a house in Turner's Lane. A board over the door displayed 'Cave's Seminary Academy for Boys and Girls of both sexes; Reading, Writing, Arithmetic, Grammar, Mensuration, the use of the globes.' In 1839 Cave also became Clerk to the Feoffees of the Free School, but some years later the feoffees found it necessary to prosecute him, probably for appropriation of funds.[16]

53 *Extract from the minute book of the feoffees, listing properties and rents. The school owned 35 properties, including many several plots and cottages, and a total of 88 acres of land. The properties had been considerably added to since the time of the first endowments.*

The unsettled conditions of the 1820s, with their hardship for the labourers and poorer inhabitants, favoured further growth in nonconformity. In 1836 Henry Miles, a surgeon of St. Martin's Street (Queen St), sold to the trustees of the Wesleyan Society a plot of land for £10 for a chapel and burial ground. This building still stands and is known as Portland House or Portland Cottages, and is divided into dwellings. By its side the Wesley Garden is the former burial ground, and some stones still remain (Plate 16). The Methodists or Wesleyans were by no means united, and early in the nineteenth century a 'breakaway' group known as the Primitive Methodists came into being, placing a strong emphasis on open-air evangelism. By 1826 they had established themselves in Motcombe, and in 1836 they built a chapel in Gillingham on Tantrins Lane, now Turners Lane, a building which still stands as a dwelling. In 1842 it is recorded as being in the ownership of Sarah Dunn, who may have been a trustee for the group. The Primitives and Wesleyans were fiercely independent of each other, the former having a more working-class membership and regarding the latter as 'front room Methodists'.[17]

The Baptists had also established themselves in Newbury by 1840, with a chapel and baptising pool.[18] Kelly's 1848 directory records that 'there are chapels for the Baptists, Wesleyans, and Primitive Methodists [and also that] a building of large dimensions has lately been erected by Mr. Edward Neave, one of the Society of Friends, called the Temperance Hall, in which lectures are given in temperance and morality.' The latter building stood on a site now occupied by the National Westminster Bank at the top of Station Road. The Neaves were one of several Quaker families in Gillingham at this time, as were the Hannams, owners of the silk mill. There was no Quaker meeting house in Gillingham, so Neave and Hannam regularly travelled to Quaker meetings at Shaftesbury, Sherborne, Marnhull, Wincanton, and even Bridport.[19]

Alongside these concerns with the moral condition of the townspeople, there were some steps towards an improvement in the town's material environment. In 1837 the Gillingham Gas and Coke Company was established by some of the leading townspeople and businessmen. The Directors were Henry Deane the vicar, Samuel Hannam, Richard Light, Robert Goldsborough, and Henry Miles; the Treasurer was Edward Neave. There were 160 shares of £10 each. The company bought a site from Sherborne School by the side of the lane leading towards Rolls Bridge. For a number of years the lane was known as Gas House Lane. It produced coal gas for cooking and lighting, and sold coke and tar as by-products. Coal came from the Somerset coalfield, at first brought in by horse and cart and later by the railway.[20]

In 1848 Pigot's directory noted that the town was lit with gas, but this may have been only to private consumers, and there was no consideration of public street lighting until the Vestry meeting of November 1858. It was subsequently agreed that gas lighting should be installed for a distance of a mile from the church on each side of the main roads, on byroads for up to 100 yards, and for all properties which abutted on to public roads for up to a quarter mile from the church.[21]

Henry Deane: Church and National School

With the ministry of archdeacon John Fisher, the established pattern of church life in Gillingham had seemed destined to change little. Like his predecessors, Fisher was often an absentee and spent much of his time at his other living at Osmington, much of his work in Gillingham being done by his curates. As we have seen, he found Gillingham a picturesque place well suited to his artistic temperament and altruistic inclinations. But he may also have found his social round in the town somewhat limiting:

> What can a man have to say, living in Gillingham and dining occasionally with a few routine parsons, who have 52 sermons and on New Year's Day turn the leaf?

Nevertheless Fisher probably expected to live out his clerical time at Gillingham or at Osmington, hoping for a long, uneventful ministry. This, however, was not to be, and following failing health he died in 1832 at the early age of 44.[22]

His successor took a very different view of his ministry. Henry Deane, a law academic and Fellow of New College, Oxford, soon

Henry Deane

Henry Deane (1799-1882) was the elder son of Henry Boyle Deane, an advocate of Deal, Kent. He went to Winchester College and then to New College, Oxford, where he studied law and held a fellowship until 1833. He was ordained a priest in 1826 and in 1833 married Jane Caswall of Devizes. He was appointed Vicar of St. Mary the Virgin in Gillingham in 1832.

His 50-year incumbency of Gillingham was notable for his energetic approach to church building and education. Unlike his predecessors, he spent much of his time in the town and was able to devote his time fully to the revival of Anglican church life. He was recognised in the parish for his personal generosity, his conscientious ministry, and his devoted attention to family. He was a successful farmer and landowner, building up an estate of property, mostly in East Stour. Jane Deane had artistic talents, and several of her paintings and drawings can be seen in the Museum.

54 The Reverend Henry Deane

His children with Jane were Jenny (b.1834, died age 8) Henry (b.1838), and Ellen Mary (b.1845). Jane Deane died in 1849. In 1851 Henry Deane married Katharine Mary Smythe of Battersea; their child was James (b.1852). Both brothers went to Winchester and Oxford and took Holy Orders. For a number of years James was able to help the elder Henry with the Gillingham ministry.

Henry Deane's ministry is represented by a brass plaque in Gillingham church. After his death his parishioners gave to the church a pulpit and eagle lectern. The portrait above is in Gillingham Museum. Jane Deane also has a memorial in the east window, but this is obscured by the later reredos.

(Based on J. Ash, *Victorian Vicar, The Story of Henry Deane*) saw his new parish as a challenge to his ambitions and abilities (Fig. 54). Deane came from a family which for a century had followed successful careers in the church. His background, and also his own not inconsiderable wealth in land and property, gave him the confidence and resources to actively pursue the regeneration of his church and parish. He made an early start, for during his first winter he held an evening school in reading for boys and men. At Enmore Green a cottage was converted into a day school and also used for Sunday evening services until a new church could be built. In 1837 Bourton church, only built in 1812-13, was lengthened and widened.[23]

His main energies soon became directed towards the rebuilding of the Gillingham church. By this time the Gillingham benefice had become a wealthy living, the value of the glebes and parsonage having advanced from the £140 of 1650 to £2,000. Thanks to the energies of parson Hume half a century earlier, the tithes were also highly valuable. The church itself however had been neglected, being little different from that of Davenant and Jesop's time. Its cramped conditions have been described in Chapter 7. In a letter to the Incorporated Church Building Society seeking financial assistance, he drew attention to the growth of the population in a town (nearing 3,000) for which the church could provide no more than 200 free sittings. He argued that there was 'need of additional pews for persons in a class of life above the occupants of the free sittings, but not possessing any of the properties to which the pews were attached'.[24]

Henry Deane's thinking was no doubt influenced by what he saw of the success of the local nonconformist churches in attracting worshippers. He noted that these were churches in which the people could not only clearly see the preacher but also each other. He recognised that church-going was fast becoming a social occasion in which people wanted to see their fellow worshippers and be seen by them. 'Sunday morning was a time when men and wives could leave their counters, cowsheds, and kitchens to show the world by their broadcloth coats and stylish bonnets how the world fared for them.[25]

Deane considered different possible plans for his new church, and in the vicarage he was frequently to be found in a 'room littered with half-unrolled plans.' One plan involved the retention of much of the existing structure with the enlargement coming from the extension of the side aisles behind the chancel. However, the adopted scheme was bolder, involving the reconstruction of all but the medieval chancel. The new church was to be longer and higher than the earlier one, with the tower moved back by twenty feet and clerestory windows above the nave. A new floor was to be inserted 18 inches above the level of the old one. The new height allowed the insertion of galleries above the aisles, reached by staircases from the porches. In this way the seating capacity could be increased to 1,100, giving the town a church worthy of its status as the major place of north Dorset. The architect was Henry Malpas of Frome. In the long term the galleries may not have been all that popular, perhaps because they darkened the church; there was an unsuccessful proposal to remove them soon after Deane's death in 1882, and they were finally taken down in 1918.[26]

The list of contributors to the building of the new church is in itself something of a profile of landed wealth in the Gillingham area. Towards the £3,000 needed for the restoration Deane gave £550. He himself was a landed proprietor, whose estates at his death in 1882 included a farm at Eccliffe and further land and property in East Stour. He also had shares in the Gillingham Gas and Coke Company. Even with his Gillingham donation he was able to contribute to his other church-building projects. The Matthews family of Milton gave £265. From the early eighteenth century they had been building up their holdings around Milton, and also had a stock farm on Exmoor; by the time of the church rebuilding they were also the town's maltsters and millers. Another landed family anxious to show their generosity (£185) were the Grosvenors of Motcombe, whose 'wheatsheaf' symbol is to be found on many farmhouses and on buildings in Shaftesbury, of which they owned the greater part. Lesser contributions came from the Bell, Card, and Mortimer families, and others involved in business activities around the town. All these and many other worthies would have heard the first sermon preached on 5th December 1839. The celebration was rounded off by a lunch in the new schoolroom, where 106 people sat down to a meal which lasted until 4pm.[27] A dinner was also provided at the Red Lion for the 22 workmen. The Salisbury and Winchester Journal of the 9th December recorded that:

> Too much praise cannot be given to the vicar, the Rev. Henry Deane, for his indefatigable exertions in erecting this noble edifice in lieu of the late inconvenient church, and adding so much more room for the inhabitants of the largest parish in extent … in the county of Dorset.'

The opening of the new church was not the end of expenditure, for the following year alterations were made to the chancel. George Follett, the Cucklington builder of the new church, was paid £288 for alterations which included work on the vestry arches and the moving

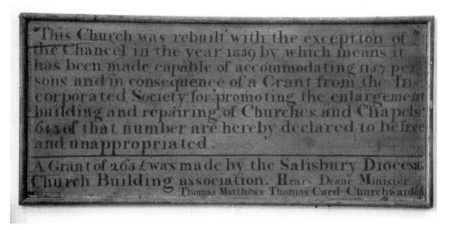

55 A plaque in Gillingham church celebrating the rebuilding of the church by Henry Deane in 1838.

of monuments; this probably referred to the removal and refitting of the Dirdoe, Read, and Jesop monuments in their present positions.[28]

While the rebuilding of Gillingham church was proceeding, Deane was also moving on with his plans for his other churches. At West Stour the church and nave were rebuilt and the work completed by October 1840, with Deane contributing a third of the cost. The following year East Stour church was completely demolished and entirely rebuilt in a Norman style; in later years a second Henry Deane was to become curate of the church built by his father. Motcombe was rebuilt in 1846, notwithstanding the objections of Lady Westminster to the services being held in the Wesleyan church while the building was taking place. Deane's final church building project was somewhat later and at Milton, where there had been no place of worship since the 1540s; here St. Simon and St. Jude was opened in 1865 on land given by Thomas Matthews. The vicar paid for the church organ.[29]

Deane's commitment to church building was paralleled by an equal dedication to educational improvement. Other than the long-established Free School, the only other school in the town was the 'Academy' of Daniel Cave, described above. Deane recognised that there was a need to provide basic schooling for children from poorer families and his solution was the creation of a 'National' school in Gillingham. The National schools originated from the *National Society for the Education of the Poor in the Principles of the Established Church,* a body which grew out of the work of the Society for the Promotion of Christian Knowledge. In August 1839 the following leaflet appeared around the town:

> A National School for girls and boys will shortly be opened at the new School Room, near the Vicarage. All the children will be taught reading, writing, summing, and knitting, and the girls will be taught needlework. Each child will pay one penny a week. No child can be admitted under six years old; nor any who does not know the

alphabet. Parents wishing to send their children to this School are requested to call at the Vicarage any morning between eight and ten o'clock.

The new school was housed in one of the buildings which lay behind the vicarage. The 1805 engraving of the church depicts a two-storey structure which most likely originated as one of the enlargements made by William Douglas or John Perne. This building was now reduced to a single storey. Stone windows and door mouldings from the old church were incorporated into the structure, which is still known today as the Vicarage School Room.[30] It continued to provide elementary schooling in the town until the establishment of the Board schools in the 1870s.

The remodelling of the churchyard area probably dates from this time. Until then the churchyard had been open to the streets, and at various times it had been used as a drying ground, a playing field, and a place for drunken brawls. Deane had the burial ground now properly enclosed, and it is likely that the building of the retaining wall to the street dates from around this time. Within little more than a decade Henry Deane had transformed the appearance of the church and vicarage area, and with it the position of religion and education within the town.

Trade and business

B Y THE 1850s Gillingham was already starting to change from a town linked to its neighbouring countryside only by agricultural needs into one where people could look at the wider business opportunities in the world beyond. Such aspirations were to become more fully realised after the opening of the railway in 1859, but even in the preceding decades there are signs of a greater commercial opportunism. The general expansion of business and trade can be seen in the increasing number of entries in the trade directories of the time. In 1830 Pigot's directory listed 61 commercial entries for the town, and this had grown to 90 by 1844 and 99 by 1852. Slater's 1852 directory listed no fewer than 10 boot and shoe makers, 4 stonemasons, 4 butchers, 4 milliners and dress makers, 4 tailors, and 7 beer retailers. This could indicate that, despite the many poor labourers, the population contained enough people sufficiently well off to expect some choice in their shopping. Pigot's 1823 Directory records a 'small market' held on Friday, and there were also annual fairs on Trinity Monday and 12 September for horses, bullock, and sheep, held on Lodbourne Green. This commercial activity was sufficient to persuade the Wiltshire and Dorset Bank to set up its first branch in the town in 1836. However, its success was limited to a few years, and by 1847 the branch had closed. For a while the town's banking needs were met by Edward Neave, the Quaker grocer and general dealer, acting as an agent for Thomas' and Storey's Bank. In 1855 the Wilts and Dorset returned, no doubt encouraged by the prospect of improved trade from the imminent arrival of the railway. Insurance agencies also grew in numbers, there being no fewer than six in the town in 1859.

Some Gillingham traders took stock of the vulnerability of their farming neighbours to the unpredictable market conditions of the time, and some saw the need to spread their activities widely. Those who diversified into notably different pursuits included Joseph Dunn, who in 1848 was a bookseller and stationer as well as being a linen and woollen draper; Thomas Smith who could both make shoes and sell beer; and Elizabeth Silverthorn, both grocer and brickmaker. However few had as diverse a business career as Edward Neave. He is listed as a grocer, tea dealer, draper, china dealer, chemist, druggist, and agent to the Sun fire insurance office. He also owned the printing works on Church Walk, his name being on most of the posters and flyers printed in the town at that time. By 1859 he had become manager of the newly built Wilts and Dorset Bank in The Square.

Another trader who took full opportunities of the times was Shadrach Dunn, whose business career is well described by Barbara Kerr in *Bound to the Soil*. Born in 1799, Dunn began his career on a small tenement at Silton, selling corn and seeds to his neighbours. In 1832 he moved to Gillingham to concentrate on selling seeds. He was particularly successful with a strain of Dorset marlgrass clover, which he sold at the markets at Gillingham, Shaftesbury, Stalbridge, Wincanton, and Salisbury. On the Salisbury market day his dedication was such that he would often leave at 3 am and not return until 9 pm. He bought grain heavily after a good season in 1846 and then sold it profitably two years later when harvests were ruined by the rain, and is said to have made £10,000 from these dealings. From his profits he built a new mansion at Springfield, from where he still continued to run his grain business. He was a determined opponent of the Salisbury and Yeovil Railway which cut across his new property, even though he may have eventually profited by it, and the costs of the battle damaged his business. After his death in 1867 it was carried on by his son, James, and many years later was moved to Bournemouth and then again to Salisbury, where it flourished as one of the country's most popular seed companies.[31]

Perhaps the most notable example of a rise to commercial predominance from modest beginnings is that of the Matthews family of Milton (p.255). From the mid-1700s they were acquiring properties from the old Dirdoe estates and by the 1820s Thomas Matthews was the principal landowner in the village (Chapter 6). At a much earlier time the family appears to have been connected with an inn in Wyke known as the Drum and Monkey, later the Buffalo, which like all inns had its own brewing premises. In 1830 Harry Matthews is recorded as a wine merchant at Wyke, and by the 1840s Joseph Matthews was well established as a brewer and maltster. It was to strengthen this business that the family bought Purns Mill about 1850. George Blandford Matthews continued flour milling but added a malting floor in order to supply the Wyke business. Soon afterwards the Wyke brewery was substantially rebuilt into its later form and became the principal supplier to public houses in the Gillingham area.[32] In 1865 the new church was built at Milton on land given by Thomas Matthews, and the church has a stained glass window to his memory. More detail on the individual members of the Matthews family at this time and their later history is to be found in Chapter 11.

The commercial spirit of the time extended even to the clergy. Henry Deane was also a farmer and businessman, and took his farming interests just as seriously as his clerical ones. In 1858 he purchased 37 acres of land in East Stour and wrote to his son, Henry, that he now had 28 cows, having just acquired three more. His letters to his son Henry invariably contain references to farming, the progress of land drainage, and other agricultural activities. Even his church congregation could not escape his enthusiasm: George Butler of Madjeston Farm was once leaving St. Mary's after morning service when Deane hastened down the aisle towards him calling, 'George, George, don't forget to look out for a bull for me at the market'.[33]

1 *Gillingham from Bowridge Hill, with Queen Street in the middle distance. The town has maintained its rural character well into recent times.*

2 *Gillingham from the Common Mead. This pasture, also known as the Cumber Mead, was a part of the manorial demesne from earliest times. It was used as an open meadow where all tenants were able to graze their animals. Attempts to enclose it were made from the sixteenth century, and by the end of the eighteenth century it may have become reduced in size. It was finally enclosed in 1809, when it was divided between a number of landowners.*

3 A mill at Eccliffe is first recorded in 1292. The first part of the name is derived from an Old English personal name, while the second part refers to the steep bank of the Stour at this point in its course. The mill was last used for grinding corn in 1939.

4 Donedge Lodge was one of the lodges of the medieval hunting forest. It stands close to the boundary of the deer park, which forms a dense hedged boundary running across the middle of the picture.

5 *The former medieval forest looking from Bowridge Hill across the Clear Walk towards Motcombe. The forest was enclosed from the seventeenth century onwards; in much earlier times it would have been dense woodland with clearances for grazing.*

6 *Enmore Green is on the edge of Shaftesbury but was within the Forest of Gillingham. By the seventeenth century this corner of the Forest had been widely colonised by cottagers but was important to Shaftesbury as a source of water supply from its wells. The elaborate Byzant ceremony was acted out annually to demonstrate the dependence of the one town on the other.*

7 A copy of the 1624 'Plott' of the Forest, produced at the time of disafforestation to show land already enclosed and that still remaining as open ground. North is on the left. The enclosed areas at the top (east) are all in Motcombe and Enmore Green. An outline of Shaftesbury can be seen top right. In the centre of the map towards Gillingham medieval features such as the Park fence and Kings Court are still clearly visible. The enclosures in the bottom centre of the map represent Newbury and the eastern end of the town; those in the bottom left are towards Bowridge and Huntingford. East Haimes, the seat of the Fee Forester but now disappeared, is the large building shown just below the Barrow Gate to the Park. Bay Lane, passing close to Bowridge Hill, was not the through road to Hindon of today, but turned to curve around the outside of the Park boundary. The original version of this map shows far more detail than is shown here, including many more buildings and names.

8 *The arms of James I in Gillingham church, probably dating from 1618. Royal arms were often displayed in churches to remind people of the crown's position as head of the church. Although Gillingham was still a royal manor, this was a time when much of the crown's property was soon to be disposed of through enclosures and leases.*

9 *The fourteenth-century chancel is the only surviving medieval part of the Gillingham's parish church of St. Mary the Virgin, the remainder of the church having been rebuilt in the nineteenth century. Medieval features of the chancel include its priest's door, sedilia or seats for the priests, and piscina where the vessels of the mass were washed. People would have seen little of the celebration of the Mass as the chancel was separated from the nave by a wooden screen.*

10 Part of the widely
scattered estates of
Sherborne School in
Gillingham in 1733. The
lane crossing to the left
is Common Mead Lane,
with the Common or
Cumber Mead lying to
the south. The enclosures
in the Common Mead
are encroachments made
by the School's tenant
farmers. The Chantry
House (B1) can be seen,
with the church shown

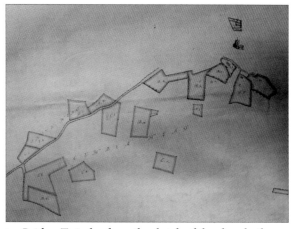

facing it across the Chantry Bridge. To judge from the sketch of the church, the
draughtsman had obviously never seen the building.

11 A map of Gillingham made in 1820. This is the earliest known map to show the
whole town, and is comparable in detail with the tithe map of 1841. At this date
Newbury was still mostly located around the junction with Hardings Lane. Oldlands
Lane, later New Road, is seen here before its realignment by the railway. On the right
the map has been subsequently annotated with detail of the railway and of some
later industries.

12 South Street, formerly known as Back Lane, one of Gillingham's medieval streets. The building on the left is the rear of the Phoenix, perhaps originally its brewing house, more recently occupied by the Gillingham town band. Further along is the Lock-up, also known as the 'Blind House' because of its dearth of windows. It was in use until 1890 when the new Police Station was opened. On the other side of the street from the Lock-up there was access to the garden and coach house of the Phoenix hotel.

13 Gillingham's first fire engine, dating from 1790, is now preserved in the Museum, along with a length of hose and the keys to the engine house.

14 Constable made four oil sketches and paintings of Parham's or Purn's Mill, one of which was exhibited at the Royal Academy in 1827 and is considered to be one of his finest works. It was painted in his Brighton studio two years after the mill had been burned down. The rebuilt mill, shown here, was despaired of by the vicar, John Fisher, for its ugliness and modernity.

15 Waterloo Mill, Silton. The mill at Silton, just outside the parish, was one of several along the Stour and Shreen used by Gillingham and Milton people. The large wheel is not from this mill, but is from the former Silk Mill at Gillingham.

16 *The Wesley Garden in Queen Street is the burial ground of the first Wesleyan Methodist Church built in 1836. One of the few remaining stones is that of Ann Lawrence (d.1852), whose grocer's shop in the Square later became a pharmacy.*

17 *A view of the High Street much changed from Victorian times. Most of this scene was the site of the house of South Lynn, built for the wealthy grocer Thomas Herridge. It was further altered in the twentieth century by the Stickland motor company, before being redeveloped into a supermarket and new shops.*

18 A chartered special in July
2007 recreates the age of steam
in Gillingham. After the line
was single-tracked in 1968
the loop in Gillingham station
provided the only passing place
between Sherborne and Wilton.
A further loop was later added
at Tisbury.

19 Behind the High Street the
buildings and small plots of
ground have a history of use
as small workshops going back
to the nineteenth century and
earlier. This row was once the
slaughterhouse of the butcher's
shop facing on to the street.

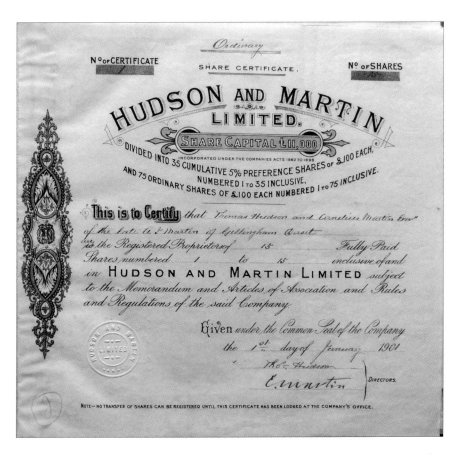

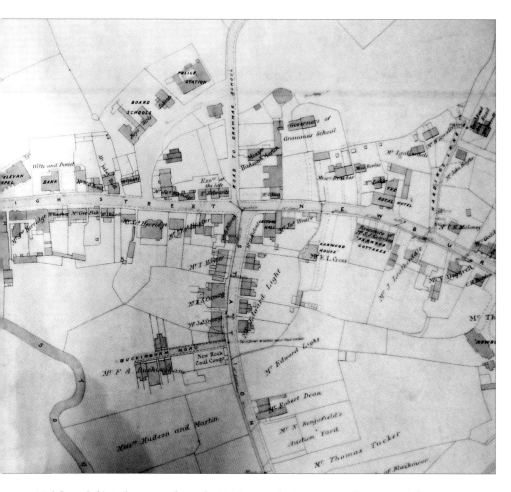

20 (above left) A share certificate for Hudson and Martin, issued in 1901. Albert Martin had recently died, and his shares were divided amongst members of the Hudson and Martin families.

21 (left) A letter heading of the Gillingham Brick, Tile, and Pottery Company from 1938, giving a view of the brickworks.

22 (above) An extract from a map showing sewers in the Newbury part of Gillingham around 1895-1900. The names are those of the owners of properties, not necessarily the occupiers. At this time the High Street was not included in the main drainage system.

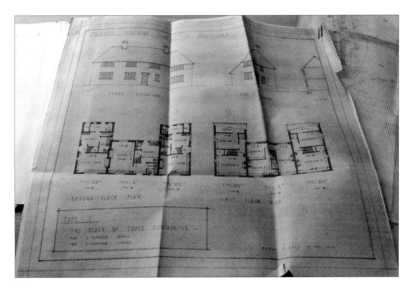

23 Plans for a type of house intended for the Lodbourne Farm (Fairey Crescent) development. This layout was one of seven types of houses intended for this housing project in the late 1930s. By the time the scheme was completed in 1946-47, these plans had been discarded for alternative layouts.

24 The Old House at Milton, as painted by Elspie Langdon-Down, who lived in the house in the early 1950s. In earlier centuries the house was associated with the Dirdoe family.

25 A stained glass window in St. Mary's church recalls Reverend Abbott's time as a teacher at Salisbury Theological College, now Sarum College.

26 The busy Wednesday market of Le Neubourg, Gillingham's twin town in Normandy.

27 The Gillingham Imperial Silver Band steps out at the Carnival in 2002.

9

AROUND GILLINGHAM ON THE EVE OF THE RAILWAY AGE

THE REVEREND HENRY Deane, his family, and his contemporaries, would have recognised a town which still lay in two parts. Around the church and vicarage was the main part of the town, with its two squares north and south of the church. This was separated by the Shreen from Newbury, at that time still a straggle of cottages and workshops extending towards the junctions with Hardings Lane and Oldlands Lane. Some street names were different from today, with the thoroughfare between The Square and the Town Bridge being known as Bridge Street, and then continuing as Newbury from the Town Bridge to Lodden Bridge. The name 'High Street' was not used at that time. New Road, not yet diverted by the railway, was then Oldlands Lane. Behind The Square, today's South Street was Back Lane. The lane towards Rolls Bridge, west of the church was, confusingly enough, also known as Back Lane until it became Gas House Lane. The road between The Square and Lodbourne Green was known as St. Martin's Street until around 1860, when it became Queen Street.[1]

The ground outside Henry Deane's vicarage door was the largest single piece of estate in the main part of the town, including both the vicarage lands and the church with its burial ground. The rebuilding of the church in 1838 has been described in an earlier chapter in some detail, and it is likely that the final boundaries of the churchyard were established at this time. Sketches and early photographs depict the vicarage as a three-bay structure with almost symmetrical frontage, a style which suggests that some substantial rebuilding had occurred since the time of John Jesop (Fig. 48). Deane had also recently built or rebuilt the Vicarage School Room to house his National School, and in so doing appears to have incorporated dressings and windows from the old church. Around and behind the vicarage were other buildings, perhaps deriving from the enlargement schemes of Archdeacon Douglas. The sketches and paintings of the vicarage also show the extensive vicarage gardens, which reached from Queen Street to the Shreen, thus including all of the present-day town car park.

The Square, Wyke Street, and Rolls Bridge

T HE SQUARE BEFORE 1860 was the commercial focus of the town, with many of the shops and business premises being found in the roads leading away and opening off from it. On its south side a short street led to the three-arched Chantry Bridge which gave access to the houses now known as Chantry Cottage and Chantry Ford Cottage (Fig. 56).[2] From here a path crossed Chantry Fields, now occupied by the supermarket car parks, and continued southwards towards Madjeston.

The view across the Square from the Phoenix was towards a row of fashionable houses with sash windows. These properties, and neighbouring buildings extending round the corner towards the bridge on Wyke Street, were in the hands of Edward Neave. For forty or more years he had a varied business, trading in groceries, clothing,

56 Chantry Bridge, a photograph
of 1939 showing a scene unchanged
for many decades. The crossing
originated as a ford in medieval
times for a road or trackway to
East Stour. The three-arched
bridge was demolished in 1967 and
replaced by the present structure
to improve the river flow. The
photograph suggests that wider
wheeled traffic forded the river.

and other commodities, which he
carried on from these properties.
Most of the range of buildings has
altered little, the exception being
the northern end of the row, which
was later rebuilt as a department
store by the Slade family (Chapter
11).[3] Neave himself lived further
along Wyke Street at Plank House,
an eighteenth-century house with
a garden now much reduced by
the relief road and its junction.
Further along this side of Wyke
Street, across the 'County Bridge'
of 1807 with its two semicircular
arches, were several stone cottages.
The one now called Little Chantry
was a blacksmith's shop in the 1830s
and 1840s; next door, the cottage
now called Folly's End is considered
to be the one shown in Constable's
Entrance to Gillingham sketch.
Further up the hill past some
later buildings was Wyke Court,
occupied in 1841 by the corn dealer,
Shadrach Dunn, before he built his new mansion at Springfield. Further
on again is the cottage now known as the 'Old Toll House' known in
the later nineteenth century as Knapp Cottage. Nothing is known of
its use as a toll house during the turnpiking era, but it is recorded as
being used as a public house by the later part of the century.[4]

The south side of Wyke Street appears to have been open space
between the Square and the river. Across the bridge, extending round

into Common Mead Lane, were a number of cottages belonging to the Chantry properties of Sherborne School. Nothing is known of their appearance since they were soon to be swept away by the building of the larger house called 'The Chantry' for Robert Freame. Across Common Mead Lane was Knapp House, which belonged to the solicitor, William Read Bell. Bell, born in 1801, was a prominent figure in the town throughout his life and held several public offices, including that of Coroner of the Liberty of Gillingham. He was frequently involved in public matters and chaired many meetings relating to town and parish affairs. Under his son, John Williams Bell, his legal practice later became joined with that of R.S. Freame. He also owned substantial landed property adjoining the town, and in his time Knapp House was much extended and rebuilt.

Knapp House stands at the corner of Wyke Street and Common Mead Lane. From this corner the Lane ran up the hill where Constable made his sketch, and then across the fields of the old Common Mead, enclosed thirty years earlier, towards Thorngrove and Eccliffe (Fig. 57). North from the Square is the little thoroughfare of St. Mary's Place, which today leads into a car park. Before the building of the relief road this was the lower end of Cemetery Road, but before 1860 was known as Back

57 The view from Common Mead Lane towards Wyke Street. At this date the lane was entirely in open countryside.

Lane, the name changing to Gas House Lane with the building of the gasworks in 1838. Further along this lane became Rolls Bridge Lane, leading through fields towards Rolls Bridge and its farm at the bottom of Coldharbour. For many years the two round gasholders were a landmark of the town; the site of now lies beneath the relief road and the adjoining car parks.

Between Gas House Lane (or St. Mary's Place) and the church path are a number of distinctive looking buildings which to judge from their appearance are of variable dates. Some are stone cottages dating from the early nineteenth century or earlier; others include brickwork and window types which indicate a later date, after 1860. These premises are now entirely residential but around 1850 were occupied by a printer, a brickmaker, and shoemakers; altogether there were no fewer than four shoemakers in and around this neighbourhood.[5] An especially interesting building is the shop at the end of the path facing towards the Square. This belonged to Ann Lawrence, who is described as a shopkeeper and dealer in sundries. She occupied the shop from before 1830 well into the 1850s, when it passed to William Samways, and it was probably from his time that it was rebuilt at the back and extended. His family and later owners occupied it continuously as a pharmacy until 2008. This indicates a continuous use as a retail business extending over the best part of two hundred years.[6]

St. Martin's Street and Lodbourne

O N THE NORTH side of the churchyard along the church path were properties belonging to the Phripp family. The Phripps were long-established stone and monumental masons in the town, and there are memorials in the church which bear the legend 'Phripp of Gillingham'. Their cottages, now called Ivy Cottage and Briar Cottage, date from this time. Church Cottage has an interesting frontage, incorporating fragments from the old church. Some of the space around these houses must have been the mason's yard. Within St. Martin's Square there were premises occupied by William Lodder or Loader, a coachmaker, and James Bell, the manager in 1844 of the first Wiltshire and Dorset Bank before it moved to The Square. The north side of St. Martin's Square is bounded by the house called Broadhayes and carries a datestone of 1842, consistent with its architectural style. This house would appear to have been built for Mrs Penninah or Parminah Stone, a flour dealer and baker. Adjoining and behind the house, facing on to the street, was a lower, plainer looking building, which when it was demolished in 1986 was found to contain bread ovens.

Beyond this bakery, the present access from Queen Street on to the town relief road of Le Neubourg Way was the lowermost end of Turner's Lane. On the far side of Le Neubourg Way the Lane leads towards Cemetery Road; on the right can be found the Primitive Methodist chapel of 1836, now used as a dwelling but easily distinguishable by its deep windows. On the opposite corner, now disappeared, was the house of Daniel Cave, the schoolmaster of the 'Academy' (Chapter 8). Further along the west side of St. Martin's or Queen Street beyond Turner's Lane, was a house and land belonging to Joseph Coombs, a tallow chandler, a site which was later occupied by Tower House. Further along again towards Tomlins Lane was a block of land belonged to Thomas Card. He is referred to in the tithe returns as 'Thomas Card the maltster' to distinguish him from Thomas Card the landowner who lived at Pierston, and was one of the principal townspeople. From his time can be dated the row of cottages which included the former Queen's Head inn, which is first recorded in an 1852 directory. The adjoining stone building may have been Card's brewing premises. Around this time he also owned the house adjoining the Vicarage School Room, where malting is known to have taken place (below).

Tomlins Lane, now also severed by the relief road, led at this time from St.Martins Street into an area of old common fields often recorded as the 'Tomalands', an area now covered by housing. The area, which had originated as encroachments from earlier common fields, was part of a more general district of small cottages and tiny plots, the homes of labourers and journeymen tradesmen extending further northwards along Wavering Lane and Peacemarsh. It is now entirely covered by the building developments of Coronation Road and adjoining roads, but occasional cottages can be found scattered amongst the later developments.

On the east side of St. Martin's Street opposite the church was the Vicarage School Room, the rebuilding of which has already been described (Chapter 8). On its north side was the house now known as The Barton. This house has a long and varied history; ownership of the property is traceable back to at least 1747, when it was owned by Edward Cox, a maltster (Chapter 7). Around 1823 it belonged to Edward Martin, and then to James Giffard, a surgeon. Around 1830 it was in the hands of Thomas Card, the maltster, who also owned the Queen's Head. By 1834 it was occupied by George Matthews Marack, an excise officer, and by 1841 was let to Peter George, listed in 1840 as a grocer and draper. The lease includes reference to a malthouse. On the rear wall of the house is an iron pulley which may relate to this period of its history. It is thought to be the last house in Gillingham to display a fire insurance badge, that of the Sun fire company. During the 1840s and 1850s it was owned by the vicar, Henry Deane. Its later history is that of Shephard's tailor's shop, a feature of the street until recent times.[7]

Next door, Lime Tree House is a mid-eighteenth century house with windows and other features characteristic of the period. This house and the 'Barton' may be representative of similar houses of this part of Gillingham which were eventually lost to fire or later developments. The house was called 'Gynns' for most of the 1700s, the earliest reference being a lease from John Chubb to Edward Reeves in 1705. He stayed at Gynns until his death around 1739, by which time the ownership had passed to the Tinney family. In 1770 it was let to William Tinney, the attorney, the Tinney family retaining an interest in the property until 1867. In 1840 it was occupied by Mrs Mary Le Hardy, who was clearly a person of status in the town since she is listed in the directories under 'private residents'.[8] Both The Barton and Lime Tree House are notable for their long gardens stretching back to the river, and may be survivors of a pattern of medieval town plots that was once more extensive along this side of Queen Street.

58 *A part of Queen Street, appearing much as it would have been in the 1840s. The Vicarage School Room (third from left) had recently been built out of materials from older buildings.*

On its north side, Lime Tree House adjoined the property of Henry Miles, the town surgeon. His house and extensive land and orchard are no longer there, but can be seen in an early picture of St. Martin's Street from the church tower. The nearer part of the site later became the home of Thomas Hudson the builder, and eventually the present adult education centre; the further part remained undeveloped until the building of the St. Martin's care home. In 1836 Miles sold to the Gillingham Wesleyans the far northern end of this property for the building of their first chapel, now Portland House (Chapter 8). This is a plain structure by comparison with the later Methodist church, and is still recognisable as a chapel despite much alteration and conversion into dwellings. The adjoining Wesley Garden has some standing memorial slabs from the former burial ground (Plate 16).

Further along the street before 1860 were a number of trading and manufacturing premises, but their exact location cannot be fixed with certainty. John Peters had rope and twine making premises, perhaps now the building which houses the food takeaway. Perhaps this was shared with the workshop of Isaiah Mitchell, a dowlas and bed ticking manufacturer, the last in Gillingham. Although by this time the industry was in decline, his was an important business since he may have employed numbers of outworkers around the town. James Dewey, a veterinary surgeon, had premises here a little later in 1871. Charles Williams, a shoemaker, had premises towards the end of the street near to Lodbourne Green.

At its northern end, St. Martin's Street opened out into Lodbourne Green, which then represented the northern end of the main part of the town. This was a triangular-shaped area, larger than the green space of today, and included land now occupied by the row of shops and the road junction. The green was used for fairs and other town events until it was built over in recent times. Facing on to the Green was the Great House farm. Its farmhouse could be Gillingham's oldest building, containing as it does the remains of a Tudor roof within its later structure. The occupier, William White, farmed the land immediately behind the farmhouse and also some fields on the northern side of Wavering Lane. On the north side of the green, the farmhouse of Lodbourne Farm can still be found amongst the later housing. This was a large farm with property which included most of the land subsequently built on by the Gyllas Way and Claremont Avenue developments, as well as further land at Colesbrook which had originally been part of the Northmoor commons.

Bridge Street and Back Lane

T HE THOROUGHFARE FROM The Square towards the Town Bridge was at that time known as Bridge Street. On the north side of the street, backing on to the church yard there was, as now, a row of premises. Opposite the Phoenix, the art shop of today has had a number of functions in the past, and around 1850 was occupied by a shoemaker. At the far end of the row on the corner is a handsome double-fronted building with a shop window facing across towards Spring Corner. For much of the last century this was the offices of Senior and Godwin, auctioneers, but in 1840 it belonged to the school feoffees and was the home of James Read, the schoolmaster. Read was also the town's postmaster. Earlier in the century around 1810 it had been occupied by Read's predecessor, Hugh Hansford, for we read in the feoffee's records of 'one other messuage or tenement called the Church House now converted into a school house with the curtilage adjoining …'. This property has windows and pilasters all characteristic of the period, the shop frontage in Queen Street being added later.[9]

Across the corner of Queen Street is Spring Corner, where the sinking of a well by Archdeacon Douglas in 1802 has already been described (Chapter 8). From here the wall of the vicarage garden extended towards the Town Bridge, and is the one depicted in Constable's painting of the bridge. Constable's painting depicts a gate here with a building which is thought to be the coach house of the vicarage. The bridge, of two arches, was built by the order of the county justices in 1800, and has a plaque commemorating Constable's painting.

On the south side of the street were premises extending back to South Street, or Back Lane as it was then known. Facing the church gate was the Phoenix inn, one of two inns in the town which can be traced back to at least the seventeenth century and may well have existed earlier. It is here that Robert Frampton had his confrontation with Quartermaster Gage during the Civil War (Chapter 5). In 1841 the publican was Robert Goldsborough, one of the better off townspeople, who owned the inn and the land behind it, and also occupied several other pieces of land in and around the town. The building itself has several units including a three-storey wing, and the rearmost section may have been the brewhouse, but nothing more is known of its early architectural history. The frontage was altered considerably at the end of the century (Chapter 13). Rounded corners to the street indicate the need to restrict damage to passing coaches. The coach house and garden were both on the far side of Back Lane, the access being directly opposite the Lock-up (Plate 12). In common with the Red Lion and with the larger inns of towns generally, the Phoenix was frequently used for official events such as meetings of the manor courts or of the church vestry.

Next door to the Phoenix is a building of equal historical interest, its blue plaque identifying it as the site of the Free School. The history of the school has been given in earlier chapters, and it would seem that by 1600 the school was occupying the building which now stands. In 1836 a Charity Commission which visited the school noted its two rooms, one above and below, for each of the two classes. The ground floor room has a ceiling considered to be of the sixteenth century. On the rear roof, recent tiles mark the position of the old school bell. On some of the windows of the long upper landing, the names of former pupils, Fred Bowles and C. King were scratched in 1870. The rear view, with its casement windows, may give a better impression of its frontal appearance before the Victorian windows were added. In the Museum there is a picture of James Sheppard, the last headmaster of the School, and his pupils in the yard behind the building. The rear yard of the school was occupied by the Lock-up, which like the school has been described in an earlier chapter. In the 1850s it would have appeared as it is now, except for the later added window at the eastern end.

The narrow building to the east of the Free School appears to be of later build, but the rest of the block eastwards would have existed in 1850, although some frontages are later. The present solicitor's office was the property of the feoffees, occupied in 1840 by Thomas Martin. The shoe repairs and pet supplies shop was occupied by Samuel Harris, a grocer who also sold clocks and watches; by 1860 it had passed to William Downs, a butcher, and continued to be a butcher's shop for many years.

An opening separates this block from the other Gillingham inn, which already had a long history by the mid-nineteenth century. Ownership of the Red Lion is recorded back to 1698, when it belonged to John Jones. By 1738 it was owned by the Phripp family, who were involved in an ownership dispute with Mary Jones, the case being heard in the Court of Chancery. Between 1741 and 1753 there are several bills containing many items including roofing, tiling, and glazing which point to a considerable rebuilding. Items mentioned in 1741 include 71 loads of walling stone, 222 feet of Kington stone, '22 joists of 3 by 4' and '54 ft of crown glass.' Stone from Kington (Magna) and Marnhull is recorded. Brick tiles and pan tiles were used, which may have come from the brickyard by Kings Court. Some of the rebuilding refers to the woodhouse and stables. By 1768 the owner was Robert Phripp.[10] Throughout this time the manor courts and vestry meetings were sometimes held here. Around 1800 the inn was known as the 'Katharine Wheel', and was owned by James Knight. By 1823 the owner was Richard Light, who occupied it until the 1850s. He also owned much of the land around the back of the inn and just across the Shreen. Next

59 A parade by the Southampton Police Band in 1912 marches past the Grosvenor Arms and neighbouring terrace of cottages. This row was built shortly before 1855 and was demolished in 1996, its site being marked today by a stone wall.

to the Red Lion, the adjoining properties in 1840 appear to have been houses rather than trading premises. The end property, now a takeaway, was occupied in the 1840s by John Edwards, a saddler and collar maker.

Pedestrians walking from this point towards Newbury will notice a low stone wall by the side of the narrow pavement. This is all that remains of a terrace of buildings demolished in 1996. The nearer, three-storey building was the Grosvenor Arms, built by 1840, when the publican was Thomas Young. The adjoining group of four cottages had appeared by 1855, when all were used as dwellings and occupied by labourers (Fig. 59).[11]

Along Newbury

I N 1840 NEWBURY still referred to the stretch of street extending across the whole of the higher ground between the Shreen and the Lodden. It was still detached from the main part of the town west of the Shreen. Walking from the Town or Shreen Bridge up the hill, the north side would be seen to be largely open land as far as approximately the present-day junction with School Road. All this land, later to include the sites of the Methodist Church and the Wilts and Dorset Bank, belonged to Barnaby's Farm and Charles Helyar. He had further fields on the other side of Newbury and elsewhere around the town. Eastwards towards Hardings Lane, School Lane and School Road had not yet appeared, but a number of small plots extended back from the street, some lying behind other plots. Further behind these plots again lay a larger field which was owned by the school feoffees; this was to be of some importance in the years to come, providing the site of the new Grammar School.

These plots have now all but disappeared from the modern map, but some are shown on a map from 1844 representing a possible alignment for the later railway (Fig. 61). West of the present School Road was the premises of Thomas Edwards, a blacksmith and cooper. A few yards further along is a house at the western end of the present ironmonger's shop, a double-fronted property with iron railings leading up to the disused front door. This was occupied in the 1860s by James Dunn, the seedsman and son of Shadrach Dunn. Behind this house is Clay Pitts, dated 1762. The ironmongers and other shops along this range extending to School Lane were much altered by the Stickland family later in the century. Further along, the 1844 'railway' map clearly shows the cottages behind the present furniture shop, once occupied by Bracher Brothers for several decades. The corner plot with Hardings Lane at the time of the 1841 census was lived in by Shadrach Dunn, who subsequently appears to have moved to Wyke Street; the site would later be occupied by one of Gillingham's landmark buildings, the now demolished Railway or Royal Hotel.

On the opposite corner of Hardings Lane is The Laurels, a handsome house notable for its wrought iron door hood and original fireplace surround. The tithe survey records the plot as being owned and occupied by Amy Lush, although her name does not appear in the 1841 census. It is clearly depicted on the railway map of 1851, where it is shown in the possession of John Helyar. Eastwards from the Laurels, across the present-day roundabout and railway bridge, walkers and riders would have found mostly open land except for the first Baptist church, a predecessor of the later structure, which was built next to it. A group of dwellings including the house of Lodden Farm, still to be found, completed the descent to Lodden Bridge.

The south side of 1850's Newbury, going back to the Town Bridge and walking eastwards, bears little relationship to the High Street of today. Almost all of the present-day buildings along this part of the street have resulted from later developments. The first few yards beyond the bridge was open land, but beyond here a number of irregularly shaped plots fronted the street, with further plots lying behind. All these were in the occupation of various tradesmen as cottages and workshops; some recorded occupations include a cooper, shoemaker, thatcher, carpenter, and carrier, as well as several labourers. One larger business was that of John Edwards, a saddler and collar maker. He occupied the long building which now extends behind the Chapman Moore estate agents, and was later used as a slaughterhouse (Plate 19). The supermarket higher up the street is only the latest occupier of much of this space, the developments of the later nineteenth century at this point being discussed in Chapter 13. The future Station Road then existed only as a gap or track between some of these plots.

A few yards beyond this gap, in the space later occupied by the Stuckeys (National Westminster) bank, was the Temperance Hall or Lecture Hall, built by Edward Neave around 1840. Further along again, set back from the street and so easily missed today, is Harwood House. The oldest part has been dated to the earlier seventeenth century, and it can be found on the forest map or 'plot' of this time. A datestone of 1694 is to be seen. The 1844 'railway' map depicts it as standing in spacious grounds with paths, and at that date it was occupied by the Reverend William Lloyd Collett. Harwood House and properties eastwards were in the hands of Richard Light, the innkeeper of the Red Lion. His land extended as far as the present Blackmore Vale House, a house of similar age to The Laurels opposite, possibly one of several similar houses once found in this area.

This part of Newbury was later to be fragmented by the coming of the railway, and much later by the relief road and associated developments. A survivor from an earlier period is Newbury House, the largest property at this end of Gillingham at this time, but now easy to miss from the main road. The main part of the house is a substantial five-bay mansion, which is flanked by slightly lower wings perhaps of a later date. In 1841 it was owned by George Pollard and appears to have had various occupiers at this time until shortly before 1859, when it was acquired by Henry Kaines, a solicitor, landowner, and notable public figure of the town. It is now part of a complex of flats and sheltered accommodation, the later road improvements taking away much of its former grounds. The eastern boundary of Newbury House was the former junction of Oldlands Lane and Newbury.

East of Newbury House the tithe map indicates perhaps half a dozen houses on sites now occupied by the railway bridge and down the hill towards Lodden Bridge, but most have not survived into modern times.

Outlying areas: Peacemarsh, Milton, Ham, and Wyke

O UTSIDE THE MAIN part of the town, the most densely populated district was that around Peacemarsh. Here, on either side of the road from Lodbourne Green towards Colesbrook, there was a sprinkle of small plots and cottages, many of which can still be found standing amongst the area's more modern housing developments (Fig. 60). These cottages had their origins in the enclosure of the common lands along the sides of the road, and were occupied almost exclusively by farm labourers, and by tradesmen such as carpenters or masons, several of whom were established enough to merit entries in the trade directories. There was a particular cluster around the meeting of Peacemarsh and Wavering Lane, and more cottages were to be found westwards further along Wavering Lane. Numerous women and girls from this district were employed in the silk mill. The census returns suggest that the population may have been more numerous than first appears, with some houses being occupied by more than one family. The Dolphin Inn and the Peacemarsh Farm are two specific properties which are readily distinguishable amongst the many dwellings houses mentioned in the census returns; the Crown was another public house which may also have existed at this time.

Eastwards from Lodbourne Green the only buildings towards the bridge were the parish workhouse on the south side, the earlier history of which has already been fully described (Chapter 7). On the north side was the Bay Farmhouse, which still stands between Fairey Crescent and Shreen Way. Beyond the bridge a cluster of cottages formed the hamlet of Bay, looking much as it does today, apart from the addition of the few more recent houses. At the end of Bay Lane

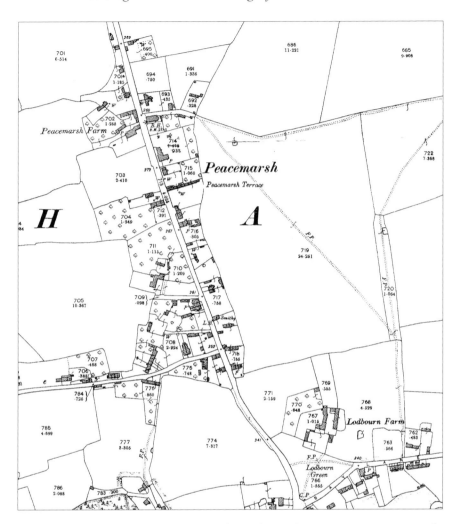

60 Peacemarsh in 1901, an extract from the Ordnance Survey map. Until the earlier decades of the twentieth century Peacemarsh consisted entirely of cottages and workshops standing in small plots close to the road, a product of earlier enclosure of the roadside commons. Many of these cottages are still to be found among the more modern developments.

was another farm and farmhouse, which bears a datestone of 1674. Up the hill along Bloomers Lane on to Bowridge Hill, plots and cottages lined the road on each side, the largest of these being the Malthouse Farm, a substantial house of five bays width dating from the early eighteenth century, and at the present day used as a care home. At this time there was no road along the top of Bowridge Hill towards Colesbrook.

North of Peacemarsh, the turnpiked road passed the toll house at Colesbrook and the Fir Tree inn, before passing through Milton on Stour and continuing along Martins Lane to Bourton. The village of Milton at this time lay in two parts. The older area lay south of the Stour and included the centuries-old estates of the Old House and Pierston. The former, by then in the hands of Thomas Matthews, was extensively rebuilt in the nineteenth century, but still retaining elements of the seventeenth-century house of the Dirdoes. Pierston Farm, largely of the eighteenth century, also has nineteenth-century additions. To the north of the Old House there was a further spreading of cottages and small plots towards Little Marsh and the Bourton road. Milton Lodge was until 1847 the home of George Whieldon, later being acquired by Thomas Matthews. Milton at this time was almost entirely agricultural, most of the households being those of farm labourers.

East of the town, beyond Lodden Bridge on the Shaftesbury road, there was a notable concentration of cottages along a track (later King's Court Road) running in the direction of the medieval King's Court site. This site adjoined a field used around this time as a brickworks. In 1841 it belonged to Elizabeth Silverthorne who lived at Newbury, and is recorded as brickmaker or grocer in contemporary directories. The 1851 census continues to record her as a brickmaker, and also her son, John, as a potter, but by 1859 he seems to have become a corn merchant. The works appears to have produced mostly poorer quality bricks, largely used for garden walling and chimney stacks, but also produced pipes and drains, for which there was a developing market amongst farmers wanting to improve their land. The works ceased operation soon after the opening of the new brickworks next to the railway after 1860. Nearby was the thatched house known more recently as the 'Haywain'; in 1841 it was lived in by Robert Barter, listed in the census and directories as a maltster. It has also belonged to the Westminster estate and has been known as Grosvenor Cottage. Yet further along the road, and on the same side, there was a brick and tile kiln at Parkhouse Farm, a site which has now been absorbed into Orchard Park.[12]

On the western side of the town, Wyke was as yet separate from Gillingham, having not yet been linked by the chain of villas which was to advance up Wyke Street and Coldharbour from later in the century. There was little to disturb the tranquillity of Wyke Hall, now lived in by James Mortimer. When he died in 1847 his widow, Anne, married George Whieldon of Milton, who was appointed High Sheriff of Dorset in 1863. Around this time much of the Hall was rebuilt both inside and outside, a rainwater head dated 1853 being a reminder of these changes. From the Hall and its park the extensive Wyke estates spread out southwards and westwards, all in the tenure of John Newman of Wyke Farm. The earliest part of the farm itself is thought to date from before 1700, but was much rebuilt during the nineteenth century, a period of security and prosperity for many tenant farmers. A notable feature still to be seen is the octagonal granary and dovecote resting on staddle stones, perhaps also dating from the middle of this century.

To the south-east of the hall the village of Wyke consisted of a group of cottages along the Wincanton road at the end of Lydfords Lane. Along Lydfords Lane and the later Clarendon Close were further cottages, facing each other across an open field. The occupiers of these included a barrel washer, carter, carrier, brewer, and carpenter, all occupations linked to the new brewery business being developed by Joseph Matthews just across the road. In the 1848 directory we read of an 'extensive brewery', perhaps indicating substantial rebuilding into its later, imposing form, complete with 'medieval' towers, a striking monument to the start of a wider prosperity in Gillingham and its surrounding countryside.

10

THE COMING OF THE
RAILWAY

I N M A N Y P L A C E S the arrival of the Railway Age is written about
as an unexpected event, something which, when it happened,
took the community by surprise. In the case of Gillingham, far
from being unanticipated, it had looked likely for a number of years
that the town would be served by the spreading railway network. As
early as 1835 there had been a proposal for a railway from Salisbury
through north Dorset to Exeter and Falmouth, with a route through
Gillingham, but the idea never got as far as Parliament. In 1838 the
railway from London reached Basingstoke, and in 1847 reached
Salisbury from Southampton. In 1846 a meeting was held in Sherborne
Town Hall to petition parliament in favour of a London, Salisbury, and
Yeovil line, and in 1848 a Salisbury and Yeovil Railway Act received
royal assent. This route, to be operated by the London and South
Western Railway, was to run from Salisbury through Wilton, Tisbury,
Gillingham, and Sherborne. Thereafter for several years the project
became mired in conflicts between different railway companies and
proposals, the financial crises of the railway mania years, and the
disagreements over whether Exeter should be reached via north Dorset
or from Dorchester. By 1853 the powers of the 1848 Act had expired,
and it looked as though the project might be completely lost.[1]

A new Act was obtained in 1854, which set up the Salisbury and Yeovil Railway Company (S & YR). This was an independent company whose main shareholders were local people from around Gillingham and Sherborne. It was supported by the London and South Western Railway, which was to provide the train services on the line, seeing it as a vital link in achieving its goal of reaching Exeter. Salisbury was reached from Basingstoke in 1857, placing Gillingham on a direct route to London. In Gillingham the railway was welcomed by the town's business interests, and it is likely that some of the growth of commercial activity in the town through the 1840s and 1850s was in anticipation of the railway's arrival. Sales details of land and property at this time sometimes referred to proximity to the proposed railway as a desirable feature.[2] Not everybody was initially enthusiastic; at Sherborne Lord Digby had opposed the line, but he was succeeded by Mr. Wingfield Digby who agreed to his land being crossed to permit a straighter line running closer to the town centre. In Tisbury Mr John Bennett, MP for South Wiltshire, at first opposed the line going through his property but changed his mind when it was pointed out that the value of his land might increase by 20 per cent as a consequence.[3]

Rather less persuadable was Shadrach Dunn, who had just bought a new property at Bugley, through which the new line was intended to pass. Although the line would have helped his business as a seedsman, he nevertheless decided to fight the project, and may have been discreetly backed by the Earl Grosvenor, Marquis of Westminster, 'whose concern for progress may have found an outlet in the development of his London estates, not in railway building on the periphery of his Dorset property.' Grosvenor perhaps saw this issue as part of his wider rivalry with John Rutter of Shaftesbury, a committed supporter of the line, who received from the people of Gillingham a silver salver for his endeavours in its promotion. Dunn's long legal battle with the railway company was only settled in 1863 in the company's favour, and his financial losses forced

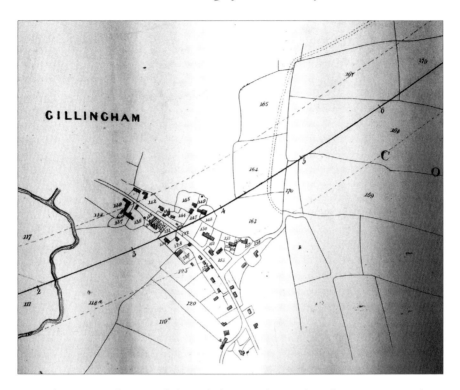

61 The proposed route of the Salisbury and Yeovil Railway in 1844. This was one of several proposals for the railway route during the 1840s and 1850s. Under this scheme the route would have passed to the north of the final alignment and is shown cutting through Newbury where the School Lane and Station Road junctions are at present. By 1851 the line had shifted slightly south again to meet Newbury by the present bypass roundabout, and was to shift a few yards south yet again by the time that building began in 1856.

him to mortgage his property.[4] His conflict with the S & YR included a disagreement in 1858 over the price to be paid for a piece of ground of just over five acres; Dunn claimed that the project would cause damage to some of his other land, and claimed £1,200 in compensation. A sheriff's jury eventually settled the amounts at £230 for the land, and £270 for additional damages.[5]

The various proposals produced different alignments for the scheme. The 1835 proposal would have carried the railway somewhat to the north of the town, across Peacemarsh and to the north of Wyke. Later schemes would have taken the line through the built-up parts of Newbury, destroying much of this part of the town. The final alignment was decided on only in 1854 (Fig. 61).[6] When construction began in 1856 the S & YR had little capital, and many of the payments to contractors, surveyors, and lawyers were made in shares. The contract to build the line was initially awarded to Leslie and Davidson, a previously unknown firm, but was soon transferred to Thomas Brassey, a highly prolific builder of railways of great reputation. By 1847 he had built one-third of the railways in Britain and by 1870 had built one mile in 20 of every railway in the world. The construction

62 The first turf about to be turned on 3rd April 1856. The ceremony was performed by Miss Louisa Caroline Seymour of East Knoyle, sister of the S & YR Chairman Henry Danby Seymour, who was M.P. for Poole. This was a day when the weather 'whirled sheets of water on our heads, blew garments into ribbons, and cast our speeches back into our teeth.' The decorated wheelbarrow and spade are in the Gillingham Museum. An etching from the Illustrated London News.

engineer was Joseph Locke, who like Brassey, had a high reputation for his railway work. He started his career by working with Robert Stephenson on the Liverpool & Manchester Railway, and during his career progressed on to many later projects including the West Coast main line across Shap Fell.

The first sod was cut at Gillingham on 3rd April 1856, at a lavish ceremony which included lunch for 300 people and numerous speeches (Fig. 62). The turf was lifted using a specially made silver spade and decorated barrow. The journalist, Louis Ruegg, who was also a principal shareholder, graphically reported the event for the *Sherborne Mercury*, later describing it again in his *History of a Railway* of 1878. One of the most memorable aspects of the day was the weather, with the proceedings being deluged by wind and rain; but even rainwater trickling into the champagne glasses could not prevent the day being successful.[7]

The initial land acquisitions were from several landowners, including the Marquis of Westminster, Sherborne School, and Henry Kaines, a Newbury solicitor who had land south of the town. The Sherborne School records include some of the notices of intent of land purchase which were sent to the School Governors during these years, most of which were not acted upon because the proposed railway was not built. The notice for the 1845 scheme specified purchases from four fields, three of which were in the occupation of Robert Goldsborough, publican of the Phoenix. The notices of intent to purchase were followed by surveys of the land to determine the value that should be paid in compensation. In 1857, a year after the first sod was turned, two surveyors were appointed, one by the school and the other by the railway company, to value a small piece of land of just over an acre. In the event, only the school's surveyor appeared at the site, duly valuing the land and reporting also on the need to provide adequate drainage since an embankment was intended. The school was eventually paid £148 13 9 for the loss of its land. Such surveys, however small the land parcels involved, were an essential and routine procedure throughout the length of the line.[8]

The manor court rolls of 1859 record numerous conveyances of land from landowners to the railway company, and the sums they received in compensation. Several were for small parcels of an acre or less, awarded where the line cut through a corner of a field or a tenement or orchard. The largest single award was £794 to the school feofees, who lost some seven acres. Another large award was £675 to the solicitor John Williams Bell, whose house and estate on the ridge at Sandley lay directly in the route of the railway. Instead of the intended cutting through the ridge, the company settled instead for a tunnel beneath, leaving the property undisturbed. Shadrach Dunn, despite his various objections, did well from the loss of his five acres. Mary George had £225 for a cottage and half acre of orchard in Newbury. In 1865 and 1866 further payments were made of £150 and £200 to Shadrach Dunn and William Bell respectively consequent upon the need for more land to make the line double-track.[9]

The first section of the line to be completed was that from Salisbury to Gillingham. It was opened for public services on 1st May 1859. As at the start of construction three years before, a lavish ceremony and dinner were held, but this time involving the whole town. Ruegg again reported the event for the *Sherborne Mercury*. Everywhere was decorated with flags and arches, bands played, the church bells rang out, and 'more than 2,000 of the working classes' were given cake and tea or beef and bread in large marquees on Chantry Field. A dinner was held in the Phoenix, and the day was concluded with fireworks which cost £25, one of the most expensive items of the whole celebration. Public train services began the following day with the 7.15 am to Salisbury.[10] Nearly £34 was left over from the celebration fund, and it was decided to use this to provide pumps and wells to improve the water supply around the town, at Bay, Colesbrook, and elsewhere.

A view down the line

THE LINE WAS built initially as single track, but with land purchased and bridges built for a double line. Locke's approach to the S & YR was to limit construction costs by having few major works such as tunnels or viaducts. There was only one tunnel on the entire line, but this meant having instead several gradients, which in turn depended on sufficient locomotive power. This can be seen in the eastern approaches to Gillingham; from Tisbury the line climbs on an average gradient of 1:241 (1:145 maximum) before dropping through 1:117 into Gillingham. A major consequence for Gillingham of the economies of construction was the decision not to provide a separate bridge for Oldlands Lane across the line to Newbury. Instead the lane was diverted eastwards to join the Shaftesbury road, so that traffic from East Stour would use the bridge on this road to reach the town centre. This scheme for the 'New Road', as it was thereafter known, has had road traffic consequences for Gillingham down to the present day.

The station building was the work of Sir William Tite, who worked with Joseph Locke and William Brassey on the buildings for much of the L & SWR. He was a distinguished London architect, who also worked for the Metropolitan Board of Works and was involved in the building of the Victoria Embankment and Royal Exchange; he designed cemeteries and their monuments, including the new Brookwood cemetery at Woking. He was also an MP for Bath. The station building had a S & YR three-storey station house with Tudor-style steep gables and tall chimneys; the latter were removed in more recent times. Through the front door was the booking hall with doors to booking and parcels offices, and booking office window. On the up platform were doors to ladies' and waiting rooms, parcels, and porters' offices. The only building on the down side was a brick waiting shed.[11]

After running level through the station, the line then climbed for two miles on an average of 1:178 (1:100 maximum) towards the Sandley (or Buckhorn Weston) tunnel. A principal engineering work on this section was the Eccliffe Viaduct, a substantial three-arched structure in local stone and brick. The viaduct made necessary the re-alignment of the junction of local lanes which met at this point. Further on the builders encountered their main obstacle, the Buckhorn Weston tunnel of 742 yards. This was the only tunnel on the line, but proved troublesome because of water from the Greensand, and additional shafts were needed to improve the drainage. In 1900 further drainage work involved the piping of surplus water down the line to Templecombe where it could be used for locomotive supply.[12]

The line was opened to Sherborne on 7th May 1860, and a month later to Yeovil. With the opening of the L & SWR line from

63 Frome, an early type of engine used by the London and South-Western Railway. At this time trains from Gillingham took nearly four hours to reach London.

Yeovil Junction to Exeter in July, Gillingham was now connected
to both ends of the London to Exeter route (Fig. 63). In 1862 an
important connection was made from the S & YR line to the Dorset
Central Railway at Templecombe, which shortly afterwards became
the Somerset and Dorset Joint Railway, giving Gillingham people rail
access to wide areas of Dorset and Somerset. However, Gillingham
and the north of Dorset never achieved anything approaching an
easy connection with the county town at Dorchester, and even at the
time of the railway system's greatest extent, this was always a slow and
circuitous journey.

Station Road and after

A N IMMEDIATE CONSEQUENCE of the arrival of the
railway was the laying out of the first new thoroughfare in
Gillingham for several centuries. The location of the station
to the south of the town at a site not already served by a lane or track
necessitated a new road to link it to the town. Station Road, some 330
yards, joined Newbury at a point where there was already an existing
gap between properties. By 1863 a number of new properties had
already appeared along it. Over the next half century the railway was
to redefine the commercial shape of Gillingham, with the focus of
business shifting away from the old centre around the Square and
church, and towards Newbury and Station Road; these developments
can be followed in a later chapter.

With the growth of traffic the original single track soon
became too congested. The line was doubled to Semley in 1866 and
to Templecombe the following year. The first signal box was opened
in 1875, and continued in use until its replacement in 1957. The
footbridge was installed in 1886 following an accident involving
passengers using the foot crossing. A distinctive feature of the station

was the 'Dando' or wind-powered pump, which pumped water from a well to be used by the locomotive water tanks and the various taps and appliances around the station. In the first two years of the S & YR there were five recorded accidents, one of which was serious enough to warrant a Board of Trade investigation. On 25 August 1859 two carriages ran down the incline from Semley to Gillingham where they hit some wagons. Another accident took place between Gillingham and Templecombe in November 1860, injuring nine passengers and the fireman and guard; the train had been travelling too fast and derailed as it came down the slope from the Buckhorn Weston tunnel, damaging the bridge over the River Cale. The damage was estimated at between £2000 and £3000.[13]

The S & YR prospered from the beginning, paying substantial, increasing dividends throughout the 1860 and 1870s. The growth was largely due to the link with the Somerset & Dorset railway at Templecombe, and the S & YR was considered to be the most successful railway company in the country. In 1872 the L & SWR made an attempt to buy out the S & YR, but the offer was rejected. A much better offer made in 1878 was accepted, and thereafter Gillingham and other stations along the line became part of the L & SWR empire extending from Waterloo to Padstow.[14]

The development of the station and goods yard area can be followed in the minutes of the S & YR and then the L & SWR. In 1859 it was noted that William Goddard wanted to use land at the station approach as a site for a bacon factory, marking the beginnings of this long-enduring employer in the town. In May 1859 land was to be sold to Joseph Matthews, the brewer, for an inn, most likely the South-Western Hotel opposite the station frontage. Throughout the 1860s and 1870s there were discussions and agreements to enlarge the area of the goods depot and extend sidings to take longer trains. One note in 1877 was for two new sidings; one on the north side, to relieve coal and mineral traffic, 550 yards long, with a brick bridge over the river (cost £1,847), and the other on the south side, again needing a bridge, cost £700. In 1893 there were notes concerning additional cattle pens, new cranes, and a new siding and platform extension.[15]

In 1905 the Parish Council wrote to the L & SWR asking the company to improve the station accommodation for passengers, pointing out the lack of shelter from the weather, and the need to provide a waiting room on the down platform; a petition with 458 signatures was collected. The following year the line superintendent requested additional roofing for the up platform, but the covered shed on the down platform remained unchanged.[16] These and other notes indicate the steady growth of traffic throughout the Victorian period. A consequence of the establishment of the brick works south of the line was that there was no proper approach or outlet for goods traffic on the south side of the station, so that most movements to and from the station had to be made along Station Road and through the streets of the town.

The coming of the railway brought about a reordering of horse-drawn coach and carrier services. The long-distance stage coach and mail services which had thrived up to the 1840s quickly disappeared, but were replaced by more local services using Gillingham as a railhead for the surrounding countryside. One which ran in 1859 before the Sherborne and Yeovil sections were opened was the *Telegraph*, which left Sherborne to call at Milborne Port, Henstridge, and Stalbridge, to reach Gillingham in time for the 10.25 am Waterloo train. Others came from Wincanton and Bourton, and from Sturminster Newton and Marnhull. These services disappeared once the other railway lines in the area developed. Mere was especially well served from the beginning of the railway era, with the station signboards displaying 'Gillingham for Mere' from the beginning. There were four horse-drawn omnibuses each day in each direction between Gillingham and Mere, the journey taking 45 minutes. The Phoenix Hotel provided a coach to meet all principal trains.

64 *A typical station scene around 1900. An up train passes the goods yard as it approaches the platform, which bears the sign 'Gillingham for Mere'. Milk churns are waiting to be loaded for a journey to London.*

Two new hotels were soon established to meet the needs of overnight visitors. Opposite the station the South-Western Hotel appeared, built on land purchased from the railway company; from here carriages and flies could be hired, and the hotel later proved popular with commercial travellers. On Newbury at the corner with Hardings Lane was the Railway Hotel, perhaps so-named to suggest to visitors that it was nearer the station than was actually the case. It was later renamed the Royal Hotel, and became a landmark building of the town until its demolition in 2006.

Passengers and goods, far and wide

WHILE OVERALL TRAFFIC to and from the town grew rapidly, passenger services were limited, given the size of the town. Despite its direct link with London, the number of through services to Waterloo remained much the same throughout the nineteenth century, most growth being in local services to Salisbury and Yeovil. One reason was that most of the fast expresses to the south-west passed through the town, making their first major stop not at Gillingham but at Templecombe. In 1859, when the line still terminated at Gillingham, there were four up passenger services per day, all to Waterloo; the journey time was around four hours. The 1889 timetable showed six services to Waterloo, with an additional morning train to Salisbury on Mondays and Tuesdays for the markets. Most London trains had a journey time of up to three and a half hours.

The 1914 timetable shows the system of passenger services through Gillingham at the time when the pre-1923 railway system of smaller companies was at its most flourishing. On weekdays there were 13 upline departures. Of these, four were direct trains to Waterloo, the remainder being all local services terminating at Salisbury. The 6.42 am departure reached London at 10.11, a journey time of nearly three and a half hours. People from villages west of Gillingham could reach London quicker from Templecombe, a stopping point for expresses, with some journey times of around two and a half hours. Salisbury journeys took 45 minutes, all trains calling at Semley, Tisbury, Dinton, and Wilton. On the down line there were 16 weekday departures, mostly of local trains to Yeovil Town. The first of three through trains to Exeter was the 10.28 am, which reached Queen Street, now Exeter Central, at 12.50, but at other times of the day it was possible to achieve similar journey times by changing to faster services at Templecombe or Yeovil Junction. At this date a first class return fare to Waterloo was 30s 8d, a second class 19s 3d, and a third class 17s 6d. There were also cheaper Saturday to Monday tickets available in both directions.

The railway system gave Gillingham people leisure opportunities not available to earlier generations. By changing at points westwards, a range of resorts and other places of interest were brought within easy travelling distance. Along the south coast Bournemouth, Weymouth, Lyme Regis, Seaton, Sidmouth, and Exmouth, could be reached; as could inland towns such as Salisbury, Bath, Wells, and Glastonbury. Some of the journey times might seem slow by present-day travel standards, but still gave scope for a reasonable day out. In 1914 the 8.29 am down train, with a change at Yeovil Junction, allowed Sidmouth, Budleigh Salterton, and Exmouth all to be reached before midday; returns could be made to be home at Gillingham by 7.47 or 10.04 pm. By taking the later 9.07 am down train and changing at Templecombe, the day tripper could be in the popular resort of Bournemouth by 11.01 or the cathedral city of Wells by 11.07. A slower journey home from Wells on the 5.10 pm meant that Gillingham was not reached until 7.47.

Besides the regular services, there were in addition many excursions run at holiday times and summer weekends at cheaper fares to local resorts and events such as race meetings and football matches. One such recorded in the Gillingham Parish Magazine of October 1879 was a church choir picnic to Seaton, which left Gillingham at 9am and returned at 9pm, 'the London and South-Western Company kindly running a special train from Templecombe to Gillingham at a later hour than usual.' This would seem to be a public service unlikely to be repeated today. A rail excursion with an even wider impact was the annual Sunday School outing to Weymouth. An entire train was chartered by the combined churches, and left early in the morning with perhaps 500 aboard, emptying the town of most of its children. This excursion continued, with breaks, until the late 1950s. A memorable event involving arrival rather than departure was the arrival of Prime Minister Gladstone in 1885, who visited the town to rally his Liberal supporters.[17]

Freight movements through Gillingham station were generated by a number of local enterprises, mostly set up soon after the arrival of the railway, which enabled them to deliver to customers well outside the local area. The diverse traffics included bacon, butter, cheese, timber, watercress, bricks, and pottery, together with livestock from the cattle market and a wide variety of general merchandise. The importance of the railway to these businesses can be seen in their tendency to locate close to the station area, with the south end of Station Road becoming an industrial estate focused on the station and goods yard (Fig. 65). One of the most notable customers was the Oake, Woods bacon factory, which had premises adjacent to the goods yard, and took daily deliveries of pigs; after curing, the sides of bacon were forwarded to Oake, Woods agents all over the country. Another was the company of C.E. Maloney, which made glue from animal bones, some of them brought in from Southampton Docks; this company were also coal merchants and had their own private fleet of wagons. J.H. Rose & Sons were also coal merchants with their own fleet of wagons. Hudson and Martin's sawmill made pit props

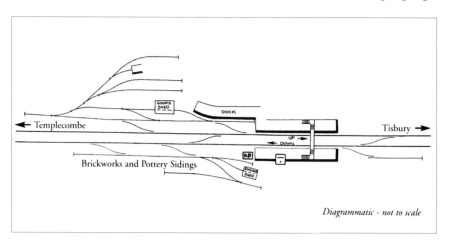

65 The station and track layout in 1894, reflecting several decades of alterations and additions. The dock was used to unload pigs destined for the bacon factory. The brickworks had its own sidings on the south side of the line. It is likely that the engine shed was no longer being used as such by this time.

from local timber, which were forwarded to collieries in returning empty coal wagons (Fig. 66).

Perhaps the most visible presence around the station were the milk churns of the Gillingham and Semley Dairy Company. The traffic in liquid milk quickly became the staple of all the stations along the Salisbury and Yeovil line, and throughout much of the day the platforms could be seen crowded with churns waiting to be loaded on to the next milk train to London. In 1860 and 1893 the platform had to be extended to cope with the number of churns, which were loaded on to the three milk trains from Yeovil Junction or Templecombe; the scheduled loading time could be as little as four minutes. In 1909 the milk train departures were 7.05 am, 6.02 pm, and 8.26 pm. In 1913 Gillingham forwarded ten loaded milk vans daily to Waterloo, and was the most important station on the line for this type of traffic. Watercress from the beds at Wolverton was another regular traffic to London, carried in the passenger trains.

On the south side of the station a private siding served the brickworks of the Gillingham Pottery, Brick and Tile Company, enabling the characteristic red bricks of Gillingham to change the appearance of towns and villages for many miles around. An important incoming traffic was coal, which was supplied to the gasworks at Gillingham and at Mere, and to the kilns at the brickworks. This came from the Midlands and from the Mendips, using the Somerset and Dorset Railway and the junction at Templecombe. Coal for the brickworks used the Pottery Siding, from where wagons were horse-shunted so that the coal could be tipped directly into the kilns; a turntable was used to turn the wagons. Other coal was delivered to the gasworks and elsewhere in the area in the wagons of J. Wiles and Co.

Perhaps less remembered but characteristic of rural towns like Gillingham was the horsebox traffic. From the beginning of the railway there was a demand from the gentry and well off families of

66 An advertisement for J.H. Rose & Son, whose railway wagons could be regularly seen in the station yard.

the surrounding countryside for the transport of horses and carriages. The animals went in their own boxes, while the carriage could be drawn up on to a 'carriage truck'; the family travelled first class. With the opening of the Compton Stud Company Farm at Sandley, later the National Stud, the demand for horse transport grew steadily, often involving special horse trains from Gillingham to Newmarket.[18]

The coming of the Railway Age changed the personality of Gillingham and stimulated a new phase of population growth. From being a country town meeting the limited needs of its surrounding farming countryside, it became a main industrial, collection, and distribution centre for north Dorset and neighbouring areas. For the first time, its population overtook that of its near neighbour Shaftesbury. In some nearby towns, the impact of the railway was to help people to move away elsewhere, but Gillingham saw its population continuing to grow over the next half century, a growth reflected in the appearance of new businesses and the changing face of the High Street.

11

1860 TO 1914: GILLINGHAM
AT WORK

I N THE CENTURIES before 1860 the growth of Gillingham had
been closely related to the fortunes of its farmers and landowners.
The well-being of Gillingham townspeople had depended in all
sorts of ways on the trade and produce from the countryside around
them. From the fields and the villages came the farmer looking to
the blacksmith to provide new shoes for his horses' feet, and to the
shoemaker for new soles to shoe the farmer himself. Out of the farms
and fields also came the livelihoods of the corn millers at the parish's
three mills along the Shreen and Stour; and from the comfortable
homes of the gentry came the 'sons of gentlemen' to be taught by
Hugh Hansford and James Read at Gillingham Free School. The issues
talked about in the Red Lion were likely to be the cost of poor rates
and land taxes, or of farm labourer's wages. The portfolio of William
Read Bell, the town solicitor, was one of cases to do with principally
landed property or probate. The important voices in local and public
affairs were those of the wealthier farmers and principal landowners.

By 1850 all this was beginning to change. The rural economy
began to lose its dominance in the town and had to co-exist with a
growing industrial interest, which over the next generation was to
turn Gillingham into the workshop of north Dorset. From now on

the conversations in the inns and beerhouses were as likely to be about the cost of coal, bricks and drainpipes, as they were about farm labourers' wages. Town and parish affairs were increasingly led by the voices of the industrial and retail community. Yet since so much of the new industry centred around farming and the products of the countryside, the rural interest was ever present, and the town was able to maintain its agricultural roots well into recent times.

The coming of the railway provided a stimulus to change by affording people a new outlook on opportunities and possibilities. Those who saw their lives in Gillingham stretching out into endless years spent mending hedges, digging field drains, or milking cows, were at least enabled with a means of escape. It was now possible to consider a different livelihood in Portsmouth, Bournemouth, Bristol, London, or elsewhere. To others, especially those looking to expand their existing trades or businesses, the railway provided new opportunities by opening up access to materials and markets beyond the immediate countryside. There were yet others outside the town, and often with no previous connection to it, who were able to see the potential offered by a location with good linkages to more distant places. By 1880 many of the principal businesses were operated by people unknown in the town twenty years earlier. The outcome was the gradual appearance of a new generation of businesses and industries, and of a more general growth in the town's commercial life.

The transition was moved along by a brisk market in land and property. At an earlier time in the history of Gillingham, the disposal of the lands of the old royal manor and forest had meant that land had passed into the hands of numerous different owners, rather than remaining in the control of a single proprietor. Although much Gillingham property remained copyhold of the manor, the copyholds were readily leased or sold through the surrender and admission process in the manor courts. Indeed, by 1850 much

Gillingham property was in the ownership of parties who lived many miles outside Gillingham. Subletting of dwellings and land had become commonplace. The frequency of property transactions is illustrated by the number of admissions which appear in the manor court books; between 1851 and 1855 some 264 admissions were recorded, growing to 360 between 1855 and 1861, 344 between 1861 and 1865, and 381 between 1865 and 1870.[1] Several of the land and property owners of the town were themselves involved in industries or business, and saw advantages in the ready availability of workmen and labourers. These conditions made it relatively easy for small plots or buildings to be acquired, which could be used to expand or set up trades or businesses. One outcome of this was the piecemeal nature of development, particularly in Newbury and the new Station Road, where town houses, labourers' cottages, shops, and trade premises all grew up next to each other within a space of a few hundred yards.

The Kelly Directory of 1889 records something like a hundred trades and businesses in and around the town, not counting a smaller number in Milton and outlying parts of the parish. Examples of almost every type of trade and business of the period can be found, from builders to butchers, gas engineers to grocers, and saddlers to stationers, making the town self-sufficient in its needs. Consumers could choose between any of seven tailors and drapers, four coal merchants, and seven shoe makers. Refreshment could be taken at any of eight hotels, inns, or beer houses. The total number of traders was not many more than had been recorded by earlier directories in the 1850s, but what was noticeable was a greater capitalisation of business. Before 1850 almost all trades were family affairs involving the master and his family, with perhaps an apprentice or one or two hired labourers. Larger businesses such as the silk mill were the exception. But from the 1850s Gillingham became dominated by a number of company enterprises employing larger numbers of people, and giving the town a more overtly industrial character. The change was gradual, with some major businesses not appearing until the 1880s.[2]

One of the first enterprises to take advantage of the enhanced trading opportunities was the new market. Kelly's 1859 Directory had recorded that 'Friday is the market day, but it is only nominally so, the market having declined,' but then went on to add 'a great many new buildings have been erected [including] a market house, and a new market is proposed to be opened to meet the needs of the inhabitants.' By 1863 there existed the Gillingham and Blackmore Vale Market Company, with its yard immediately to the north of the station (Fig. 67). The market may have been the creation of Messrs Bell and Freame, the solicitors who were the secretaries to the company. In 1889 it was recorded that 'the market is held every alternate Monday, and on the same day two cattle auctions are conducted by Messrs Senior and Godwin and Mr Nathaniel Benjafield.' The latter also had his own yard a little further up Station Road. The Blackmore Vale market soon

67 The cattle market in Station Road, around 1890, from the station gates. The market was opened with the coming of the railway and was a main feature of the Gillingham trading scene for almost a century. For many farmers and traders it was both a social occasion and place of business.

became noted for its calf sales, for which it was considered second in the country. By 1905 a third auctioneer in the town was Jeffery & Son of Donhead, whose cattle auction yard occupied a site on the corner of Buckingham Road and Station Road.[3]

Bacon and dairy products

ANOTHER OF THE new enterprises, and also the most lasting, was the bacon factory. The trade signs of Messrs Oake, Woods & Co. proudly proclaimed the establishment of the business in 1847, and it has been widely assumed that, with some considerable foresight on the part of its owners, the business had been deliberately set up close to where the railway would eventually pass. The actual story is rather different from that which is widely accepted. The factory was the creation of William Goddard, a native of Donhead St. Mary (b.1814), who by the mid-1850s was a partner in the firm of Goddard & Tamsett, bacon curers of Commercial Road, Landport, in Portsmouth. In 1858 he acquired for £160 from Henry Kaines, the Gillingham solicitor and landowner, an acre of the field called Dryshays, 'bounded on or to the east and south by the land of the Salisbury and Yeovil Railway Company', and this was the land on which the bacon factory was first built. In 1873 this property passed on the death of Goddard to his son, another William Goddard (b.1836). The property was then described as the 'dwellinghouse and outbuildings, stores, sheds, stables, lawns, garden, and yard etc adjoining Station Yard in Gillingham, 1 acre.' In 1879 the younger Goddard paid Kaines £620 for another five acres of Dryshays, presumably with a view to extending the business. During this period the parent company remained in business in Portsmouth.[4]

In 1887 events took an unexpected turn, for by this time William Goddard had been committed to an asylum in Devon, being of unsound mind. Following this, a lease is recorded to William Oake, late of Islington, but now of Gillingham, a bacon curer; to John Woods of Fairlight, Sydney, in New South Wales; Gilbert Burrington of Bridgwater, a banker; and to Evan Roberts Down also of Bridgwater, an architect. By this time the property had become more extensive, comprising a 'dwelling house and factory with singeing chamber, ice cellars, offices, outbuildings, premises, a close of meadow and 3½ acres next to Station Yard.' The lessor was Ellen Tamsett of Southsea.[5]

It was from this time that the business became known as Oake, Woods, & Co., although it is possible that Oake and the other lessees had already been part of the enterprise for some time, as Evan Down

68 An advertisement for Oake, Woods bacon from the early 1900s. The company, which was founded by William Goddard, achieved an international reputation for its 'Royal Gillingham' bacon based on its distinctive curing process. Its site, on Station Road, meant that it was the first of Gillingham's businesses to greet the rail traveller to the town.

became the company's managing director. The bacon was already acquiring its reputation as a high quality product derived from Oakes' distinctive 'patent auto-curing' method. By the 1870s it was already winning international prizes and by 1885 their 'Royal Gillingham' cured bacon was being exported to the continent and to America. Advertisements depicted the company's prize medals from the British Dairy Farmers' Association, and the 'royal appointment', courtesy of the Prince of Wales, later King Edward VII (Fig. 68). Many pigs were brought in by rail, but others came from local villagers, many of whom still kept a pig in their garden. The finished products went away mostly by train. The company also maintained a retail shop in Station Road. Oake, Woods was one of the largest employers in the town until its closure in 1984. Its only legacy is the slaughterhouse, now used by J.H. Rose; and the new adjoining housing development named 'Oakewoods'.

The coming of the railway brought about a revolution in the marketing of dairy produce in the whole of the Blackmore Vale. Until 1859 dairy products, mostly butter and cheese, had been sold mostly through local markets. The arrival of the railway, with its direct connection to London, opened up an entirely new market for liquid milk sales, and from this time London became the principal outlet for the area's produce. To begin with, local farmers made their own marketing arrangements, taking the milk to the station in churns inscribed with their names, but this soon gave way to marketing through companies and farmers' co-operatives. The scale of business was such that some 70 horse-drawn carts laden with churns arrived in Gillingham each morning. In 1875 one Thomas Kirby started buying milk from local farms and built a depot near Semley station. By the 1880s his company had opened another milk depot and cheese factory at Gillingham and in 1889 was trading as Semley and Gillingham Dairies; from 1890 this became the Salisbury, Semley, and Gillingham Dairies Co. Ltd. The factory buildings on

Station Road are marked on the 1889 Ordnance Survey map as the 'Gillingham Dairy Farm' and on the 1901 map as the Cheese Factory; it was also known as S.J. Taunton's dairy factory. The Station Road factory was large enough to have its own churn-making department which employed ten tinsmiths. From here milk and other products were sent regularly to London on the several milk trains serving the station daily.

Besides the large Gillingham and Semley establishment, a number of smaller dairy processing factories appeared around the town. One was that of the Gillingham Dairy Farmers' Association, managed in 1889 by Edward Bell of Knapp House and of the solicitor family of the Bells. This would have been a co-operative marketing organisation set up by local farmers, but nothing more of it is known. The Shutes, a family who at this time were farming at Bugley, Shearstock, and Lodden Bridge, were also active in marketing farm produce. In 1892 Edwin or Eden Shute started a butter factory in New Road, using cream bought from surrounding farms. His 'Golden Melon' brand was primarily sold locally but he was able to take advantage of proximity to the station to make his product popular in the London shops. He also bought butter from farmers which could be sold under his own brand.[6] Around six people were employed and eggs and cheese were also sold. Water came from a well behind the factory. Around the same time other members of the Shute family had a butter factory in Turners Lane on a site now demolished for the building of the relief road. This building, with its cellars, thick walls, and small windows, was ideally suited for butter storage. Another Shute premises was the milk factory in the Square, built around 1880 and run by Harry Shute in partnership with a Mr. Sims; this is now part of the Farnfields solicitor's building.

Some of these small dairy enterprises had a limited life as independent producers, and were soon absorbed into the business of the Wiltshire United Dairies company, a Trowbridge-based organisation which took over many small dairies in the Wiltshire area. Once it had acquired the Salisbury, Gillingham, and Semley business, all United Dairies production was concentrated at Station Road. From 1920 the company was acquired by United Dairies (Wholesale) Ltd; the name is still to be seen on the side of one of the Station Road buildings. Production at Eden Shute's factory continued until 1937 when the business was sold to Aplin & Barrett of Yeovil, producers of St. Ivel products. Shute's site today is marked by Prospect Close. Shute had also owned the land on the opposite side of New Road, which he sold to the Sturminster Newton and District Farmers' co-operative for the building of a milk depot. This remained as a milk factory well into recent times, later owned by Highnams and Hunts dairies. The site is now occupied by a lighting shop and the modern terrace known as Rufus Court.[7]

One already established business which developed notably at this time was the Matthews brewery at Wyke. This had its origins earlier in the century, when it flourished under the brewer Joseph Matthews. By 1860 George Blandford Matthews had rebuilt the existing brewery premises into the imposing structure with its distinctive fortress-style features seen today (Fig. 69). The brewery used malt from Purns Mill, also owned by the Matthews family, and had its own wells which supplied water for steam, heating, and cooling. Coal came by rail from the Somerset coalfield. Opposite the brewery he erected a stable building with a large arched doorway which has carved above: 'G.B.M. 1884'. Along both sides of the road towards Gillingham a number of cottages were built for the brewery employees, still distinguishable by their uniform appearance, giving Wyke the character of an industrial village. A charging buffalo became the company's trade mark; a reminder of this today is the inn called The Buffalo which still stands in Lydfords Lane.[8]

A drinks business of a different sort was that of the mineral water factory at the far eastern end of Newbury near Lodden Bridge.

The Matthews family of Milton

The Matthews family rose from being farmers at Milton to being major landowners in Milton and Gillingham, and owners of the Wyke brewery and Purns Mill.

Thomas Matthews (1793-1865) became a major landowner in Milton, with 600 acres and 32 labourers in 1851. He owned Milton Lodge and gave the site opposite his house for the church of St. Simon and St. Jude. This was built shortly after his death.
Harry Matthews, his brother (b.1801), is recorded as a woolstapler (1823) and wine merchant at Wyke (1830).

69 *A delivery wagon stands outside the brewery at Wyke, around 1900. The brewery eventually supplied all the public houses in the town. When it was sold in 1963 it had 64 tied houses in Dorset, Somerset, and Wiltshire*

Joseph Matthews, another brother (b.1811), is recorded as a brewer at Wyke between 1841 and 1861. He lived at Wyke House, with Harry Matthews and another wine merchant, John Furmedge (b.1816).
George Blandford Matthews (1827-1908) was the son of Thomas Matthews. He married Charlotte Parham and purchased Purns Mill from the Parham family around 1850. He rebuilt the Wyke brewery around 1860, and under his ownership it greatly expanded the number of its outlets. He lived first at The Old House in Milton before moving to The Kendalls. G.B. Matthews was well known in Gillingham and Milton for his roles in public life including those of churchwarden and Grammar School governor.
George Gerrard Matthews (1859-1925) was the eldest son of George Blandford Matthews. By 1890 he was a master brewer living at Wyke House. His eldest son and last of the brewery owners was Gerrard Blandford Matthews (Chapter 14).

This was first established by Ambrose Collis, who in the 1870s and 1880s had been operating as a coal, hay, and corn merchant from Station Road. In 1889 he is listed as a mineral water manufacturer at Newbury (Fig. 70). In 1895 the business was being run by Ernest J. George, from whom it was purchased by W. Slade, the owner of the department store in the Square. From this time it was known as the Gillingham Mineral Water Works, and developed a local reputation for its lemonade, ginger beer, soda water and peppermint, and still ginger wine. The drinks were sold in pressurised bottles which were prone to explosion, so that the workers had to wear protective clothing and masks. Up to six or seven men could be employed. Competition from other mineral water factories which were using motorised transport brought about the factory's closure in 1920.

70 Slade's Mineral Water factory was a well known building along the approach to Gillingham from Shaftesbury. The building and the lettering stood for several decades after the premises had ceased to make mineral waters.

Brickworks and sawmills

PERHAPS THE ENTERPRISE that did most to change the appearance of Gillingham, and of many other places round about, was the opening of the brickworks on a site south of the railway line in 1865. There had been previous brickyards in Gillingham including a site belonging to the Silverthorn family at Ham, but they were small-scale enterprises producing mostly tiles and drains for fields, and bricks of limited quality. The new business, named the Gillingham Pottery, Brick, and Tile Company, was on a much more industrial scale. Its proprietors and original shareholders included the solicitors, J.W. Bell and R.S. Freame. They saw the potential of the 90-feet deep bed of Kimmeridge Clay, which could be dug from a site immediately next to the railway line. The coal for the kilns could be loaded directly from wagons, and the finished products taken away by train. The railway made it possible to exploit a resource immediately adjoining the town in a way which had not been possible previously.

Over the next few years the 'brick fields' gradually spread over the fields on the west side of Oldlands Lane. As this clay became worked out, the diggings were extended across to the other side of the lane, the clay being hauled to the brickworks by wire-operated tramway. The site of the pits is now occupied by the Lodden Lakes.[9]

An advertisement from the turn of the century indicates the range of products from the yard, which were of 'every description'. There were many different sorts of bricks, which could be supplied in many shapes and sizes. They were classified as of semi-engineering quality and were of a distinctive harsh red colour. Tiles were made for roofing and for garden edgings. Drain pipes were made from two inches diameter up to 16 inches. There was a wide range of garden ornaments and vases, and any clay product could be made to order (Plate 21).

The Gillingham brick works

The brick works was at one time the town's largest employer, with up to 65 men working at the height of production. Until the 1930s the clay was dug by hand, usually worked by a dozen men along a 20-foot face, using long spades or 'grafts', and then loading the clay into trucks, which were then moved by hand or by donkey. In 1938 hand digging was replaced by a specially designed clay-digging machine.

71 Clay wagons wait to be hauled up the tramway to the top of the brickworks incline. A scene from shortly before the closure of the brickworks in 1966.

To weaken the clay to the consistency needed, old tiles, bricks, and stones were ground to dust, and added to the ground clay which had been squeezed through a series of rollers. A pug mill forced this into a machine which extruded it in the shape required; it was then cut into the correct lengths by wire cutters. It was next stacked on long lines of platforms to dry. Care had to be taken to make sure that the bricks did not dry out too quickly and so shrank and cracked.

The bricks, along with the tiles and pipes, were then placed for firing in an open top kiln, which had to be carefully loaded with bricks at the bottom and tiles and pipes higher up. This took several days, during which the temperature had to be carefully controlled so that the contents of the kiln baked and shrank evenly. This required considerable judgement and experience from the brickmaker.

All movement was carried out by wheelbarrow. The long barrows used could each carry about 40 bricks, but there were also larger barrows for 60 bricks used for loading and unloading the kilns. All the barrows were made and repaired on site by a resident wheelwright.

Coal for the boilers and kilns came in by rail via the brickyard siding. From here it was shunted on to a turntable rotated by hand and the trucks were then drawn up to the boiler house by a winch and a wire rope. Other trucks were drawn up near the kilns and the coal was wheeled up to the kiln holes in barrows. There were several buildings on the site, including a round kiln for the pottery products. There was also a 'long kiln' with a chimney 99 feet high.

(Based on a description of the brickworks in Charles Howe's *Gylla's Hometown*.)

The works closed in 1968. As has happened with many brickworks, the site has now entirely vanished, and apart from one or two small buildings is represented only by the names 'Brickyard Lane' and the Brickfields Business Park off New Road. The most enduring legacy of the brickworks has been the many red brick buildings around the town and more widely, the products being used across the south of England, especially in the Bournemouth area.

In 1865 the businesses of the town were joined by that of Thomas Hudson (b.1832), who originated from Norfolk. He saw that the expansion of industries and building in Gillingham required a specialist supplier of building materials and services, and opened his builders' merchants yard in the town. His 1875 directory entry reads 'Auctioneer, timber merchant, steam saw mills & building material merchant, Newbury.' In 1885 his daughter married Albert James Martin, who joined the business, which from this time was known as Hudson and Martin. Martin managed the business until his early death in 1900 at the age of 45. In 1900 it became a Limited Liability Company, the first directors being Thomas Hudson and Cornelius Martin, the brother of Albert (Plate 20). By this time the business had become well established in Station Road on the site most recently occupied by the Focus DIY store, where it centred round the company's steam-driven sawmills.

The company was a major producer of sawn timber in the area, which it sourced both locally and from timber brought in by train. Much timber was moved by heavy horses, which were kept on the company's farm at Ham. Sawn beech was sold to chair makers in High Wycombe for chair and furniture making, while oak and elm were used by local builders and for making coffins. The company's steam boilers were specially adapted to burning wood and sawdust.[10]

An 1889 directory shows that by this time Hudson and Martins had wide interests, including the supplying of slate, cement, and stone pipes; and also as auctioneers, property appraisers, and surveyors. Their builders' merchants yard was along both sides of School Lane. A staff photograph of 1924 shows almost sixty employees. Hudson prepared the plans for many buildings, including the new Methodist Church and the mansion of South Lynn. The Adult Education Centre in Queen Street was built by the company as a residence for both the Hudson and Martin families, its decorative features designed to show off the abilities of the firm. As the major building firm of the town, the company was involved in the design or the building of many of the smaller houses and terraces built at around this time.

Gillingham's new entrepreneurs

Thomas Hudson and **Albert Martin** Thomas Hudson (1832-1914) came from Pentney, near King's Lynn. By 1865 he was in business in Gillingham as a timber and builders' merchant. In 1885 his daughter married Albert Martin, who joined the business and managed it until his early death in 1900 at the age of 45. In 1901 both the Hudson and the Martin families were living in the Hudson-built mansion in Queen Street which is now the Adult Education Centre.

72 Thomas Hudson (left) and Albert Martin (right)

Hudson and Martin had a sawmill in Station Road, a builder's yard in Newbury, and in later years, a showroom in the High Street. Recently the business became absorbed into Sydenham's builders.

Edwin Robert Stickland (1853-1911) came from Milborne Port, but arrived in Gillingham in 1882 from working in ironmongery in Birmingham. He set up his ironmongery and smithy business in the High Street. The business expanded under his son, Edwin John Stickland, (1880-1952) and came to embrace cycle repairs and eventually motor dealership. The original site is today still occupied as an ironmonger's store.

73 Edwin R. Stickland

Charles Maloney was born at Radstock in or around 1869, the eldest son of Arthur Maloney, a Somerset farmer. By the 1880s the family was living at Westbrook Farm, and by 1891 Charles and his brother Bertram had already established themselves as coal merchants in the town. In 1901 he was living in The Laurels at the corner of Hardings Lane with his wife, Mary Anne, and young family. He later acquired the mansion of Newbury House.

Maloney's account books show that by the 1890s he already had thriving coal and corn businesses. However he is best known in Gillingham for his opportunistic establishment of the glue factory in Station Road, which remained in production until 1970. Charlie Maloney was a well-known figure in the town, a parish councillor, and also a conductor of musical entertainments.

74 Charles Maloney

Charles Maloney: coal, corn, and glue

P ERHAPS THE MOST striking example of economic opportunism in the decades following the coming of the railway is that of Charles Edwin Maloney. He came from Radstock, and by his early twenties was already established in Gillingham as a coal and corn dealer, along with his younger brother, Bertram. By 1900 he had his own fleet of railway coal wagons in the station goods yard and also had a coal depot at Tisbury. His coal ledgers for around 1890 show that he had over 600 credit customers indexed, with deliveries extending as far outside town as Bourton, Mere, Wincanton, and Warminster. The ledgers also list his coal suppliers. There were many deliveries from the Mendips, especially from the Writhlington and Clandown collieries at Radstock, and the Edford and New Rock collieries at Stratton, near Bath. He also bought coal from the Midlands coalfields, including the Butterley, Cossall, and Bolsover collieries near Nottingham, which arrived via the Midland and the Somerset & Dorset Railways. The coal types listed were 'small', coke, and culm. The latter was largely dust or 'slack' and would have been used in the kilns of the brickworks, or in similar industrial uses.[11]

On the corn side of the business, Maloney opened a corn mill further along Station Road on its east side and dealt in all manner of grains and animal feeds. He was one of five corn dealers in the town at this time, the demand coming especially from the feed needed by the many horses used for carting and industrial work. His account customers were a mix of farmers, businesses and private residents from all around the town and the nearby countryside, his deliveries extending to Mere, Silton, Buckhorn Weston, and the Stours. His suppliers included Spillers grain depot at Bristol and the Maloney family's own farm at Westbrook.[12] The company also undertook general carting work in timber and building materials; around 1893 it was involved in carting for the firm of J. Parnell & Sons of Rugby, who were building the new mansion at Motcombe, the accounts listing the many materials being moved from Gillingham station to the construction site.[13]

The coal and corn businesses represented only the start of Maloney's enterprises. He was soon to notice the plentiful availability of bones in the district from the slaughtering of animals in the bacon factory and elsewhere. On the basis of this he began the manufacture of glue, and the site on Station Road gradually became transformed into the Gillingham glue factory. The range of products included Carpenters' Slab, Pearl, Bone, Skin, Chinese Bone, and Crystal glues, as well as Bloom and Pigskin gelatines; samples of these can all be found in the Gillingham Museum. A by-product was low-grade fat which was used in margarine, and after 1914 in the manufacture of explosives. The glue making process in turn led on to the manufacture of soap, the products including toilet soap, shaving soap, and soap for washing animals and preparing them for showing. 'Maloney's Super-Fatted Shaving Soap' was one line advertised in the *Grocer's Gazette*. The toilet soap had a distinctive smell, the local saying being that 'you could tell a Maloney worker by day by the smell of the bones and after work by the smell of the soap'. Water came from the factory's own well. By this time Maloney had sold his coal business to a competing coal merchant, John H. Rose.

Maloney's factory was highly unpopular in the town for the smell it generated and for the rats and maggots attracted by the heaps of bones. Others valued the factory for the jobs it provided.[14] At the time the factory was sold in 1954 it comprised no fewer than 33 different production sections and buildings. It included stables, a loading gantry, and drying tunnels where trolleys of wet glue would take a week to move through currents of warmed air. The site extended all the way from Station Road to Newbury, including Maloney's own home of Newbury House. Much of the site is now the 'Old Market Centre' with a range of businesses and a fitness centre.[15]

Maloney was a notoriously hard employer to work for, but his business drive never faltered. He was constantly searching for new business enterprises, his later ventures including breeze blocks, a brickworks at Dinton, and mushroom growing, but in these he was much less successful. An altogether more successful product of

Charles Maloney's later years was his 'Lion' petrol engine, used widely by local farmers but also exported.[16]

Engines and engineering

T
HESE NEW BUSINESSES could not have been so productive without making use of technological developments which had been taking place in a far corner of the old, original parish of Gillingham. Bourton might seem to be an unlikely location for an iron foundry and its products, having no local supplies of raw material nor direct access to water or rail for transporting them. There had long been a linen making factory at Bourton based on the village's water power, and in the early 1800s Daniel Maggs established a foundry and agricultural engineering works which made threshing machines and waterwheels. He was able to use a vein of fine sand suitable as moulding sand for the castings from his blast furnace. By the 1870s the business was in the name of the Hindley family, and was advertising portable and fixed steam engines, cider presses, apple mills, and boilers. Over the years the range of products greatly expanded. By 1900 the company was into the manufacture of steam lorries, gas and oil engines, pumps, dynamos, hoists, and saw benches. Many types of agricultural and food processing machinery were also manufactured.[17]

The company had its offices in London and exported globally. The boilers and other large machinery were hauled to Gillingham station by steam wagons for rail shipment. At Bourton over 200 men were employed, including many people from Gillingham. A notable feature of the factory was the massive overshot water wheel of 60 feet diameter, reputed to be the largest water wheel in England. It produced all the power needed in the factory until 1918, when steam power was installed. Many of the Hindley engines found their way into the local farms and industries, including the engine in the brick yard and a steam wagon used by the Maloney company.[18]

Details survive of the engine supplied to the Gillingham brickworks in 1866. The tender was for: a 30-horsepower engine (£305); evaporator and condenser (£100); and Cornish boiler (£225). The engine was later adapted to 60-horsepower. This engine remained working at the brickworks until 1973; a model of it is to be seen in the Gillingham Museum.[19]

Engineering of a different sort was associated with the Light family of Gillingham. The Lights had been a prominent business family in Gillingham throughout the nineteenth century, but the family linkages are not easy to establish. William H. Light was a noted racing cyclist in the 1880s, and around 1889 started a bicycle-making workshop in his house in Peacemarsh around 1889, later moving to a site in the High Street. His 'Magnet' cycles became widely used in the Dorset police force, and he later moved on to retailing motor cycles, a business which continued until the late 1980s. Light's garage in Newbury continued to trade until 2000.

Work for ladies' hands

WHILE THE INDUSTRIES described so far were all about men's work, the women of the town would look for employment at the silk mill. The development of the silk mill has been described in an earlier chapter. It remained in the hands of the Hannam family, who in the middle of the nineteenth century were in partnership with a nephew, Thomas Thompson. During this time it continued to be the principal employer of the town's younger and poorer women. Some 38 women gave silk throwing or winding as their occupation in the 1871 census, although others may have been employed from outside the parish. The era of girl apprentices in the outside building was long past, none being recorded in the censuses from 1841. Later in the century the Samuel Hannam Stephens company continued to run the mill until overseas competition brought about its closure in 1895.

The trade directories list a number of dressmakers and milliners, some of whom worked for the larger shops, or operated from their homes. Some employed other women and girls, several of whom appear in the censuses of this period.

A particularly important contributor to female work was glove making, using workers to do the stitching in their own homes. This was an important industry in the Dorset and Somerset areas close to Yeovil, where there were several glove factories. In 1871 Edward Greenwood, a native of Cirencester living in Station Road, is recorded as employing 500 in the manufacture of gloves. While this may seem a high figure, some 67 glove workers are recorded in the same census, spread all around the town and farming areas, with a notable group in Bay. Greenwood may also have used others from outside the town. Surprisingly, his enterprise is not mentioned in the directories of the time. Around 1900 the Founds or Fownes company had a glove factory in Newbury. Outworkers were trained at the Newbury premises and eventually were supplied with sewing machines to use at home. The business was still operating at Newbury in 1923.[20]

Shops and hotels

THE CHANGING FACE of industry was accompanied by comparable changes in retailing and services. Earlier in the century much retailing in the town had been in the hands of a small number of traders who described themselves merely as shopkeepers, grocers or general dealers. They had seen themselves largely as suppliers of basic commodities such as grain, draperies, or utensils to the farming and town communities. But needs and tastes were changing: by the later nineteenth century retailing was taking on a more consumerist approach, with a wider choice and range of goods being presented to meet the needs of the better-off farming and business families. New shops began to spring up around the Square and along Newbury, many associated with families whose origins lay outside the town rather than within it.

The earliest of this new generation of traders was Silvester Edgar, who had been born in Crewkerne in 1827. By 1851 he was established as a clock and watch maker in the premises opposite the Phoenix. In 1856 he was appointed Postmaster, succeeding James Read, the master of the Free School. Two years later he remarried, to Hannah, daughter of Robert Goldsborough, landlord of the Phoenix. His business was soon to become very diverse, as this 1859 directory entry shows:

> Clock & watch maker, jeweller, stationer, bookseller, perfumer, cutler, gunsmith, toy & fishing tackle warehouse, tobacconist, fancy repository, & agent for Hornimans pure uncoloured tea, & postmaster.

Edgar's business was to remain in the same premises for the next half century; some later directory entries merely describe the business as that of jeweller, stationer, and printer, but that of 1889 records two entries, one for the watches, jewellery, and engravings part of the business, the other being that for printing, bookbinding, music sales, and fancy goods. The business was still to be found at this location in the early years of the next century.

On the opposite side of the church gate was the shop of William Samways. He came from Yeovil and was of the same age as Silvester Edgar. During the 1850s Samways acquired this business from Ann Lawrence, who had traded here as a grocer and general dealer since before 1830 (Plate 16). Samways' business was that of a chemist as well as a grocer, and he also became an agent for the London wine merchants Gilbey and Co. In the 1870s he married as his second wife Alice, a daughter of Silvester Edgar. In 1886 Samways acquired the postmaster business from Edgar. The family continued to run the pharmacy business until the 1960s, and it remained in use as a pharmacy until its closure in 2008.

Another rival business to that of Edgar faced into the Square from its western side by the corner with Gas House Lane. Earlier in the century this had belonged to Edward Neave, the general dealer, trader, printer, and prominent townsperson (Chapter 8). By 1859 he appears to have retired from his retail activities, for the store was then being run by John Davis, described in 1875 as 'linen and woollen draper, hatter, outfitter, undertaker, china, glass and earthenware dealer, ironmonger, and druggist'. By the 1880s the business had passed on again into the Slade family, who originated from Stockton in Wiltshire. Their façade proclaimed 'china, lamps, hardware, ironmongery, and house furnishing', but they were also milliners, dressmakers, outfitters, hosiers, and drapers. Out of this they created a substantial department store, particularly notable for its house furnishings. In 1904 the store was substantially rebuilt in the latest Edwardian style with an even more prominent façade advertising its different departments. The family also acquired the mineral water business in Newbury, as related earlier in this chapter.

It was, however, across the Shreen in Newbury and the higher end of Station Road that the greatest changes took place. Prior to 1860 this had been an area of cottages and workshops which had grown up gradually over the centuries. It was now transformed by a phase of rebuilding and new building, which although led by retail developments, also included other trade premises, banks, and houses both large and small. The outcome was the creation of new street frontages dominated by shops and other services. The trade directories of the time show the range of businesses developed, there being space here to refer to only the most prominent and enduring. Around 1866 Edward and John Bracher, cabinet makers from Semley in Wiltshire, opened an upholstery, cabinet making, and decorating business in Station Road. They later added furniture removals, building, and undertaking to their range of services. In 1896 they relocated to Newbury, occupying a site which is still used as a furniture store at the present day, although the Bracher firm itself now operates only an undertaking business. Another general retailer was G. and E.J. Fish, who occupied Cheapside House on the south side of High Street for their haberdashery and outfitting business, and a further building on the north side for groceries, provisions, furniture, and ironmongery.

Retailing was still a trade which required commitment from younger employees through apprenticeships. In 1898 Joseph Fish was apprenticed to John White for four years, promising to learn the trade under very stringent conditions, notably to:

> 'faithfully serve his (master's) secrets, keep his lawful commands … not waste the goods of the said master … not contract matrimony within the said term, nor play at cards or dice tables or any other unlawful games … not haunt taverns or playhouses, nor absent himself from his said master's service day or night unlawfully.'

It would be surprising if many young employees today would find these conditions acceptable. At the outset of the contract Joseph paid a £20 premium. His wages in his first year were 4 shillings weekly, rising to 7s weekly in his final year of apprenticeship.[21]

The town at this time could boast several specialist outfitters, drapers, and hatters to suit all tastes and pockets (Fig. 75). These included the store of George Pitman, born in Paddington, whose grandly named 'Paris House' stood at the corner of High Street and Station Road; and Robert Cuming of Devonport, whose store was also in Station Road. Particular mention can be made of George Shephard, who had a tailor's shop in Queen Street in the house now known as the Barton, previously referred to in its earlier use as a maltsters (Chapter 9). The day books of the business from the 1860s show that it catered for the better-off end of the townspeople and country society. A regular user was the Reverend Henry Deane, who on 15 April 1868 paid 19 shillings for a pair of striped trousers, and another shilling for a further trouser repair; on 6 June he bought another pair of Oxford trousers for £1 4s. John Edwards, a town blacksmith, also visited the shop on 15 April for a suit for which he paid 3 guineas (£3 3s). George Whieldon of Milton Lodge in May and June paid for alterations to a brown coat and silk trousers and purchased a tweed 'stable' suit for £3. James Bartley of Malthouse Farm bought fashionable hats and trousers around this time. Military uniforms were a speciality, with a uniform suit of the 11th Dorset Rifles being supplied for £2 10s. An

75 A Gillingham tailor's workroom around 1902. This may have been the workroom of Shephard Brothers on Queen Street, or of Beaton & Scovell on the High Street, since there were several tailors in the town at the time. The business was still heavily dependent on traditional hand sewing skills.

especially valuable item of business came from one Samuel Round, who in 1870 purchased a complete indoor and outdoor outfit at a cost of £11 18s 2d.[22]

Just as Charles Maloney is the best example of economic opportunism amongst the town's industries, the corresponding figures in the retail trades are James Herridge and Edwin Stickland. In 1859 Mary Herridge had a grocery business in the town, while in 1863 James Herridge (b.1835) is shown as the owner of the field south and east of the Town Bridge, with a frontage on Newbury, now the High Street. During the following years he built up a thriving grocery, ironmongery, and furnishings business, and also bought other land in the town including part of the Stickland site further up Newbury on the other side. Local reputation has it that he made his money selling groceries to railway navvies. In any event, his success was such that in 1872 he was soon able to commission Thomas Hudson to build for him the grand mansion of South Lynn further up the street, one of the largest houses in the town.

Edwin Roberts Stickland was born in Milborne Port, apprenticed to an ironmonger at Bruton, and subsequently worked in Hereford and Birmingham, where he married (p.262). He came to Gillingham in 1882 where one of his brothers was a shirtmaker, and opened an ironmongery and smithy business in the High Street (Fig. 73). On his first day's trading he sold only a bucket, nails, a mouse trap, and a hoe. However, the business gradually prospered, with good fortune falling into his lap in 1906 when he was able to buy out his rival, B.P. Edwards, who had an ironmongery and smithy business right next door to his own. His business was continued and expanded by his son, Edwin John Stickland, who in the early part of the new century took it into cycle repairs and agencies, and eventually into car dealership and franchises. He remained in control of the firm until his death, by which time it included premises on both sides of the High Street. It is still represented in the town by the ironmonger's shop of P. & G. Crocker, which occupies the site of the original Stickland premises.[23]

Until the 1860s the provision of refreshments was still largely in the hands of the two centuries-old inns, the Phoenix and the Red Lion. Other beerhouses which had been in existence for some time were the Queen's Head in Queen Street, and perhaps also the Dolphin, Fir Tree, and Buffalo in Wyke. At this time these older houses were joined by the Grosvenor, opposite the Town Mills, the South-Western Hotel opposite the station, and the Railway Hotel in Newbury. The South-Western occupied a prime position for incoming visitors by rail and was aimed particularly at commercial travellers. From the hotel they could hire carriages and traps and visit the neighbouring villages to show off their samples. Being close to the market yards, on market days the hotel was crowded with farmers and livestock dealers, who parked their carts and wagons nearby so that the staff could look after the horses. Around 1900 its proprietor was G.F. Bignal, who issued his own public house tokens. The hotel is now closed and has been converted into flats.

At the far end of Station Road, just round the corner in Newbury, the Railway Hotel was built at the corner with Hardings Lane. By 1889 the Railway was in the hands of Frank Ford, whose advertisement read: 'Railway Hotel and posting house (within three minutes walk of the L & SWR), billiards & pool, everyday market at one o'clock.' By 1895 it had become the Royal Hotel, and like the South-Western was owned by G.F. Bignal. Other beerhouses trading at the turn of the century were the Crown at Peacemarsh, and the Mead family house at Westbrook. For travellers seeking non-alcoholic accommodation, James Weare had a Temperance Hotel in Newbury, which he also ran alongside a bakery business.

Farming and the Gillingham Agricultural Society

A LONGSIDE ITS FLOURISHING new industries, Gillingham remained firmly wedded to its agricultural roots, reflected in the establishment of its livestock market immediately following the coming of the railway. The calves in the market and the milk on the station platform demonstrated the importance to the town of the many livestock farms scattered around the parish. The 1871 census records the size of a few of the farms, and also the number of people employed. Many farms were small family affairs, with up to 50 acres being looked after by just the farmer and his immediate family. Above this size, there was a need to employ additional men and boys (Fig. 76). In the census, 'dairyman' is often given as an occupation distinct from labourer, implying a higher status. Some of the largest farms were John Honeyfield's property at Peacemarsh of 380 acres, which employed 12 men and 3 boys; and George Parham's Milton farm (the Old House) of 500 acres, with 14 men and 3 boys.

The prosperity of farmers from the increase in the London milk trade no doubt encouraged many to think about how their productiveness could be increased still further. Farming generally was in a period of change, with new scientific approaches to husbandry, breeding, and land management gradually eroding the older centuries-old ideas. A pioneer not many miles away from Gillingham was the Reverend Anthony Huxtable, whose 'model' farms at Sutton Waldron employed all the arts and techniques of the new farming, and he became especially known for his application of steam engines to husbandry.[24] In grassland areas field drainage was seen as a key to land improvement, and larger brickworks such as

76 A threshing machine at work on Ernest Mills' farm at Bugley, around
1930. For many people in the rural areas around the edges of the town,
farmwork and agricultural labour remained the most common form of
livelihood until after 1945.

the Gillingham one could now supply drainpipes to farmers in larger
quantities.

Farmers everywhere could begin to feel more of a distinctive
identity, increasingly defined by their specialist knowledge of good
farming practice. The need to share and develop the new techniques,
and for farmers to find a voice in county and national affairs, led to
the formation of agricultural societies. Besides national bodies such
as the Royal Agricultural Society, others were formed at county and
local levels. In the west country the Bath and West Society soon
became the best known. While lectures, discussions, and training
courses were always popular activities for these groups, much of their
energy was directed towards the holding of the annual agricultural
show. It was at this event, lasting a whole day or longer, that excellence
in farming practice could be demonstrated for all to see.

The Gillingham Agricultural Society was formed in 1860
and held its first show in that year, possibly in one of the livestock

markets in Station Road. The neighbouring society of the Shaftesbury Farmers' Club and Agricultural Society came into being just three years later. In 1886 there was an unsuccessful proposal to link the Gillingham, Shaftesbury, Dorchester, and Melplash events into a single show. Meetings of the society came to be held regularly on market days in the South Western Hotel, when many of the members could be guaranteed to be in town. In 1908, the Station Road site having become too small, the show was moved to a field in Hardings Lane now occupied by the Football Club and school playing field, and remained there until 1952. In 1913 Gillingham suggested that the Gillingham and Shaftesbury shows could be amalgamated, but this was not achieved until 1930, when the two societies were merged.[25]

The subscription lists printed in the show programmes of the early 1900s suggest the wide support for the society across the rural and business communities of Gillingham and its surrounding countryside. The 1904-5 subscription list contained 139 names, entered according to subscription levels. At the top of the list were a dozen or so names each paying between £2 and £5 subscription, comprising mostly landed gentry and including Lord Stalbridge, Sir Henry Hoare, and Viscount Portman, all major landowners in and around Dorset. The bulk of the subscribers paid a guinea or less, often ten shillings or five shillings, and included owners of shops and businesses in the town, as well as many of the farmers. Charles Maloney, Eden Shute, Edwin Stickland, and Evan Down, all owners of thriving businesses, were among the subscribers. In 1911 the list had expanded to 155 names.[26]

The show programmes of the early 1900s also illustrate the pastoral nature of local farming, There were competitions for cheese, butter, horned stock, horses, pigs, and sometimes roots, but little mention of corn. A notable event at the shows was the awarding of 'premiums' to labourers for service to a member of the society over a long number of years, and who 'have during that period borne a good character', a feature clearly intended to foster loyal, conscientious attitudes among the farm workers. In 1906 an award of £1 was made to Henry Evill of Gaspar, near Stourton, then aged 70, who had given 48 years service in the employ of C. M. Balch. Among the younger workers to receive an award was Harry Hinks of Milborne Port, who at the age of 30 had already been with the same farmer since he was 12. Other labourers and their masters visited the shows of this time from Stourton Caundle, Kilmington, Crichel, Compton Abbas, Ebbesbourne Wake, Sutton Waldron, and Fonthill Bishop, indicating that the show was attracting visitors from well beyond Gillingham and its immediate area.[27]

Services to business

THE GROWTH IN industries and retailing, together with the greater capitalisation needed in farming, led to an increased demand for the financial and other services required to support these businesses. By the 1850s the Wilts and Dorset Banking Company had become established in premises in the Square, but in 1878 they moved to new, grander premises on the High Street, and traded there until 1914 when they were taken over by Lloyds Bank. By 1880 Stuckey's Bank, by that date a well-established banking company in west country towns, had opened an agency of their Wincanton branch in the Square, and in 1900 opened their new branch at the corner of Station Road and Newbury. The new building, to a design by Bristol architect G.H. Oakley, stood on the site of the town's former Lecture Hall. For a short time the company was taken over by Parrs, who in 1923 became part of the Westminster Bank. By 1900 the National Provincial Bank had premises in the later Masonic building in Station Road, subsequently opening a branch on a corner opposite the Westminster Bank.

Insurance agencies also became more in evidence. In 1848 Edward Neave had acted for the Sun Life office, and James Read for the Royal Farmers, but by 1859 there were seven agencies on offer, and 14 in 1875 and 1889. From this date agencies are no longer identified in the trade directories, but the number by this date is clear evidence of the growth in demand for insurances for businesses and property.

Printers were kept busy by the demand for letter headings, invoices, delivery notes, advertisements, labels, packaging, and all manner of commercial stationery required by the town's businesses, as well as the many posters and news sheets promoting the social life of the town. Earlier in the century most printing had been done by Edward Neave, and by the 1850s Silvester Edgar was also involved in printing. By 1880 George Ridout had opened a printing works in the High Street, which by 1900 had become Compton Press. For a while this produced the newspapers called the *Weekly Record*, *Three Shires Gazette*, and *North Dorset Herald*, but they were all eventually absorbed by the *Western Gazette*. Compton Press continued in business until 1952. Around 1900 Brickell and Nicholson took over part of the disused silk mill for printing, but this partnership later dissolved, with Nicholson moving to Station Road and Brickell to Newbury; the latter later occupied the buildings of the old Leatherdale School.

The growth in population and the increase in property transactions brought about a busy time for the town's legal services. In the middle of the century these demands had been served by the attorneys, William Read Bell of Knapp House and Henry Kaines of Newbury. Around 1852 W.R. Bell retired and passed on his business to his son, John Williams Bell (b.1827), who went into partnership with Robert Sadler Freame as Bell & Freame. They used the premises in the Square vacated by the Wilts and Dorset Bank. By 1880 Henry Kaines had retired, leaving Bell and Freame for a while as the sole legal practice in the town. When J.W. Bell retired in 1893, Freame continued in practice with his brother, Edward Bell. By 1902 Freame was in partnership with Edward Light, the business later becoming Freame, Light, and Wyld. By this time a rival business had been established in the town by the Shaftesbury firm of Rutters. Much later, the Freame business was purchased by Farnfields, which still continues in practice from the premises in the Square used continuously since 1878.

The Freame and Light business of around 1900 looked over a town very much changed from that known to William Read Bell and his son, John, half a century earlier. At that time Gillingham was known mostly as a supplier of goods and services to its surrounding farming society, but by the turn of the century had become a town of milk and butter factories, timber and coal merchants, and more fashionable High Street shopping. While there had been some signs of greater commercial development before 1860, much of the subsequent growth had derived from the enterprise of individuals, some of whom came from inside the town and others outside, building on the stimulus provided by the coming of the railway. However, a wider perspective might be that with one or two exceptions, the new businesses remained largely localised and unable to develop wider, national markets for their products. Some of the businesses barely expanded beyond the small premises where they originated, or were eventually absorbed into larger organisations based elsewhere. As a result Gillingham was never able to develop into a more obviously industrial town comparable with Yeovil, Chippenham, or Swindon. This domination by small businesses, making it a workshop for the neighbouring countryside, was to define the character of the town for several decades.

12

1860 TO 1914: THE
GILLINGHAM OF THE
FREAMES

ROUND 1850 A young solicitor by the name of Robert
Sadler Freame came to live in Gillingham. He was the son
of the solicitor, Edmund George Freame, of London and
Corsham. Soon after settling in Gillingham he formed a partnership
with John Williams Bell, whose father, William Read Bell, had already
practised in the town for several decades. The partnership of Bell and
Freame was to dominate legal work in the town for the remainder
of the century, eventually becoming the firm of Freame and Light.
Freame married Agnes Hussey of Marnhull, and by the early 1860s
they were living in a new house on Wyke Street which they called 'The
Chantry'. For forty years and more Freame held many public offices in
the town, and was an owner of land and several properties, including
the town brickworks.[1] His son, Bertram, was similarly active in town
affairs and public life. His daughter, Ethel, kept a diary for much of her
adult life, and some extracts have been published by the Gillingham
Museum, providing a vivid picture of the lifestyle of an upper class
lady in Gillingham from Victorian times to the 1930s. Robert Freame
remained an Anglican for most of his life, but his wife and children

were staunch Catholics and were to eventually establish the town's first Catholic church.[2]

The society of the Freames' time comprised in 1901 some 3,380 people in the town and in Milton on Stour. Opening a public meeting of townspeople in 1894 Robert Freame succinctly summarised the three 'interests' or divisions of the parish: property (by which he meant land and rents), trade (such as manufacturers and shop owners), and labour. At the higher end of this society in terms of wealth and means was a small group to which the Freames belonged: a cluster of town and country gentry readily identified by their ownership of land and property, pursuit of professional businesses, and a leisured lifestyle based on rural sports such as riding, hunting and shooting. Among their near neighbours of similar status in the early 1900s were Major Cecil Jackson at Knapp House, Alfred Manger J.P. at Stock Hill, George Blandford Matthews at The Kendalls in Milton, Carlton Cross

77 Wyke Hall, the history of which extends back to Elizabethan times or earlier, was much rebuilt in the mid-nineteenth century. In the early 1900s it was in the hands of Captain Ernest Birch, and in 1905 was bought by Carlton Cross JP, a Lancashire cotton manufacturer.

The Freames of Gillingham

Robert Sadler Freame (1825-1910) was the son of Edmund George Freame (1773-1855), a solicitor based in London and Corsham. Robert was educated at Grosvenor College, Bath, and admitted to the legal profession in 1848. He settled in Gillingham around 1855 and soon afterwards began a solicitor's practice. By 1865 he was in partnership with John Williams Bell, son of William Read Bell. After Bell's retirement in 1893 he went into partnership with his brother, Edward Bell. The practice later continued as Freame and Light.

Freame married Agnes (d.1901), the daughter of John Hussey JP of Nash Court, Marnhull, and had two children, Bertram and Ethel.

78 RobertFreame

The family lived at the house known as The Chantry in Wyke Street.

Robert Freame was a prominent figure in Gillingham public life. He held many public offices, including clerk to the magistrates of Sturminster Newton, Shaftesbury, and Gillingham, positions which he held for many years; chairman of the Grammar School governors; chairman of the Parish Council; alderman of Dorset County Council; and Deputy Steward of the manor of Gillingham. He owned land and several properties in and around the town, and was part owner of the Gillingham Pottery, Brick, and Tile Company. He was a founder and later captain of the Gillingham company of Dorset Volunteers.

Bertram Edmund Freame (1856-1936) was the only son of Robert and Agnes Freame. He was educated at Downside Abbey, near Bath, and developed a career as a land agent. His clients included the Smedmore (Kimmeridge), Lulworth, and Wardour estates, and properties of the Irish peer, Lord Carbery, who had land in Gillingham.

Like his father, he was very active in the town affairs of Gillingham, becoming Chairman of the Parish Council, He also commanded the Volunteers company for a time. In business he became the Chairman of the Gillingham Pottery, Brick, and Tile Company. He established the Catholic church in Cemetery Road.

Bertram Freame with Lord Arundell

Ethel Freame (1859-1952) was the only daughter of Robert and Agnes Freame. Like her brother, she never married and was well known in the town for her voluntary and charity activities. Her diaries cover the period 1886-1936 and provide a record of her life and times in Gillingham.

Bertram and Ethel gave The Chantry to the Carmelites in 1925, and moved to a new house at Higherfield in Common Mead Lane.

Ethel Freame

J.P. at Wyke Hall, and Capt. Geoffrey Hornby J.P. at Sandley (Fig. 77). Of a somewhat higher status nearby, but part of the same social circle were Sir Harold Pelly (1863-1950), fourth baronet Pelly of Upton, a prominent Conservative who lived at Thorngrove; and Lord Richard Grosvenor, first Baron Stalbridge, a Liberal Unionist politician who rebuilt Motcombe House in 1895.

Looking down the social ladder, Robert Freame might also expect to rub shoulders with the managers of the town's larger businesses such as Evan Down (Oake, Woods) and Mark Churchill (Gillingham and Semley Dairy) whom he often met in the course of public duties such as school governance and parish council business. Generally however the Freames saw themselves as being distinct from the many traders and shopkeepers who formed the town's commercial community, many of whom have been identified in the previous chapter. The traders in their turn were recognised as superiors by Freame's third 'interest', the mass of the labouring population who lived in Ham, Bay, and Peacemarsh, the one group paying the wages of the other.

Local government, old and new

F ROM HIS PROMINENT position in public life, Robert Freame was well placed to observe the many changes which were at work in the town during the later nineteenth and earlier twentieth centuries. One of these was the gradual modernisation of the governance and administration of the town, which had remained largely unaltered since Tudor times. In 1850 Gillingham was administered almost entirely through the machinery of the parish vestry, the overseers, and the feofees. By mid-century this system was becoming increasingly unable to deal with the growth in population and the demands of a newly industrialising town. At first these needs could be acknowledged through the creation of boards to deal with particular functions, such as the Burial Board or the Lighting Inspectors. But these were soon overtaken by the overall reforms in local government imposed by national legislation. Notably these were the creation of the Shaftesbury Rural Sanitary District (1875), a body based on the framework of the Shaftesbury Poor Law Union, to deal with water provision and drainage; the modern Dorset County Council (1889); the Shaftesbury Rural District Council (1894), which superseded the Sanitary District; and the Gillingham Parish Council (1894), which took over all those non-ecclesiastical responsibilities of the old church vestry not dealt with at the Rural District and County levels. In May 1894 a public meeting took place at the Lecture Hall to consider the election of a parish council. At first it was proposed by Robert Freame that the councillors should be elected by an appointed committee, but his proposal was amended to allow direct elections by the townspeople. In December 1894 400 people attended an open meeting at the Cheese Market House (Market Hall) to elect 33 candidates for 15 seats as Parish Councillors. At a meeting on 19 February 1895 standing orders were drafted and committees set up, including Burial, Lighting, and Finance. The first of regular annual public meetings of the new body was in March 1895 when 50-60 people attended.[3]

One of the first proposals to be discussed by the new Council was the provision of a new council building to include offices, a debating chamber, a strong room for records, a fire station, and clerk's house. A newspaper advertisement invited builders to submit proposals, and a prize of five guineas was to be given for the most suitable scheme. One proposal emerged as a winner, and a site was made available 'facing the new Road (School Road) opposite the Police Station'. However many modifications were needed to bring it within budget, and eventually the idea was dropped. This left council committees without any special meeting place, and for many years afterwards the full meetings were held in the Police Court room, and the committee meetings in Cemetery Cottage, the Board School, or councillors' homes. In 1896 a very different idea explored was that of providing ten new cottages for working people under the Houses for Working Classes Act of 1890. A letter was written to the Shaftesbury RDC, but they expressed no interest in the idea, and the town had to wait for more than twenty years before the first council houses appeared.[4]

Both of these proposals, although very different, suggest that 1890s Gillingham was increasingly identifying itself as a proper town rather than a large place within a Rural District. As early as 1884 the churchwardens looked into the possibility of constituting the town as an Urban District, but nothing seems to have been taken further. In 1898 the matter was revived, and a committee was formed to report on its desirability and feasibility. A map was produced showing the proposed area of the new urban authority, and an estimate made of the number of houses and their rateable values. Circular letters were sent to other towns which had recently made the transition, such as Wimborne, Swanage, Crewkerne, and Ilminster, asking them for their views and details of the costs, particularly the value of rates, but the replies were inconclusive. The matter was taken no further, a consideration being that much of the parish comprised outlying rural areas which would have to pay urban rates without benefiting from the enhanced utilities and amenities. The matter was revived in 1910, when once again some nearby Urban Districts were consulted, but no further action was taken.[5] In 1932 yet another unsuccessful bid was made to give the town urban status (Chapter 14).

By 1860 a pressing need was to provide the town with more burial spaces, the parish churchyard having by now become inadequate for this purpose. In order to comply with Burial Acts of 1853 and 1855 a Burial Board was set up under the Reverend Henry Deane to acquire land for the purpose of creating a town cemetery with both consecrated and unconsecrated spaces. The Burial Board was permitted to borrow the sum of £1,400, and the Carmins Orchard near Rolls Bridge was purchased from J.W. Bell for £600. In November 1860 a contract was awarded to the builder Thomas Doggrell, the schedule of work to include the grounds and drainage, a lodge and entrance gates. It was agreed that, for a beginning, unused spaces within the grounds were to be rented out as allotment gardens.[6] This proved to be only a temporary solution, and by 1880 it was recognised that even more space was needed. In 1887 a second cemetery was authorised on land belonging to John Westover further along Cemetery Road on the north side; and the need for a chapel where services might be held was also discussed. All these works were completed during the following years. In 1900 a water supply, pump, and tool shed were provided.[7]

As the town was growing in buildings and property, the need for adequate fire protection became more pressing, the only cover being that of the horse-drawn engine from earlier in the century (Chapter 7). The matter was first raised at the Easter Vestry meeting of 1893, and in November a committee recommended the purchase of a steam fire engine capable of providing 200 gallons per minute; the present manual engine was to be repaired; and the appliances were to be kept in a new house built at Newbury for the purpose. Nothing was done immediately, and it was left to the new Parish Council formed in 1894 to pick up the matter. It then became absorbed into the wider project for the new Council House, which would have included a fire station. Throughout 1896 and 1897 there were protracted council discussions over the type and cost of a suitable engine. The appliance eventually selected was a Shand Mason model at a figure of £406, and a piece of ground at the bottom of the Grammar School drive was made available for the fire station. This building, a corrugated iron structure large enough to house both the existing manual engine and the new steam appliance, was completed by the builders, Flower &

Barnes, and by early 1898 both engine and building were in use. In 1903 a new Volunteer Brigade was set up, the council agreeing to bear half the costs of maintenance and meeting the cost of larger items of equipment.[8] The twenty members of the brigade were not paid, but had 7d an hour when attending fires. They were called out by a system of call bells in their homes operated from the Police Station. There were two further alarm bells in the town, one at the Fire Station and the other at the south gate of the church. The latter enabled any nearby member to go out into the fields near the church and catch the horses. Funds for the upkeep of the brigade were raised through a variety of local functions. A major fire was that of 1911 when Senior and Godwin's auction ring in Station Road was completely destroyed.[9]

Water supply became another major issue. This came from a number of wells and pumps, some of which had been provided and paid for from the surplus money left over from the railway celebrations (Chapter 10). By the 1890s there were wells at Ham, Wyke, Wavering Lane, Hardings Lane, Spring Corner, Queen St, Bay, Colesbrook, Cemetery Gate, School Road, and Tomlins Lane. Several of the businesses, including Matthews Brewery and Oake Woods, had their own wells. In several parts of the town, notably at Bay, Colesbrook, and Ham, this provision was increasingly inadequate. In 1895 the Water Supply Committee, with the approval of the Rural District Council, authorised new pumps at Bay and Colesbrook, the cost to be shared between the council and the ratepayers. The new well at Bay was in a corner of the Malthouse garden, and was made to a depth of 112ft. It was also agreed to erect a further pump in Tomlins Lane using water from a well in front of the Primitive Methodist Chapel.[10]

This enhanced provision was still far from satisfactory. The Parish Council was reluctant to take on the maintenance of the wells and pumps, considering that they belonged to the users who had subscribed to them. In the meantime the number of complaints multiplied, some thirty problems being brought to the notice of the

Water Committee between 1897 and 1912. These concerned the quality of the water, which varied greatly in hardness and purity; the constant drying up of wells, the unfitness of pumps for use and incidents of damage and vandalism. A frequent complaint was of farmers using the wells to water livestock, thus depleting the public supply.[11]

Not surprisingly, public pressure began to grow for the provision of a piped water supply. In 1909 special Parish Meetings were held to consider the merits and costs of the issue, with over 400 attending a meeting in November, and representations were made to the District Council. Sources of supply from Mere, Bourton, Bainly and elsewhere were considered, but no decision could be reached. In 1912 the Bourton proposal was rejected on grounds of possible contamination, and the Bainly proposal seemed to be the most favoured. In August 1913 the *Three Shires Advertiser* reported on the public enquiry held in the Market Hall to consider an application by the Shaftesbury RDC to the Local Government Board to borrow £14,000 to provide Gillingham with a piped water supply from Mere. At the enquiry the inspector heard about both the Mere and Bainly proposals, the latter being supported by a petition of 505 inhabitants. It was concluded that although the Bainly scheme was cheaper, the Mere proposal gave more assurance of supply and its supporting evidence was more factually based. It was this scheme which went ahead, the first piped supplies reaching the town in 1914 (Fig. 79).[12]

The provision of drainage and sanitation was equally behind the demand. From 1875 these were the responsibility of the Shaftesbury Sanitary Authority, and from 1895 of the Rural District Council. Around this time a map was produced showing the extent of sewers and main drains in Gillingham (Plate 22). One system took drainage from Tomlins Lane, Queen Street, Gas House Lane, The Square, and South Street, and discharged it into the rivers through outfalls at Chantry Bridge and close to the confluence of the Stour and Shreen. A

79 Gillingham's first piped water supply came from the chalk aquifers near Mere. The waterworks was opened in 1914.

second, quite separate, system took sewage from Newbury, Hardings Lane, and Station Road, and led it to an outfall on the Stour behind the milk depot. This left several roads without mains sewerage, including the commercially important High Street east of the Town Bridge, and also New Road and Turner's Lane. The map gives no indication that any of the sewage was treated before discharge. In 1899 the Parish Council proposed laying a new sewer at Wyke; the owners of the new villas would be asked to pay a quarter of the cost, while the District Council would pay the remainder.[13]

Roads and streets left much to be desired. The turnpike trust roads through the town became increasingly unsatisfactory since the revenue raised in tolls failed to keep up with the need for repairs. The coming of the railway quickly ate away at much of the traffic, but in fact the more the roads were used, the more they deteriorated and the more they cost to repair. In March 1861 the vestry was informed that the Blackmore Vale Trust had no funds for road repairs, and the parish agreed to fund the repairs itself. In 1865 the Shaftesbury and Sherborne Trust refused to pay for any more repairs, and it was agreed in the vestry that the chairman should sign a petition urging the trust's abolition; the Shaftesbury Division of this trust was dissolved in November 1865. Its functions were taken over by the Shaftesbury Highways District. The Vale of Blackmore Trust struggled on until November 1882, and the following March the parish vestry recommended the removal of all gates across public roads. In 1888 all former turnpiked roads became the responsibility of the Dorset County Council.[14]

Within the town, streets were the responsibility of the parish, and there are several references in the vestry and parish council minutes to problems with streets and pavements. In 1859 the Road Committee agreed that, with the coming of the railway and the increase in traffic, the roads around the town required immediate improvement, and that flint surfaces should be trialled between Common Mead Lane and the railway bridge; and that a special roads account should be opened at the Wiltshire and Dorset Bank. In 1878 the widening of the Town Bridge was recommended to the Highways Board.

Pavements were first proposed in 1860, but were slow to appear. In February that year a tender was accepted to provide 500 yards of kerbstone around the Square and as far as Station Road, but in May the tenders were considered too high, and instead the work was to be done by the parish waywardens. In June 1861 the Road Committee asked that they should be completed in Newbury as far as Station Road and towards Lodbourne, and as far as the turnpike gate. In March 1886 there were comments on the dangerous state of the footpath on the north side of High Street and the east side of Station Road, especially on Market Day. It appears from early photographs that the south side of the High Street had a broad footway, while the north side had none at all. In 1888 the north side of the High Street still had no footway, as had only one side of Queen Street; some considered that footways on both sides would make the roads too narrow; others that footways without kerbstones were of little use. A scheme of road widening at St. Martin's in Queen Street was discussed in November 1899. In 1905 further tenders were invited for the improvement of the footpaths on the north side of the High Street. In March 1897 it was agreed to put steel name plates at The Square, Bay, Lodbourne, Colesbrook, Common Mead Lane, Tomlins Lane, Turner's Lane, and Hardings Lane. Those at Bay and Lodbourne can still be seen. An improvement for the inhabitants of Bay was approval in December 1901 of the cinder path from Bay to Hardings Lane. Four iron turnstiles were authorised at a cost of £7 8s, and two of these are still in place on the path near Bay.[15]

Street lighting improvements eventually arrived. The area required to be lit had been fixed in 1858 (Chapter 8), and in 1863 this was extended to include Station Road and the station premises. In January 1882 it was reported that better lighting was needed around the church path, and this was raised again in February 1883, along with the need for more lighting at Lodbourne and Station Road. In March 1887 it was recommended that lamp standards in Station Road should be moved out of the way of the traffic. In 1893 additional lights were requested for Railway Terrace, Oldlands Lane, and Lodden Farm, and in 1901 for outside Newbury post office. The cost of lighting the town in 1900 was £114 10s 10d.[16]

In early 1914 the parish council pressed the Postmaster General, through the town's M.P., Sir Randolph Baker, to have the telephone service installed in Gillingham, since neighbouring towns and villages had enjoyed this service for some time. The provision of a new full-time Post Office building was also requested. The Post Office replied that the provision of the new service was being held up through lack of funds from the Treasury. In July a further note received stated that a start was about to be made on the new building, but linking businesses to the telephone exchange at Shaftesbury could not yet be undertaken. The new Gillingham Post Office in Station Road eventually opened in 1915.[17]

Dustcart collection of house refuse was considered at a committee meeting in September 1910. A collection area was mapped out which included all the built-up area of the town, as well as parts of Wyke, Peacemarsh, and Bay. The contractors invited to tender were John E. Wiles, Mrs. Collis of Stock, John H. Rose, and Charles E. Maloney.[18] Refuse disposal sites were to be the brick fields and at Bleet.

One forward-looking step taken by the new Parish Council in 1894 was the setting up of an Allotments Committee; this was to comply with the Allotments Act of 1887, which required that local authorities should provide allotments if there was a demand for them. In February 1895 the Committee agreed that 11 acres should be made available, and invited certain landowners to make offers of land which they could spare. Various parcels of land were offered, but some proved unsuitable for various reasons. Eventually offers were accepted of lands at Langbury Hill, Smiths Mead, Coldharbour, and Huntingford, and these were then leased to tenants for rents.[19]

The protracted and piecemeal arrival of basic utilities and amenities spread over the half century before 1914 might lead to the conclusion that Gillingham lost out by failing to achieve urban status in 1894. Unable to raise urban levels of general rates, it lacked the resources to finance much needed improvements that might have flowed from higher rateable values of property, and had to depend on lower, more rural levels of funding. This in turn was rooted in its failure to achieve borough or corporate status in an earlier period, a product of the many centuries spent as a royal manor and estate. In later centuries the residue of this estate had been parcelled out between a number of landowners whose main interests lay elsewhere, rather than in the town itself. These influences continued to shape the town until the arrival of modern local government in more recent times.

Gillingham goes to school

UNTIL THE NINETEENTH century, education in Gillingham had been almost entirely in the hands of the feoffees of the Free School, and was available only to a small number of pupils from well-off families, many of whom came from outside the town. From 1839 the National School based in the Vicarage School Room provided some elementary education to children from working families, but it was not until the 1870s that more substantial changes took place. These changes derived from the Endowed Schools Act of 1869, which aimed at reforming the ancient educational charities to make them provide a more comprehensive system of post-elementary education; and from the Education Act of 1870, which laid down that every district was to have an elementary school maintained by a local committee and financed by an education rate. From December 1870 the feoffees met frequently to discuss the implications of these measures, and to formulate a new system of education for the town. After considering several schemes, it was eventually decided to leave the provision of an elementary (or 'Board') school to the government, and to proceed with the foundation of a new secondary school. This was to take shape as the Gillingham Grammar School.[20]

The scheme agreed in 1872, besides establishing the new Grammar School, also provided for the relief of the poor and the repair of bridges, as had been done by the feoffees of the old Free School. In 1879 the amount to be spent on poor relief was reduced, and the bridges obligation was deleted. The feoffees themselves were to be superseded by a new governing body which included

James Sheppard

James Sheppard (1819-1895) was the last headmaster of the Free School. This picture was taken at the rear of the school in South Street, perhaps in the early 1870s; Sheppard is almost certainly the seated figure on the left (Fig. 80). Sheppard was also parish clerk for fifty years and for a time assistant overseer, rate collector, postmaster, and foundation governor of the new grammar school. In his later years he lived on Cemetery Road. He is commemorated by a plaque in St. Mary's church.

80 The boys of the Free School with their master, James Sheppard. The group was photographed in the yard behind the school, adjoining the Phoenix.

representatives from the feoffees, the church, the County Council, and the Parish Council. The school was to be a day and boarding school for boys, the feoffees at this time being reluctant to admit girls, stating lack of funds as the problem. The fees were to be between £2 and £6 a year for day boys and £30 a year, plus tuition fees, for boarders. No boy could be admitted to the school before the age of eight and could not remain beyond the age of 15 except by special permission of the Governors.[21]

81 The original Grammar School of 1876. Although all these buildings have now disappeared, the foundation stone can still be found in the hall of the present-day Gillingham School.

The new governors first met in March 1874 under the chairmanship of Robert S. Freame to consider the site for the new school. After some disagreement with the Endowed Schools Commissioners, land belonging to the feoffees close to Hardings Lane was finally chosen. The school was built on land belonging to the feofees by the local builder, Thomas Doggrell, for a price of £1795. The main part of the original building was the single teaching room, where all classes were taught until the erection of a partition in 1908, but there was also a dining hall and dormitory for boarders (Figs. 81, 82). The other principal structure was the head master's house.[22] The new school opened in 1876 with 30 pupils and the Rev. James Mountain as head master. He resigned in 1880, his successors being the Rev. Charles Trew (1880-92), Rev. Alfred Wilson (1892-95), Walter Le Sueur (1895-1903), and Rev. Charles Wimberley (1903-5). In 1905 Alfred H. Mumford (b.1870) was appointed, and he remained

82 A sketch of the Grammar School from around 1900, showing the school dining hall. Taken from A.F.H.W Wagner's history of the school.

in office until his retirement in 1930. He had previously served as an assistant master at Gillingham earlier in his career. The register of staff records his first salary as £60, but by 1919 this was £400 and by 1922 was £600.[23]

In 1889 a new wing was added to the head master's house to provide him with a better study and living accommodation. By the start of this year 70 pupils were enrolled. By 1894 there were three assistant masters, the governors agreeing to them using one room in the school as a common room. Around this time the governors sold the piece of land opposite the police station to the School Board for the erection of a school house for the new Board School. In 1898-9 a science laboratory and workshop were added to the school. The Education Act of 1902 brought the school more under County Council control, the Council becoming more significant as a funding body.[24]

An inspection carried out in 1903 revealed various inadequacies, including the poor qualifications of some teachers and the need to increase the number of governors. The principal criticism was the failure to provide an appropriate education for girls, something which had been resisted when the school first opened. By this time there existed in the town a private High School for Girls in Station Road belonging to Miss Sarah Dunn, and it was considered that the problem could be remedied by absorbing Miss Dunn's school into the Grammar School. Under this arrangement the girls' school would be managed by the Grammar School governors, with Miss Dunn remaining as head mistress. This was accomplished in 1906, with the School prospectus proudly advertising the dual school. The Gillingham Grammar School for Boys was described in the following terms:

> Excellent and healthily situated premises, including Laboratories, Class Rooms, Carpenter's Shop, Assembly Hall, Dining Hall, Bath Room, well equipped Gymnasium, Fives Courts, Miniature Rifle Club affiliated to the N.R.A. ,

and other sporting amenities. Attention was drawn to the wide curriculum which included chemistry, physics, commercial subjects, and land surveying. Boarders were under the care of the head master's wife. The prospectus now included

> Under the management of the same governing body, Gillingham Grammar School for Girls …

and referred to the commodious premises in Station Road with its large assembly hall, kindergarten under its specially trained mistress, and modern science course. As a further attraction, each boarder might expect to find a separate cubicle.

The new dual school opened with 40 boys and 26 girls, but the outcome was less than satisfactory. An inspection in 1908 found the separate functioning of the girls' school to be 'uneconomic' and pressed for a mixed school. The governors pointed to the cost of new buildings and asserted that there was still 'a great deal of local objection to a mixed school.' The outcome was that the management of the girls' department was terminated the following year, and it reverted to private status under the control of Miss Dunn. It was not until 1916 that the governors were persuaded to accept mixed status and admit girls on equal terms, recognising that 'after the war, the women of the future must have a greater share in the Nation's work than before'.[25]

In 1912 the Grammar School acquired a new amenity, the School Swimming Bath. This was built on land at Bay sold by the school governors, and although owned by the school was available for public use when not needed by the school. An unanticipated outcome was that the construction of the pool brought about the archaeological finds detailed at the very beginning of this book.

The pages of the school admission register reveal something of the background of its pupils at this time. The occupations of the parents typically included landowners, farmers, shopkeepers, publicans, and other trading and business activities. Only a few pupils had attended the Board schools, most being drawn from the various small private schools around. Only a minority came from within the town itself, the greater number having addresses in the neighbouring towns and villages, such as Mere, Wincanton, Tisbury, Cucklington, Milton, Silton, Kilmington, East Knoyle, Buckhorn Weston, Semley, and Yeovil. A small number, clearly boarders, came from many more miles distant.[26]

Alongside these developments in secondary provision, important changes were taking place in elementary or primary education. Following the 1870 Education Act and the decision of the feoffees not to endow a new primary school, a new elementary school was established under the control of the newly created local School Board. The site was land adjoining the Grammar School, and the new school had separate boys', girls', and infants' sections While the new building was taking shape, the school was housed in the National School premises in the Vicarage School Room.[27]

The boys' section of the school opened here in January 1875 with William Tidmarsh as master, and the log book records some of the problems of the opening months. The school opened with an attendance of 45, but several children were sent away because they were clearly younger than seven. The master graded the children as best he could, but found that many were backward in most subjects. He received some help from Mr Bell, the chairman of the School Board, and also depended on the assistance of older boys who wanted to become pupil teachers. To begin with there were hardly any teaching resources, but in the first few weeks a harmonium and reading books were acquired, so that singing and grammar could be taught, and the teaching subsequently extended into scripture and geography. By Easter attendance had increased to around 60, but illness and bad weather often kept pupils away from school. By May the new cricket club was becoming popular with the boys, affording them much enjoyment in the evenings. The following January the girls' part of the Board School opened under Mary Thomas. This had only seven pupils to begin with, but gradually numbers increased despite bad weather and illness. In 1882 the boys' master could report that there were 137 boys on the roll, but average attendance was only 110.[28]

Further schools were opened in Milton (1868) and Wyke (1875). The Wyke School reflected the growth in population at the western end of the town, particularly in the 'village' around the brewery. This school was enlarged in 1898. In 1911 the capacities, average attendances, and head teachers of the Elementary schools were:

Gillingham boys	110	97	Robert Atkinson
Gillingham girls	110	118	Emily Truebridge
Gillingham infants	140	128	Lucy King
Milton on Stour	108	50	J. Slater and Nora Clarke
Wyke		140	104	Caroline Northeast [29]

A reason sometimes given for the poor attendance of boys, especially from outside the town, was the need for them to help with farm work.

Glimpses of some of the aspects of school life can be seen in the pages of the log book of the girls' school for 1911-1912 (Fig. 83). On September 5 eleven girls were excluded by the school medical officer for verminous heads, but were allowed to attend again from the 18th. On October 23 the inspector for religious instruction reported that he was much pleased with the school, the standard of the third division being especially high. By early December colds and illness were taking

83 A class at the Girl's School in the late 1870s. At School Lane there were
separate schools for boys, girls, and infants.

their toll of attendance, and on the last day of the term many girls were absent so that they could receive their annual bread tickets. Floods and snow after Christmas again reduced attendance to around 113 out of 124. The log book records the regular visits of school managers and inspectors, who paid particular attention to attendance and standards of work. On April 1 the school was closed for polling, but 30 girls were taken to Sherborne to take part in a singing competition. In June pupils visited the new baths recently opened at the Grammar School.[30]

A very small number of children had no acquaintance with the Grammar School or the Board Schools, but instead attended one of the small private schools which sprang up in the town from time to time. One of these was the establishment of John Leatherdale in the present Blackmore Vale House on Newbury. Leatherdale was a Suffolk man who had set up the school by 1870. In 1871 it had eighteen pupils between the ages of seven and fourteen. All were boarders, mostly from Middlesex and London; none were from Gillingham. He was also the owner of several other properties around the town. By 1889 the school was being run by his daughter, Edith. Further along the street at Newbury House, Annie and Gertrude, the daughters of Thomas Tucker the builders merchant, had a day and boarding school for young ladies in the 1890s.[31]

Gillingham goes to church

F OR A LARGE number of townspeople, public worship and social life continued to focus on the parish church of St. Mary the Virgin. Until 1882, parish life was dominated by the ministry of Henry Deane, the spiritual architect of the rebuilding of the church in 1838, and of several other churches in the parish (Chapter 8). In his middle and later years Deane continued with his prominent role in public life, and was a driving force behind the creation of the new Board School in the town and new schools in East and West Stour. By this time he received regular assistance from his son, James, in his parish duties.[32]

In the years following his death in 1882 a number of alterations were made in the church. The remaining appropriated seats with doors were removed and converted to free seats. This did not prove popular with everybody, and in 1898 there was a proposal by some parishioners at the annual meeting to have them reintroduced. It was decided that there should be no appropriated seats, 'other than that which had hitherto held of custom and usage … such allowance conferred no right on any person to prevent anyone else entering the seats' or to ask people to leave them. In 1885 new chancel stalls were fitted. A new pulpit and lectern were bought from public subscription to Deane's memory. In 1883 a major piece of building was the new vicarage, now Rawson Court, designed by the Stony Stratford architect E. Swinfen Harris. In 1907 it was agreed to erect a monument to the late Charles Bealing, who had been sexton for 37 years. The most striking alterations were those of 1908-10, when the tower was rebuilt to a design by the Wiltshire architect, Charles E. Ponting. The tower improvements were paid for by the vicar, the Rev. Walter Sotheby. At the same time the west gallery was taken down, a new belfry floor was inserted, and a new west window was installed as a gift from Evan Down, the owner of the town's bacon factory.[33]

In 1873 a new Parish Magazine was started, and some surviving copies from 1878-9 give glimpses of church life at the time. In 1878 over 200 children were attending Sunday schools, held twice each Sunday, and 163 Bibles and hymn books had been given out during the year. The annual Sunday School feast had been attended by 280 children from Gillingham and Milton. There was a choir of around 28, and a train trip to Seaton had been organised for choir members. The church had a branch of the Society for the Propogation of the

Gospel, and regularly raised funds to support missionary work; there was also a separate Ladies' Association. The church was linked to the Gillingham Aid Society, which raised funds to provide for urgent cases of hospital need.[34]

Despite the continuing importance of parish life to many in the town, there were signs that the wider influence of the Anglican church was beginning to wane. Henry Deane's successors are much less well remembered, and it is likely that in their ministries they were unable to match the vigour of Deane's earlier years. Statutory changes in local government gradually removed from the parish vestry the control over town affairs which it had exercised in previous generations, and after 1894 the church became entirely an ecclesiastical body. While individual Anglicans could continue to shape the affairs of the town through their membership of bodies such as the new Parish Council or school governing boards, the church was now one interest among several which sought to have a view on how Gillingham should be developing.[35]

The principal forum for local Anglicans in the Gillingham church was the annual Easter Vestry meeting, which was the basis of the Annual Church Meeting of more recent times. In 1898 some fifty people attended this meeting, a number which might be expected to include a good cross-section of Gillingham's churchgoers. Of those who can be identified, at least a third to a half were professional people or owners of businesses, indicating a strong middle class church membership. The names included Joseph Mullings (bank manager), R. Le Sueur (headmaster), Alfred Manger (landowner of Stock Hill), Clarence Shephard (tailor), John Rose (coal merchant), William Samways (pharmacist), and Robert Freame (solicitor). All these were playing an active role in church affairs at this time.[36]

The Anglican church in Gillingham was now being challenged by the more forward image projected by the nonconformist congregations. By the 1870s both the Wesleyans and Primitive

Methodists had outgrown their existing chapels built earlier in the century. In 1875 the Primitive Methodists sold their chapel at Turner's Lane for £75 and used the money to build a new a chapel on Queen Street. The group became known as the Queen Street Society. The chapel still stands, having for many years been used as a toy factory. Despite now having a larger premises than before, the Queen Street Methodists always considered themselves to have a more outdoor, evangelical, approach than their Wesleyan counterparts (Chapter 8). At almost the same time, the Wesleyans bought land for a new chapel from Josiah Hannam, the silk throwster, for £320, on a site formerly occupied by Barnaby's Farm. Here they built a new chapel at a cost of £2,750, on an elevated site directly facing across towards the Anglican vicarage and church beyond. It was designed and built by Thomas Hudson, a principal builder in the town and a trustee of the new

84 An artist's sketch for the Wesleyan chapel, designed by Thomas Hudson and built in 1876-7. The final result (Fig.40) is similar to this but differed in some details.

church. It was completed in 1877 (Fig. 84). A proportion of the cost was raised by sponsored building stones, which can still be seen to the rear. In 1903 further land was bought from the adjoining Wiltshire and Dorset Bank (now Lloyd's bank) for an extension including extra schoolrooms.[37]

Some 126 names have been identified as trustees and regular attendees of the Wesleyan church from around 1870 to 1900. These included a number of the owners of businesses and the larger shops, often employers of some importance, including Thomas Doggrell (builder), William Goddard (bacon factory owner), Charles Maloney (coal and corn merchant), and Thomas Hudson (timber merchant and builder of the church). Most of the rest of the congregation were smaller shopkeepers, tradesmen, or labourers. Many of the wealthier Methodists were in a position to contribute generously to the society and its new chapel. The comparable Primitive Methodist list has 107 names, but there are far fewer large business owners and more labourers, with a few farmers, and a more distinctly working class membership. Both of the Methodist societies drew many of their adherents from Peacemarsh, Bay, and Ham; in addition Eccliffe was the source of some Primitive Methodist families.[38]

At the far end of the town in Newbury, the Baptists continued to build up a following. Their first chapel of 1840 was replaced in 1892 by a new larger structure with seating for 400, the old building continuing in use as a school room. The minister around 1895 to 1905 was the Reverend George Scott.

Funerals of prominent people could involve not only friends, relatives, and churchgoers known to the deceased, but crossed religious divisions and might bring the whole town to a standstill. At the funeral of Edward Light in November 1908 all shops closed for an hour and a half, all blinds were drawn, and Station Road near his house was filled with people. The procession was the longest known for half a century, such that when the head of the procession reached the church the rear portion was still some way up the High Street. The newspaper report listed by name over 150 in the procession, almost everybody of note in the town and round about being present.[39]

Health and well being

U NTIL THE LATER nineteenth century, only a minority of the townspeople expected to have access to doctors when medical need arose. In the middle of the century the only doctor in the town was Henry Miles and his son, Edwin, who lived on St. Martin's Street (Queen Street) opposite St. Martin's Square. In 1875 the practice was joined by the young Theophilus Woods from Ireland (Fig. 85), who later took over the practice when it moved to The Square. For the next few years he was the only doctor in the town. Like many general practitioners of the time, he was expected to be medical officer to the many businesses and organisations around him. In the 1890s he was joined by William Branson and then by Charles P. Allen. Woods was a highly respected figure who, despite his busy practice, held a prominent position in the public life of Gillingham until his early death in 1900.[40]

Another Irish doctor, Thomas Hanly, came to Gillingham in 1898 and bought the new mansion of South Lynn in the High Street. He built a surgery and waiting room next to the house, and like Woods, he became medical officer to several businesses as well as to the Shaftesbury Union. Being a Catholic, he became consultant to the Freames and other Catholic families around, some from considerable distances, including the Arundells of Wardour. Hanly was one of the first people in Gillingham to own a motor car, a Humber he purchased in 1906. George Stewart started a practice at Harwood House on Newbury, where he was followed by Arthur Walker. Walker later served in World War I and was a founder member of the Sir

Theophilus Woods

Theophilus Woods (1834-1900) was the only doctor in Gillingham in later Victorian times. He began his work in the practice of Henry Miles in Queen Street. By 1880 it had become Woods' own practice and had relocated to The Square opposite the Phoenix. In the 1890s Woods was joined in the practice by William Branson and then by Charles P. Allen.

Woods was also Factory Surgeon to the London & South-Western Railway Company, Assistant Surgeon to the Volunteer force, Medical Officer to the Gillingham District of the Shaftesbury (Poor Law) Union, and also to almost every club or society in the town. Alongside his busy practice Woods found time to Chairman of the Parish Council, Alderman of the County Council, governor of the Grammar School and member of the School Board. He died suddenly in 1900 at the age of 56.

Douglas Haig Club. The first listing of a dentist in Gillingham is that of Arthur Griffin in 1889, who attended Butt's shop in the High Street on Mondays.[41]

Many working people paid for the visits of doctors and for hospital treatment by joining one of the town's Friendly Societies, the subscription being a form of health insurance. One was the Oddfellows, formed in 1888, which had monthly meetings in the Vicarage School Room. The Ancient Order of Foresters also met monthly, in the Phoenix Hotel. The Red Lion and Queen's Head public houses had slate clubs, a name derived from the original practice of chalking the members' names on a slate. Besides being a means of mutual support, the meetings of these clubs provided opportunities for members to meet socially. People without any means of support were dependent on whatever charitable help they could find. At the annual public meeting of the Parish Council the financial position of each of the town's official charities was always reviewed. In 1904-5 Read's charity had expended £150, Dirdoe's Charity £19 5s 7d, and the Grammar School £30; these were long-established charities which have been previously described (Chapter 7). Further relief had been given by Doggrell's coal charity (£166) and (in Milton) Phillips' blanket charity (£9).[42]

There also existed a Gillingham Aid Society. Its objective was to ensure that all cases of urgent medical treatment could be promptly dealt with, and it provided tickets of admission to the hospitals at Bath, Dorchester, Salisbury, Shaftesbury, Sherborne, and Weymouth. Hot dinners could be provided for deserving cases. In 1878-9 it collected subscriptions to the value of £21 18s 1d. It had its own larder, and in 1879 it reported that there were in store seven bottles of wine, 21 pots of beef essence, and three bottles of gin, which suggests that it might have been providing something more than basic level nutrition. The society kept a wheelchair for loan, looked after by Robert Freame, but its use for long-term disability was clearly not envisaged since it was requested that it should always be returned by the evening of the day on which it was borrowed. During the hard winter of 1878-9 the Aid Society opened a soup kitchen for ten weeks at Knapp House, to make 12 gallons of soup twice a week. By the end of February when it closed, 1,700 quarts (over 400 gallons) had been made, half as much again as had been expected.[43]

A major development came with the decision of the Parish Council to seek the services of a District Nurse. In 1897 the Parish Council looked at several ways of celebrating the Queen's jubilee in the town, and agreed to the building of a house where a District

Nurse could be based. The house can still be seen in Queen Street. A Hospital Carnival was held every year until 1914 to raise money for a Gillingham hospital, but this ambition was never realised and instead the money was eventually given to Shaftesbury Westminster Hospital.[44]

Social life and leisure

F OR MANY OF the labouring families of the town, long working hours and the needs of large families meant that there was little time for leisure outside the family home. However, an increasing number of people, both labouring and middle classes, were finding more opportunities for meeting others and finding some relaxation beyond their own hearth. Old photographs record something of the diversity of leisure activities. Much leisure time centred around church and chapel, with early photographs often depicting groups of people ready to go on outings or involved in activities such as Sunday School treats for children. There was a variety of musical life to suit a range of inclinations; this included a Gillingham Choral Society, which in 1878 was sufficiently accomplished to put on a performance of extracts from Handel's *Judas Maccabeus* and the following year of Haydn's *Creation*. The main venues for these and similar events were the Lecture Hall at the top of Station Road (until 1901) and the Market Hall. A Town Band was in existence in the middle of the nineteenth century; many of its members were builders or from the brickworks. It played at fetes and fairs and also accompanied the Volunteers on their marches through the town. By the early 1900s Charles Walford, a travelling film presenter, had established Gillingham's first cinema in the Market Hall; it was known as Walford's Electric Palace. In 1911 the Constitutional Club was opened in Buckingham Road and the cinema moved to the upper floor of the hall; the name 'Palace' was retained and appeared on the canopy over the door (Chapter 14).

Local sports around the turn of the century included a Gillingham Football Club, and also a 'Lumsden Lambs' Football Club, named after a Bible class led by the Reverend Lumsden. St. Mary's church also had a football team. Many of the town's sports and other activities were played out on Chantry Fields on sites towards the railway bridge. From 1912 the Grammar School swimming pool was available to the townspeople. The town's Friendly Societies such as the Oddfellows also provided a social focus for their members as well as being a form of health insurance. In 1898 a Masonic Lodge was established, known as King's Court Lodge No. 2689, named after the lodge or palace of the medieval forest. It began with 16 founder members who met in rooms behind the Phoenix, and formed a charity association which made donations regularly to the town's hospitals during the First World War.[45] Major events within the town included the Gillingham Agricultural Show, which has already been described (Chapter 11), an annual carnival, fairs, and circuses; the latter two were normally held on Lodbourne Green. The Blackmore Vale Hunt regularly passed through the town. Almost all organisations and firms had regular outings for their employees; the largest exodus was that occasioned by the combined Sunday schools annual trip outing to Weymouth, when the town was virtually emptied of its children. Many of these activities and events were able to cut across class barriers, uniting all sectors of the town in common enjoyment.

For many of the younger men of the town, leisure came in the form of the local Volunteer force. In 1859 the solicitor, Robert Freame, formed the Blackmore Vale Rifle Corps, financed by a subscription list headed by the Reverend Henry Deane. Freame himself was the company's first commanding officer. The company started off with around 20 men and by the 1880s had become 'L' company of the First Volunteer Battalion, Dorsetshire Regiment, variously commanded by Philip W. Matthews, O.H.A. Maggs, and from 1888 by Bertram Freame.

86 A game of cricket on the field behind the Grammar School around 1900

The company increased in popularity and had grown to around 80 men by 1889 and 100 by 1895. In 1907 the Volunteers became a unit of the new Territorial Army. In 1911 the units recorded in Gillingham were the D Squadron, the Dorset (Queen's Own) Yeomanry; and the Right Half of E Company, the 4th Battalion the Dorsetshire Regiment, mustering about 100 men. It was these companies which went to war in 1914.

To many of the younger men, the Volunteers provided a welcome break from their daily work. There were drills, shooting competitions, and camps, with members at first having to provide their own equipment. Rifle ranges were set up at Duncliffe and Bleet. A significant development was the building of the first Drill Hall in Gas House Lane, perhaps about 1870. It remained in use until the new Drill Hall was built in 1930, now used as the Youth Centre.

The view from The Chantry

ETHEL FREAME SPENT much of her life at The Chantry, continuing to live there with her brother, Bertram, after her parents had died. She would often write more than a page a day in her diary, mainly about household matters, visitors, her brother Bertie's comings and goings, and particularly her attendances at church. She also travelled extensively elsewhere in the country and abroad, and gives her impressions of the places she visited, but most of the diary is to do with her life around Gillingham. Her journals were written for most years between 1886 and 1936, a period of profound changes in the town; the published extracts cover the period 1897-1900.

Ethel was a devout Catholic churchgoer even though her father was an active member of the Anglican St. Mary's congregation in Gillingham. As there was no Catholic church in Gillingham at the time, she frequently travelled to masses at Catholic chapels at Marnhull, Bonham, and Wardour.[46] Many of her acquaintances were Catholics, but even Ethel could tire of too much Catholic society. One acquaintance was a Mrs. Doyle who 'never travels without a Catholic Directory etc and really one does get weary of nothing but clerical conversation after a while'. She could be sharp with priests whose sermons she didn't like, such as the Mr. Richards of Bonham whose 'most unpatriotic sermon made me boil', and told him that he should 'make his remarks where one could answer him'. She had especially hard words for some of the Protestant clergy she encountered, such as the new vicar of Motcombe and his wife, who '…are rather awful specimens and I feel sure that if they knew we were Catholics they would not care for our acquaintance – they look bigoted to the last degree.'

Her social circle was largely drawn from acquaintances and relatives at her own social level. A regular visitor was her cousin, Gerald Arundell, the son of Lord Arundell of Wardour, who often came by train to see Ethel and Bertie, who was also his land agent. Knapp House and Stock Hill were among the local gentry households Ethel regularly visited on her many social rounds. The town's doctor, Theophilus Woods and his family, were well known to her, and she also

87 *The River Lodden, painted in 1898 by Henry Woodcock of Woodwater Farm. He was the son-in-law of John Leatherdale, who established the Blackmore Vale Academy in Newbury.*

met the doctor regularly through her work on the Nurse Committee. She seldom wrote in her journals of the town's tradesmen and working people since they only occasionally came into her day-to-day life, for instance when alterations or repairs were needed around the house. The Chantry had several servants, and the diaries show her caring disposition towards their health and well-being. Ellen Hann, who seems to have fallen ill frequently during the winter months, was sent to her sister Julia in Shaftesbury for a break, but 'I don't expect she will spend her full time up there, at this season (September) it would be cold on the hill.' Over the winter 1899-1900 Ellen, Frank, and Cook were all ill, giving Ethel more of the housework to do herself, so that 'already I feel pretty well done … a little sunshine would be such a boon.'

A lady of Ethel's social standing was expected to be involved in various good causes for the less fortunate in the community. We learn of her work as Secretary of the local branch of the RSPCA or her 'Beast Committee' as she called it. The cause occasioned a visit to the wealthy Lady Pelly at Thorngrove, not her favourite person, who to Ethel's surprise contributed a guinea of her own towards the cause and a further twelve shillings from Sir Harold. Perhaps of more direct concern to the town and its people was the Nurse Committee, formed to support the work of the District Nurse who had recently been established in the town. Ethel was Honorary Secretary of this body, on which she worked closely with Theophilus Woods. This organisation appears to have functioned in a rather bureaucratic way, since she records that it held meetings at executive, general, and public levels, all in the course of one evening. She found herself at the centre of a row when the nurse threatened to resign, allegedly because of Ethel's sharp speaking towards her, but the matter seems to have been suitably resolved and the nurse stayed.

Ethel Freame was a keen horsewoman and rode extensively. She recounts her experiences of a new mare called Bess, which seems to have given her a rough ride from time to time. The exasperated rider was moved to write 'If she is going on like this she will be very little use to me except for harness.' A new development for her was the new bicycle or 'tin gee-gee'. She clearly enjoyed riding the new contrivance around the local lanes, and claims to have notched up a thousand miles in less than two years. Her travels around the district took her to many social events, including dances, plays, concerts, and equestrian activities. She particularly enjoyed watching the exercises and manoeuvres of the Volunteers, of which her brother was the commanding officer for much of his life.

In Ethel Freame's diaries, the view of Gillingham from The Chantry can sometimes be that of a society rooted in the slower, gentle pace of past times, but her lifetime spanned a time of huge social and technical changes embracing the railway age, the motor age, and beyond. While these changes were based on the drive and energy of a generation of profit-minded opportunists, many of the very same people gave their spare time to public service as councillors, school governors, church managers, and the like. The majority of people holding voluntary public offices in the town were also members of one of the town's churches, and their dedication to public life was well rooted in their moral and religious convictions. Taken together, these influences all meant that for the majority of people, the material conditions of life in 1914 reflected a changed world from that which had heralded the start of Gillingham's railway age.

13

AROUND GILLINGHAM AT
THE TURN OF THE CENTURY

W HEN THE TRAVELLER, Sir Frederick Treves, visited
Gillingham shortly before 1906, he could not have
been less complimentary about it. His description of
it as a 'sprawling, uninteresting town' characterised by many new
ugly red brick houses contrasts with his picturesque accounts of
the surrounding countryside. Treves had reached Gillingham from
Shaftesbury after a pleasant ramble round Mere, Motcombe, and
Silton, and the markedly different appearance of the industrialising
town clearly took him by surprise. He may not have realised the extent
to which Gillingham, unlike some of its neighbours, had undergone
a generation of transformation. The mid-nineteenth century town
had been one of grey or buff coloured cottages and workshops, barely
changed for centuries. By the time of Treves' travels at the turn of
the century, new housing and factories built with the characteristic
bricks and tiles of the new brickworks had changed the dominant
colour from grey to red. But not all observers took such a dismal view
of the town, another contemporary description being: 'Contrary to
the general condition of towns in this part of the county, Gillingham
may be defined as a bustling, thriving, rapidly improving place, with

an increasing population and a future before it.' Setting aside their particular views, both observers would seem to agree that Gillingham was a town which attracted some attention.[1]

Gillingham's new builders

THE CHANGE FROM stone to brick had been spread over a number of years, there being only a few all-brick buildings in the town before the 1880s. The oldest all-brick dwellings in the town may be the Cemetery Cottages of 1860, but generally a mix of brick and stone was in favour for many years, with stone often used for the main parts of new buildings, and brick for the quoins or cornerstones, and for dressings around doors and windows. From the 1880s new terraces of cottages began to appear: the earliest may be Harwood Cottages on Newbury, with a datestone of 1886. From this time onwards into the early 1900s the redbrick house and terrace became widespread. Stone continued to be used for some of the more prominent buildings, including both Methodist churches (1876 and 1877), the new vicarage (1882), Stuckeys (now the Natwest) Bank (1902), and some of the larger country houses such as The Kendalls.

The rebuilding of the town which had so dismayed Treves was the work of a small number of local builders, several of whom had been busily at work since the 1860s. Thomas Doggrell, a farmer from Ham, had a builders' yard on Newbury and in 1871 was the employer of 32 men. In 1860 he built the structures for the first cemetery, now the Remembrance Garden, and in 1875 was awarded the contract to build the new Grammar School. He continued in business until around 1890. James George built houses in Newbury and Station Road. Later builders were the timber and builders' merchants, Hudson and Martin, who numbered amongst their projects the High Street mansion of South Lynn (1872), the Methodist Church (1875), and their own house on Queen Street. Around 1900, smaller builders were Alfred Barnes and Charles Barnes, with businesses in Cemetery Road and Hardings Lane respectively, and Frank Flower in Tomlins Lane. Bracher Brothers are thought by some to have been involved in building work in the town, although this interest never features in their advertisements as cabinet makers and house furnishers.

Portions of New Road were sold for building developments as soon as railway construction started and the road appeared. In June 1858 an auction took place of 'Sites for building purposes with frontages to the Shaftesbury and Sturminster roads and immediately adjoining the station'. Twelve lots were offered, mostly of around 20-30 perches, each with a frontage of around 40 feet. In 1863 we can read of 'six cottages of Joseph Light's in Station Road', suggesting some building activity in the new street. In 1868 Joseph Light conveyed to Edward Light a parcel of ground in Newbury together with a pair of dwellings 'now in course of erection', and in the same year Josiah Hannam, the miller sold to William Bond a 'dwelling house and shop now in course of erection in Newbury'.[2]

Prospective buyers could make use of a Gillingham General Permanent Building Society. In 1861 it advanced £500 to James Herridge for his Newbury (High Street) shop. His repayment subscription was to be £4 15s 6d monthly over 14 years. In 1862 George Davis borrowed £160 from the Society for a cottage in Bourton. However when in 1865 James George and George Cave wanted to borrow £1,054 for the pair of houses they were building in Station Road, they obtained the advance from the London-based Temperance Benefit Building Society. Again, the term of repayment was 14 years.[3]

Treves might have been more impressed had the town been able to display entire areas of new, carefully planned streets. Instead the building boom produced few new residential streets but much rebuilding of older properties and infilling along existing roads. This was a reflection of the piecemeal nature in which the new developments

88 *The 1889 edition of the Ordnance Survey 'six-inch' map captures Gillingham shortly before Treves' visit, thirty years after the arrival of the railway had started to transform it into an industrial town. Much of the edge of the town was gardens and orchards.*

occurred, mainly by small local builders lacking the capital to finance larger speculative ventures. New Road, the diversion of the northern end of Oldlands Lane, was a necessary new thoroughfare caused by the building of the railway. Station Road and Railway Terrace also appeared with the arrival of the railway, the former having a mix of houses, shops, and industries. Many townspeople continued to live along the High Street and Newbury. The only truly new residential street from the later years of the century was Victoria Road (1897), which remained an unadopted road until the 1970s. Other new thoroughfares were School Road and School Lane, but these were not intended as residential roads. Away from the town's main streets the provision of utilities lagged behind the building of the houses, and it was to be several decades before piped water and mains sewerage reached all parts of the town.

An important change for the townspeople was the renaming of several of the town's older thoroughfares. By 1861 St. Martin's Street, from Spring Corner to Lodbourne, had become Queen Street, although St. Martin's Square, next to the church, has continued to be known as such. With the building of the first cemetery in 1860, the continuation of Gas House Lane (now St. Mary's Place) towards Rolls Bridge became Cemetery Road. Back Lane behind the Phoenix became more officially known as South Street. The most significant renaming was that of Newbury and Bridge Street. In earlier times Newbury had extended from the Town Bridge on the Shreen as far as the bridge across the Lodden. Sometime around 1875 to 1880 Bridge Street, together with the western part of Newbury as far as Station Road, was renamed High Street. While this renaming may have reflected the contemporary fashion for creating 'high streets', it was also an acknowledgment of its new position as a main shopping thoroughfare of the town, and of a shifting of commercial activity eastwards towards Newbury and the station.

The Square, Cemetery Road, and Queen Street

T HE SQUARE OF 1900 was much as it had been half a century earlier, with some notable changes. The western side going round the corner into Wyke Street was now owned by Dr.

Theophilus Woods, whose house door with its day and night bells is still to be seen. The northern end of this range was a general store which until around 1880 belonged to John Davis, who advertised himself as a draper, outfitter, ironmonger, druggist, china and earthenware dealer, and undertaker. Soon afterwards the building was acquired by the Slade family, and around 1904 William Slade carried out extensive rebuilding. His new department store was a substantial structure of three-storeys, with modern large windows to attract shoppers and the range of goods proudly proclaimed around its fascias. Inside it could boast the latest interior fitting and 'tube' transfer system for cash payments. The building still dominates the Square as the present day Slade Centre and bar.[4]

Across from the Slade store by the church gate was the pharmacy of William Samways, which to judge from the mix of stone and brickwork was probably built earlier in the century and then rebuilt around this time. It eventually came to include the buildings extending further behind, and also incorporated the post office, which was accessible by a separate door to the left of the pharmacy entrance.

On the south side of the Square is one of Gillingham's most imposing buildings, the 'Dutch' style offices of Farnfields, solicitors. It is most likely to have been built around 1855 for the Wilts and Dorset Bank, with part of the building being the home of the bank manager. The style is that of Thomas Doggrell, the builder of the Grammar School. After 1875, when the bank moved to the High Street, it became the offices of the solicitors, Bell and Freame, and has always remained a solicitors' practice.[5] Attached to the western end is a very different building, the lower half of stone and the upper half brick. This started life as a milk factory before becoming a car factory, a glove factory, and in more recent years has become part of the solicitors' premises.[6] Also on the south side of the Square some older cottages led into Back Lane, by now officially known as South Street. Little had altered here since a generation earlier, but a major change in 1895 was the closure of the Lock-up, following the completion of the new Police Station in School Road. This left the Lock-up without any specific use, and it was sold to the brewery owner G.B. Matthews, who used it as a store.

On the north side of the Square, today's St. Mary's Place is blocked off by Le Neubourg Way, but to the residents of Victorian and Edwardian times this was Gas House Lane, which led into Cemetery Road. Much of what was here has long disappeared under the relief road and car parking. On the east side was the first Drill Hall, a low stone building with lancet windows, built for the Volunteers around 1870. Beyond here was the gas works established in 1837, recognisable by its round gas holders. Further on some older buildings clustered around the top of Turners Lane; a little further on again was a house lived in until 1895 by James Sheppard, the retired schoolmaster. This adjoined a pair of cottages which were later given by Bertram Freame for the new Catholic chapel (Chapter 14). Next to these are the gates to the 'new' cemetery of c.1889. On the south side of Gas House Lane a pair of small cottages looking towards the church date from about this time, while on the far side of the present relief road another pair of larger cottages bear the datestone 1895.[7] Further along are the cottages built for the keepers of the first cemetery, now the Garden of Remembrance, built in 1860. The keepers' cottages were built by Thomas Doggrell in a 'Gothic' style which he developed more fully in his design for the Grammar School

89 The Cemetery Cottages, built by Thomas Doggrell in 1860 in a style which he used some years later in the new Grammar School building.

some years later (Fig. 89). The mortuary chapel at the far end of the garden dates from 1881.[8]

Around the Church Walk or path most of the houses date from an earlier period, and have been described in an earlier chapter. Pedestrians of the time would have noticed a passage between these buildings opposite the west door of the church; this was to enable the movement of biers and coffins from the church to the cemetery, and has remained a right of way for the church until recent times. In Queen Street, Church House, jutting out into St. Martin's Square, was used by Robert Freame as his offices until 1875, and afterwards by Bertram Freame. From here the view from its now blocked-up windows along Queen Street showed significant changes from half a century earlier. On the east side of the street The Barton was at this time the tailor's premises of Shephard Brothers, followed by Lime Tree House, unaltered in appearance. But this in turn was now flanked by the grand new mansion built by the builder, Thomas Hudson, for his own family. The scale and appearance of this building, with its bright red brickwork and decorative detail, may have been intended to show off the capabilities of the builder to prospective customers. In 1901 the house was occupied by Hudson's own family and also the widow and family of Albert Martin, his recently deceased business partner. Early photographs show it bounded by a higher wall to the street, with a wider gate and pillars. In later times it has seen use as a private school, clinic, and adult education centre.

Adjoining the Hudson house on its north side was a smaller, older house, the remains of a once larger orchard, and then the chapel of 1836, since deserted by the Wesleyans for their much more spacious accommodation on the High Street. This building was now divided into several dwellings, and along with the remaining cottages towards the end of the street was occupied by mostly labouring people. A veterinary surgeon, James Dewey, was also here. Towards the end of the street the public house or wine bar of recent years was used as a

90 A view of Queen Street from the church tower, taken around 1895. On the east (right) side of the street, the mansion of Thomas Hudson, now the Adult Education Centre, has yet to be built; the house shown on the same site is that of the surgeon Henry Miles. On the west (left) side, Tower House, built around 1890, has a notably higher 'observation tower' than at present. Towards the top of the view is Lodbourne Green, with the cottages of Bay Road straggling away towards top right.

baker's shop. Next door was a row of thatched cottages, now gone. At the end of the street the pair of redbrick cottages, perhaps built in the early 1900s, were known as Queen's Villas.[9]

Looking along the west side of Queen Street from Church House, the older buildings around St. Martins Square and beyond had been joined by several newer properties. The square itself now included the redbrick Myrtle Cottage (dated 1901). Further along, on the corner of Turners Lane, is the interesting-looking property of Tower House, complete with pilasters, dentilled eaves, and with observation tower in the roof. In 1901 this was the property of Harry Shute, a butter and cheese merchant, whose factory adjoined the houses; the factory building disappeared entirely when the relief road was built. In Turners Lane itself is a terrace of brick cottages with the name 'Victoria Terrace, 1897'. Returning to Queen Street and adjoining Tower House is the house erected for the District Nurse. This was built in 1897, the year of the Queen's Jubilee, and bears a plaque with the names of the different parts of the Empire. Beyond the older row of houses with the Queen's Head inn is Octave Terrace, a row of eight brick cottages similar in style to Victoria Terrace, built by the brickworks for its employees. Next comes a detached brick villa, The Haven. On the corner with Tomlins Lane is the Primitive Methodist Chapel of 1876, built in stone with its twin towers and large schoolroom annex behind.[10]

The northern end of Queen Street opened out into Lodbourne Green, flanked by the farms of Lodbourne and Great House, largely unaltered from previous generations. Along Peacemarsh and Wavering Lane there was little new building, these neighbourhoods retaining much of their previous character as areas of labourers' cottages together with some smaller trades. In Bay Road a row of four brick cottages dates from the early 1900s and has a mansard roof and buff coloured bricks which are used decoratively to imitate dressings and string courses. Further along is another row of four cottages in a plainer style with the plaque 'Elm View Terrace'; and beyond the bridge another pair of brick bay-fronted semi-detached houses of about this date. In Wavering Lane a pair of semi-detached houses with large bay windows are in stone, in contrast to the brick building which was becoming normal everywhere else in the town by this time.[11]

Wyke Street and Wyke

BY CONTRAST WITH Peacemarsh and Wavering Lane, the area towards Wyke in 1900 was developing as the more fashionable end of the town. This part of Gillingham, with its elevated locations and good views, increasingly attracted the attention of the landed and business classes as the place to build their mansions and villas.

The view into Wyke Street from The Square in recent times has become more difficult to visualise because of the building of the relief road, but on the south side there was still in 1900 a short open stretch from the end of the butter factory across the bridge to The Chantry or Chantry Farm. The Chantry property has been entirely redeveloped in modern times, making it even more difficult to appreciate what previously existed. In the 1840s this had consisted of a row of cottages bending round the corner into Common Mead Lane. It was then acquired around 1860 by the solicitor, Robert Freame, who seems to have entirely remodelled it, replacing the cottages with a farm and outbuildings, behind which he built a mansion with spacious grounds. Little is certain about the appearance of Freame's Chantry since it always lay behind high hedges and walls and was later demolished for redevelopment. The only known picture shows it as a long stone building in an earlier vernacular style, perhaps unlike other traditional houses around Gillingham, and more similar to the buildings around Corsham from where Freame had originated. Southwards of the house the open Chantry Fields extended to the railway line and beyond. The site is now entirely occupied by the houses of Common Mead Avenue. The Freame family lived here until 1925, when they moved further up Common Mead Lane, and the property was given to the Carmelite religious order (Chapter 14).[12]

The corner of Wyke Street and Common Mead Lane was a pleasant corner of the town overlooked by the wooded grounds of both The Chantry and Knapp House. The latter, facing The Chantry from across the Lane, was an eighteenth-century mansion altered and extended by its Victorian owners. These were the solicitor William Read Bell, earlier in the century, followed by his widow Agnes (d.1886), and his younger son Edward by 1880. By 1902 the occupier was Major Cecil Jackson. Knapp House and its grounds included the entire corner between Common Mead Lane and Wyke Street, and it was on the very edge of the town, with uninterrupted country extending to Thorngrove along one road and Wyke along the other. Perhaps as a sign of things to come, a handful of redbrick villas were already beginning to appear further along Wyke Road. These were the homes of some of the better off business owners in the town, who, attracted by the open, elevated location, were taking the opportunity to move out of their existing residences close to or on top of their businesses. These were Elmcroft, built for Evan Down, the owner of the bacon factory (by 1895); Fairview, the home of Joseph Mullings, bank manager (before 1905); and Oakleigh, belonging to the ironmonger Edwin Stickland (by 1911). Others would be added later.

On the north side of Wyke Street the view towards the hill first of all took in Plank House, for many years the home of Thomas L. Parkes, a building stone merchant. Across the bridge the row of cottages, including Little Chantry and Folly's End looked much as it did earlier in the century when Constable had sketched the view from Common Mead Lane. Next came Rosebank, a brick house with the datestone 1870, making it perhaps the earliest of Gillingham's redbrick villas. Further up the hill, beyond the older Wyke Court and Knapp Cottage (today's Old Toll House), other villas from this period were Wyke Hill House, Mountview, and the three semi-detached pairs of houses towards the Coldharbour junction. The junction itself was then occupied by the small thatched Beehive Cottage, a vestige of a previous era. Next came Wyke House, a handsome property with a different frontal appearance from that seen today, the home in 1900 of the brewer, George Gerrard Matthews.[13]

It was further along beyond Wyke House that the scene was most changed from half a century earlier. The focus of change was the Wyke brewery, built by the Matthews family around 1860 and described in Chapter 11. This was followed by the construction of cottages for the brewery employees. Four pairs of semi-detached dwellings were built on each side of the road, to a uniform style with double fronts, mansard roofs, stone walling, and brick dressings (Fig. 91). The building and occupation was most likely spread over several years, since in 1871 two cottages remained uninhabited and the 1901 Ordnance Survey map shows two blocks on the north side of the road still not built. The parallel rows, with the striking brewery building at the end, gave the scene something of the character of a 'factory village' when approached from the town.[14] At the end of the southern row are some interesting looking frontages, which might have been intended as the start of another brewery building which was never completed. At this time the brewery building itself had only one tower. Opposite the brewery are the substantial stables which bear a tablet with the initials of GBM and the date of 1884. Further along on the corner

91 Wyke Road, with company cottages lining the route to the Matthews brewery building. Today the brewery is Milford Court and is divided into private apartments.

of Lydfords Lane, the village character was further enhanced by the building of the first Wyke primary school, a Board School building of 1890, and now a private residence.

High Street, School Lane, and School Road

T HE ADOPTION OF the name 'High Street' for the thoroughfare between The Square and Station Road may have represented a change in perception by residents of the shape and ordering of their town. Until the 1860s Gillingham was largely seen as being focused around the church and its two squares, where most business and trading had taken place since medieval times. Newbury was considered an extension of the main town, commercially significant but nevertheless detached and tributary. But from this time onwards the impetus of retailing activity was generally understood to have extended across the Shreen to the newly named street which had been so much rebuilt since the middle of the century. The rise to prominence of the High Street and adjoining roads was reinforced by their proximity to the railway station and to the area being chosen for the site of public facilities, notably the new schools, the police station, magistrates' court and fire station.

The lower, western end of the High Street remained the least altered by new developments, although the view from the town bridge was now dominated by the large, modern edifice of the Slade department store. On the corner of The Square access to the Phoenix Hotel for wheeled vehicles could still be had through the front of the building, a space occupied in recent years by the hotel's dining room. Across the street is a double-fronted shop of striking appearance, built of three storeys with decorative stonework. This was the premises of

Silvester Edgar, who occupied the site for half a century with a varied business which included watchmaking, jewellery, printing, and bookbinding. Further along on the other side opposite Spring Corner was a butcher's shop, occupied in the 1870s and 1880s by William Down and in the 1890s by J. Wastfield and Son. This butcher's shop had its own slaughterhouse at the rear, on the other side of South Street.

Beyond Spring Corner was a development of a different nature. Henry Deane had been content to live in the old vicarage occupied by his predecessors stretching back to the Jesops, but in the year following his death it was taken down. In its stead there arose a much grander structure built to a design by the architect, Edward Swinfen Harris. He came from Stony Stratford, now part of Milton Keynes, and was an advocate of the Arts and Crafts style, designing numerous churches and other buildings along these lines, mostly in and around Buckinghamshire. On the front of the Gillingham building, now Rawson Court, the influence of this style can be clearly seen in the use of rubble walling, mullioned windows, and arched doorway, making it strikingly different from the town's other buildings of this time.

It was further along the High Street across the Shreen that the most notable changes occurred. From the bridge up to Station Road the street was almost entirely rebuilt. On the north side the mill remained much as before, but beyond here the entire street became newly built up. The dominating building was the new Methodist Church of 1877, built to a design by the builder and trustee, Thomas Hudson, and occupying an elevated position facing across the Shreen. The rear extension, with its extra rooms, dates from 1903. Next to it came the Wilts and Dorset Bank of 1875, in a very different style from the company's earlier premises in the Square, with Corinthian columns, carved porch, and dentilled eaves. This was extended with a new wing on its western side around 1910. Further along is Fernbank, a bay-windowed house with a garden which once extended to the road but is now occupied by a travel agent. Next door the pharmacy of today was a house and shop belonging to Bowles, a hatter and outfitter. In 1906 the adjoining site was used for a shop occupied by G.E. and J. Fish, a dealer in general provisions, furniture, and ironmongery. This was a distinctive-looking shop, modern for its time, with three doors, broad-angled fascias, and curved plate glass windows at either end.[15]

Across School Lane, the whole range of land and buildings extending to School Road gradually came under the ownership of the Stickland company, the growth of whose ironmongery business has been described in Chapter 11. The house on the corner with the steps to the front door and iron railings was once the home of James Dunn, the seedsman. Adjoining is a section of building with wrought iron balcony, followed by several ranges with gable end to street. While these gabled sections may appear to be all of one date, they were in fact built at different times, and until the early 1900s a gap in the frontage gave direct access from the street to the yards at the rear.

The south side of the High Street was notable for its broad pavement, contrasting with the north side which for many years had no pavement at all (Fig. 92). A few yards beyond the Shreen, a detached, double-fronted shop was built and occupied as a butchers by the Hann family. This family were trading as butchers in the town at least as early as 1840, and were still in business as butchers in the early 1900s. Behind the shop was their long slaughterhouse which still stands, occupied now as dwellings (Plate 19). Across the alley today is a range of terraced shops in stone, part of which was owned by James Herridge, a general grocery and provisions' dealer, and house furnisher.[16] Further along again was a house, partly of stone and partly of buff-coloured brick, then lived in by Joseph Kingsbury, a retired glover and tea dealer, and occupied today by an optometrist. Slightly higher up again was Cheapside House, a tall, substantial shop with its name proclaimed on the eaves, still looking remarkably similar today as the town's post office. This was the other shop of

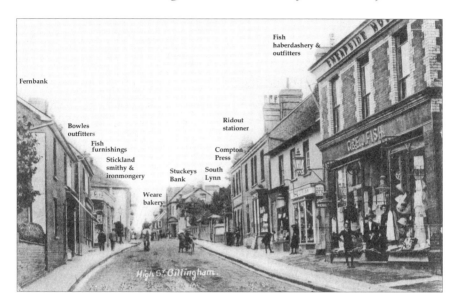

Fernbank

Bowles
outfitters

Fish
furnishings

Stickland
smithy &
ironmongery

Weare
bakery

Stuckeys
Bank

South
Lynn

Fish
haberdashery &
outfitters

Ridout
stationer

Compton
Press

High St. Gillingham.

*92 The upper part of the High Street around 1910. By this time the north
side (left of picture) was made up with a proper pavement. The high
wall on the south side was that of South Lynn, hidden behind the nearer
buildings.*

the Fish family, whose business therefore occupied both sides of the
road, Cheapside House being the fashion and outfitting departments.
Adjoining this was Stedman, a printer; and then one or two more
doors along came Compton Press with its distinctive semicircular
arched doorway, the property of the Ridout family. Next came one
of the last traditional cottages of the High Street, a rubble stone and
thatched structure which was not demolished until 1904, the site later
becoming Stickland's motor showrooms.

Adjoining this site was one of the most substantial buildings of
the High Street, of which no trace now remains. This was the mansion
of South Lynn, built by Thomas Hudson in 1882 for James Herridge,
the grocery entrepreneur and owner of several other properties along
the High Street (above and Chapter 11). This was a tall stone building
with recessed frontage and several gables, the frontage displaying
deep mullioned windows and a grand arched doorway approached by

steps. A tall curtain wall formed the boundary with the street, giving the building the appearance of a school or public building rather than a private house. After building the house, Herridge found that he could not afford to occupy all of it. In 1898 it was sold to Dr. Thomas Hanly, who established his general practice here and added an extension, which he used as a waiting room and surgery. The building was later bought by Jack Stickland to use as his home and offices for his growing motor business, and much later the frontage was turned into a filling station. Today nothing can be seen of South Lynn, the house and neighbouring premises all having been demolished to make way for a supermarket and adjoining shops (Plate 17).

Beyond South Lynn was Clive Vale House, a double-fronted bay-windowed house, occupied around this time by another doctor's practice. Little can be seen of this frontage since much more recently a pair of shops were built in front of it. A little further up on the corner with Station Road was Paris House, a grandly named three-storey store built for the draper and milliner, Thomas Pitman. Only a fragment of this building can be found today as the newsagent's shop in Station Road, the remainder being demolished to make way for the later National Provincial Bank.

On the north side of the High Street, School Lane and School Road were laid out. The former was the original driveway to the new Grammar School. By the 1890s the road was flanked by the builders' yard of Hudson and Martin and the new fire station before becoming a tree-lined drive bending upwards towards the school. The building, which occupied an elevated site overlooking the town, was the work of the local builder, Thomas Doggrell, and its origins have been described in an earlier chapter. By 1901 other buildings had appeared behind the main structure, but none of these remain today. School Road originated as a drive leading to the new Board Schools, which had separate buildings for boys, girls, and infants. Only part of the original buildings remains, much having been destroyed in a fire in 1977. The two roads became joined following the building of the Police Station and School House.

Station Road and Buckingham Road

T HE MOST IMPORTANT new road to appear in the town was Station Road. Besides linking the town with the station, it provided the only access to the market and the various yards which were grouped around the station. But even with this commercial impetus it never became completely built over and two distinct parts were always recognisable. The part nearer the town was one of shops and houses; the lower end by the station was that of the yards and depots of the various businesses clustered around the station.

Starting with Pitman's store at the corner with the High Street, a walk along the west side of the street around 1900 would have first passed a number of cottages, which are still to be seen. One of these was the home of Albert Chubb, a coachbuilder.[17] Next came a three-storey block with two shops. This was an imposing frontage with carved brackets to the windows. The first shop was that of Collihole, drapers and costumiers, shortly to become Ayles and Owen; the further shop was Styles, with menswear. The building was demolished in recent times for a new block of flats named Paris House. Further along were a pair of similarly substantial houses, which always seem to have been dwellings until their recent use as a flower shop and betting shop.[18] These adjoined one of the most interesting and least-known buildings of the street; this started life as the Girls' High School of Sarah Dunn, and was subsequently used as a bank, a wartime hospital, and most recently as a Masonic Lodge and office of the Agricultural Society. Over the years the rebuilding of the outside, involving replacement or removal of doors and windows has greatly changed its external appearance. In 1901 the upper floors of these buildings were homes to several households with occupations suggesting that they were connected with the businesses below or nearby. Further down, beyond what was to become Buckingham Road, was a yard owned by the New Rock Coal Company, which had a colliery near Radstock. By 1905 this had become the yard of the auctioneer, John Jeffrey of Donhead.

Further along again towards the station was the extensive premises of the larger businesses, of which now little remains to be seen. Hudson and Martin occupied the area which has recently been Focus DIY and the relief road. Behind their sheds and boiler house facing on to the streets, an area stretching back to the river was filled with piles of timbers and tree trunks, the raw materials of the saw milling trade. Next came a small field used from time to time as allotments, and then the Gillingham and Semley dairy factory, of which an L-shaped range of buildings remains standing; and finally the Oake, Woods bacon factory on the edge of the station yard, of which only the slaughterhouse still stands. The station yard, a scene of bustle and noise, housed a collection of sheds and huts with signs advertising the businesses of the various traders and activities. The origins and development of all these enterprises have been described in Chapter 11, and they formed a continuous corridor of trade and business linking the town with the station.

Turning round opposite the station to return towards the town along Station Road, the first building to be encountered by the rail visitor was the South-Western Hotel, with its signboard over the front door and distinctive frontage of gabled barge boards with 'Commercial Hotel' written over its windows. Beyond it and around it extended the yards and buildings of the market. On market day the area around the hotel would be full of the carts and carriages of farmers and dealers, whose horses would be looked after by the hotel staff. The most important of the market buildings to the town community was the Market Hall, a long narrow building which stretched

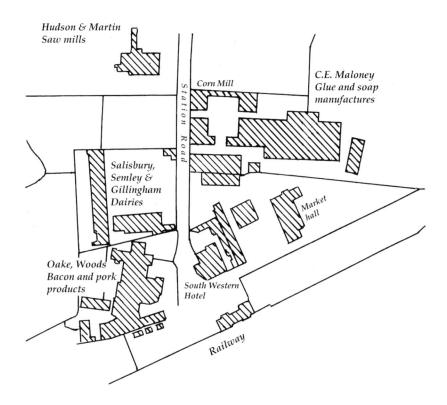

Hudson & Martin
Saw mills

Corn Mill

Station Road

C.E. Maloney
Glue and soap
manufactures

Salisbury,
Semley &
Gillingham
Dairies

Market
hall

Oake, Woods
Bacon and pork
products

South Western
Hotel

Railway

93 Station Road around 1900-1910. The Maloney premises may include
some later extensions to the factory.

behind the Hotel and was the venue for many public meetings and
entertainments. These included Walford's Electric Palace Cinema,
where the townspeople first saw films and heard a phonograph record.
Walking back towards the town, the next piece of ground had been
open land until about 1890 when it was acquired by Charles Maloney
for his building of a corn mill. After 1900 his premises considerably
expanded as he used the site for the development of his glue factory,
which eventually grew to cover much of the space stretching back
from Station Road to Newbury House, which Maloney then bought
for his own residence (Fig. 93). Fronting the street opposite Hudson
and Martins were a pair of houses and a saddlers' shop. The whole of

this area beyond the hotel towards the relief road is now represented by the recent developments of the Old Market Centre.[19]

The upper part of Station Road on its east side beyond Maloneys had belonged since the late 1860s to Edward Light of the Freame legal practice. He owned a field which was used until 1908 for the Agricultural Show. From there to the top of Station Road was entirely cottages, mostly built soon after 1860.[20] The appearance of the top of the street was greatly changed some decades later in 1900 with the demolition of the old Temperance Hall and the building of the new Stuckey's Bank (Chapter 11). This act of construction finally consolidated the position of the top of Station Road as the focal point of commercial and social activity in the town; from here the streets gave direct access to the station, market, schools, police station, fire station, larger shops, banks, and hotels.

Buckingham Road appears to be of later development, the name not appearing in directories until after 1905. The name comes from the owner of the properties on the south side of the street. On this side the most significant building was the Constitutional Club, built in 1911, which housed the town's first cinema on its upper floor. On the north side John Jeffreys, the Donhead auctioneer, opened an auction yard.

Around Newbury

B Y 1880 THE name Newbury was used only for the part of the main street eastwards of Station Road. In earlier centuries this had been a populous, if detached, part of Gillingham, with many cottages clustered around the meeting of the main street with Hardings Lane, and at the turn of the twentieth century the new redbrick terraces and houses quickly intermingled with the older properties. On the north side the view down Station Road

94 Victoria Road, which dates from 1897. The street remained unadopted until the 1970s.

was dominated, as now, by the handsome façade of Strange's shoe shop, used today as an estate agent. Further along was a shop used by George King, a tailor, and behind this were various buildings belonging to the building business of Hudson and Martin. By 1901 Sidney M. Peach had a hairdresser's in one of two timber shed structures which were to remain until quite recent times when they gave way to the supermarket. The next building was the new premises of the Bracher Brothers, furnishers, builders, and undertakers, whose business is described in Chapter 11. This was built in 1896 after the business moved from Station Road, and is still used as a house furnishers, now occupied by the Woods furniture store. A few yards along again was one of the most striking buildings in Gillingham, the Royal Hotel. Its frontage was notable for the two decorative lions above the portico, and until its closure in 2005 was a town landmark. On market day the front was crowded with the wagons and carts of farmers and traders.

Further along past Hardings Lane was The Laurels, a handsome house from earlier in the century lived in around 1900 by Charles Maloney, the coal merchant. Further on again, a large shop now facing on to the roundabout was occupied by Jesse England, a grocer and postmistress. A few doors along was a house belonging to the minister of the Primitive Methodist Church, Thomas Phelps. Next door to this were the two Baptist churches, the one dating from around 1840 but still used then as a Sunday School, and the other newly built. Beyond here some pairs of redbrick houses from the first decade of the new century lead towards an older shop on the edge of the railway bridge, occupied in 1901 by Samuel Reakes, a retired bootmaker. Beyond the bridge was a redbrick villa, The Elms, the property of James George, a retired builder.[21]

On the north side of Newbury some older cottages were to be found around the junction with Hardings Lane, while 'The Firs' is an attractive stone-built property with a datestone showing 1900. The significant development here was the building of Victoria Road, the only new residential road in the town. A 'Jubilee' datestone on one of the houses identical with that in Queen Street identifies the construction date as 1897, and the name clearly reflects the royal event of that year (Fig. 94). Thirteen houses were built in short rows, several with the red brickwork of the walls balanced by the buff brick dressings around the doors and windows. The occupants were invariably the better-waged manual workers and tradesmen rather than the poorer paid labourers. Further along Newbury, opening off by the bridge, was Railway Terrace, with some fifteen houses in two rows, the nearer row dating from the 1860s, the further row possibly a little later. In 1901 all householders were people with low paid labouring or other manual occupations, and altogether 72 people were housed in these rows, making it the most densely populated road in the town.

Much of the south side of Newbury was completely rebuilt around this time, in red brick with much use of buff coloured dressings

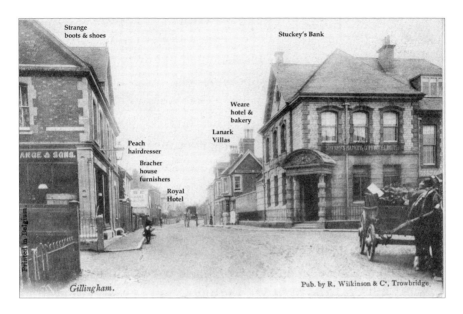

Strange
boots & shoes

Stuckey's Bank

Weare
hotel &
bakery

Lanark
Villas

Peach
hairdresser

Bracher
house
furnishers

Royal
Hotel

Gillingham.

Pub. by R. Wilkinson & Cᵒ, Trowbridge.

95 A view of Newbury in 1905, showing the newly built Stuckeys Bank on the corner with Station Road.

for windows and doors. Adjoining the new Stuckey's Bank was the Temperance Hotel of James Weare. The advertisement proclaimed 'Every accommodation for the gentleman and cyclist' and the name was posted along the eaves and across the back of the building as well as at the front. Adjoining the hotel on the side of the bank, Weare also operated a bakery. Next came a pair of shops with private residents living above, and then the driveway to Harwood House, a much older property. The next block was Lanark Villas, reputedly built by Bracher Brothers in 1907, and today housing a dental practice. Opposite the Royal Hotel and Hardings Lane was Harwood Cottages, a block of six, built much earlier than the adjoining terraces, in 1886. Several of the occupants of these properties in 1901 were living on private means, while others had higher waged occupations, making this a 'respectable' part of the town to live in.[22]

Further along, Blackmore Vale House was the academy or private school of the Leatherdales. Some years earlier under John

Leatherdale this had been a flourishing institution with nearly twenty boarders; it was later run by his daughter, but in 1901 no pupils are recorded in the census. The adjoining long building was once part of the school. Further along again, redevelopment and the building of the relief road has removed other houses, notably one which belonged to Thomas Doggrell, the builder of the Grammar School. Beyond the relief road the most prominent building was the mansion of Newbury House, the earlier development of which has previously been described (Chapter 9), and which by the later nineteenth century had probably achieved its present appearance. In 1901 it belonged to the coal merchant, Thomas Tucker, and was soon to pass into the ownership of Charles Maloney. Across the railway bridge on the far corner with New Road was Wesley Villa, a later nineteenth century building which was the home of the Wesleyan Methodist minister, in 1901 the Reverend Samuel Whitaker. A little further down the hill was the building of the mineral water works started by Ambrose Collis, which later passed to William Slade, its gable end proclaiming its products to all entering Gillingham from the Shaftesbury Road. Behind the Collis buildings lay the Lawrence Cottages, a terrace of ten brick cottages built in the 1880s or 1890s, very plain in style; in 1901 all were inhabited by low-waged manual workers, including several railway employees. Further along Shaftesbury Road area a few more pairs of brick cottages of a similar date.

Opening off the south side of Newbury, the junction with New Road was always one of the busiest in the town, a consequence of the Sturminster road not having its own bridge over the railway. From this time onwards the name Oldlands Lane appears to have lapsed and the entire road towards Madjeston became known as New Road. The land on the eastern side of New Road, between the road and the railway, was owned by Eden Shute, and remained undeveloped apart from a pair of houses. It was later sold to the Sturminster Newton Farmers Co-operative as a dairy factory. Further on round the corner new houses only appeared after 1900; the first terrace of six brick cottages is dated 1906 and has the buff dressings found elsewhere in the town. Further on are another pair in a similar style with bay windows. Beyond Brickyard Lane are the three pairs of Pottery Villas cottages, built for brickyard workers in 1913. Along Brickyard Lane only two buildings remain from the former brickworks: the office and the manager's house. The former, a redbrick bungalow, was often to be seen on the company's letter headings (Plate 21).

On the eastern side of New Road land for building was being sold as early as 1858 (above). One of the purchasers was John Hayter, who by 1871 had a farm on the site, and by 1895 this was in the hands of Eden Shute, who developed his new butter factory there (Chapter 11). Shute also built a new house, Prospect House, which remained until 1981 when the site was developed. By 1900 a number of other brick cottages had appeared beyond his factory, but once round the corner the buildings ended and the brickfields on the western side marked the edge of the town.

In the rebuilding of Gillingham between the coming of the railway and the First World War, two phases might be might be recognised, an earlier building boom of the 1860s, and a later one between the 1880s and early 1900s. Between them they changed the character and appearance of the town as new red brick houses, factories, and shops intermingled with the stone cottages and workshops of an earlier era. While the focus of commercial activity shifted from the old town around the church towards Newbury and the station, the scale of change was not enough to basically alter the geography of the town. There was much infilling along existing streets, but few new streets were created, and until the mid-twentieth century Gillingham remained much within its earlier limits. Perhaps the people who benefited most from the changes were the higher wage earners of tradesmen, shopkeepers, foremen, and clerks, whose incomes now enabled them to rent houses in the new terraces appearing around Newbury, and to even venture an entry as a 'private resident' in the Kelly directory. The labouring classes continued to be found largely in the older cottage areas around the edges of the town in Ham, Peacemarsh, and Bay. Gillingham, so refashioned, was to persist for some decades to come.

14

GILLINGHAM IN WAR AND PEACE, 1914 TO 1939

I N 1911 THE population of Gillingham reached 3,570, the highest level it was to achieve until 1961. The last half of the nineteenth century had been a time of great social and economic changes for the town, but by the early years of the new century there were signs that this period of change was coming to an end. By 1910 there was less new building going on and much of the pattern of trade and business had already been established for half a century. A few people in the town now had motor cars, but it was to be several more years before they made much impact on the general pace of life.

By the middle of 1914 the possibility that the country might soon find itself at war was beginning to be understood around the town. Ethel Freame wrote in her diary on 30 July: 'The dread of European war grows deeper every day. Ireland seemed bad enough but if this does come it will beat all previous records of horror and magnitude'; and again on 3 August, the day of a fete: 'The feeling of dread and anxiety which has come upon us all today will never be forgotten. The scouts fete had to be gone through somehow but it was a great strain.' On the following day her thoughts took a more pragmatic turn: 'We seem to be on the very brink of war so it behoves every woman to keep her head and do all she knows to help'. These practical leanings were soon to be called on in the months ahead.[1]

The Great War and its aftermath

THE GROWTH OF volunteer military units in Gillingham had made it inevitable that the town would be involved in the war from the beginning. In 1907 the volunteer company established by Robert Freame half a century earlier had become a unit of the new Territorial Army, known as the Right Half of E Company, the 4th Battalion the Dorsetshire Regiment. The Gillingham TA was now under the command of his son, Major Bertram Freame. Alongside it were mounted volunteers of the Dorset (Queen's Own) Yeomanry. These companies mustered around 100 men. At the outbreak of war in August 1914 E company were training on their summer camp at Bulford. From here they were sent directly to Devonport to guard the docks. Freame's age and health prevented him from joining his company, but he spent much of the next few months travelling around the area helping with recruiting.[2]

In October the 4th Battalion was sent to India. From 1916 it served in Mesopotamia, and also in Egypt and Palestine. The Dorset Yeomanry were first based on the east coast on defence duties, and for a time used cycles instead of horses. In 1915 they were sent to the Dardanelles where they played a full part in the unsuccessful Gallipoli campaign, suffering heavy casualties. They later served in Egypt, where they performed their famous but costly cavalry charge at Agagia in 1916. Some Yeomanry detachments took part in the Palestine campaign and the capture of Jerusalem. Many other local men served with other regiments, the Royal Navy, and the Royal Flying Corps, and saw service in other theatres, including the Western Front.[3]

In Gillingham itself the most noticeable change was the greater number of uniformed people around, many being billeted at the various farms and houses around the town. The town's main contribution to the war effort was the provision of its two Red Cross hospitals and the participation of many townspeople in the Voluntary Aid Detachment (VAD). The Plank House hospital was set up in the home of the solicitor, Henry Wyld, lent by its owner for the purpose. The hospital opened on 5 November 1914 with twelve patients under the command of Lady Parr, who remained as Commandant until July 1918 when Mrs. James Anstruther of Knapp House took over. By 1916 the number of beds had increased to 24, and an operating theatre was in service. The hospital dealt with tuberculosis cases and also performed major operations and amputations. Some thirty women served as officers and nurses, with men also employed as orderlies. Plank House hospital closed in January 1919. The other hospital was in Station Road, in the former girls' grammar school, later the Masonic Lodge building. This hospital opened in October 1914 with 25 beds, and had 62 beds when it closed in March 1919. Its commandants were Mrs Leatham (1914-17) and Miss S. Leatham (1917-19). A theatre was improvised out of the adjoining building of the National Provincial Bank, with a door between the two premises. 792 patients were treated in total, the busiest years being 1915 (286) and 1918 (283). Over 40 people gave their services here at different times. The Medical Officers to the hospitals were Dr. W.W. Farnfield and Dr. B. Pope-Bartlett.[4]

The patients were moved to these hospitals from the camps and military hospitals at Codford, Sutton Veney, Cosham, Bournemouth, and elsewhere. The movement of sick and injured war personnel, and their care while in transit, was the duty of the Gillingham VAD, one of 1,990 Detachments set up nationwide by the Red Cross (Fig. 96). Its Honorary Commandant was Sir Harold Pelly of Thorngrove, who also sometimes drove the Detachment's one ambulance. In his report of the work of the VAD, he wrote of the difficult journeys made in the winter months by the ambulance crews across the Wiltshire Downs. He drew attention to the problem of finding enough people to be properly trained, which meant that the Detachment was never properly registered. Altogether nearly 170 people gave service to the VAD during these years.[5]

Once the initial impact of being at war had been taken in, townspeople not directly involved in the services began to think of what they could do. In the middle of August 1914 Ethel Freame could write 'We are beginning to lose the dreadful feeling of paralysis which took possession of our minds and hands during the first few days of the month. Now everyone is craving to do something to help.' She forthwith turned her energies into cutting out shirts for soldiers, and was given leave by her Catholic priest to carry on with the work on Sundays. This soon became part of a wider effort by Gillingham people to supply clothing and food parcels for the war effort. In September 1916 Ethel Freame and Grace Christmas wrote to the Three Shires Advertiser about the funds raised from a fete at Pensbury House in Shaftesbury, and of a forthcoming jumble sale to be held in the Drill Hall. 'So far our work has been exclusively for the 1st Battalion of the Dorsets, but this particular sale is for the first and fourth, equally divided … Nothing will be too small to send, nothing too large. We have again heard how much our socks are appreciated at the front,' and the letter ended with a list of the parcels sent during August.[6]

Within the town the war years were mostly uneventful, but one highly unexpected episode took place in the early hours of June 29, 1917. Following a day of exceptionally heavy rain the wall of a retaining dam collapsed on the Stour upstream at Gasper Lake. The deluge which followed overwhelmed the Bourton foundry and then swept on southwards to Gillingham, where the river level around the Wyke Street bridge rose in a matter of minutes to flood all surrounding buildings to a depth of four to five feet. At Plank House

96 A scene repeated on Gillingham Station many times during World War I. Stretcher parties of Red Cross volunteers carry war wounded from the train to the hospitals at Station Road or Plank House.

Hospital the event had the potential to be a disaster, and many of the patients downstairs and in the open-air shelters were saved only through the determination of a small group of hospital staff and other patients. The *Western Gazette* reported that 'It is entirely due to the heroic efforts of Sister Jones, Nurse Brock, Dr. Farnfield, Corporal Williams, and Private Robinson that no lives were lost, and too much praise cannot be accorded to them for their splendid work.' Other premises in the area similarly flooded included the Freame, Light, and Wyld office, the Wiltshire United Dairies premises, and many of the cottages around the low-lying parts of the town.[7]

Many men returned from the war with decorations for gallantry and with mentions in dispatches for bravery, and a collection of medals is to be seen in the Museum. As everywhere else in the west country, this service was at considerable cost to families and communities, since recruitment drew heavily on the labouring poor of rural counties. In Somerset 11,000 men were killed in the war out of a total population of less than 450,000. In Gillingham, war dead can be difficult to calculate exactly because lists of honours often include men only marginally connected with the town. The Roll of Honour in St. Mary's church has 38 names, while the War Service Book in the church has 93 names of war dead. The War Memorial in the town lists 82 names. A Roll of Honour Board at Gillingham School lists 23 names of past pupils, and at Milton on Stour the War Memorial has 11 names. These lists include some people born in the town but who had since moved away from their families; people from nearby villages; men not originating from Gillingham who had perhaps died in the town's wartime hospitals; and some names whose connection with Gillingham is not known. In the cemetery there are a further 14 Commonwealth burials to be found. The Milton memorial includes the names of three men who all died during the same incident.[8]

The losses were from across the social spectrum. They included Herbert Hooper, a journeyman baker from Portland Cottages in Queen Street; Gideon Stone, a farm labourer; and George Edwards, from a High Street family of decorators and painters. James Foote was a maker of wooden boxes for Hudson and Martin, while Frederick William Bracher came from the Bracher cabinet-making family at Newbury, although by now he had left home for the Metropolitan Police. William Down came from the family which managed the Oake, Woods bacon factory, while John Manger was the youngest son of the landowning Manger family of Stock Hill. An interesting entry on the Roll of Honour is that of Lionel Sotheby. He was not of Gillingham but his father's cousin was the town's vicar; Lionel is known for his War Diary, which was published in 1997, a record of his letters and journals from the Western Front.[9]

A little more is known about Bertram Hiscock (born 1889), whose death in Gallipoli was reported in the *Three Shires Advertiser* of the 18 September 1915. He came from a farm labourer's family, and by 1911 he was living in St. Martin's Square with his widowed mother, brother, sister, and niece. Bert was a clerk in the bacon factory and was also known as a member of the Constitutional Club and a worker for the Red Cross. He was recruit no. 758 for the D Squadron of the Yeomanry, becoming a Lance Corporal. A letter survives written by Bert to his brother Edwin from Cairo, where Bert had been stationed three weeks earlier. In it he comments on the quality of Egyptian cigarettes, the heat and the flies, the ready availability of dancing girls, but also the beautiful buildings. He writes 'I have knocked about a bit since I left Gillingham and there is no place like home. I shan't want to leave it again for a time when I get back there'. The issue of the Advertiser reporting his death also included the death of Lionel Churchill, the son of Mark Churchill, the dairy factory manager. Like Bertram Hiscock, most of the war dead shown on the Roll of Honour and War Memorial were men in their early and middle twenties.[10]

The Gillingham War Memorial, with its 82 names, was unveiled by the Earl of Shaftesbury on November 18, 1920. It originally stood by the Town Bridge, but is now to be found inside the neighbouring car park. The Milton memorial was unveiled the following year, and has eleven names from the Great War. While most of the war dead are known now only by an inscription upon these monuments, a handful were fortunate enough to be remembered by individual memorials. At the rear of the church is a plaque to William Down, son of the bacon factory owner, Evan Down. At the front of the church is a far more prominent monument, the finely carved stone reredos behind the altar. This was given in 1925 by George Matthews of Wyke House as a memorial to his two sons. It was carved by the acclaimed sculptor, Nathaniel Hitch, who also did work in Westminster Abbey and in Bristol and Truro Cathedrals. However, the most striking memorial to be added to the church was an extension of the church itself. This was the building of the Good Shepherd Chapel by Carlton and Emily

Cross of Wyke Hall in memory of their son, Reginald, killed in action in France. It was dedicated on 23 January 1922. The architect was W.D. Caroe, who also worked on the east end of the Lady Chapel of Sherborne Abbey. Within the chapel there is a plaque to Reginald, and a further plaque to his mother who died in 1927. At the Grammar School a cricket pavilion was erected in memory of former pupils lost in the war.[11]

Perhaps the most distinctive memorial to Gillingham's war losses was not within the town but a mile outside it at Langham, and had been planned even before the start of the conflict. Alfred Manger (b.1850) had lived at Stock Hill House since 1890 and had long had the idea of building a church for his family and estate workers. He died in 1917 before his plan could be carried out, and it was left to his son, Lt. Col. Charles Harwood Manger, to build the church on his return from the war. In the meantime its purpose had been altered by the conflict (Fig. 97). It now became a memorial chapel to Charles' youngest brother, John, killed at Ypres in 1915, and other members of the Manger family from outside Gillingham killed in the conflict.[12] Manger chose as his architect Charles Ponting, who was well known as an architect of many churches in the Wiltshire area and had redesigned the Gillingham church tower some years earlier. Ponting, normally reputed for his adherence to Gothic style, chose instead to build it as a thatched church in coarse squared rubble, a design reflecting arts and crafts influence rooted in the English vernacular tradition. Its plain, simple interior, taken along with its dedication to St. George, patron saint of soldiers, expresses a deep belief that the sacrifice of lives was for a noble cause, the preservation of the peace and tranquillity of traditional English life. The Langham church, completed in 1921, was built over the graves of Alfred and his wife Elizabeth.[13] It has since been maintained by a trust of the Manger family.

Even while the war was continuing, returning servicemen, many of them injured, began to meet socially as the 'Comrades of the

97 *Langham Chapel was built as a memorial to the members of the*
Manger family lost in the Great War. The architect was Charles Ponting,
and the inspiration for the design was the thatched church of St. Agnes at
Freshwater on the Isle of Wight, built in 1908. Among the Manger family
commemorated is Robert Lancaster, son-in-law of Alfred Manger and the
father of the cartoonist Osbert Lancaster. The young Osbert made several
visits to his grandfather around this time.

Great War', using a hutted hospital building in Station Road. The hut
itself was later replaced by a site in School Lane and was opened in
1920 as the 'Sir Douglas Haig' Club. The founder members were R.
Bracher, Ernest A. Martin, and Dr. Arthur Walker (p.361). At the time
of opening it had 98 members. It remained in use until 1978 when it
became the Gillingham branch of the Royal British Legion and was
rebuilt soon afterwards (Chapter 16).[14]

Business and trade; the depression years

THE PATTERN OF business and trade between the two wars
was not greatly different from Edwardian times. All of the
major businesses established before 1900 were still present

in the town. By the 1920s the dairy factory on Station Road belonged to United Dairies, a large organisation which listed the 'Gillingham Creamery' as one of its 37 dairy factories.[15] Oake, Woods & Co. continued to be a main employer in the town, but during the 1920s passed into the hands of C. & T. Harris of Calne. The former Bell and Freame legal business was now known as Freame, Light, and Wyld until it passed to Farnfield and Nicholls of Mere in 1940. It continued to own the Gillingham Pottery, Brick, and Tile Company. Other businesses also stayed with the same owners or within the same families, often a number of generations on from the founders. In the station yard J.H. Rose was the principal coal merchant for the town and outlying villages, and was also a furniture remover. The Rose business, now concerned with builders' materials, continues from the old station yard to this day. Hudson and Martin bestrode the town's timber and building supplies needs, while Maloney's glue factory was one of several enterprises still being run by their founders.

Most of the new businesses which came along after the First World War were linked in some ways to the rising motor trade. The first motor vehicles had appeared in the town in the early 1900s, and by the next decade they were a more common sight among the better-off townspeople, such as Major Freame and Dr. Farnfield. During the War there were relatively few new registrations, and many of these were commercial vehicles that could be used to contribute to the war effort. In 1919 Charles Maloney, the glue manufacturer, showed the way ahead when he registered for his private use a 30 hp. Cadillac Cabriolet. In 1912 Percival Baker had opened a posting stable on the east side of Station Road, and by 1919 had changed from horses to motor vehicles. He became the owner of a number of Ford Model-T cars. Over the next few years he built up a business based on the delivery of newspapers and mail, car hire, taxis, haulage, petrol sales, and vehicle repairs. For many years he held the contract for all deliveries from the station. The other main motor business was that

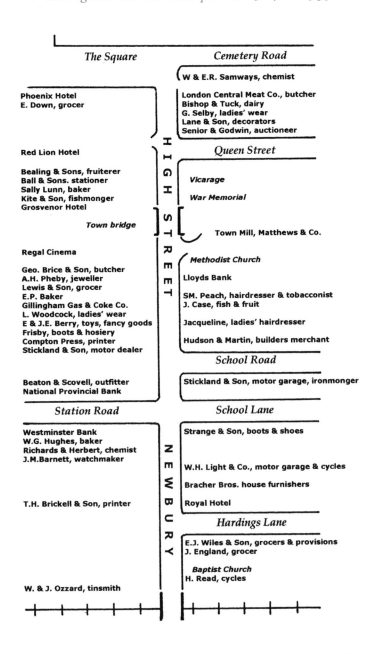

The Square

Cemetery Road

W & E.R. Samways, chemist

Phoenix Hotel
E. Down, grocer

London Central Meat Co., butcher
Bishop & Tuck, dairy
G. Selby, ladies' wear
Lane & Son, decorators
Senior & Godwin, auctioneer

Red Lion Hotel

Queen Street

Bealing & Sons, fruiterer
Ball & Sons. stationer
Sally Lunn, baker
Kite & Son, fishmonger
Grosvenor Hotel

Vicarage

War Memorial

Town bridge

Town Mill, Matthews & Co.

Regal Cinema

Methodist Church

Geo. Brice & Son, butcher
A.H. Pheby, jeweller
Lewis & Son, grocer
E.P. Baker
Gillingham Gas & Coke Co.
L. Woodcock, ladies' wear
E & J.E. Berry, toys, fancy goods
Frisby, boots & hosiery
Compton Press, printer
Stickland & Son, motor dealer

Lloyds Bank

SM. Peach, hairdresser & tobacconist
J. Case, fish & fruit

Jacqueline, ladies' hairdresser

Hudson & Martin, builders merchant

School Road

Beaton & Scovell, outfitter
National Provincial Bank

Stickland & Son, motor garage, ironmonger

Station Road

School Lane

Westminster Bank
W.G. Hughes, baker
Richards & Herbert, chemist
J.M.Barnett, watchmaker

Strange & Son, boots & shoes

W.H. Light & Co., motor garage & cycles

Bracher Bros. house furnishers

T.H. Brickell & Son, printer

Royal Hotel

Hardings Lane

E.J. Wiles & Son, grocers & provisions
J. England, grocer

Baptist Church
H. Read, cycles

W. & J. Ozzard, tinsmith

HIGH STREET

NEWBURY

98 Traders in Newbury and the High Street around 1935. The information comes from the directories of the Gillingham Chamber of Commerce and Industry. Not all of the traders in these streets may be represented here.

of E.R. Stickland, now led by the founder's son, Edwin John Stickland (1880-1952). As early as 1904 he had been an agent for Humber cars, and after the War he took the firm beyond its well-established ironmongery and cycle business further into car dealership and servicing. He secured a franchise as a main Ford dealer in 1921, and other franchises came to include Lucas and Exide. He built a new showroom on the opposite side of the High Street on a site adjoining South Lynn, a building which the firm acquired in 1918. By 1927 he was also a main agent for Morris cars, advertising a vehicle that could be bought for as little as £148 10s. The firm sold tractors, delivered oil and petrol to farms, and maintained charabancs for local outings.[16]

Along Newbury another trader who successfully made the transition from cycles to the motor age was William Herbert Light, who many years earlier had started with cycle repairs in Peacemarsh. By the 1930s his main business was selling motor cycles, and he also sold petrol. Another motor-cycle dealer of the 1920s was Nevill and Haines, at the far end of Queen Street. On Station Road Samuel Braddick, a blacksmith from Milton, opened his agricultural machinery business in 1917, later dealing in Austin lorries and tractors. On Shaftesbury Road Hines Brothers developed a heavy haulage and removals business, first using steam tractors before moving on to motor haulage. They also had quarries and a building materials business in Ringwood, delivering by road throughout Hampshire, Dorset, Wiltshire, and Somerset. Hines were a large employer, carrying out most of the council road contract work of the time. To service the area's growing petroleum needs, oil depots and storage tanks appeared around the station. Shell, BP, and Anglo-American all had depots as early as 1908; the spirit was brought in by rail and until the 1920s distributed by horse and cart. By the 1920s all the oil companies were using motor lorries for distribution, and had built new depots in the field adjoining the brickyard. The site is still in use as an oil supplier's depot.

A different sort of motor enterprise in Gillingham, and one that was short-lived, was the manufacture of a motor car. This was made by the Vitesse Motor Car Company, which around 1933 had premises in Wyke Street, in the building later used by Southcombes gloves and most recently by Farnfield and Nicholls. The company produced a single-seater racing cycle car initially known as the Gush Special, which was raced at Brooklands and broke several records. It also produced a prototype two-seater road car which it intended to market commercially. In 1935 the company collapsed, and its assets were sold to Buddens of East Stour.[17]

In his lively history of Gillingham, Charles Howe describes the personality of a town which had become the workshop of the countryside for many miles around. He estimates that the various main industries provided jobs for around 600 to 700 men, as well as a smaller number of women in departments such as packing and despatch. He illustrates the hard working conditions of the time, compared to what might be expected at the present day. Labourers found little in the way of comforts in the workplace, or any basic shelter from the elements. They would expect to cover their clothes with sacks to keep off the rain, and to wear the same patched hard-wearing trousers for many years. Evenings at home might be spent in the repair of hobnailed boots, or indeed of the footwear of the whole family. He goes on:

> Between six and seven in the morning there were five factory whistles blowing. Those who were late for work were docked half an hour's pay. At midday and evening it was a job to drive down Station Road for the mass of men coming up on foot or on bikes. Many of them walked in from the villages, some as much as ten miles away, and they seldom stayed away because of bad weather or were late.

All building or construction work required large numbers of labourers, every operation being carried out by hand. On building sites all materials such as plaster or paint were prepared as needed from the basic raw materials. Trades such as joinery would be carried out entirely with hand tools, the tradesman supplying his own tools, which he would expect to last a lifetime. Health and safety considerations were largely unknown; scaffolding comprised wooden poles tied together, with the uprights inserted into old milk churns. Long working hours could be expected; in May 1923 two full-time roadmen were hired for the parish, with hours of 7am to 5pm weekdays and 7am to 4pm on Saturdays. The rate of pay offered was 5s 6d per day for each day worked.[18]

Around the town the many shops expected to stay open later in the evening, especially on Saturdays when there were perishable goods to be disposed of cheaply. A lot of retail trade was done by door-to-door deliveries from hand carts, particularly by the town's bakers, butchers, and greengrocers. The liveliest day of the week was market day, when the station yard would be crowded with people selling cheap goods, patent medicines, and other items of dubious value. Howe remembers many of the traders, pedlars, and street characters of this period; one well known personality was

> Joey Frugal (real name Fuoco) an Italian by birth. He used to come down from Shaftesbury where he kept a 'doss house' and took in anyone who had the price of a bed. He travelled around the district playing a small drum organ which he carried on his back. With his monkey on his shoulder and with the few coppers he picked up, he nevertheless owned his own property and when he became old he returned to Italy to end his days.[19]

One area of the town where small shops and businesses had considerable local importance at this time was the Queen Street-Lodbourne area. North of St. Martin's Square many of the buildings which are now dwellings were then local shops. At various times the different premises included a public house (the Queen's Head), chip shops, butcher, motor cycle repairs, car repairs, post office, bakery, hairdressers, menswear, china, tobacconist, and Co-op store. There were further small shops in Bay and Peacemarsh. Despite changes of occupier and business, many survived as retailers into the 1960s.

Outside the town, farmers and farm workers led an often isolated life which had changed little for decades. Joan Green, who was brought up at Forest Side Farm, Huntingford, in the 1920s and 1930s, recalls that the farm was at the end of a no-through road accessible to motor vehicles only by a ford. The family had no electricity or telephone, and lighting was by candles and oil lamps. All milking was by hand, the milk being tipped from pails into ten-gallon churns which were then loaded on to a horse-drawn van and carted across the ford to a platform where they were left for collection. Feed came from Gillingham and Purns mills. Eggs were collected daily for sale at the Station Road market, and pigs were sold to Oake, Woods. The children had a two and a half mile walk to the school in Mere. Eventually a tractor replaced the horse power, making easier tasks such as haymaking or chain harrowing. Winter jobs included ditching and hedge laying.[20] This was a period of low farm profits and wages for farm workers, and any incapacity or failure to work could have serious consequences. Throughout this time the interests of the employers, the farmers, were maintained through the Gillingham Agricultural Society and its annual show. The show was discontinued for the war years but was resumed in 1920. In 1930 the Society joined with the Shaftesbury Farmers' Club to form the Gillingham and Shaftesbury Agricultural Society. It was agreed that the venues would alternate between the two towns and that the first show would be held in Gillingham 'because it had been established longer and had better transport facilities'.[21]

All this commercial activity nevertheless has to be seen within the wider depressed economic conditions of the time. The Gillingham area, with its dependence on dairy-related industries, may have fared less badly than some arable farming areas of southern England where competition from imports kept farm prices down. Nevertheless, much of the local economy was in a stagnant state. Some statistics for traffic passing through Gillingham Station show over the period 1928-36 a 35% fall in passenger tickets issued, a 46% fall in the tonnage of goods forwarded, and a 14% drop in coal movements. However, quantities of milk forwarded went up by 13% and numbers of livestock trucks received doubled. During the early 1930s Oake, Woods bacon factory was running at about 40 per cent of its capacity of 1,250 pigs a week; in 1937 35,573 pigs were killed, and in 1939 this figure was 28,873. Decline in production was attributed to foreign competition. Hudson and Martin's sales figures declined between 1931 and 1933 but rose in most other years between 1922 and 1937.[22]

It was these unpromising commercial conditions which led in 1930 to the formation of a Gillingham Chamber of Trade to promote the business interests of the town. It had its first meeting on 9 July 1930. Evan B. Down of Oake, Woods & Co. was elected President, and an Executive Committee of twelve was formed, all being prominent business people of the town. Its early meetings looked at a wide range of issues affecting commerce in Gillingham; these included shop opening hours, the nuisance of itinerant stallholders on market day, the unsightly appearance of poles for the new electricity supply, and the need for more working-class housing in the town. Its main interests soon came to focus on two means of promoting the town's commerce. One of these was to have an exhibition tent and trade stands at the Agricultural Show. This first appeared at the August 1930 Show. The other was the introduction of a Shopping Week, first planned for the summer of 1931 but then moved to early December. The events and activities came to include extended opening hours, a window dressing competition, the Town Band, whist drive and dance, and a production of the Operatic Society. Some of the factories

Albert Chubb (1865-1954) was born at Motcombe and worked first in Shaftesbury, where he learned his trade as a coachbuilder. He moved to Gillingham in 1888, opening his first business in Station Road, later moving to the High Street. He was a well-known public figure in the town, serving for many years as a Justice of the Peace, member of Shaftesbury Rural District Council and Gillingham Parish Council, and a Grammar School governor. At one time he served on no fewer than 36 public bodies. He was a Trustee of the Wesleyan Methodist Church and a member of the Gillingham Masonic Lodge. During World War One he served as coal and meat controller for the Gillingham area, and after the war he was actively involved in promoting the welfare of disabled soldiers.

99 Albert Chubb, seen here on a seaside trip to Weymouth.

Dr Arthur Walker (1879-1939) was in general medical practice with Thomas Hanly at South Lynn by 1911, later moving to Harwood House. He joined the Territorial Army as a Medical Officer and saw active service in France, being awarded the D.S.O. On receiving his decoration from George V the town laid on a full reception for him. After the war he was a founder member of the Sir Douglas Haig Club, to become the branch of the Royal British Legion, and did much work to enable ex-servicemen to acquire disability pensions.

opened their premises for public visits. Hudson and Martin laid on conducted tours of the sawmill, apologising in advance for the mud in the yard and requesting that visitors should 'ask all questions of your guide and do not speak to the actual workmen.' A handbook was produced for the event, advertising the members of the Chamber and promoting the events of the week.[23]

Despite the low commercial conditions of the time, examples of enterprise could still be found. Mrs. Louisa Woodcock borrowed £500 from William Slade, the owner of the stores in the Square, to open a new grocery store in Wyke. A condition of the loan was that during the time of the repayments, she should buy all her goods and supplies from Slades. Within a few years she had not merely repaid the loan, but had made the shop prosper to the extent that she was able to sell it and open two new shops in Gillingham, selling ladies' and gents' clothing respectively.[24]

Gillingham's train services retained much of their pre-war pattern, although the timings had changed since 1914. There were ten up trains each weekday, mostly stopping services to Salisbury. The fastest London journey of the day in 1927 was the 9.07 am departure, which reached London at 11.14, but for most other departures journey times to London were three to three and a half hours, mostly involving a change at Salisbury. The station and goods facilities remained much as in pre-war times, with the Southern Railway agreeing in 1924 to provide an additional siding and alterations to the milk dock. An ongoing issue was passenger access across the line to a pathway through the brickyard towards New Road and Madjeston. The station staff would act to stop people from crossing the line, claiming that the right of way had been extinguished in 1874. Representations were made from the RDC in 1918 and 1924, but to no effect; in 1937 a further complaint was made by the Parish Council, but the position of the railway company continued to remain the same.[25]

In 1931 United Dairies modernised its milk depot at Semley to allow milk to be loaded in bulk directly into rail tanker wagons. This meant that from now on much less milk was being handled at Gillingham, and milk trains eventually ceased to call at the town. The milk factory itself went into decline and by the start of the Second World War was largely empty. It was a sign of the industrial changes that would affect the town more profoundly in the years ahead.

Housing, living conditions, and local government

I N   H I S   B O O K   *All Done from Memory* the cartoonist, Osbert Lancaster, then a young boy, recalls the visits he made to stay with his maternal grandfather, Alfred Manger, at Stock Hill House in the closing years of the war. At Stock Hill he found an upper class household firmly rooted in the routines and ceremonies of Victorian days, but one where daily ritual could be readily discarded in the interests of spontaneous leisure. He found himself free to spend the days playing around the gardens and woods, or around the stables with the groom, 'a splendid, primeval rustic figure who had never been further than Shaftesbury in his life.' Much of the time the household revolved around the unpredictable personal needs of the grandfather. Lancaster depicts Manger as a recently accepted member of the county gentry, something he had achieved 'thanks to an engaging presence, thirty years residence, and a stable full of hunters.' Manger, a county Justice of the Peace, was nevertheless acutely aware of his place in the local class system – well above the tradesmen and labourers of the town, but not to be placed on the same level as the 'local baronet'. These class differences were to be placed under considerable pressures in the years to come.[26]

The visiting young Lancaster was always picked up at Gillingham station by the chauffeur, and apart from noticing the smells of the town and the dreary brick station yard, saw nothing of the housing and living conditions of its labouring population.[27] At the end of the war many labouring people still lived in cottages which were up to two centuries old, especially around Ham, Wavering Lane, and Peacemarsh. While the main streets of the town had benefited from new mains water, sewers, and gas, these utilities had not yet reached the more outlying neighbourhoods. Around 1918 the Shaftesbury Rural District Council (RDC) had to deal with a number of instances of overcrowding and poor living conditions. A cottage inspected at Peacemarsh in 1918 had three male and two female adults, and a child living in two living rooms and two bedrooms; comments were made on its general state of dilapidation and unsatisfactory ventilation. Other nearby cottages at Crown Yard were described as being in a similar state, many dwellings depending on unsatisfactory pail closets. At Dolphin Lane two living and two bedrooms were shared by one man, five women, and two children. Another Peacemarsh cottage inspected in 1920 had no through ventilation, no sink drains, and shared with another cottage a privy closet with no pit.[28]

Some of the houses built around the start of the century were little better. At Ham the drains from four recently built cottages discharged to an open ditch, while the Elm View houses on Bay Road and Octave Villas on Queen Street still had no mains water supply. The primitive sanitary conditions were also found in some of the town's workplaces, such as the Rotary Engineering works on Station Road, where 36 employees shared two pail closets; and the same company's New Road premises, where nine employees had no facility. Similar conditions existed at the Dairy Factory by the station. At these industrial premises new water closets were ordered to be fitted, but it took some time before these requirements were complied with.

During the early 1920s mains water and sewerage gradually reached the more outlying neighbourhoods. In August 1918 plans for a new sewer on Bay Road from Lodbourne to Bay Bridge were reported as completed (Fig. 100). In 1922 the RDC was borrowing money from the Ministry of Health for the 'Gillingham Water Extension' supply scheme; in January 1923 it accepted a tender for a water pipleine from Wyke Corner to Quarr, with a service tank at Langham Hill. In 1925 payments were made in respect of the provision of a public sewer to Ham and King's Court, and in January 1927 a tender was accepted to extend this further along the Shaftesbury Road. By this time tendering had long ceased to be an affair for purely local firms, and for this project tenders had been received from firms as far distant as Parkstone, Weymouth, and Bristol. In September of 1927 the Ham sewer extension was reported as completed. By this date there are fewer references in the Council minutes to insanitary conditions, suggesting that progress was being made with these problems. In 1931 the Gillingham Gas and Coke Company was supplying 655 consumers through six miles of gas main, and opened a new showroom in the High Street to retail gas appliances. In 1923 the RDC was approached with a proposal for a private electricity scheme for Gillingham, but it was decided not to pursue it at this

100 Public utilities were slow to spread to outlying parts of the town. The new mains sewer from Lodbourne to Bay Bridge was completed in 1918. At that time this block of terraced houses, newly built a few years earlier, looked across open countryside.

time but to include it later in a wider scheme for the entire Rural District. The first electricity reached Gillingham in 1928. In 1933 the Lighting Area (by gas) was extended to include Wavering Lane as far as Slaughtergate, Bay Lane to Allotment Gate, and the further parts of Common Mead Lane, together with other parts of the town, bringing street lighting to 117 new homes.[29]

Regular refuse collection was not established until this time. Although the Parish Council had agreed to have dustcart collection in 1910, this was not yet happening, and in 1922 the Parish Council asked the RDC to provide a dustcart and collection scheme. In November 1922 this was tendered for, and the tender of John Wiles was accepted. Several roads and streets remained in a poor state. In 1919 the residents of Victoria Road asked the RDC to adopt and make up their road, which consisted of broken rubble with no footways, kerbs, or drainage. After some discussion by the Council, it was decided to take no further action. St. Martin's Square seems to have been at a lower level than Queen Street, and work was authorised in 1920 to raise it up. In 1924 work on widening Common Mead Lane was completed, and in January 1925 tenders were received for major works on the Shaftesbury road. In 1926 several roads were given a tar covering in response to the many complaints about dust caused by the loose macadamised surfaces.

The need to provide rented housing for labouring people had been recognised by the Parish Council some years earlier, but the RDC had been unable to respond to the problem (Chapter 12). This now became obligatory through the 1919 Housing Act and the 1924 Housing (Financial Provisions) Act, in which the government provided subsidies to local authorities to house working-class people. This was part of a wider government programme to deal with the mounting social concerns of the time and provide the 'homes fit for heroes' which had been promised during the war. The RDC minutes of April to July 1919 refer to the Council's plans for 40 such new houses in Gillingham. Under the scheme, approval had to be sought from the Ministry of Health for each new dwelling to be built. The first houses to be built were almost certainly the 20 dwellings of Addison Terrace on New Road, built before 1921 and named after Viscount Addison, the Minister of Health behind the 1919 Act (Fig. 101). In September 1924 the RDC considered that it needed 150 new houses over the next 15 years, and recommended the building of 28 at once,

101 The Sturminster Newton road, formerly called Oldlands Lane, but later known as New Road. On the right the six red brick houses in three pairs are Pottery Villas, built by the Gillingham Pottery, Brick, and Tile Company for their employees in 1912. On the left, Addison Terrace, dating from 1921, was Gillingham's first council houses.

of which 20 should be in Gillingham. In October 1928 contracts were agreed for the erection of 12 houses in Wavering Lane (Waverland Terrace), completed in April 1930. At Peacemarsh the 20 houses of Lodbourne Terrace were being built at around this time. After 1930 attention turned to Shaftesbury Road, where an initial eight were built, followed by a further 26 which make up Lockwood Terrace.[30]

All these houses were built to a similar style, mostly in blocks of four. Long gardens extended front and behind, since working people expected to grow much of their own food. Rents varied depending on house size, but were around seven shillings a week. Firms and private owners could also apply under the scheme for employees' housing; in 1925 the Matthews' brewery applied for subsidies for two cottages, and in 1927 the Mere Co-operative Society also applied for two subsidies. A later local authority development was at Orchard Road, where sixteen semi-detached properties were completed in 1936.

In 1936 plans started to take shape for a new development at Lodbourne Farm in Peacemarsh. This was to be a scheme of forty houses on land east of the farm, stretching northwards from Bay Road. The initial design was more ambitious than the 1920s schemes, envisaging a 'village' layout with houses facing each other across a curving green (Fig. 102). The architect was W.J. Morrish of Wyke. By 1937 the plans had been considerably revised to allow for 60 houses. The road now shifted round westwards behind Lodbourne Terrace to join the Mere road, giving space for even more housing, and producing the now familiar form of Fairey Crescent. By 1939 the project had reached a further stage, the alignments having become regular in shape to include a close and an infant Bourne Way. The plans indicated no fewer than seven different types of house to be built, varying in size from one-bedroom bungalows to five bedroom family houses (Plate 23). The sketch elevations, with their hipped roofs, casement windows, and dormer bedrooms, suggest an indebtedness to the 'garden city' ideas of the period. As with the 1920s houses, the long gardens were expected to provide for much of the family's food needs. The substantial room proportions and inclusion of indoor WCs, bathrooms, and fuel stores, were well beyond what most working-class families of the time might have anticipated. The coming of war put an end to all these expectations, and when the houses were finally built, it was to a plainer and less varied style (Chapter 15).[31]

Other than the local authority housing, there appears to have been little new private building during these years, in contrast to the

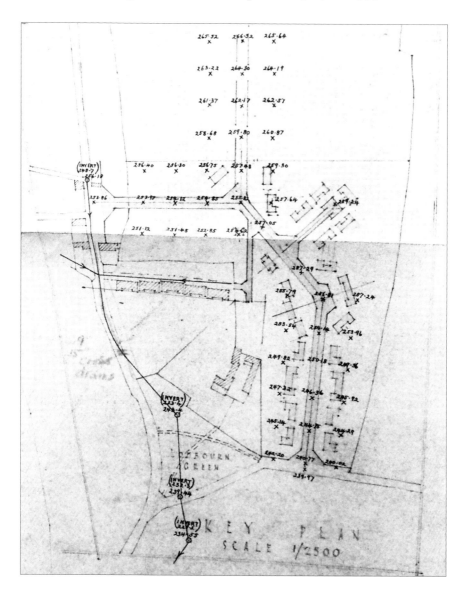

102 The 1939 key plan for the Lodbourne Farm housing scheme. Sixty
dwellings are shown here, with the planned roads providing spaces for
many more. One of the several house types envisaged is shown in Plate 14.

generation before the war. A number of new villas appeared along
Wyke Road, extending the built-up area of the town towards the

brewery village, and 'Wyke' was a popular address for many of the private residents listed in the Kelly directories.

In 1930 the County Council met to consider the implications of the Local Government Act of 1929, which allowed authorities to adjust district boundaries in order to create new county districts which could deliver services more efficiently. Gillingham Parish Council took the opportunity to press for the town to be designated an urban authority, something which it had first aspired to at the end of the previous century (Chapter 12). The County Council agreed that 'the Gillingham Parish Council be informed that the County Council view with favour the creation of a suitable area of the Parish into an Urban District' and asked for views from both the Parish Council and RDC. The County Council recognised that Gillingham had a large area of agricultural land, but the town proper was developing and was quite urban in character; key considerations were population size and financial strength. The Gillingham Chamber of Commerce and Industry discussed the matter in November 1930, with members supporting the view that 'they all felt they could manage their little town better than other people could do it for them.' The Shaftesbury RDC discussed the issue in March 1931 but came to the conclusion that:

> it is not in the interests of the Rural District that Gillingham should be taken away from the Rural District, as although this may give Gillingham greater financial strength, it cannot help but tend to impoverish the portion of the District then remaining, which might in all probability have insufficient resources to provide all the necessary sanitary and other services without special assistance.

A committee of the Parish Council had concluded that the future lay in keeping the whole of the parish together within the same authority, since the outlying parts would be using the same utilities and amenities as the town, such as the cemeteries and fire service, and 'would be more likely to get consideration from a local body on which they had representation.' The RDC for its part produced a map showing a boundary for a possible Urban District, which took in a much smaller area – the outer points here were Madjeston, Eccliffe, Wyke Hall, Milton, Pierston, Spicketts Farm, Purns Mill, Colesbrook, Malthouse Farm, King's Court, Park Farm, and Cole Street. In April 1931 the Chamber of Commerce wrote to the County Council urging it to accede to the formation of an urban authority. From this point the idea seems to have been taken no further; later references to the District Review in the County Council minutes make no mention of the Gillingham proposal.[32]

Community, schools, and leisure

WHILE LOCAL GOVERNMENT was endeavouring to reshape the town in different ways, community life tended to follow the patterns established in pre-war days. St. Mary's church remained the focal point for the town's Anglican community, its appearance enhanced by the building of the Good Shepherd chapel. In 1914 the Rev. Walter Sotheby had a new clock installed, the intention being to have two faces illuminated by gaslight. However, the Parish Council declined to pay for the gas, and so only one face was installed, with no illumination. Between 1916 and 1925 the vicar was Robert Abbott, who went on to be the first Bishop of Sherborne, the only vicar of Gillingham to become a bishop (Plate 25). By now the congregation was declining in size, and in 1918 the opportunity was taken to remove the galleries which had been a principal feature of Henry Deane's new church of 1839. The vicarage became a clergy house in which the vicar and his curates lived together and administered the parish as a single unit. In 1932 changes came to the town's two Methodist churches, when the different strands of Methodism in Britain merged to form a single united Methodist Church. The Queen Street and High Street congregations clung on to their separateness for many years, the smaller Queen Street group not giving up their church until 1963.

In the 1920s Bertram and Ethel Freame took steps to advance the Catholic cause to which they were so dedicated. In 1924 they built a new house on their land higher up Common Mead Lane, which they called Higherfield, using stone from the old silk mill annex. They then gave the Chantry house and farm to the Carmelite order, for use as a convent. In March 1925 the convent was visited by Cardinal Bourne, Archbishop of Westminster, to complete its enclosure. The nuns subsequently made notable alterations, including building a church. The sisters later applied to use the site as a burial ground, but this was refused by the Shaftesbury Council. The community remained until 1945, when they left Gillingham. Bertram Freame's other donation was to the town's Catholic population, which at that time was around twenty families. This was a gift of two houses on Cemetery Road for use as a Catholic church. It was dedicated to St. Benedict and opened around 1923, but in 1929 tragedy struck and the new church was badly damaged by fire. A new church was built by Freame on the site soon afterwards, and was subsequently enlarged in 1952 after a legacy from Ethel Freame, and again in 1976.[33]

The Fire Brigade continued to operate as a volunteer brigade under the control of the Parish Council. A Thorneycroft motor tender was purchased in 1926, and Dennis motor pump in 1930, considerably updating the brigade's equipment. Much of the funding needed for these purchases was raised from social events. Other community services which depended on volunteers were the Nursing Association and Ambulance League; by 1931 the League had acquired a new Morris ambulance which it kept in a garage next to the Fire Station.[34]

Rev. Canon Robert Abbott and Vera Brittain

Robert Crowther Abbott (1869-1927) was appointed Principal of Salisbury Theological College in 1907. After incumbencies in Cambridge and Weymouth he became Vicar of Gillingham in 1916, and inaugural Bishop of Sherborne in 1925. During his time at Gillingham the vicarage became a 'clergy house' where the vicar and his curates lived together. A window in St. Mary's church recalls Canon Abbott's time as teacher and bishop (Plate 25).

A visitor to the clergy house in 1923 was Vera Brittain, author of 'Testament of Youth', who came to give some lectures to the Gillingham clergy. She recalled her visits as follows:

'For four weeks in succession I was entertained to luncheon by the Clergy House at Gillingham, where half a dozen raw, cheerful young curates consumed enormous platefuls of cold beef and boiled potatoes. The cleric then presiding over this animated table was the Rev. R.C. Abbott, a courteous and intelligent man with a strong sense of humour, who afterwards became, for two years, Bishop of Sherborne. Although a scholar of Trinity and the Seventh Wrangler of his year, he was accustomed to keeping his youthful curates in a good humour by regaling them with ludicrous parish anecdotes or simple schoolboy 'howlers' of a Scriptural variety'.

(From Vera Brittain, *Testament of Youth*, Gollancz,1933.)

By the 1930s the Southern National Bus Company was providing some services to neighbouring places. Service no.16 provided four buses on weekdays to Shaftesbury, Mere, and Wincanton, with two on Sundays. Service no. 73 gave a bus to Sturminster Newton on Monday (market day) and Wednesday, two on Thursday and Sunday, and three on Saturday, but none on Friday; additional buses served Mere. Another service (no.52) brought people into Gillingham from Wincanton and Buckhorn West on alternate Mondays for the market. The pattern of services was clearly intended to fit in with local needs.[35]

The Grammar School came increasingly under the control of the County Council, and in 1926 the Governors agreed to accept all their grants from the County, who in return became responsible for paying the salaries of the staff. In 1930 Mr. Hill Mumford retired as Headmaster and was succeeded by Martin Perks, who held the post until the end of 1956. Under Mr. Perks' leadership the school expanded in numbers from one hundred to three hundred and the staff from five to eighteen. Soon after his arrival boarding accommodation was withdrawn and in 1936-7 the school was substantially rebuilt and expanded. Academic standards were raised through the establishment of a Sixth Form and developments in Science teaching.[36]

A very different educational development was soon to arrive on the doorstep of the Grammar School in the form of the County or Modern School. This was intended to provide for pupils between the ages of 11 and 14 who were not able to attend the Grammar School. While Secondary Modern Schools are usually associated with the 1944 Education Act, some authorities had already started to establish them before 1939. In Dorset (outside the Poole area) 22 Secondary schools were planned, of which four were ready by 1939, Gillingham being one of these. The school was built on land directly adjoining the Grammar School, but the two schools always functioned as separate entities. The original frontage is still to be seen, now part of the present Gillingham School. In September of 1939 the new school was hastily occupied by pupils from the Primary School to prevent its use for billeting. It eventually opened as a Secondary School in 1942 with Robert Lock as headmaster, and in 1946 had 142 pupils. Reorganisation also affected the younger levels of education, the boys' and girls' Board Schools merging in 1923 to form a new Elementary School. On September 3 the first page of the new school log book, headed 'Gillingham Council Mixed School' proclaimed 'This school, consisting of the boys' and girls' departments, amalgamated to form one mixed department, was opened on this date.' The adjoining

Infants' School remained separate. Wyke School had several changes. In the 1930s it was used for all age 7-11 pupils in the town; in 1942 most of the pupils moved into the town school, and by the end of the war it had only 14 pupils, all infants. The school closed in 1945.[37]

In 1920 the building on Station Road which was formerly the school of Miss Dunn and the Red Cross Hospital, was acquired by the Gillingham Masonic Lodge, who now vacated their existing rooms at the Phoenix. The Station Road building has continued to be used as a Lodge to the present day.

A new departure in social life and entertainment came with the establishment of the Gillingham Amateur Operatic Society in 1921

103 The Operatic Society production of The Chocolate Soldier in 1934. This was the first of the Society's productions to be staged at the newly opened Regal Cinema.

(Fig. 103). The driving force behind this was the Rev. Canon Robert Abbott, who was its first President. The performances were staged in the Market Hall. The Musical Director was Charles Maloney, the owner of the glue factory, who could use the opportunity to show the town that his talents extended beyond the manufacturing world. The company concentrated entirely on light opera, beginning with *HMS Pinafore* in 1921. In 1934 the company moved its productions to the newly opened Regal Cinema. In the same year a breakaway group calling itself the Gillingham and District Light Opera Company staged an alternative production in the old Market Hall venue, but this group subsequently came to nothing. In 1938 the parent company also collapsed as a consequence of falling audiences, cinema competition, and rising costs, particularly entertainment taxes.

Meanwhile the cinema was becoming increasingly popular. In 1911 the Electric Palace in the Market Hall had moved to the Coronation Hall in Buckingham Road, where it was still known as The Palace. It was here that the 'talkies' were first seen and heard, the new medium proving so popular that a coach was soon running each evening from Wincanton, Bourton, Zeals, and Mere. An advertisement for a week in 1931 read:

> Sat. Dec. 5. Evelyn Brent and Robert Ames in *Madonna of the Streets*
> Mon to Wed. Dec. 7 to 9. Lillian Gish, Conrad Nagel, Rod La Roque, Marie Dressler in *One Romantic Night*
> Thurs to Sat. Dec. 10 to 12. Reginald Denny and Lillian Roth in *Madam Satan.*

The programmes were no doubt seen as a useful extra attraction to the town's Shopping Week of the same dates. By this time the cinema was in the hands of Mr. R.W.M. Robinson. In 1933 he had a brand new cinema built in the High Street by the Town Bridge, and when he moved to the new premises he changed its name to the Regal. This was a building in a modern style, and by all accounts was well fitted out and luxurious, with a stage and dressing facilities for dramatic and operatic productions. It is said that the floor material had to be carefully chosen to cope with the debris of the boots of the bacon factory workers who were regular patrons.[38]

One amenity severely lacking in the town until this time was a public open space or recreation ground. In many other towns public gardens, parks, and recreation fields had arrived through the generosity of a benefactor, but Gillingham had not been so fortunate. This was eventually remedied through the purchase of a piece of ground from Lodden Farm, between the railway and Hardings Lane. Its opening took place on 5 July 1926, the ceremony being performed by Lady Pelly. It was attended by the fire brigades of Mere, Wincanton, and Gillingham, and music was provided by the Bourton Prize Band; presentations were made of long service medals to members of the Gillingham Fire Brigade. The field was later to become the site for the new swimming pool and Gillingham Leisure Centre. The Football Club had two teams and played in two leagues, and used the Show Field in Hardings Lane. The Bowling Club, with its hedged green off School Road, was considered a beauty spot of the town. There were two troops of Boy Scouts from St. Mary's church, one of which consisted entirely of church choristers. The company of Girl Guides was described as 'doing useful work in the moulding of character in keeping with its [the association's] tenets.' The Gillingham Imperial Silver Prize Band was a popular addition to many civic and social occasions.[39]

Gillingham on the eve of the Second World War was in many ways a town little changed since the beginning of the earlier conflict a generation previously. It still had the same employers and workplaces, the same noises and smells, and the same unmade roads. Apart from the addition of some council houses, all of the town would have been instantly recognisable to anyone who had left in 1914. But the town of 1914 had been able to look back on a period of growth which had seen many people become better-off in real terms; this boom time was now long past, investment in the town over the last two decades had been negligible, and the population was in decline. The slow spread of modern utilities to the outlying neighbourhoods was more characteristic of a rural place than an urban one, and many people felt frustrated by the town's failure to achieve urban status and control over its own affairs. The coming of war meant that several more years had to pass before these issues were again addressed.

Gillingham's photographers

Many of the street photographs of Gillingham were taken by the town's own photographers. **Charles Johnson** had a photographic business at the end of the nineteenth century, but little of his work has survived and very few pictures can be definitely accredited to him. **William Edgar Samways**, the proprietor of the pharmacy in the Square until the late 1930s, took many pictures to sell as postcards. His work included parts of the town away from the High Street, such as New Road, Lodden, and Peacemarsh, and can sometimes be identified from the backward sloping captions on the negatives. **Ernest Berry**, who had a newsagent's shop in the High Street in the 1930s and 1940s, was a prolific photographer of High Street scenes (Fig. 104). When his stock ran low he would go into the street with his camera and capture yet another image.

104 A view of the High Street photographed by Ernest Berry in the early 1920s. The pedestrians are walking past South Lynn towards Stickland's new car showroom, opened in 1920.

15

GILLINGHAM IN WAR AND
PEACE, 1939 TO 1974

The Second World War

B ETWEEN THE WARS the Territorial Army had remained popular in the town. They were now the 7th and 8th platoons of the 4th Battalion of the Dorset Regiment. A new Drill Hall had been built on Cemetery Road, with a house for the Drill Instructor; the old hall was eventually sold to the gas company. In 1927 the commanding officer was Capt. G.B. Matthews, and in 1935 it was Lieut. E.R. Found. The company met twice weekly at the Drill Hall and also for rifle practice at the Bleet, Eccliffe, range on Sunday mornings. At the start of the war the company was training at Verne Barracks, Portland. It was moved to Bourton to do duties which included guarding the railway tunnel. In March 1940 the Company moved to Berkhamsted and Hertford, and subsequently to Dover Castle, Sandwich, Herne Bay, and Bexhill.[1]

The Second World War made a more immediate and deeper impact on Gillingham than the earlier conflict. From the start the army took over empty and not-so-empty buildings including the butter factory, the dairy depot, the bacon factory, Thorngrove, Wyke Hall,

Purns Mill, Woodwater Farm, Milton Lodge, the Grammar School, and the Chantry. Martin Perks, the Grammar School headteacher, became the Billetting Officer for the town, and troops were billeted in these buildings and in many houses around and outside the town, making the military presence widespread. Hine Brothers became the government's local wartime transport organisation. The Eden Shute butter factory was used as the Air Raid Warden's Headquarters. From September 1939 evacuees arrived, and were first taken to the Grammar School from where they were distributed to their new homes. The Methodist Church Schoolroom was used as the school for evacuee children. Motcombe House was used as a prisoner of war camp for Italians.[2]

One evacuee, Mrs. Theresa Suter, recalls clearly her move to Gillingham during the war. At the age of three she travelled to Gillingham with her mother, carrying a black gas mask in a cardboard box. The family had already been divided, with other members having been evacuated to Devon. Daughter and mother were first billeted in Victoria Road, the mother finding work as a chambermaid at the Phoenix Hotel. Theresa first went to school with other evacuee children at the School Road primary school, but was later moved to school at Wyke. In 1940 the family were reunited and rehoused in Dolphin Lane. When the mother obtained new work at the Malthouse, the family moved again into a cottage nearby. By now some evacuees had returned home, but the family was one of many which remained in Gillingham. Theresa recalls wartime charabanc outings to Weymouth, films at the Regal Cinema, and dances at the Market Hall, which were popular with the many servicemen billeted nearby.[3]

A unit of the Local Defence Volunteers was formed, soon turning into the Home Guard (Fig. 105). It was part of a group of units co-ordinated from Sturminster Newton, and characteristically comprised three groups: young men awaiting call-up, middle aged

105 Gillingham's Home Guard, perhaps in 1944. Almost all of the people shown in this picture are identifiable.

and older men, and those in reserved occupations. All had normal daytime jobs, including farm work and brickyard work. When rifles became available, the unit used the TA ranges at Bleet for shooting exercises. The most important local site for guard duties was the petrol depot at Brickyard Lane, now Tincknell's depot. A pillbox was built here. A half-ton lorry was provided by Sticklands; this was to be used for all movements in event of invasion. An Auxiliary Fire Service was formed and a group of the Air Training Corps was set up at the Grammar School. An Observer Corps post was set up on the school field by Hardings Lane to watch for enemy plane movements; this became especially important at the time of the Bath blitz, when the red glow over the city could be seen from Gillingham. It remained in position throughout the war. The Home Guard was stood down in November 1944.[4]

Gillingham's direct experience of enemy action came from the air. In the area around Mere, Gillingham, and Wincanton, there were some twenty recorded air crashes, mostly flying accidents or collisions, but some resulting from hostilities. The opening of Zeals airfield in 1942 meant that the local airspace was kept busy. On 4th July 1940 a Heinkel bomber came down at Forest Side Farm. This plane had been on its way home from an attack on Bristol docks or the aircraft factory at Filton, when it was intercepted over Weston Super Mare. Three German airmen were killed and were buried in Gillingham cemetery, before being removed to the German war cemetery at Cannock Chase in 1962. In late 1940 bombs were dropped in a field at Milton, probably by returning bombers endeavouring to jettison their load; some residents believe an unexploded bomb still lies there. Another bomb damaged property behind the Red Lion in the town. In September 1942 a pair of Seafires, a naval version of the Spitfire, crashed at Sandley.[5]

In December 1940 three general hospital units were set up in Gillingham, before being posted to Africa in 1941. Doctors and medical officers were billeted in the Lodbourne area, and nurses at Wyke Hall. Later in the war, in preparation for D-day, the US 7th Cavalry were encamped under canvas in Langham Lane. At the end of the war piles of US ammunition could still be seen in fields between Gillingham and Wincanton. The 4th Dorsets took part in the Arromanches landings in Normandy, and were subsequently involved in a

106 Private Cliff Lloyd was a member of the 4th Battalion TA Dorset Regiment when he was called up in 1939 from his employment at the International Stores. He spent much of the earlier part of the war in coastal areas of Britain but later took part in the D-day landings and the Normandy campaign. He subsequently took part in the later, withdrawal stages of Operation Market Garden, the battle for the bridge at Arnhem.

ferocious battle for Hill 112 at Caen. An account of this action has been given by a Gillingham participant, Cliff Lloyd (Fig. 106). The War Memorial of 1949 on Castle Hill at Mere is a replica of that erected on the hill itself to commemorate the action. The former Grammar School headmaster, John Webster, has also described his recollections of the Normandy campaign, including the liberation of the town of Le Neubourg, with which Gillingham was eventually twinned. Cliff Lloyd took part in further action in 1944 when the 4th Dorsets were involved in the withdrawal stages of the unsuccessful Operation Market Garden, the assault on the bridge at Arnhem.[6]

The war inevitably brought additions to the war memorials at Gillingham and Milton. At Gillingham there are eighteen names, of which twelve are also recorded on the Roll of Honour in St. Mary's church. There is just one entry on the Milton memorial. Two Commonwealth burials are to be found in the Gillingham cemetery. Those who died from the Gillingham congregation are remembered by the installation of lighting in the Good Shepherd chapel of St. Mary's church, itself a memorial of the earlier war. A small wooden plaque reads:

> To the glory of God and in proud and grateful remembrance of the men of this congregation who fell in the war 1939-45, lighting was installed as an aid to worship in this chapel.[7]

The early post-war years, 1945 to 1959

GILLINGHAM'S YOUNG PEOPLE of the 1950s, born during the 'baby boom' years straight after the war, grew up knowing a town which in many respects had changed little since their parents were children. The Gillingham of the early decades of the century remained almost entirely intact into these years, apart from the addition of a few rows of council houses, and a new secondary school. Some of the occupiers of shops and businesses had changed, but the shopper could still expect to find much the same mix of shopping and the school-leaver the same choice of jobs. Leaving the town meant travelling on trains which ran to much the same schedules as half a century earlier. A major difference from an earlier generation was the far larger number of motor vehicles in the streets, which were now causing congestion and parking problems. By the 1950s, modern utilities such as mains sewerage, water, and street lighting, had at last reached all parts of the town, but gas and mains sewerage remained absent from Milton and the rural parts of the parish. A new clinic in Queen Street provided for all basic health needs.

One of the effects of the Second World War had been to halt projected public works or developments of every kind, leaving places in a time frame of 1939, modified only by the lesser or greater effects of war damage. Having been fortunate enough to escape the direct effects of enemy action, Gillingham entered the late 1940s with a backlog of building and property repairs, housing shortages, and overstretched ageing utilities. The war years and immediately afterwards were a time when licences from the local authority had to be sought to carry out repairs of the most minor sort, and it was to be some time before the appearance of the town notably changed.

A priority for the Shaftesbury Rural District Council was the completion of housing schemes which had been planned before the war but postponed. By June 1945 new plans and layouts for Lodbourne Farm had been prepared, and the work was completed during 1946 and early 1947. The layout was similar to 1939 with modifications, but the range of housing plans envisaged a decade earlier was discarded in favour of just two semi-detached house types. Some 60 new dwellings were completed, forming Fairey Crescent and adjoining closes. By 1951 another scheme was getting under way across Peacemarsh on land belonging to Great House Farm. This development took place on one large field which had remained unchanged in size and shape since medieval times; on it were built new roads named Coronation Road, Abbotts Way, and Deweys Way (Fig. 107). By February 1953 74 dwellings had been completed. These were mostly three-bedroomed houses, but there was also a number of two-bedroom properties and bungalows. Despite these additions to the housing stock, there were still 120 entries on the Gillingham housing waiting list at this time. These included a number of families still living in properties requisitioned during the war, notably at The Chantry, where thirteen families were accommodated. It was considered that the demands should be met by moving tenants from older pre-war houses into the new houses, thus freeing up the older properties for the Chantry tenants. The housing list also included a number of families living in agricultural tied cottages, who were given special consideration on the waiting lists. Figures for the Rural District as a whole show that in

107 New houses in the appropriately named Coronation Road, built in 1953 as part of the Great Farm development.

1951-2 there had been 56 lettings of new properties, in 1952-3 38, and in 1953-4 73 new lettings. The majority of these were in Gillingham. A rent card for a house in New Road shows a weekly payment of 18s 6d, made up of 10s rent and the remainder for rates and water rates.[8]

To cope with the demands of more houses, a new water main was laid from Common Mead Lane through Eccliffe and Bugley to Bowden Reservoir, together with a new pumping station. It now became possible to pump water from the Gillingham waterworks at Mere to Bowden, where it could serve the rural area round about, and also be pumped from Bowden to Gillingham should the need arise. The new main also served Eccliffe and Bugley, the only remaining areas of Gillingham still not connected to the council mains. A comprehensive sewerage review of the town was undertaken to take account of the needs of the Great House development and adjacent areas, and to remedy the continuing pollution of the River Stour from sewage and factory effluents.[9] In 1949, following the nationalisation of the gas company, the Parish Council signed an agreement with the Gas Board for the supply of gas to the town's one hundred street lamps. In 1955 the gas lights were replaced by sodium electricity lamps, of which there were 146 in the town. In the same year the High Street bus shelter was erected by the Parish Council with the permission of the then vicar, the Reverend Seager.[10]

The employment alternatives for anyone returning home in 1945 were much as they had been for half a century. Some of the town's factories had now passed out of the hands of their original owners into larger organisations, but the products remained much the same. The milk factory on Station Road had largely closed at the end of the 1930s, but still belonged to United Dairies, who used parts of it as an egg packing factory; this employed up to 35 people, mainly women. Part of the old milk factory was now occupied by the Gillingham and District Modern Laundry. United Dairies itself became part of Unigate in 1959. The Sturminster farmers' milk depot in New Road now belonged to Highnam's Dairies, while on the opposite side of the road the butter factory founded by Eden Shute belonged to Aplin & Barrett of Yeovil, makers of St. Ivel products. On Station Road Oake, Woods was linked with the C.T. Harris bacon company of Calne, while further along, the glue factory started by Charles Maloney was sold in 1954 for £45,000 to Union Glues and Gelatines.

Some issues relating to Gillingham's industries refused to change. For decades the town had endured the noxious smells of the glue factory in the interests of livelihoods and employment, but by the 1950s this nuisance was becoming less acceptable. In 1959 the District Council refused an application from the company to take over the (now redundant) market hall for an extension to its premises on the grounds that the company could give no guarantee that the nuisance would not be further increased. Worse was to come for the company, for in the same year the Parish Council got together a petition with 244 signatures which it passed to the town's M.P., Col. Sir Richard Glyn, who lived at Knapp House. The petition was to be presented in Parliament using the constitutional rights of any individual or individuals to petition government and Parliament over a grievance. The petition drew attention to the annoyance and discomfort caused to residents, the depreciation in property values, and the general adverse effect on business in Gillingham; all caused by the 'abominable stench of raw, putrid flesh and bones, and the cooking of material'. The petitioners prayed that some action be taken, but were careful to point out that they had no wish to bring about the closure of the company's business. The petition had the ritual ending 'And your petitioners, as in duty bound, will ever pray'. However, the petition appears to have had little outcome, since two months later the Parish Council found it necessary to write to the District Council, still complaining about the problem.[11]

The town's railway facilities continued to play an important role in its commercial life. While the quantity of some traffics had fallen since pre-war times, the railway was still vital for many businesses. On the following page, Sam Braddick describes the dependence of his family's agricultural machinery company, based in Station Road, on the railway goods yard. He also recalls the cargoes which turned up regularly on the station platform: the twittering of day-old chicks from Zeals hatchery, the brace of pheasants with no wrappings and only a label for identification, the watercress from Wolverton, fish from Mere, and bundles of brushes from the Mere Brush Company. The signal box, damaged in a shunting accident in 1956, was replaced by a new box the following year. Passenger services retained much the same pattern as in earlier years, with journeys to London often involving a change at Salisbury. A popular event was always the annual Sunday School trip to Weymouth, on a special 14-coach train which was so long that it had be loaded at the station platform in two sections. Sam Woodcock recalls:

> Every year the vicar, the Rev. Seager, would hire a complete train to take us on this pilgrimage. Hundreds of children from Gillingham and surrounding villages would muster with their parents or families in the Station Yard. Sunday School pupils had a roll call and were given a shilling each to spend. The others were less fortunate. The whole scene was reminiscent of wartime evacuee children, but this time buckets, spades, and picnic sandwiches replaced gas masks and suitcases.[12]

Another train memorable for its length was the Sunday evening departure to London, a 12-coach service packed with returning weekend trippers, and known as the 'Sunday Long'. Advertised weekday bus connections for the regular services in 1947 were six Southern National services between Gillingham station and Mere, and five from Gillingham to Shaftesbury.[13]

While the pattern of life for the working people of Gillingham seemed to be firmly set, that for the town's younger people was

Gillingham's goods yard in the 1950s

Sam Braddick describes the importance of the railway goods service to his family's agricultural machinery business in the 1950s:

One of our main suppliers of agricultural machinery was International Harvester, whose spare parts business was based at City Road in London. Once a day they would dispatch parcels from the main line stations to their dealers around the country, from Waterloo to Gillingham in just a few hours. Larger consignments would be put into steel containers mounted on castor wheels. These were delivered from Gillingham on a railway lorry from the 'Goods Shed.' Up until the 1960s almost all the tractors and farm machinery deliveries from manufacturers throughout the country would have to be made via the railway network. On arrival in Gillingham, many of the flat wagons were parked along the loading bank from where we could unload them. Tractors, dung spreaders, trailers, balers, and a whole range of farm machines arrived fully assembled, although some needed to be lifted off by the railway's crane, which was located at the end of the loading bank, near the cattle pens. Not only did we receive parts and machinery by rail, but we made extensive use of the service to dispatch goods from Gillingham to neighbouring stations from where the farmer would collect.

The Gillingham Goods Yard always seemed to be a very busy place; there were the coal yards for Messrs Rose and Wiles, who both used parts of the yard as their depots. There were several stores for agricultural animal feeds, which were delivered to the farm by the railway's own lorry.

Reprinted from Carver, B. *Gillingham* 2009: *a brief history celebrating* 150 *years of the Railway.*

undergoing important changes. The Secondary Modern School, after experiencing a difficult start in the war, flourished during the 1950s, with numbers rising to around 350 most years. In 1951 the school was opened up to pupils from neighbouring parts of Somerset and Wiltshire. It developed a broad curriculum with a strong emphasis on practical skills and rural skills, which could draw upon the farming backgrounds of many of the pupils. The school had its own pig farm, its own annual 'agricultural show', and each year a number of pupils went on to further studies at Salisbury Technical College and the Dorset College of Agriculture. At a visit by HM Inspectors in 1953 the school was considered 'much improved' since the previous visit in 1947, and commended for its good behaviour and children taking pride in their school. In 1954 Major Perkins became Acting Headmaster.[14]

The following year, discussions began over the future of secondary education in Gillingham, with the County Education Committee recommending that both the Grammar and Modern schools be combined into a 4-form entry bilateral school. This was eventually accepted by both governing bodies, and in January 1957 Mr. John Webster was appointed head of a Grammar School which was now required to become a fully comprehensive school. However, the integration plans were delayed since some governors decided too oppose the proposals. It was agreed that additional buildings and facilities would be needed to bring the new combined school up to standard, particularly the construction of a new Assembly Hall where the entire combined school could meet. When the new school opened in September 1959 as a five-stream comprehensive, it was known as 'Gillingham School'. For a while the 11+ was retained as a means of determining the ability level of incoming children, but a new house system was also introduced which cut across academic divisions. The new Assembly Hall was finally achieved in 1966. An outcome of the integration in the following years was the expansion and development of sixth form teaching.[15] The school at this time also housed the Gillingham Evening Institute, the town's provider of adult education.

On July 3 1952 the town received a visit from Her Majesty the Queen and HRH the Duke of Edinburgh, who had been visiting the

Duchy of Cornwall estates and the Newton Abbot show (Fig. 108). The royal couple arrived by train from Yeovil Junction and were received by the Earl of Shaftesbury, the Lord Lieutenant of the County. They were presented with a copy of *The Marn'll Book*, a history of the north Dorset area, compiled by the Women's Institute for the Festival of Britain the previous year. Afterwards the Queen was driven to local engagements, including the National Stud at Sandley, and the Hill Brush factory at Mere. For the Coronation in 1953 a Committee was formed to organise the town celebrations. The programme of events included dances, the town band, a children's fancy dress parade and carnival, fireworks, a bonfire, and a united churches service. Mugs were purchased for all children up to the age of 16, and crowns were given to children born on the Coronation Day. Television viewings were provided at the schools, and for many people this would have

108 The new Queen Elizabeth II arriving at Gillingham railway station on 3 July 1952. On the far left is Mr. E. Batho, chairman of the Parish Council.

been their first opportunity to view the new medium of entertainment. Surplus funds from the celebrations were used to purchase wooden seats for the Recreation Ground, carved to commemorate the event.[16]

The issue of Gillingham becoming an urban authority refused to die, and in 1954 was being debated in the pages of the *Western Gazette*. Perhaps it was in relation to this, and to the diminishing possibility of Gillingham ever having a mayor, that the Parish Council went ahead with the purchase of a chain to be worn by the Council Chairman. Discussion took place over possible heraldic insignia, initial ideas based on the slaughter of Danes by brave Saxon townspeople being discarded because of doubtful historical authenticity. Instead, a coat of arms was devised based on sounder history: a background depicting the three rivers which meet at Gillingham, a stag's head representing the long history of the early forest, and a crown, a reminder of royal authority in earlier times. This insignia still represents the town at the present time.[17]

During these years new social and leisure amenities were slow to arrive. For many people, the traditional community life which had long been centred round the town's churches, together with the cinema and public houses, were the principal leisure attractions outside the home. By 1947 the town had a public lending library, which until 1974 was housed in rooms in the Methodist Church. After the war a 'Victory and Memorial' fund had been set up to commemorate the victory, and it was eventually decided to use this to build a new open-air swimming pool in the Recreation Ground on Hardings Lane. This was opened in 1959 by Sir Richard Glyn M.P. A plaque was erected, 'To those who serve, 1939-45'. A major loss to the town's entertainments came in 1963, with the closure of the Regal Cinema in the High Street, a reflection of a the general decline in cinema-going and the growing popularity of television. The site was redeveloped for new shops.

An important step was taken in 1953, when the Gillingham Parish Council decided to sponsor the formation of a Gillingham

Well known townspeople of the post-war years

Ernest Rowsell Samways (1885-1986) was the younger son of the pharmacist William Samways. Ernest left home at 17 to work and learn the pharmacy business. In 1936, on the retirement of his elder brother Edgar, he returned to work in the town and took over the pharmacy in The Square until his own retirement in 1964. In 1958 he donated to the Local History Society the two cottages which became its first Museum. In his retirement he wrote the novel *Dorset Barnaby*, a tale based on local life during his boyhood; in the novel the names of people and places are recognisably linked to Gillingham. In his time he was a parish councillor, school governor, and president of the bowls club.

Gerrard Blandford Matthews (1890-1976) came from the Matthews brewery and mill-owning family (Chapter 11). He owned the brewery until its sale to Hall and Woodhouse in 1963. He was always known as Blandford Matthews and took a prominent role in town affairs. He was Chairman of the Grammar School Governors for many years and first President of the Gillingham Local History Society.

Ven. Edward Leslie Seager (1904-1983) was born in Hartlebury, Worcestershire. He came from a wartime role as an army chaplain to be Vicar of St. Mary the Virgin, Gillingham, from 1946 to 1979, and was Archdeacon of Dorset from 1954. He was a governor of the Grammar School and other local schools, and of Wellington College in Somerset. Canon Seager was well known around the town as a scout leader and for his involvement in community life generally. He was the last vicar to live in the Victorian vicarage which is now Rawson Court.

Arthur 'Dinger' Bell (1891-1976) was born in Wyke. He began his working life as a butcher's boy, but after war service he worked at the Wyke brewery, where he remained until his retirement in 1956. He was a founder member of the Royal British Legion and the Gillingham Silver Band, and became Vice president of the Football Club. He was a founder member of the Gillingham Carnival and a main influence behind its revival in the 1950s. He is well remembered as a Gillingham 'character' and for his robust representation of the town in public life. In this picture he is leading the town procession, mounted on a donkey.

Reginald Shute (1891-1982) was the son of Eden Shute, the New Road butter manufacturer. He was a Parish Councillor and County Councillor for many years, and also a staunch supporter of the Methodist Chapel in Queen Street. He was a founder member, first Chairman, and President of the Local History Society.

Local History Society. The aims of the society were to be the promotion of the study of the town's long and varied history through speakers and lectures; and the establishment of a collection of local artefacts and records which could be housed in a museum. A particular need was to find a place for the collection of Freame family artefacts and papers which were now in the hands of Sidney Carter. Initially the new collection was housed in a room in the Secondary Modern School, while the search went on for a suitable museum site. This was realised in 1957 when Ernest R. Samways donated a pair of cottages in Church Walk behind his chemist's shop for the use of the society as a museum. The Gillingham Museum officially opened in November 1958. Lt. Col. C.R.A. Wallis, a founding member and a driving force behind the museum project, remained its first curator until his death in 1962.[18]

Industrial decline and change

THE PROSPERITY OF Gillingham from 1860 had been built on the coming of the railway and on the economic opportunism of local entrepreneurs, who saw in the railway new possibilities for the development of their rural-based businesses. Nearly a century later these conditions were greatly changed. The railway, once a key to the town's prosperity, was now a declining mode of freight transport and seen as increasingly uncompetitive with road haulage. This eroded a major advantage of Gillingham's location as a railhead for local products. Although the town was not far from the A303, this had not yet developed into the main route which it is today, and the town's businesses lay entirely off secondary roads, sometimes accessible only down narrow streets unsuited to modern, larger vehicles. This was also a time of the growth of corporate businesses nationwide, so that smaller companies which had started as family firms now found themselves as branches of larger organisations. As the parent companies increasingly sought economies in larger, more modern plants, it was the smaller parts of their business, often distant from their centres of operations, which were increasingly at risk. By the 1950s a number of Gillingham's businesses found themselves in this position, since they were now owned by companies whose principal interests lay elsewhere. Another ingredient was the lack of capitalisation and investment; all around the town, industrial buildings and plant had seen little investment for half a century or more, limiting performance and competitiveness.

1959 saw an event which augured badly for the future of the town in the years ahead. The auctioneers Senior and Godwin, who had run the livestock market behind the station since the 1880s, decided to close the market and to concentrate their auctioneering functions on their yard at Sturminster Newton. The fortnightly Monday market for calves, described in pre-war directories as having a 'wonderful reputation' and the 'second largest in the kingdom', had been a centrepiece of commercial life in Gillingham, its location next to the station ensuring large attendances. Its closure was to be followed by the disuse of the market yard, and the eventual demolition of the Market Hall and the use of the space for a station car park.[19]

The closure of the livestock market, the first closure of a major Gillingham business for many years, was the first of several more to come. In 1940 Hudson and Martin had converted their sawmilling works to diesel power and in 1950 to electric operation, but in 1960 finally closed the timber part of their business, bringing to an end nearly a century of saw milling on Station Road. The main reason was the high costs and increasing scarcity of locally grown timber compared with imported material. This brought about significant job loss, especially among people who had worked for the firm for much of their lives. The company continued to flourish in Gillingham for many years to come as a builders' merchants, but disposed of the wood yard

110 Baxter's butcher's shop in the 1960s. The shop is now Scenes arts materials and picture framing.

111 Small tradesmen and shop owners depended heavily on their deliveries to outlying parts of the town and nearby rural areas. This is the van of Sid Kite, a High Street fishmonger, about 1950.

and mill at Station Road. In 1963 the Matthews company sold its Wyke brewery and its tied houses to the Blandford brewer, Hall and Woodhouse. Soon afterwards, brewing came to an end, and with it the disappearance of the Matthews 'Buffalo' label. The company retained the Wyke site as a soft drinks and bottling plant, until this in turn was closed and the process transferred to Blandford. In 1966 the Matthews company also moved out of the Town Mill, concentrating its feed manufacture at Purns Mill, and bringing to an end centuries of corn milling in Gillingham town centre. In 1964 a loss of a different sort was the closure of the National Stud at Sandley and its transfer to Newmarket.

An even more visible change to Gillingham's industrial face came in March 1968 with the closure of the brickworks of the Gillingham Pottery, Brick, and Tile Company. This had been the material source of much of the building boom of Victorian and Edwardian times, with the products of the works giving Gillingham the distinctive appearance which had so dismayed Sir Frederick Treves many years earlier. Over the decades the workings of the plant had expanded to the eastern side of the Sturminster road, and a mechanical digger had long ago replaced the original manual extraction. However, the Gillingham plant was tiny when compared with the giant operations appearing in the Bedfordshire area, where massive dragline excavators could easily swallow up the efforts of the Gillingham clay pits. In the Vale of Marston in Bedfordshire there were already in the 1930s 167 brickworks' chimneys, and the Stewartby site of the London Brick Company employed 2,000 men producing 500 million bricks each year. Moreover, the cost of coal and wages was rising, and while the Bedfordshire brick makers could depend on imported Italian labour, it was becoming harder in small rural places like Gillingham to find local men still willing to undertake the hard, manual work. By this time, the best of the clay had already been worked out. The brickworks' chimney, a Gillingham landmark, was felled in September 1972. An irony is that the shutdown came at a time when much more private new building was about to take place, but a positive outcome of the closure was the release of a large area of land to the south of the town where new, modern industrial development could be encouraged to locate.

Another Gillingham industry to disappear at this time was the glue factory built by Charles Maloney earlier in the century. In 1954 this had been bought by Union Glues, and in 1960 the manufacture of glues from bone was discontinued in favour of synthetic glues. Union Glues was in turn taken over by Carborundum, an American-based manufacturer of abrasives, and the Gillingham factory closed in 1970, to the relief of many local people. On the opposite side of Station Road towards the station, the United Dairies' egg packing plant closed in 1970; in its heyday it had provided 35-40 jobs. A longer survivor was the bacon factory; since the 1930s this had belonged to C.T. Harris, which in 1962 became part of the Farmers' Meat Company group. Production at Gillingham and the use of the Oake, Woods name continued, with a throughput in the 1970s of 1,300 pigs weekly, many from direct contracts with farmers. When the factory closed in 1985, along with its retail shop, it ended almost a hundred and thirty years of production of pork products at the Station Road site.

These several closures changed the character of the lower part of Station Road and the area around the station. From being an area of thriving activities, it became quieter, with some of the empty buildings standing derelict, part occupied by smaller businesses, or used for storage. The closures were partly offset by the appearance of new business names bringing with them welcome new jobs. These included Sherman Chemicals, a manufacturer of a range of chemical compounds, including materials used in the electrical industry. This company took over the sawmill premises on Station Road in 1962, later moving to the Brickfields industrial estate. Other new industrial faces were those of glove manufacturers, attracted by the availability of outworkers and reviving an industry which had once been traditional throughout north Dorset. One was the Yeovil manufacturer, Southcombe, who located in Wyke Street in 1959; the other was Chester Jeffries, a Slough glove manufacturer, who in 1963 opened a factory in Buckingham Road. This firm still occupies the same premises today as a maker of high quality handmade gloves. Nevertheless, unemployment became a major concern. At a meeting of the Parish Council in August 1970, it was estimated that unemployment in the town was twice the national average. A proposal was made to seek the support of the Rural District Council in having the district declared a depressed area, but this was not carried.[20]

In 1963 disquieting rumours of a different sort began to circulate. In March 1963 the government had issued the Beeching report 'The Reshaping of Britain's Railways' and accepted its findings, which already included closure of the Somerset and Dorset line through

Templecombe. Some months earlier, management of the Exeter route west of Salisbury had been taken over by the British Railways Western Region, which was known to be considering whether two routes from London to Exeter were necessary. During the months which followed, reassurances were sought from Western Region management about the future of the line, and representations were made to local MPs and to Dorset County Council. In February 1964 the shape of a revised service was revealed. Steam locomotives were to be replaced by diesel units, giving a direct service to Waterloo and to Exeter St. David's, with a timetable accelerated and revised to serve the principal intermediate stations, which included Gillingham. However, services to the smaller stations west of Salisbury were to be discontinued, and Templecombe was to close in its entirety. A revision of freight services was also announced, centralising distribution on key centres accessible by road, with the closure of all other freight depots.[21]

The outcome had mixed consequences for Gillingham. The new passenger timetable of September 1964 gave the town its fastest and most regular service to London and major destinations along the line. However, when the smaller stations closed in 1966, all the stopping trains were withdrawn; this had a particular effect on local journeys, especially children travelling to Gillingham School. In 1965 the goods yard was closed and Gillingham lost its stationmaster as part of a management reorganisation. In 1967 the line was singled, but Gillingham retained its double track through the station as a passing loop, serving both platforms (Plate 18). The signal box, and an engineer's siding were also retained. Eastwards, the long, 19-mile single line section to Wilton was to be the cause of many delays for years to come. In 1969 the Shellstar fertiliser company opened a distribution depot with a siding, a train arriving weekly from Ince and Elton in Cheshire. This depot distributed fertiliser over a wide area, the company later trading as UKF Fertilisers. The traffic and depot continued in operation until 1993.[22]

Changing directions: the Overspill proposal

I N THE EARLY 1960s Gillingham found itself having to consider a proposal which would have changed the character not only of the town itself but of much of the countryside around. The origins of this lay in the county development plan of the Dorset County Council. This envisaged meeting the needs of future population growth by creating a 'new town' of 60,000 in the north of the county, a project which would have absorbed not only Gillingham, but Shaftesbury, Motcombe, and Mere. The magnitude of the proposal meant that it soon met with widespread opposition from the local authorities involved. As a consequence, a special meeting of the Parish Council and Chamber of Trade in May 1965 took place to consider an alternative proposal. This was to participate in the Expanded Towns or 'Overspill' scheme of the Greater London Council. 'Overspill' was a response to the consequences of enemy bombing and the large amount of substandard housing in inner London, and had been given statutory authority by the Town Development Act of 1952. Overspill involved the movement of population out of London to new housing estates built by the GLC in the expanded towns, and the creation of industrial estates in the towns to bring in more jobs. Eventually 29 towns took part in the scheme; most overspill towns were in the south-eastern counties, but a few were more distant from London; the nearest to Gillingham were Andover, Basingstoke, and Swindon.

The Gillingham proposal involved expansion on a smaller scale than the original new town idea, an initial target being growth to 20,000 over ten years. In October 1965 a Gillingham councillor reported back on a visit he made to the established overspill towns of Haverhill and Thetford, and indicated that they were prospering under the new initiative. The following month a Parish Council motion to accept the proposal was virtually unanimously approved. The motion called for expansion to 15,000 by 1981, this being the lowest figure that the GLC would accept; and for the expansion to take place entirely within the existing parish, thereby leaving places outside the parish unaffected. The parish councillors no doubt saw in the proposal the means to achieve the new jobs and housing which were badly needed in the town, and also a means by which the town could finally take control of its own affairs. However, opposition to the proposals came from the villages and rural places nearby. A campaign called 'Dorset in Danger' depicted the project as a first stage in a wider government policy of urbanising much of the county of Dorset. It portrayed a Gillingham expanded to 17 times its existing size, with the town under the control of a huge, imported overspill majority. In March 1966 the Gillingham councillors passed a motion to press the Shaftesbury RDC to increase the representation of Gillingham on the council in view of its growing population, no doubt in anticipation of a critical vote that was to come. In August a poll was held around the town, which showed that the population was largely behind the scheme.[23]

The argument reached its climax at a special meeting of the Rural District Council on 8 September 1966. After an evening of intense debate, preceded by Dorset in Danger demonstrations outside the Shaftesbury Town Hall, the motion was finally defeated by 19 votes to 14. The Gillingham councillors voted for the motion, while those of the villages, mainly to the south of Shaftesbury, voted against it.[24] Had the project been carried, the proposal would have brought the greatest changes to the north Dorset area since the coming of the railway. As it was, even without overspill, the population continued to grow in the years ahead, albeit more gradually. An irony was that the growth occurred largely through an influx of incomers, although perhaps of a different type from those envisaged by the overspill scheme. Much of the proposed new housing was to arrive through private developments, but without the necessary improvements in infrastructure which the overspill scheme might have brought.

While the attention of the townspeople was focused on the major issues involving the future of the town, a significant disappearance of Gillingham's past was taking place, although perhaps less noticed. This was the loss of the three-arched Chantry footbridge, dating from 1821. In 1967 the water authority decided that the arches were impeding the flow and contributing to the flood risk, and so the bridge was rebuilt, this time with a single span, thus removing one of Gillingham's most distinctive features.

The 1971 *Local Plan and after*

T HE COLLAPSE OF the overspill scheme, together with developments in national planning legislation, made necessary the preparation of Gillingham's first Local Plan. By the mid-1960s the population, which had remained largely static since earlier in the century, was starting to grow again, and it was agreed in 1967 by the local authorities concerned that a figure of 6,000 by 1981 should form the basis of future planning policies for the town. There was also the pressing need to offset the continuing loss of local jobs in the old-established industries by encouraging the location of new businesses. In 1969 a draft consultation plan was issued which had four main objectives: to make new land available for industrial development; to consolidate existing approved developments and curtail the spread of development into nearby rural areas; to build a new relief road round the town; and to enable some segregation of vehicular and pedestrian movements where appropriate. By this time housing needs had already led to the first releases of land for private building development for many years, with new housing already appearing in Shreen Way, Lodbourne Green, Clarendon Close, Common Mead Avenue, and Addison Close. By November 1968 permissions had been granted for a further 700 dwellings on 95 acres, mostly on land east of Peacemarsh. The final version of the plan appeared in 1971.[25]

The housing allocations in the 1971 plan, both existing and proposed, were to lead to housing developments in a number of areas. The largest new development was at Peacemarsh, north and east of Fairey Crescent. Here the principal new roads were the remainder of Shreen Way, Broadacres, Claremont Avenue, and Downsview Drive, with associated smaller roads (Fig. 112). This was a more substantial development than anything so far seen in the town, much of it comprising retirement bungalows. A second area was off Common Mead Lane, where the Maple Way and Laburnum Way neighbourhood was built. The latter was a development for London families, and the scheme may have been an offshoot of the earlier overspill proposal. Smaller developments were at Barnaby Mead, Bridge Close, and Wessex Way. Development of Hyde Road, with over 130 flats and houses, extended the Great House Farm local authority estate. It was recognised that such housing growth would eventually require a new primary school, and a site somewhere in Peacemarsh was considered to be the most suitable location.

In looking at future industrial developments, the plan considered that the older Station Road industrial area no longer had space for new, modern, industrial development. It proposed that this should be concentrated in two areas: the now abandoned clay pits area and brick works south of the railway, and a smaller area on Chantry Fields which would be close to the new distributor road. Approval would not be given to industries generating smells, dust, and other nuisances, and existing industries in the town centre would be encouraged to relocate in the new areas.

112 Downsview Drive, a product of the extensive building of retirement bungalows in Gillingham in the 1970s and 1980s.

A critical feature of the 1971 plan was the provision of a new distributor or relief road. There was a recognition that the existing roads through the town centre could not be widened without unacceptable damage to the buildings and environment, and a route had been fixed as early as 1965. The objective was to carry the Shaftesbury to Wincanton or Mere (and A303) traffic to the west and south of the town centre, keeping through traffic off the town streets and also giving direct access to the Station Road industrial area. New car park areas south of the High Street could also be accessed. The original route was that largely followed, the exception being the northern end. Here, the route had been initially designed to rejoin Queen Street around Turners Lane, but was later extended to rejoin further north at Lodbourne Green. It was noted that funding would probably not allow this route to be built for some years, and this turned out to be a longer wait than many people would have hoped for.

Many of the proposals in regard to housing, industry, and a distributor road were to be realised in the years ahead, but it was the ideas relating to the central area of the town which were not so readily implemented. The plan noted that the mix of functions in the High Street, a result of its piecemeal development over a long period of time, made it vulnerable to uncoordinated development. It proposed that at the Station Road end of the High Street and Newbury, change of use and new developments would be restricted and approval given only in limited circumstances. Instead, new town centre development would be encouraged at the lower end of High Street, west of the Town Bridge, especially on land which lay behind the Phoenix and Red Lion. Here, the plan saw the opportunity to develop a modern town centre, linked to the distributor road by a service road, and containing the town's principal car park (Fig. 113). In the event, much of the vision was never realised, and some of this land is still awaiting a proper role to play in the functioning of the town centre. In August 1969 the local builder and developer M.P.Osmond submitted a scheme which would be at variance with the proposed plan. This was to redevelop the Town Mill, and land to the front and rear, involving filling in the mill pond, but the proposal was rejected. The 1971 plan also envisaged a greater provision of pedestrian routes around the town. One of these would have been a riverside path linking the new town centre and Town Mill with Lodbourne; another would have linked Gillingham School with King's Court and Ham housing areas via a path under the railway. Forty years later both of these are still awaited.[26]

In April 1972 the Parish Council clearly felt that changes and improvements in the town were not making sufficient progress, and a motion was proposed and agreed, that in view of the likely population increase over the next five years, a four-point policy should be pursued. This was to press the County and Rural District Councils to advance the date for construction of the distributor road; to provide adequate parking for at least 200 vehicles; to take the steps needed to provide a new library and pedestrian crossing; and to give high priority to the provision of new, light industry.[27] One consequence of

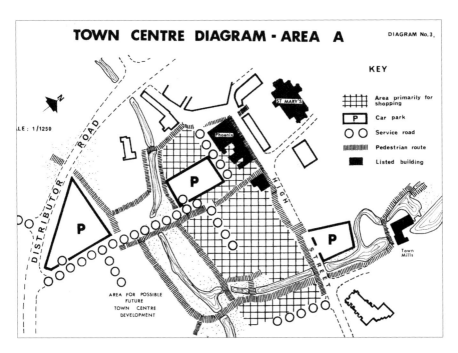

113 *The redevelopment of the town centre, as envisaged by the 1971 Local Plan. The area behind the Phoenix and Red Lion would have become the town's new commercial hub, with service link roads separated from pedestrian paths.*

the 1971 Plan was that the Parish Council decided to sell for housing a site which it already owned in Peacemarsh and had been earmarked for industrial development. The scheme was to have been led by a concrete casting works, with the developer providing a service road which would have encouraged further industries to locate there. In October 1972 the Parish Council agreed that surplus money from the sale of the site ought to be used for the provision of a community and sports centre, and a covering over of the swimming bath. It was successful in persuading the Rural District Council of this need, and the project was to come to fruition just a few years ahead.[28] Another development of the same year was the opening of the new Fire Station at Peacemarsh, replacing the old Victorian station on School Road.

Besides the large issues of future developments, the Parish Council minutes of these years also record the many more minor matters and issues relating to the town. In June 1971 the Recreation Committee reported on damages to windows in the public toilets, to the kissing gates on the Bay footpath, and to the see-saw in the Hyde Road play area; 'other business' raised included the bad state of the pavement between the Methodist Church and School Road, and a dangerous hole made by the Water Board in Great House Walk. The following month new matters arising and discussed included: unsatisfactory street lighting on the Shaftesbury and Sherborne roads; the use of the Recreation Ground by Gillingham Football Club; paying council workmen for days absent through illness; and the health hazards of derelict houses in Wavering Lane. Many of these, or similar issues, raised in the closing years of the Parish Council's administration, had been the staple material of its meetings for the previous 90 years. Some of the topics might also have been debated at the vestry and overseers' meetings of previous centuries. A topic not seen before, with implications for the future, came in January 1973: the introduction of double yellow lines. This was one topic which proved to be too controversial for instant decisions, and it was agreed to leave it unresolved for at least six months.[29] Congestion and parking would continue to be an issue for many more years.

16

EXPANSION AND CHANGE
SINCE 1974

THE LOCAL GOVERNMENT Act of 1972 ushered in a new system of local administration for England and Wales, bringing significant changes for Gillingham. In 1974 the old Shaftesbury Rural District established in 1894 was abolished, and Gillingham become part of a new District of North Dorset, which included Blandford Forum, Shaftesbury, Sturminster Newton, and Stalbridge, together with their neighbouring rural areas. The Gillingham Parish Council gave way to a Town Council, which could now elect its own mayor. In this way, Gillingham achieved the official urban status it had sought over many generations, albeit as the lowest level in the new three-tier system of local government.[1] The responsibilities of the Town Council were largely those of the old Parish Council, including recreation grounds, allotments, and cemeteries. From the town's wards seventeen councillors were elected, representing a 1971 population of 4,050. All other functions, including planning applications, refuse disposal, lighting, and roads, were the responsibility of the District Council or the County Council. In 1974 the first mayor was Tony Coombes. In 1979 Gillingham was given a distinctly municipal image through the appointment of David Wathen as Town Crier, reviving a post that had been last held in 1934.

Over the years Mr Wathen, in his colourful official attire, became a familiar figure at carnivals, Remembrance Day services, and many other town occasions.[2] From 1976 until 1989 the council met in the newly built Gillingham Centre on Hardings Lane, subsequently moving to the former Magistrates Court building adjoining the Police Station.

In 1975, the Mayor of Gillingham received an invitation from Le Neubourg, to begin a twinning link between the two towns. This followed the twinning of Shaftesbury in 1974 with the town of Brionne, a neighbour of Le Neubourg situated in the *Eure*

114 The Gillingham Town Council of 1989. Back row from left: Tony Coombes, Brian Nicholson, George Joyce, Elizabeth Fricker (Town Clerk), Jim Norris, Robin Hussey, Fred Evill, Peter Crocker. Seated from left: Sylvia Dobie (Assistant Clerk), Gina Norris, Paul Harrison (Deputy Mayor), Tim Rose (Mayor), Helen Burt, Linda Knox, Elizabeth Hague. A few weeks later the Council Office was moved from the Gillingham Centre to the former Magistrates Court.

Le Neubourg, Gillingham's twin town

Le Neubourg, with a population of 4,000, is smaller than Gillingham, and is a vibrant, lively town. It enjoys a wide range of shops and services supplied by over 160 shopkeepers and craftsmen, and its Wednesday Market is amongst the most important in Normandy (Plate 26).

Although a small town, it actually offers more jobs than the population of 4,000 might suggest. Industry represents 47% of the town employment, and commerce a further 17%. Education is provided by a pre-school, two primary schools, a secondary (11-16) school, and an agricultural college.

Le Neubourg is notable for its many and varied sports facilities. These include a new Hippodrome complex which encompasses a *vélodrome* for the cycling club, football training pitches with artificial turf, used by the 250 members of the football club, and a *piste hippique* for the annual horse trotting race. The *Haut-Phare* sports complex provides a swimming pool, gym, sports rooms and community hall, while the nearby *Champ de Bataille* Golf Club has an international reputation. In all there are 18 sports clubs with 3,000 members.

Cultural facilities include a multimedia library, the *Universitié populaire,* the *Viking* cinema, Anatomy Museum, and the Museum of agricultural implements. The town holds regular exhibitions covering various topics of art and culture and there are several major festivals celebrated throughout the year.

Like Gillingham, Le Neubourg was also a town that once depended heavily on the railway. The line was important for moving agricultural produce, and was popular with people holidaying on the Normandy coast. Unfortunately it was only

115 A street sign in Le Neubourg announces the town's twinning with Gillingham.

a local line and became uneconomical, closing in 1969. In recent times it has been made into a 'green way' for walkers and cyclists.

The Town Hall of Le Neubourg displays the traditional motto *travail vaut richesse*- 'work is wealth', while the modern motto is *'une ville qui avance'* – 'a town which goes forward'.

Département of Normandy. Visits between the two towns took place and Gillingham Town Twinning Association was formed. The official charter linking the two towns was signed in France in April 1977 and at The Gillingham Centre on 12 November of the same year. This latter function provided the occasion for an unexpected meeting between John Webster, Gillingham School Headmaster, and Jean Le Norman, a former leader in the French Resistance; they had last met in 1944 when Mr Webster was serving as a captain with the 8th Royal Scots, part of the Lowland Brigade which liberated Le Neubourg.

The main aims of the twinning were to promote friendship and understanding through social and cultural interaction, as well as for each town to enjoy the other's art, history, and culture. Since 1977 many exchanges and visits have been made between the two towns. Visiting groups from Gillingham have included the Gillingham Imperial Silver Band, art and floral groups, local musicians and dancers, sports clubs, and Youth Club. School exchanges and joint art exhibitions have been held. When the Gillingham relief road was opened in 1989, it was appropriately named Le Neubourg Way.

Gillingham expands: 1974 *to* 1991

URING THE 1970s the development and growth of the town took place within the time framework of the 1971 Local Plan. While some of the plan's policies and proposals were carried out as intended, others were held back for various reasons, and by 1981 still awaited modification or implementation. During this decade the population grew to reach almost 5,500 by 1981, of which 4,700 was in the town itself, and the remainder in the rural wards. Over 840 new dwellings were built, representing a 55% increase on the 1971 dwelling stock. Much of this had taken place at Peacemarsh, with smaller amounts in the other areas of the town, as outlined in Chapter 15.

By the early 1980s it had become necessary for the District Council to review the 1971 plan and assess its continuing usefulness. In 1981 a new Dorset Structure Plan had appeared, with a requirement that between 1980 and 1996 Gillingham should accommodate a further 1200 to 1600 new dwellings, implying a population of around 6,800 to 7,600 by 1996. The county plan also required the release of further amounts of land for industrial development. An issue arising from the developments of the 1970s was that much of the private building had been in the form of small bungalows attractive to older people wishing to move into the town, while the local authority housing had been largely of flatlets and bedsitter accommodation for the elderly. This had created an unbalanced population structure, with the number of elderly people in the town almost doubling over the decade. Another issue was that while there had been some growth in new light industries during the 1970s, half of the town's working population commuted to jobs outside the town, often as far away as Yeovil or Salisbury. It was suggested that over 700 hundred new jobs might be needed over the decade ahead. Other problems identified included the need for more shopping floorspace and recreational facilities, and the urgent need to complete the relief road to relieve traffic congestion.

These ideas and issues formed the basis of the Gillingham Local Plan, the final version of which was published by the North Dorset District Council in September 1986. This provided for 770 new houses over the plan period to 1996. By the time this plan appeared, layouts and designs had already been drawn up for much of the remaining land between Common Mead Lane and Wyke Road, producing Freame Way, Broad Robin, and neighbouring roads. Additions to Addison Close were also sketched out. To these the plan added some further areas, of which the main ones were: the remainder of the Common Mead - Wyke Road area, which became the Milestone Way and Deane Avenue neighbourhoods (180 dwellings); Peacemarsh north

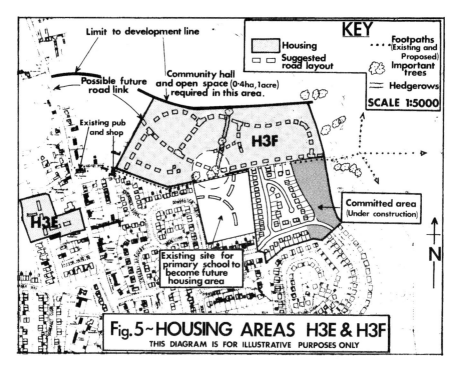

Fig. 5 ~ HOUSING AREAS H3E & H3F
THIS DIAGRAM IS FOR ILLUSTRATIVE PURPOSES ONLY

116 An extract from the 1986 Local Plan showing proposed developments in Peacemarsh. The alignment of the future Gylla's Way can clearly be seen. By this time it had been decided that the new primary school should not be at Peacemarsh but at Wyke. The suggested community hall was never implemented.

of Claremont Avenue, eventually producing the roads around Gyllas Way (120); Chantry Fields (later Church View) of 60 houses; and more local authority additions to Addison Close (Fig. 116). However, the greatest release of land for new building was at Rolls Bridge Farm and westwards as far as Pound Lane, taking in all the land between Wavering Lane and Wyke Road not so far built upon. Here, the plan allowed for the construction of 380 dwellings on 15.1 hectares, mostly of lower density with some higher density areas. This became an area of family homes, mostly 3 and 4-bedroomed detached and semi-detached. Along with this development, Cemetery Road was to be extended westwards to become Rolls Bridge Way, and a new link road, Coldharbour, was to join it to Wyke Road. All of these housing proposals were gradually completed over the following decade.

The creation of a Conservation Area to protect the town's older buildings and areas of local character from inappropriate development was seen as desirable, and this would be implemented in 1986. The new Conservation Area included the medieval street areas around the church, the Square, Chantry cottages, Victorian vicarage, and older buildings in Queen Street.[3]

The expansion in housing brought with it the urgent need to expand the town's educational provision. The need for a further school had been foreseen in the 1971 plan, and a suitable site, initially for a middle school, had been identified in Peacemarsh off Downsview Drive. However, as the number of pupils in the Peacemarsh area remained low, with most new residential development taking place in the Wyke and Rolls Bridge areas, it was decided instead to implement the new school to the west of the town. A site was found within the new Wyke housing area, and the new Wyke County Primary School opened on Deane Avenue in September 1991.

The 1986 Local Plan envisaged that most new employment would come from developments on the Brickfields industrial estate south of the railway line, and from redevelopments in the Station Road area close to the station, although possible development south of the relief road on Chantry Fields was also considered. Light and general industries, service industries, and distribution, including smaller units, were the main types envisaged. By 1986 new industrial units were being built in the former glue factory and old market areas, and further new units were appearing on the old brickworks site. A further 2,000 sq. metres of new shopping space was identified as being needed, the main area for which was to be provided on Chantry Fields between the High Street and the relief road. Here, possible supermarket sites were sketched in, together with access roads, car parking, a market site, and a new library site.

Several improvements to roads and highways were proposed. One of these was the closure of Common Mead Lane to through traffic and the creation of a new link road (Broad Robin) joining Common Mead Lane and Wyke Road. The closure of Wavering Lane to through traffic, and its separation into two parts was provided for in the plan. The most far-reaching change was the building of the relief road, Le Neubourg Way, long delayed since its inception in the late 1960s.[4] While welcomed generally within the town for its ending of town centre congestion and parking problems, concerns were raised. There was a fear that, when linked with the new supermarket plan, the road would draw shoppers away from the existing High Street shopping area to the detriment of long-established traders; and that the loss of direct traffic from Wyke Street would add to this further. The relief road opened, without modification from the plan, in 1989. An interesting outcome from the road's construction was the archaeological investigations that had to be carried out before the work could begin; this revealed important new information about the dawn of Gillingham as a settlement, which have been described in Chapter 1. Further findings of archaeological importance came in the 1990s from the construction of the Waitrose supermarket and its car parks.

Gillingham expands: 1991 *to* 2004

A LREADY BY 1991, the plan of 1986 was being overtaken by developments originating from elsewhere. A review of the plan showed that over the previous decade Gillingham had experienced the fastest rate of growth of the five towns in the North Dorset District, and the County Plan now identified it as a main centre for population, housing, and employment growth to the year 2001. Proposals for Gillingham became part of a new District Wide

Local Plan which initially looked at planning needs to 2001 and was subsequently extended towards an end date of 2011. This Plan identified the need for about 1,610 dwellings to be built between 1994 and 2011, most of which would need to be on new greenfield sites. The largest allocation was south of the Shaftesbury Road at Ham Farm, where 292 dwellings were scheduled, becoming Hine Close, Kingfisher Avenue, Chaffinch Chase, and adjoining 'bird' named roads. To the rear of Lockwood Terrace, 126 properties were approved for a development to be accessed from the new Fernbrook Lane. Behind Lodden Bridge Farm 111 houses were to be built, becoming King John Road, Queen Eleanor Road, and Palace Road, names reflecting the nearby site of the medieval King's Court. A further 90 houses were planned for the Addison Close – Meadows area for construction after 2006. At Peacemarsh, the estate to the west of the Fire Station was extended with 245 new dwellings to be built along Marlott Road, Weatherbury Road, and other roads with 'Thomas Hardy' derived names. Sixty-three new houses appeared on Chantry Fields at Church View west of Le Neuborg Way. The completion of these housing allocations during the first years of the new century was to expand the town well beyond any limits thought possible since the expansion plans of the 1960s. The continuing imbalance towards an elderly population inherited from previous years has meant that most of the new housing has been directed towards younger people and families. By the time the plan was revised in 2003, it was estimated that by 2011 the population would have reached around 9,800.[5]

The District Wide Plan recognised that in order to allow for the expansion of the town, additional provision of community infrastructure was required. This included the building of a third primary school to serve the needs of the growing Ham area along the Shaftesbury Road. This opened in September 2004 as St. Mary the Virgin CEVA School. A new community hall was proposed, with several sites looked at, and at the time of writing is intended to be realised as part of the new Riversmeet Centre. A community health centre for Peacemarsh was suggested, which eventually took shape as a new medical practice (2004) and dental practice (2007). Little of a specific nature was proposed in additional shopping, but sites behind the Red Lion and between School Lane and Newbury were seen as the most suitable sites, the latter eventually being used for the Lidl supermarket. The Plan proposed a number of footpath and cycleway developments, some of which would contribute to the completion of a Stour Valley Way long-distance path, but also opening up new amenity areas between Milton and Eccliffe.

The District Wide Plan identified a number of sites suitable for generating new employment, all on the edge of the town. The largest was the Brickfields site, where a further 3.7 ha. was made available for new development, continuing the growth of earlier years. The principal occupier of this site by this time was Dextra Lighting, a manufacturer of commercial lighting systems, whose blue lorries are a familiar sight around the Gillingham area (Fig. 117). Other names came to include Sherman Chemicals, who relocated from their Station Road site; and Sigma-Aldrich, a manufacturer of organic chemicals and biochemicals. A different sort of occupier by this time was the Stour Vale Bowling Club; this eventually became the Olive Bowl, a conference, training, and events centre, which became popular for weddings, receptions, and similar events. At Peacemarsh. 2.5 ha. became available for employment use, a site later developed by Neal's Yard Remedies, which manufactures organic-based skin and body care products in its distinctive blue building. At Park Farm on Shaftesbury Road, 4.5 ha was allocated for employment use as an alternative site to the Brickfields Business Park. From 2004 a number of small units were built here, but the principal occupier of the site is the Orchard Park Garden Centre, relocated from its earlier site at Milton.

Environmental measures in the District Wide Plan included a traffic calming and enhancement scheme for the Square and High

117 Gillingham's new industries: the Dextra Lighting factory in the Brickfields Business Park. Dextra is the largest occupier of the former brickworks site.

Street, implemented in 1991. Outlying areas of the town, particularly those with groups of older cottages, were designated as Areas of Local Character since they did not fully meet the requirements of Conservation Areas. These were Bay, Colesbrook, Eccliffe, King's Court, Lodbourne, the Lodden Bridge area, Peacemarsh, Wavering Lane, and Wyke. In these areas developments would only be approved for proposals which respected their local character. A new policy for land east of Gillingham was the Gillingham Royal Forest Project. This aimed to promote farm diversification towards woodland planting and countryside recreational activities in an area within the bounds of the old royal forest and deer park, with the boundary of the Forest Project area becoming the eastern boundary of the town's possible expansion in this direction. Within this area, development which might damage the aims of the Project would not be permitted.

The District Wide Local Plan, as revised in 2003, is still current at the time of writing, and together with earlier plans has helped to reshape Gillingham during the last thirty years. Not all of the proposals and policies in these planning documents have become reality. Some had to be abandoned for all sorts of reasons, or were superseded by later proposals. Others did take shape, but in a different way from the original intentions. Throughout the last generation, a constant pressure on the planners' ideas has been the steady rise in housing allocations imposed on the town from county and national requirements, bringing with it the need for new employment, infrastructure, and amenities. A common perception in the town is that the provision of these has never caught up with the influx of new housing. All of these forces are recognisable in today's Gillingham, modifying but not obscuring or diminishing the town of earlier generations.

The changing town centre

T HE CHAMBER OF Commerce and Industry Directory for 1991 listed 147 members around the town, a notable increase from the 95 recorded in 1978, suggesting a rise in commercial activity in line with the growth of population. Despite the arrival during this period of a number of newer business names from outside, Gillingham remained a town of mostly long-established local traders. Even today, nationally known 'high street' names are rarely seen. Until the 1990s almost every example of goods or service needed could still be found in and around the town centre, often with some choice. In 1991 there were five new and used car dealers, three carpet shops, four retailers of shoes, and five retailers of children's ware. The public houses to be found in the town centre were the Phoenix, Red Lion, Queen's Head, Smouldering Boulder, and Royal Hotel; further out were the Dolphin and Buffalo. Some businesses were notable for their diversity; Brachers combined furniture and house furnishings

118 Herbie and Alan Light with their motorcycle business in Newbury in 1987. The business had been founded some ninety years earlier by the cycle maker William H. Light. The site is now occupied by Lidl's supermarket.

with funeral undertaking, as they always had done, and also offered lighting and travel goods. The pharmacy in the Square advertised newspapers, passport photos, and recorded music. The R. & E. Hussey business was in two premises; the one in Station Road combined newspapers, toys, sports gear, and gentlemen's hairdressing; the other shop round the corner on the High Street was ladies' and mens' wear and school uniforms. Surprisingly few items to be found in 1991 have entirely disappeared from the town shops, but the choice in many has become very limited.[6]

The long-anticipated relief road of Le Neubourg Way was finally opened in 1989. It was initially expected that the road would provide a corridor for the location of new employment within the town, as well as a southern boundary to a possibly enlarged town centre. 1992 saw the opening of the Waitrose supermarket, accessible by vehicle only from Le Neubourg Way, but linked to the rest of the town centre by pedestrian paths. This quickly became a highly popular retail site, reputedly the third busiest Waitrose store in the country. A nearby site had originally been earmarked as a possible garden centre, but this failed to materialise, and instead later became the Waitrose extension car park. A further adjoining site marked for employment became what is today the town's only filling station. Further east, the Baker car dealership spread itself around the junction with Station Road, while the relocation of Sherman Chemicals to the Brickfields industrial estate enabled this site to be redeveloped as the Focus DIY store, opened in 2000.

Since 1974 the town library had been housed in the former bank premises at the top of Station Road. The 1986 plan had envisaged a new library somewhere in the area between the High Street and the relief road. When an actual site became available, it offered an opportunity for not just a library but also a rehousing of the Gillingham Museum, which had now become overcrowded in its cottage accommodation on Church Walk. The Chantry Fields site opposite Waitrose offered both library and museum a more spacious location easily accessible to users, especially to passing shoppers. The rehoused museum could potentially double the amount of space it had available. The new library opened in 1993, but the completion of the museum took rather longer (Fig. 119). The Local History Society took possession in January 1994, and the official opening was in October 1996.

In 1993 new foot bridges from the Waitrose and Museum area across the Stour to the Red Lion yard and to Buckingham Road were opened, improving access to these new amenities. In 1996 the Chantry footbridge was rebuilt to its present form, this being the third bridge to occupy this site.

On the south side of the Station Road junction with Le Neubourg Way, the former glue factory and market sites on the eastern side were redeveloped in the 1980s as the Old Market Centre,

The new Gillingham Museum

The Museum on Church Walk had served Gillingham well for forty years, but by the 1990s was no longer suited to the needs of a growing town. The lack of space had meant that the museum was unable to show exhibits to their best advantage, carry out essential conservation work, or cater for an increasing number of visitors in an expanding town. It had limited opening times, and was closed to visitors completely from October to March.

119 Queen Victoria takes up residence in the new Gillingham Museum.

The completion of the new museum involved a grant of £15,000 from the Heritage Lottery Fund, the museum having the distinction of being the very first recipient of one of the Lottery awards.

a group of new units which today includes a fitness centre, Scats store, and builders' supplies, as well as several smaller units. On the western side, change and redevelopment was slower to take place.

Part of the old egg packing factory was occupied for some years by Somdor, a steel products manufacturer, and subsequently by furniture retailers. The Oake, Woods bacon factory premises, vacated in 1984, was demolished and some of the space taken over by the sand and gravel merchant, J.H. Rose, leaving only the former abattoir standing, now used as the Rose office. The site had been envisaged as being developed for a mix of business, retail, and housing uses, but in the event, the only significant development has been for housing.

Significant change took place in the character of the Square and nearby streets, the oldest part of the town. Although the focus of retailing and commerce had shifted further towards Newbury in Victorian times, the area around the Square had still retained a diverse retail function well into recent times. In 1986 the Conservation Area was created, embracing the Square, South Street, Church Walk, St. Martin's Square, and the lower part of the High Street. It was inevitable that the construction of the relief road would bring further change by closing off the Square to Wyke Street and Cemetery Road, and making it into a no-through area. A consequence is that the Square has become progressively quieter as retailing has gradually deserted this corner of the town. Recent uses for former shop premises today include a veterinary practice, accountants, architect's practice, and kindergarten. A recent casualty has been the former pharmacy founded by William Samways around 1860, which at its closure in 2008 was thought to be the oldest continuously used pharmacy in the country. Across the corner, the former store of the Slade family became an electrical shop for several years, but in more recent times has been a bar. Above the bar is the Slade Centre, an arts centre with galleries, exhibitions, and meeting rooms, opened in 2000.

Like the Square, Queen Street has declined in retail uses since the 1980s. A walk from the High Street end towards Lodbourne at this time would have first passed Shephard's, a men's tailor's shop since Victorian times (Chapter 10). In St. Martin's Square could be found

The Gillingham Imperial Silver Band

There has been a band in Gillingham from at least 1861, when a Gillingham Town Band was engaged to play for an event of the Total Abstinence Society. The band played regularly at events of the Friendly Societies, and many of its members worked in the building trades or in the brickyard. The band disbanded during the First World War but was reformed in 1928 as the Gillingham Imperial Silver Band.

Since then the band has played a full role in the community, participating in civic events, fetes, concerts, and church services. It has been a regular contributor to the carnival, the Agricultural Show, and the Gillingham Festival. It has been highly successful in contests and competitions, reaching the national finals on several occasions (Plate 27).

The band is now housed in a room behind the Phoenix Hotel, approached by its distinctive doorway on South Street.[7]

a men's hairdresser, and also the Corbin's Tea Rooms, advertised as of 'Cozy Olde Worlde' character. By 1980 St. Martin's House, which housed the clinic, was also being used for adult education classes, and this use continued to increase during the following years, the building eventually becoming the Adult Education Centre. With the completion of the relief road scheme, the bottom end of Turner's Lane became merely a link between Queen Street and Le Neubourg Way. Further along, the former Wesleyan burial ground by the side of Portland Cottages was until 1999 in a much neglected state, before being taken over by the Town Council and turned into the Wesley Garden as a Millennium project. The walk along the street would have continued past the Queen's Head, which closed as recently as 2004; its last inn sign is to be found in the museum. The old Primitive Methodist chapel on the same side was a toy and fabrics factory. On the other side, the house notable for its large windows was for a short time the Cottage China Shop, while two doors along was a grocery store which was also the Queen Street Post Office. The motor businesses at the end of Queen Street were at this time in the hands of A303 Tyres and Stour Motors, which also had a petrol forecourt. Across on Lodbourne Green, the supermarket was being run by Scotts Foodmarkets.

Until 1989 Cemetery Road, had been a minor road serving mostly the old gas works and the cemeteries, ending as a proper road at Rolls Bridge Farm. The building of the relief road truncated it at the town end, converting this end into a no-through area and clearing away the industrial remains. For some time into the 1990s the Rolls Bridge Farm became a squash club, but this eventually disappeared with the spread of surrounding housing. At its western end beyond Rolls Bridge, the road was extended to become a local distributor road to the new housing areas between Wavering Lane and Wyke Road.

At the lower end of the High Street the Victorian vicarage in 1983 ceased to be a clergy home and property of the church, and became a care home known as Rawson Court, operated today by the Signpost Housing Association. Land from the vicarage garden, which had extended to the river, was used to extend the care home and to make a new town car park. The War Memorial was moved from its position by the bridge to a new site within the car park, a response to subsidence due to the memorial's proximity to the river bank, and the large sum which would have been required to underpin it. The new site also ensured that the Remembrance Day parade, a major civic occasion for the town, could be carried out with the necessary dignity and minimal inconvenience to passing traffic.

Not many yards from the vicarage and war memorial, a tragic loss in 1981 deprived Gillingham of one of its most notable buildings. A major fire swept through the old Town Mill, which had already been disused for several years. The 1986 Local Plan described the mill as a notable landmark, and stated that every effort should be made to rebuild it, perhaps for residential or retail use, but also acknowledged the high costs involved in so doing. The outcome was that the site remained unoccupied for several years while various proposals were considered, including a new civic centre and library. Eventually the option of retirement flats was decided upon, but progress was slow and was interrupted in 1989 by the possibility of flood damage. The development was not completed until 1992. Within the town there was some disappointment that the initial objective of restoring the mill to its original appearance had not been achieved.

Opposite the mill, the removal of the Grosvenor buildings in 1996 considerably changed the aspect of this part of the High Street by opening up a wide gap between the two parts of the town and creating a new view towards the recently built Waitrose supermarket and library. Since then this space has been used for visiting fairs and for the Gillingham Festival, which by this time had become a regular feature of the town calendar. Across the bridge, regular users of the High Street would have noticed changes of ownership in the shops extending towards School Road, but little to change the overall look of the street frontages, which still appear much the same today. A long-established name which had disappeared from the High Street by 1999 was that of the builders' merchants Hudson and Martin, who by this time had entirely relocated to Ham, and had become part of Sydenhams. In 1978 the site of the Stickland garage and the Victorian mansion of South Lynn, also owned by Sticklands, was cleared to make way for a Gateway supermarket and car park extending all the way back to Buckingham Road. Flanking the entrance to the supermarket on both sides were newly built blocks of shops (Plate 17). This gave a new aspect to the High Street and represented an increase in shopping floorspace in the town. However, it still left the town short of convenience goods retail provision, a situation that had to await the arrival of Waitrose some years afterwards. On Newbury, redevelopment took place following the closure of Light's garage and petrol station, ending another of Gillingham's old-established businesses. Their site, and that of the former Hudson and Martin yard

The Gillingham Festival

Gillingham might seem to be an unlikely place for a music and arts festival, but until recently one was held in the town continuously every year from the 1980s. The festival originated as a way of bringing together both local talent and better-known performers, and making them available to a wider audience. Recent performers at the festival have included Chris Barber, Paul Jones, Acker Bilk, Pam Ayres, Elkie Brooks, and Barbara Dickson. Young bands and tribute bands featured prominently. Gillingham's own Imperial Silver Band performed regularly, and there were orchestral performances and recitals. Non-musical events included children's items and workshops, and a classic car display.

120 The Gillingham Festival in 2007.

The festival lasted for two weeks. The first festival was held in a barn at Park Farm, but the regular venue for most events became the marquee or 'big tent' erected on the open space by the Town Bridge. Sadly, the last festival was held in 2009.

behind, eventually became available for a Lidl supermarket and car park. A major loss to the town took place in 2004 with the closure and demolition of the Royal Hotel on the corner of Harding's Lane.

This building, with its memorable lions over the porch, was a link with Gillingham's past railway age and a landmark building for visitors to the town. Further eastwards, the street view from 1989 onwards took in the roundabout of the new relief road. The road itself cut through some of the grounds of Newbury House, at that time being used by an estate agent, and later to be developed into flats.

In Hardings Lane a major development of the 1970s was the new Gillingham Centre. This was a badly needed facility for the town, and had been recognised as such in earlier town plans. The new amenity involved a rebuilding and covering of the open-air pool built in the Recreation Ground in the 1950s. It was opened in 1976 as a sports and community centre, with accommodation for 630 people for theatrical and other performances, a folding stage, and a council chamber which could be used as a meeting room. On the other side of Hardings Lane, the secondary school continued to expand as pupil numbers rose, the old Victorian buildings being gradually replaced by modern teaching accommodation. The oldest buildings on the site are now those of parts of the secondary modern school, dating from the late 1930s.

The town of the Three Rivers

IN 2004 THE North Dorset District Council published a report on the landscapes and open spaces around Gillingham, with suggestions for their future use. The main purpose of the study was to look at the landscapes of the areas around Milton, Bay, and Ham which had been acting as buffers to the town's growth, and assess their possible amenity and recreation potential. It also examined other opportunities to improve open space in the town. Among the ideas put forward were Conservation Area status for Colesbrook and Purns Mill House, a town park on the space between the Red Lion and the library, the development of sports and community facilities on Chantry Fields, and a park along the Shreen Water at Bay. The study also recognised the importance of Gillingham's three rivers in providing the chief corridors of green or undeveloped land through or around the urban area, several sections of which were not yet publicly accessible.[8]

The 'three rivers' theme was also being taken up at this time through the formation of the Three Rivers Partnership. This was a coming together of local councils and community organisations to develop community and leisure facilities appropriate to Gillingham's recent growth. The aims of the partnership, which took over the issues and concerns of the former Civic Society, were initially directed towards the provision of adequate open spaces, amenities for children and young people, and community meeting places. The project soon came to focus its attention on finding a replacement for Gillingham's ailing leisure centre on Hardings Lane. This had been built in the 1970s and had served the town well, but by the turn of the century was in need of considerable refurbishment. It eventually fell victim to District Council spending cuts and was closed in January 2008. The Three Rivers Partnership undertook the rebuilding of the centre, which was opened as the Riversmeet Centre in September 2010. It features a new swimming pool, sports hall, fitness suite, meeting room, and coffee shop, and at the time of writing a community hall remains to be added.

In 2006 the residents of Milton on Stour, together with Huntingford and Colesbrook, decided to produce their own village plan, so that they could assess the needs of the village for the future, and make their views known to the local councils. The Milton on Stour Village Plan was published in 2009. It included an action plan for the immediate concerns, and a vision statement for the future. An issue common to many concerns was the lack of information about activities and developments in the village arising from the loss of local facilities such as the Post Office, which had recently closed.[9]

2005 and 2006 saw the completion of the housing developments at Ham Farm on Shaftesbury Road. Another, smaller, housing scheme, of largely terraced town houses, was the Stour View scheme off Station Road on land previously occupied by the Oake, Woods bacon factory. In 2010 redevelopment began of the former Royal Hotel site, a scheme long delayed by planning issues. Meanwhile a housing project of a very different sort was taking shape at Cole Street Farm. Here a cohousing community and education centre was set up, at first on a pilot basis and then winning planning permission and grant funding in 2008. To date it consists of fourteen dwellings, some of which are affordable homes shared with a housing association. Residents have their own properties but share some facilities such as common room and laundry, and the centre provides courses on sustainable living. The centre is considered to be a pioneering venture in the development of cohousing schemes.

There have been a number of celebrations in recent years. In 2006 a plaque was unveiled on Gillingham Station to mark 150 years since the cutting of the first turf for the railway. The following year the town's French friends came from Le Neubourg to help to celebrate thirty years of the twinning association. In 2008 the Gillingham Local History Society marked fifty years of having a museum in the town. In 2010 the Gillingham and Shaftesbury Agricultural Society could look back over a century and a half since the society's foundation.

An especially significant celebration took place on 2 May 2009. This was to mark 150 years since the completion of the railway to Gillingham. A full day of celebrations included a procession from the High Street to the Station led by the town band, steam traction engines, and the Wessex Highlanders Pipe Band; a second unveiling of the commemorative plaque; various stalls, sideshows, and entertainments; and an evening of performance by the Gillingham Arts Workshop. The day was a reminder of perhaps the most important single event in

Relating the story of Gillingham: its past historians

Lt. Col. Charles R.A. Wallis was the brother of Barnes Wallis, of 'bouncing bomb' fame. Charles retired from the regular army in 1945 and returned to his home at Wyke House, from where he began to take an active interest in all aspects of local life. He served on the Parish Council, the Rural District Council, and the Parochial Church Council, and also gave time to Civil Defence and the scouting movement. Colonel Wallis was a principal founder of the Gillingham Local History Society and Gillingham Museum, and was its first curator. He died in 1962 while attempting a rescue in a drowning incident at Tintagel, Cornwall, for which he received a posthumous award for gallantry from the Carnegie Foundation.

Albert F.H.W. Wagner (1905-71) was educated at King's School, Pontefract, and at the University of Leeds. He joined Gillingham Grammar School in 1931 as a history teacher, later becoming Head of History, and at his retirement in 1969 was Deputy Headmaster. He developed a particular interest in the history of Gillingham, and wrote a history of St. Mary's Church and of Gillingham Grammar School. Much of his brief retirement was spent on research for a complete,

authoritative, history of Gillingham, along with William Slade. This work was cut short by his early death, after which Mr. Slade did no further work on the history.

William Slade came from the Slade family who owned the former store in the Square. Apart from Merchant Navy service during World War I he spent most of his life in Gillingham. He was a long-serving fireman, and a founder member of the Local History Society. He led the excavations of the Roman settlement at Todber, and was Curator of the Museum from 1962 to 1977.

Charles Howe (1923-85) was born in Ham, and grew up as an apprentice carpenter in his grandfather's building business. During the war he saw service as an RAF pilot in the Middle East and Burma. On his return home,

he continued in the family business, and was a founder member and President of the Gillingham Rotary Club, and Vice-President of the Royal British Legion. Mr. Howe served on the Town Council, the North Dorset District Council, and the County Council. He was Mayor of the town from 1980 to 1982, Chairman of the Gillingham Local History Society from 1976, and Curator Of the Museum from 1979. In 1983 he published *Gylla's Hometown*, a lively history of the town from its earliest times. *121*

122 Judging cattle at the Gillingham and Shaftesbury Agricultural Show in 2009.

Gillingham's history, marking the start of its transformation from an era of farms and horses into one of workshops and engines, a legacy which can still be found around the town at the present day.

APPENDIX 1
KEY DATES IN GILLINGHAM
HISTORY

Earliest times

c. 2,500 BC   Neolithic dwelling at Bay; long barrow at Longbury.

C. 100 BC   Durotrigian (Iron Age) hill fort at Whitesheet Hill.

75-350   Roman occupation in Common Mead Lane area. Late Roman cemetery at Langham.

658   Saxon victory over British at Penselwood.

1016   Battle between Edmund Ironside and Canute at Penselwood; earliest record of name *Gillingaham*, in Anglo-Saxon Chronicle.

1086   Domesday Book record of estates in Gillingham and Milton. Church of St. Mary granted by William the Conqueror to the Abbey of Shaftesbury.

1100 to 1500

c.1100   Liberty of Gillingham established by this time.

1132   Henry I's visit recorded in a charter made at Lincoln Cathedral.

1204   King John's first visit to Gillingham.

1209   John's feast to celebrate completion of King's Court.

1217   Perambulation establishes final boundaries of Gillingham Forest.

1244   Earliest record of Motcombe as a name.

1250   Henry III begins extensive additions to King's Court.

1261   Manor and forest of Gillingham granted by Henry III to Eleanor of Castile.

1267   Dominican Friary recorded at Gillingham.

1274   Survey of manor records a manor house, lands, and four mills.

1319   First vicar of St. Mary's Church, William Clive.

1330   Chantry chapel established in St. Mary's church.

1348   Black Death kills half of the population of Gillingham.

1369   Edward III orders demolition of Palace buildings at King's Court.

1378   Date of account of John Nyman of Motcombe.

1441   Earliest reference to a *guildhall* in Gillingham.

1453   Earliest known version of 'Charter of Gillingham.'

1500 to 1700

1516	Trust formed to provide education for the children of the parish; establishment of Free School.
1549	Dissolution of Gillingham Chantry, followed by granting of its properties to Sherborne School.
1553	Robert Dirdoe buys manor of Milton.
1559	First entries in parish registers. Sir John Zouche appointed keeper of the forest.
1579	John Jesop becomes vicar of Gillingham (d.1625).
1598	Chancery decree and reform of feofees constitution.
1608	Survey made of manor of Gillingham.
1615	Edward Rawson born. He was later to emigrate with his wife to a Puritan Colony in Massachusetts in America. He became the first Secretary to the Massachusetts Bay Colony.
1625	Charles I orders the disafforestation of the Royal Forest; map or 'plott' of Forest made.
1628	Forest riots; troops sent to quell disturbances.
1632	Charles I grants the manor and town to the Earl of Elgin.
1644	Church and vicarage plundered by Parliamentary troops. Vicar Davenant deprived of living.
1645	Encounters between Parliamentarians and Clubmen, a locally formed militia. Oliver Cromwell crushes Clubmen resistance at Hambledon Hill.
1648	Robert Frampton appointed Headmaster of the Free School. He quarrels with John Gage. He was later to become Bishop of Gloucester.
1651	Freke family at Wyke Hall.
1660	Manor and Forest conveyed to Sir Edward Nicholas for £21,500. Davenant's living restored.
1663	Byzant agreement renewed with Shaftesbury.
1694	Major fire destroys 40 houses and makes 54 families homeless.

1700 to 1800

1724	Beginning of Chancery dispute between Sherborne School and Frekes of Wyke Hall.
1729	Serious smallpox outbreak claims many lives.
1733	Death of Frances Dirdoe; her monument is in Gillingham church. Vicarage rebuilt by Rev. William Newton.
1736	Workhouse opened at Lodbourne.
1742	Another fire destroys 6 houses.
1750	Lock-up in South Street built around this time. Time of John Cave's Methodist sermons.
1753	Shaftesbury to Sherborne road turnpiked.
1766	Court Leet attempts to revive Charter of Gillingham.

1769	Gillingham Silk Company formed by Stephen Hannam, the town miller, together with three partners. Silk mill built on ground adjoining corn mill.
1775	Court of Exchequer dispute, Rev. John Hume and Motcombe villagers.
1776	Gillingham landowners propose a scheme of enclosure for the remaining commons.
1790	First manual fire pump purchased for the town. The pump is now on display in the Museum.
1792	First Wesleyan meeting house established in Queen Street by Henry Broadway.
1798	William Read leaves a sizeable legacy which founded 'Read's Charity'. It was originally for the relief of the poor and to provide bread on St.Thomas's Day.
1800	Town Bridge built; the date stone is inscribed 'County Bridge 1800'. Hugh Hansford is master of the Free School.

1800 to 1850

1801	Population of 1,873 recorded in first national census. Well sunk near the Vicarage (Spring Corner) by Rev. William Douglas to provide the first source of spring water to the town.
1805	Engraving of church made by John Buckler.
1807	New bridge built over the Stour at Wyke Street.
1809	Act of Parliament authorises enclosure of remaining commons.
1810	Unrest and disturbances following enclosure of Mapperton Hill.
1815	Sunday School established in the town.
1820	John Constable's first visit to Gillingham.
1823	Constable's second visit; his *Bridge at Gillingham* painting.
1825	Purns Mill destroyed by fire.
1821	New footbridge built over the Stour at Chantry.
1830	Disturbances and riots in Vale of Blackmore.
1831	Road from Sturminster Newton and East Stour to Gillingham and Bourton turnpiked.
1832	Rev. Henry Deane appointed Vicar of Gillingham, a post he held for the next 50 years.
1833	Gillingham Labourers' Friends Society formed "to improve conditions of the labourers of this Parish and to promote habits of industry among them".
1835	Earliest proposal for a railway through Gillingham.
1836	Horse-drawn manual fire pump purchased. First Methodist chapels in Queen Street and Turners Lane.
1837	Gillingham Gas & Coke Company opens new gasworks in Gas House Lane (later Cemetery Road).
1838	St. Mary's Church partly demolished and rebuilt; reopened December 1839.

1839	National School opened in the new schoolroom near the vicarage. New Poor Law Union workhouse opened at Shaftesbury.
1840	Royal Hotel built around this time. First Baptist Chapel in Newbury.
1843	Bad outbreak of Scarlet Fever, causing 41 child deaths between August and December.
1847	Wilts and Dorset Bank close their office following acute agricultural depression.

1850 to 1900

1851	Population of Gillingham reaches 2,806.
1855	Wilts and Dorset Banking Company re-open agency.
1856	First turf cut for new railway line. The spade and barrow used for the grand opening are in the Museum.
1859	Railway line opens to Salisbury on 1May; to Sherborne in 1860. Blackmore Vale Rifle Corps formed. Bacon factory and South-Western hotel opened.
1860	Brewery built at Wyke by the Matthews family. Gillingham Agricultural Society formed. First cemetery opened, now the Garden of Remembrance.
1865	New church of St. Simon and St. Jude opened at Milton on Stour.
1865	Gillingham Pottery, Brick and Tile Company formed; brickworks opened to south of railway line. Thomas Hudson starts a builders' merchants business.
1866	Bracher Brothers established in Station Road.
1874	New Wilts and Dorset Bank opened in the High Street.
1875	Board school opened in School Lane, now Gillingham Primary School.
1876	Gillingham Grammar School opened, James Mountain first Headmaster. Primitive Methodist Chapel built in Queen Street,Wesleyan Chapel built in the High Street.
1880	Slade family in business in The Square.
1882	Stickland's ironmongers established by Edwin Roberts Stickland.
1886	Ethel Freame's first diary.
1889	J.H. Rose established haulage business. William Gladstone, Prime Minister, visits Gillingham
1890	School built in Lydfords Lane, Wyke. Police Station and Courthouse built in School Road.
1892	Eden Shute's Butter Factory built in New Road. New Baptist Chapel built in Newbury.
1894	Gillingham becomes part of Shaftesbury Rural District. Parish Council formed.
1895	First Annual Parish Meeting held at the Lecture Hall.
1897	Fire Station built in School Lane at cost of £161.0.2d. Introduction of District Nurse.

1901 to 1950

1901	Population of Gillingham reaches 3,380. Slade and Sons rebuild department store in the Square.
1902	Stuckeys Banking Company open new premises at corner of Station Road and Newbury, later to become National Westminster Bank.
1903	Volunteer Fire Brigade formed.
1904	New Shand Mason Steam fire engine pump purchased for £250 to replace 1838 pump.
1905	A.H. Mumford appointed Headmaster of Grammar School. He retired in 1930.
1906	Oake, Woods bacon factory allowed to use the 'Royal appointment' by King Edward VII. First attempt to incorporate Miss Dunn's girl's school into Grammar School.
1907	Volunteers become unit of Territorial Army.
1908	Rebuilding of church tower with new west window.
1910	Parish council introduces first dustcart collection of house refuse.
1912	Grammar School swimming pool constructed at Bay; remains of Neolithic dwelling of about 2,500 BC discovered during excavations.
1914	New clock installed in St. Mary's Church. Start of new piped water supply from Mere. Plank House and former girls' school mobilised as Red Cross Hospitals.
1915	Post Office built in Station Road.
1917	Town flooded after dam bursts at Stourton Pond.
1920	Dedication and unveiling of War Memorial in High Street.
1921	First council houses at Addison Terrace.
1923	Grammar School Cricket Pavilion built by Old Boys in memory of fallen comrades.
1924	Convent established at Common Mead Avenue for Carmelite Order.
1926	Recreation Ground at Hardings Lane opened by Lady Pelly.
1928	First electricity supply.
1930	Martin Perks appointed headmaster of Grammar school; he retired in 1956.
1931	Gillingham's proposal to become an Urban District is rejected.
1932	Primitive and Wesleyan Methodist Churches amalgamate.
1934	Regal cinema built in High Street. Last meeting of Manor Court.
1939	Arrival of many evacuees and military personnel.
1941	German airplane comes down over Huntingford.
1942	Secondary Modern school opens on site adjoining Grammar School.
1946	E.L. Seager becomes vicar of St. Mary's.

1950 to 2010

1952	Queen arrives at Gillingham Station for local visits.
1953	Establishment of Gillingham Local History Society and Museum.

1956	A.F.H.W. Wagner publishes history of St. Mary's church; and of Grammar School in 1958.
1958	Museum in Church Walk officially opened; Hon. Curator is Lt.-Col. C.R.A. Wallis.
1959	Senior and Godwin close market in Station Road. Gillingham School formed from amalgamation of Grammar and Secondary Modern Schools. Open-air swimming baths opened next to recreation ground.
1960	Hudson and Martin close sawmills in Station Road.
1963	Closure of Regal cinema. Hall and Woodhouse acquire Matthews brewery at Wyke.
1964	National Stud closes operations at Sandley and re-locates to Newmarket.
1966	Matthews & Co. cease working at Town Mill.
1968	Last Gillingham bricks manufactured at the brickyard.
1970	United Dairies egg packing station in Station Road closes; Union Glues, formerly Maloneys, closes.
1971	Publication of Gillingham Local Plan.
1972	New Fire Station built at Peacemarsh.
1974	Parish Council replaced by Town Council; office of Chairman replaced by Mayor.
1977	Major fire at Primary School (25 May). Signing of Twinning Charter with French town of Le Neubourg, Normandy.
1982	Fire destroys former Town Mill.
1986	New Local Town Plan published.
1989	Town relief road, Le Neubourg Way, opens.
1991	Wyke primary school at Deane Avenue opens.
1992	Waitrose store opens on Chantry Fields.
1993	Opening of new library on Chantry Fields.
1994	Local History Society takes possession of new purpose Museum on Chantry Fields.
1996	Official opening of new museum.
1999	Restoration of Methodist burial ground as Wesley Garden.
2004	Formation of Three Rivers Partnership. Opening of St. Mary the Virgin primary school.
2009	Milton on Stour village plan published. Celebration of 150 years of railway in Gillingham.
2010	New Riversmeet Centre opened on Hardings Lane.

APPENDIX 2
SOME TERMS FOUND IN
GILLINGHAM HISTORICAL
DOCUMENTS

Advowson   The right to appoint a priest to a benefice, especially a parish church.

Amercement A fine in the manorial court.

Assart   A piece of land brought into cultivation by enclosing it from the waste.

Attachment court A court for the preliminary hearing of forest offences, sometimes merged with the swanimote court. From French *attacher*, to apprehend.

Barton The home farm of the lord of a manor.

Benefice An ecclesiastical living.

Church rate A rate levied on all households in the parish to maintain the church and churchyard.

Church-scot A payment made to support the parish priest, usually of cocks, hens and eggs.

Consistory court Courts held by bishops or archdeacons to administer ecclesiastical law in respect of, for example, the conduct of parishioners and clergy, or probate matters.

Copyholder One who holds land by the custom of the manor, as recorded on his copy of the court roll.

Court leet A court held in the manor, usually every six months, with jurisdiction over petty offences, customs of the manor, and civil affairs. It could fine and imprison offenders.

Customary or custumal The written statement of the customs of the manor, recording matters such as admittances to copyholds and the regulation of farming in the common fields.

Encroachment The illegal taking into private use of a piece of waste land for agriculture or building. Encroachments could be legalised in the manor court by the payment of a fine.

Essoin A lawful excuse made for non-attendance at the manor court.

Extent A formal survey of the value of the lands of a manor and its services, rents, profits, etc.

Fee forester The chief official of the forest, who supervised other foresters and keepers.

Fine (1) A sum payable on admission to a holding, so-called because it was final, ie only paid once; applied to copyholds in the manor court and later to leases. (2) a sum paid for an offence against the manor (eg an encroachment), also called an *amercement*.

Glebe Land assigned to the incumbent of a parish as part of the endowment of the church.

Hambling or lawing, The cutting of the front claws of dogs.

Heriot A due paid to the lord on the death of a tenant, often his best animal or a sum equivalent to it.

Heybote The taking of timber for the repair of hedges and fences.

Hide A measure of land, varying from 60 to 100 acres; in Domesday Book used for purposes of taxation. Originally the amount which could be tilled by a plough in a year.

Hundred A subdivision of the shire used for local administration. It survived for some functions well into recent centuries.

Husbote The taking of timber for the repair of houses.

Inquisition An enquiry or valuation.

Jointure Property or a fixed sum settled on a woman at marriage, to remain hers after the death of her husband.

Landshare or *lanchard* A strip in the open field (similar word to *lynchet*).

Lay subsidy A tax levied on moveable property, a tenth or fifteenth; not applied to the clergy.

Liberty A manor or estate which lay outside the sheriff's jurisdiction. Some royal estates were liberties, their cases being heard in the royal courts.

Lynchet A cultivation terrace often found on limestone and chalk lands.

Manor An estate or territorial unit originally held by feudal tenure, ie held of the lord by service.

Messuage A dwelling house or tenement with its surrounding property. A *capital messuage* was a larger property belonging to someone of status.

Pannage The right of tenants to graze pigs on the acorns and beech mast of the commons or forests of a manor; also payment by others for this privilege.

Peculiar A church jurisdiction outside the normal control of the bishop or archdeacon; royal manors were often peculiars.

Perambulation The beating of the bounds of the forest, often in order to establish the extent of the forest jurisdiction.

Peter's pence A tax of a penny paid to support St Peter's church in Rome.

Plurality The holding of several benefices or ecclesiastical livings.

Prebend A benefice belonging to a cathedral or abbey, which provided the priest (prebendary) to the benefice; the income drawn by the cathedral (or abbey) from the benefice.

Rectory (1) The benefice of a rector, the incumbent entitled to the great or 'rectorial' tithe. (2) The residence of a rector.

Purpresture An *encroachment* in a forest or other royal land.

Quarenten A linear measure, a furlong.

Serf An unfree peasant or bondman, holding by land service; by the fourteenth century many services had been commuted for rent.

Sheriff's aid A tax levied by the sheriff to assist with his expenses.

Sokeman A free peasant, more commonly used in eastern England.

Surrender Extinction of the owner's right in a property; used in the manor court as part of the process of transferring copyhold land.

Swanimote A court concerned with the administration and regulation of the forest, particularly the availability of pannage.

Tallage A tax levied by a lord, usually at Michaelmas.

Thegn A Saxon landowner or nobleman.

Tithe The ancient obligation of all parishioners to maintain their priest from one-tenth of the produce or 'fruits' of the earth.

Tithing A grouping of ten households bound together to the court leet for the good conduct of all the members.

Underwood Timber taken from below the level of the principal trees, of lower value than trunks and branches of the larger trees.

Verderer The official appointed by the king to administer the vert and venison (vegetation and deer) of the forest, and to hear cases in the swanimote court.

Vicarage (1) The benefice of a vicar, the incumbent entitled to the small or 'vicarial' tithe. (2) The residence of a vicar.

Villein A serf of a higher status.

Virgate A holding of arable land in the open fields, usually of 30-40 acres, with accompanying rights of common.

Visitation An official inspection of the parish by the bishop or archdeacon.

Worksilver A due paid by villains to the lord in recognition of their possible liability for land service.

APPENDIX 3
LISTED BUILDINGS IN
GILLINGHAM AND MILTON

All Listed Buildings are Grade 2. Some architectural description can be found in the pages of Royal Commission on Historical Monuments, Vol.4, North Dorset.

Bainly House
Barn south-east of Old House, Milton
Blackmore Vale House, Newbury
Brewery house and front fence, Milford Court
Bridge carrying Wyke Street over River Stour
Broadhayes, St. Martin's Square
Broadhayes Cottage, St. Martin's Square
Chantry Cottage
Chantry Ford Cottage
Church Cottage, Church Walk
Church of St. George, Langham
Church of St. Mary the Virgin
Church of St. Simon & St. Jude, Milton
Folly's End, Wyke St
Granary, Wyke Farm
Higher Langham House
Knapp House, Wyke St
Lime Tree House, St. Martin's Square
Little Chantry, Wyke St
Lock-up, South St
Lodbourne Farmhouse, Lodbourne Green
Lodden Bridge Farmhouse
Lower Bowridge Hill Farmhouse
Madjeston Farmhouse
Mill House, Barnaby Mead
Nos. 1 and 2 Church House, St. Martin's Square

Old Toll House, Wyke Rd
Park Farmhouse, Shaftesbury Rd
Pierston Farmhouse, Milton
Pierston House, Milton
Plank House, Wyke St
High St, former Free School
High St, premises of Rutters
High St, old schoolhouse
Purns Mill House
Queen St, former Queen's Head
Rawson Court
Springfield, Bugley
The Great House, Lodbourne
The Barton, St. Martin's Square
The Square, former Cat Boutique
The Cottage, Cemetery Rd
The Laurels, Newbury
The Old House, Milton
Phoenix Hotel
Red Lion Hotel
Town Bridge
Table tombs (three) in St. Mary's churchyard
Vicarage Schoolroom, St. Martin's Square
War memorial, Barnaby Mead
Wessex Cottage, Mapperton Hill
Milford Court, Wyke, former brewery
Wyke Farmhouse
Wyke Hall

APPENDIX 4
VICARS AND RECTORS OF
GILLINGHAM, 1318-2011

1318	William Clive	1625	Edward Davenant
1361	Reginald Typul	1680	Thomas Ward
	Roger Tyrell	1696	John Craig
1364	William de Chiltern	1696	William Newton
	William Burton	1744	John Perne
1386	Robert Symond	1770	John Hume
1429	John Nicol	1783	Edward Emily
1437	William Pole	1792	William Douglas
1439	Richard Elys	1819	John Fisher
	John Bate	1832	Henry Deane
1463	Simon, Bishop of Connor	1882	Edward Inman
	Simon Elvington	1891	Sidney Davies
1475	William Stodard	1899	William Heygate
1493	Robert Forster	1905	Walter Sotheby
1527	Edward Moore	1916	Robert Abbott
1541	John Rythe	1925	Rupert Newman
1546	Richard Brisley	1946	Edward Seager
1561	Robert Peveral	1979	John McNeish (Team Rector)
1571	Thomas Coke	2000	Alan Gill (Rector)
1579	John Jesop	2009	Peter Greenwood (Rector)

APPENDIX 5
MAYORS OF GILLINGHAM
SINCE 1974

1973	S.P. Hiscott		1992	F.H. Evill
1974	A.R. Coombes		1993	Linda Knox
1975	A.R. Coombes		1994	Susan J. Moore
1976	A.R. Coombes		1995	C.E. Dann
1977	S.A. Ballard		1996	Su Hunt
1978	G. Jones		1997	Linda Knox
1979	Helen B. Burt		1998	Liz Hague
1980	C.L.L. Howe		1999	Su Hunt
1981	C.L.L. Howe		2000	Janet Robson
1982	F.H. Evill		2001	B. Nicholson
1983	R.H. Osborne		2002	C.E. Dann
1984	G. Joyce		2003	C.E. Dann
1985	R. Hussey		2004	C.E. Dann
1986	A.R. Coombes		2005	C.E. Dann
1987	Helen B. Burt		2006	C.E. Dann
1988	B. Nicholson		2007	B. Millichamp
1989	T.S. Rose		2008	I. Stewart
1990	P.J. Crocker		2009	R.W. Evill
1991	C.E. Dann		2010	Su Hunt

Notes and References

Abbreviations used:

DHC   Dorset History Centre, Dorchester
WSHC   Wiltshire and Swindon History Centre, Chippenham
GLHS   Gillingham Local History Society
PDNHAS Proceedings of the Dorset Natural History and Archaeological Society
SDNQ   Somerset and Dorset Notes and Queries

Chapter 1: Origins of a Dorset town

1.   Treves, Sir F. (1906), *Highways and Byways in Dorset*, Ch.2
2.   The dominance of pasturage and the reluctance of farmers to drain lands for arable production may also reflect the oppressive costs of the higher tithes payable on corn. Kerr, B. (1968), *Bound to the Soil*, p.171.
3.   Howe, C. (1983), *Gylla's Hometown*, 14. The report was published in the *Morning Post*.
4.   Ross, M.S. (1987), 'Kington Magna and surrounding areas: a fieldwalking survey of the prehistory (1979-87)', *PDNHAS* 109, pp.91-104.
5.   Cunliffe, B. (1993), *Wessex to AD 1000*, from the map of causeway camp territories, p.56.
6.   Green, M. (2000), *A Landscape Revealed: 10,000 Years on a Chalkland Farm*, shows the intensive level of prehistoric settlement in one small part of the Dorset landscape. I am grateful to Peter Barker for his comments on prehistoric finds in the local Gillingham area.
7.   Putnam, Bill. (2007), *Roman Dorset*, pp.14-20.
8.   The population of the country may have risen from the 1 million of Durotrigian times to 5 million; Putnam, ibid., p.78.
9.   Hutchins J. (1868), *The History and Antiquities of the County of Dorset*. Vol. III, p.662. The 1951 findings are reported in *PDNHAS* (1951) 73, p.112, and the 1984 work in Cox, M. *PDNHAS* (1984) 106, p.118. The name *Coldharbour* or 'shelter from the cold' is a frequent occurrence along or close to Roman roads.
10. The Common Mead Lane excavations were fully reported on by Moore W.F. and Ross M.S. in *PDNHAS* (1989), 111, pp.57-70.
11. Dorset County Council (forthcoming), *Dorset Historic*

Towns Survey, Gillingham report.

12. Ross, M.S. reported on the West Stour villa in *PDNHAS* (1985) p.164. For the Kington Magna detail see the same author and volume: 'Kington Magna, a parish survey.' The Wincanton site at New Barn Farm is included in Richardson, M. (2003), *Wincanton, an Archaeological Assessment,* Somerset Urban Archaeological Survey.

13. Information on field walking finds from Peter Barker and members of the Gillingham Local History Society.

14. Hutchins, ibid., pp.326-7. The significance of the Langham cemetery and its possible relationship to the Common Mead Lane burial is discussed by Moore and Ross (1989), above.

15. 'In this year (658) Cenwalh fought at Penselwood against the Welsh, and drove them in flight as far as the Parrett.' *Anglo-Saxon Chronicle.* The strategic role of Penselwood is noted in Barker, K., 'Institution and landscape in early medieval Wessex,' *PDNHAS* (1984), p.106.

16. Mills, A.D. (1989), *The Place-Names of Dorset,* English Place-Name Society, Part III, p.9. Earlier interpretations of the name based on rivers etc are not now acceptable.

17. The wider significance of royal estates and minster churches in providing focal points for Saxon settlement is discussed by L. Keen in Haslam, J. (1984), *Anglo-Saxon towns in Southern England.* Sherborne, Wimborne, Shaftesbury, Wareham, and possibly Christchurch, are other towns based on royal manors. There is a tradition, encouraged by William of Malmesbury and the historian John Hutchins, that Edward the Confessor was proclaimed king at Gillingham in 1042, but no evidence is known to support this.

18. *Anglo-Saxon Chronicle,* ed. Garmonsway G.N., p.149.

19. There is further description of the Gillingham fragment in *The County of Dorset, Vol.4 (North),* Royal Commission on Historical Monuments, (1972), pp.16 and 30.

20. Penn K.J. (1980), *Historic Towns in Dorset,* p.65.

21. The principal report on the Saxon grain driers investigation is Heaton M.J. (1992), 'Saxon grain driers and later medieval features', *PDNHAS* 114, pp.97-126. There is a shorter note by the same writer in *PDNHAS* p.113 (1991).

22. Valentin J. in *PDNHAS* (2001) 123, p.128.

23. All Domesday Book references are to the text and notes of the Phillimore edition ed. C & F Thorn (1983). The royal manor at Gillingham was grouped with Dorchester, Fordington, Sutton (Poyntz), and 'Frome' (not easily identifiable).

Chapter 2: Gillingham as a medieval manor

1. Terms italicised in the text are to be found in the glossary at the end of

this book. Hutchins references are from Vol. III, p.615 *passim.*

2. *Cal. Patent Rolls (CPR)* Hen III 6, 736-7; Edw I 3, 451-2; Edw II 3 115-6. Hutchins p.616.

3. National Archives E142/80/1. There is a translation in *The Marn'll Book* (1952), p.62.

4. Ibid. Field sizes were described as according to the 'lesser measure', possibly 16 ½ feet to the perch.

5. Mills A.D. (ed, 1971), *Dorset Lay Subsidy 1332.*

6. Shaftesbury was a Domesday borough, and sent members to parliament in 1295; it was the largest Dorset town in 1332 with a well developed trading community. Sherborne established its new borough of Newland in 1227 and held Assizes from 1242. Penn (1980), *Historic Towns in Dorset.*

7. DHC D/GIM/M1; a transcription and translation by Drew C.D. and Mylam W., is in the Gillingham Museum. Hutchins (p.651) reproduces in full a copy from 1573, which is longer than the medieval version and includes further detail on the common fields which were not present on the original.

8. National Archives PRO C143/106/20; PRO C143/157/10. Also notes from a lecture by W. Mylam in 1957 (Gillingham Museum).

9. Sandhull is 'sand hill', a reference to the sandy nature of the soil on this part of the Corallian. The development of 'hill' to 'ley' is due to the lack of stress on the second element; Mills A.D. (1989), *The*

Place-Names of Dorset, Part 3, p.17.

10. From the Drew and Mylam transcript, p.23. A problem in assessing the total amount of virgate land in the manor is the use of the Latin word *medietas*. The literal translation gives 'mid-part', but it can also be translated as 'one half', or even as another way of writing 'medium quality'.

11. It is considered that since the labour liability was not wholly entirely discharged by payments of rent, the additional payment of *worksilver* was levied in recognition of the difference. Although by the fourteenth century lords were largely using hired labour for their demesne lands instead of villein service, the worksilver liability gave the lord the option of returning to villein service should the labour situation on the estate require it (Drew and Mylam).

12. Hutchins p.617.

13. The relationships are discussed in Haimes J.W. (1970), *The Haimes: A Dorset Family.*

14. The court rolls, for many years in the hands of Farnfield and Nicholls, solicitors, are now in the Dorset History Centre. All references to the 1296-7 roll are from the DHC transcript, D/GIM/M3.

15. Copy in Gillingham Museum.

16. Hutchins pp.643-4, makes no distinction between rectory and prebend. He gives a list of the prebendaries.

17. PRO SC8/200/9968; PRO C47/11/2/9; *CPR* Edw I 1 174.

18. Page W. (ed. 1908) *A History of the*

County of Dorset Vol.2 (Victoria County History), p.92. The nearest other Dominican house was at Wilton, founded in 1245; in 1280 the brothers moved to Salisbury, leaving Wilton as a cell. Another Dominican house was at Ilchester, founded 1221-60.

19. Hutchins p.645.
20. Hutchins pp.627, 631, 632, 645
21. *CPR* Ed III 1 501. The *Inquisition ad quod damnum* PRO C143/210 gives slightly different details for the land and property.
22. Below, Chapter 4.
23. Good, R. (1966), *The Old Roads of Dorset* p.95, where other vanished roads are described.
24. National Archives E142/80/1; DHC D/GIM/M3; Mills, *Place-Names of Dorset,* ibid. p.16.
25. Cox, P. (1992), 'Excavations at the Waitrose supermarket site, Chantry Fields, Gillingham, 1991-2.' *PDNHAS* 114, pp.127-34, also includes the original of Fig. 12.
26. Valentin, J. and Robinson, S. (2001), 'A medieval site in Gillingham, Dorset: further excavations at Chantry Fields, 1999'. *PDNHAS* 123, pp.23-50. See also the earlier evaluation in *PDNHAS* 120 (1998), p.104.
27. Ross, M. (1993), in *PDNHAS* 115, p.164, also includes the original of Fig. 14.
28. Hutchins, p.654.
29. See *SDNQ* 23, 148. There are also references to strip lynchets from aerial photographs in *Historical Monuments in the County of Dorset, Vol.4 (North),* Royal Commission

on Historical Monuments, 1972, p.35.
30. Mills, *Place-Names of Dorset,* ibid. p.14; *Historical Monuments* ibid. Hutchins, p.625. The aerial photographs are held by Dorset County Council.
31. Mills p.15, and earlier references used above.
32. Ibid.
33. Early references (from Mills, *Place-Names*) include *Roger atte Colverhouse* (Roger of the dove-cote), 1327 Subsidy Roll; *Stokkefeld* 1441 Gillingham Court Roll; *Bengeruylesgrove* 1313 Close Roll; and *Kyngmede* 1415 Court Roll.

Chapter 3: The medieval Forest of Gillingham

1. Hutchins J, *History and Antiquities of the County of Dorset,* 3rd edition (1861-70), Vol. III, pp.620-1.
2. John Rylands Library, Nicholas Papers no. 68
3. Coker, John (1732) *A History of Dorsetshire,* but considered to have been written by Thomas Gerard c.1620.
4. *CPR* Ed III 3, 513.
5. The 1624 *Plott* is to be found in the Dorset History Centre. Leland's journey : the Gillingham reference comes from additional notes to his journey of 1542; see Chandler J. (1993) *John Leland's Itinerary,* p.142.
6. Hutchins p.618
7. For example: *Cal. Lib. Rolls (CLR) Hen III 3 124 & 130,* May 21 1247, John Blanchbully to deliver 5

tuns of wine from Southampton to Gillingham; July 21 1247, a further 10 tuns. *CLR Hen III 3 293*, 1250 June 30, to the bailiffs of Southampton, to deliver 5 tuns of wine to Gillingham.

8. Haime J.W. (1970), *The Haimes: A Dorset Family*, pp.2-3.

9. *Cal. Close Rolls (CCR)* Hen III 3 258.

10. *CCR* Hen III 6 299.

11. The boundary, and its condition some years ago, is fully described in Cantor L.M. and Wilson J.D. (1965) 'The medieval deer parks of Dorset, Part 5', *PDNHAS*, p.87. 1624 *Plott*, ibid.

12. *King's Court, Gillingham*, Gillingham Museum publication, 2002.

13. *King's Court, Gillingham*; Hutchins p.618 gives some possible dimensions. *CLR* Hen III 1 415.

14. Cited in Howe C. (1983), *Gylla's Hometown*, p.22.

15. *CCR* Hen III I 54; *CLR* Hen III I 1 215; *CLR* Hen III 1 302; *CLR* Hen III 2 222; *CCR* Hen III 6 308.

16. *CLR* Hen III 3 257; *CLR* Hen III 3 297.

17. Hutchins, p.619.

18. *CCR* Hen III 7 333; Hen III 7 242; Hen III 7 370; Hen III 9 79; Hen III 10 1,2. *CPR* Hen III 4 434.

19. Hutchins, p.619; Howe p.36.

20. PRO *Cal. Of Misc. Chancery* I P P 332-3.

21. *CCR* Hen III I 54; Hen III I 64; Hen III I 240. *CCR* Hen III 6 453; *CPR* Hen III 4 100.

22. Hutchins, p.651.

23. *CLR* Hen III 2 64; Hen III 2 274.

CCR Hen III 10 9; Hen III 10, 81; Hen III 10 149.

24. *CCR* Hen III 10 272; Hen III 10 258; Hen III 10 232-3.

25. The use of Close and Liberate Rolls for tracing the destinations of the Gillingham oaks has been carried out in detail by Bill Shreeves in his series of articles for the *GLHS* journal, beginning in 1997. The detailed references which follow can be found in these articles.

26. The Gloucester Friary oaks are fully described by Bill Shreeves in the *GLHS* journal for 2009.

27. *GLHS* articles, ibid.

28. Mills A.D. (1989), *The Place-Names of Dorset, Part 3*, p.17. *Dorset Lay Subsidy 1327* (Dorset History Centre). Hutchins, p.645.

29. Hutchins, pp.645, 629.

Chapter 4: Black Death to Reformation

1. Bettey J.H. (1986), *Wessex from AD 1000*, pp.82-4. Some lynchets near Gillingham are recorded in *Historical Monuments in the County of Dorset, Vol.4 (North)*, Royal Commission on Historical Monuments (1972), p.35.

2. Bettey, ibid.

3. Forrest, M. 'The Black Death in Dorset: the crisis of 1348-1349.' *PDNHAS* (2010) 131, p.3.

4. Forrest, ibid.

5. Forrest, ibid. The payment of *worksilver* in lieu of labour services was already well established in the manor by 1300 (see Chapter 2, note 11).

6. Barker, P. (2010) 'Milton on Stour's

medieval pilgrims', in *GLHS Journal*, p.23.

7. DHC D/GIM/M3. Transcription by Joseph Fowler in *SDNQ* (1961) p.27 pp.218-20. There is a further transcription with the document in the DHC. The later part of the document now appears to be missing.

8. eg Nicholas Papers, Elgin v. Croke dispute, citing court roll of 1405-6.

9. All references are from Mills, *Place-Names,* and Gillingham Court Rolls.

10. Ibid.

11. Based on the notes left behind by A.F.H.W Wagner, W.W. Slade, and John Pinnock. The latter looked at several records in the Public Records Office relating to the 'charter'.

12. National Archives PRO C143/429/98, Chancery Inq p.m. 22 Ric 2, n.6.

13. Chantry rolls in *PDNHAS* 27, 28, and 29 (1907-9). The references to Martin's chapel are in Mills, *Place-names*; Gillingham Court Roll 1438; Hutchins p.618. In Bodmin, Cornwall, a town of 2,000, there were no fewer than forty gilds by the sixteenth century, the majority founded for religious or charitable purposes.

14. Wagner A.F.H.W (1957), *Gillingham Grammar School, Dorset: An Historical Account*, p.11.

15. Penn, K.J. (1980), *Historic Towns in Dorset*, pp. 88,95.

16. DHC D41/1, 18th century copy of 1598 Chancery decree.

17. Ibid. By the early nineteenth century the feofees had acquired considerably more property (Chapter 8).

18. DHC S235 C1/2/1

19. Hutchins, p.642. Chantry roll references as above. There had been 21 priests of the St Catherine's chantry between 1333 and 1549.

Chapter 5: 1579 to 1680: The Gillingham of John Jesop and Edward Davenant

1. Stoate T.L. (1982), *Dorset Tudor Subsidies*; PRO LR2 /214, 1608-9. All references to the 1608 manor survey are PRO LR2/214, on DHC microfilm.

2. Meekings C.A.F. (1951), *Dorset Hearth Tax Assessments, 1662-4.*

3. Gillingham Parish Registers. Hutchins also has some parish register totals, p.643. These figures take no account of people moving into or out of the parish.

4. 1608 manor survey.

5. Hutchins, pp.622-3.

6. Ibid.

7. Hutchins, p.617, p.651.

8. *SDNQ* (1915) XIV, p.158

9. There is more detail and discussion on East Haimes in Haimes J.W. (1970) *The Haimes, A Dorset Family.* However the identification of East Haimes as Bowridge Hill Farm is incorrect, the actual location being clearly shown on the 1624 map.

10. DHC D435/1 Recovery of the manor of Madjeston, 1655.

11. Wagner A.F.H.V. (1957), *Gillingham Grammar School, Dorset: An Historical Account*, pp.13-15. There

is a copy of the Chancery order in DHC, D41.

12. Horsfall A. (1995); The woodcourt of the royal forest of Gillingham', *SDNQ* 33, p.419.

13. Hutchins p.622.

14. Cantor L.M. and Wilson J.D (1965), 'The medieval deer parks of Dorset', *PDNHAS* 87, p.5.

15. This account of the Gillingham riots is drawn from Bettey J.H. (1976), 'The revolts over the enclosure of the royal forest at Gillingham, 1626-30', *PDNHAS* 97, p.21, where full references may be found. Another account is in Sharp, Buchanan (1980), *In Contempt of All Authority: Rural Artisans and Riot in the West of England, 1586-1660*. There is further detail on the enclosure itself in Hutchins, pp.649-51.

16. Bettey J.H. (1987), *Rural Life in Wessex 1500-1900*, pp.113-4. The Skimmington myth has a parallel with that of Captain Swing, the equally mythical leader of rural riots two centuries later.

17. Sharp, ibid., pp.127-8.

18. Bettey (1976), ibid.

19. eg Sir Edward Berkeley's land at Benjafield, sequestered until 1650; also lands of William Thornhill, Richard Gilden, Lord Stourton, and others; Hutchins p.637.

20. Goodwin, T. (1996) *Dorset in the Civil War 1625-65*, pp.108-10. An older, but fuller, account is Bayley A.R. (1910), *The Great Civil War in Dorset, 1642-60*, p.276-80.

21. Meekings C.A.F. (1951) *Dorset Hearth Tax Assessments, 1662-4*.

22. Hutchins p.629-30. Also *SDNQ* (1893) VI, p.297; and Stevenson, W. (1815) *A general view of the agriculture of the county of Dorset*. The name 'byzant' may refer to a gold coin or other tribute.

23. Haimes, ibid., p.26.

24. Aubrey, J. *Brief Lives,* written between 1669 and 1696.

25. Evans T.S. (1876) *The Life of Robert Frampton, Bishop of Gloucester*. This appears to be based on a much earlier manuscript of Frampton's life.

26. Several references as earlier, further references in Hutchins.

27. This account of the Rawson, Perne, and Greene families is based largely on the notes of the late A.F.H.W. Wagner and W.W. Slade.

28. I am grateful to David Lloyd and Tony Thrasher for their information on Wyke Hall and its families.

29. Hutchins, pp.619-20.

Chapter 6: 1680 to 1820: population, land, and livelihoods

1. Hutchins, p.619.

2. Meekings C.A.F. (1951), *Dorset Hearth Tax Assessments*, 1662-4.

3. D/GIM/MIC/R/1133

4. Gillingham parish register transcripts in the Dorset History Centre.

5. Gillingham parish registers.

6. Dorset History Centre, Land Tax return for 1781 QDE(L) 23/2/2, and subsequent years.

7. The earlier Thomas Freke of Wyke in 1735 presented the church with a library of 600 books. By the time

of Henry Deane's ministry only 200 remained, and are now housed in the library of Salisbury Cathedral. The name of Thomas Pile appears in 21 of the volumes. Hutchins p. 647, *GLHS* Journal for 2008.

8. Sykes estate map, 1767; sale particulars 1821. Both are in the Gillingham Museum.

9. DHC D/GIM J6/2/4; details of the charity on the church monument; Land Tax returns ibid.

10. Hutchins, p.627. Howe, C. in *GLHS* Newsletter, 1985. Further detail is given on the church monuments.

11. 1781 Land Tax return; and Hutchins, p.627. In 1781 Thomas Matthews contributed £4 17s 4d in land tax, with smaller amounts levied from William Matthews and Henry Matthews. In 1802 John Matthews paid £5 2s for his own land, which was tenanted; the land farmed from Whitchurch was valued at £6 15s and from Long at £5 10s.

12. Hutchins IV, p.104. Kerr, B. (1968), *Bound to the Soil: A Social History of Dorset,* p.179. Sale particulars, Gillingham Museum.

13. Christian Broome, nee Helme, died on the island of Nevis in 1720. The monument to her and to later Helmes family members was erected by her descendant Grace Cox in 1812.

14. Sherborne School Records in DHC, S235.

15. Stevenson, W. (1815), *A General View of the Agriculture of the County of Dorset.* Also Claridge, J (1793), *A General View of the Agriculture of*

the County of Dorset.

16. Stevenson, ibid. Sykes estate sale particulars, Gillingham Museum.

17. Read estate papers, DHC.

18. Sherborne School Records and Sykes estate details as above.

19. Sherborne School Records S235 C2/13/1, C2/10/2/1, and C1/3/2.

20. Map of survey of waste lands of Gillingham, 1777. Gillingham Museum.

21. eg 1772, Edward Card enclosing part of the common called Tomalands. DHC D/GIM N 3/1. The October 1780 Court Leet recorded William Godwin, John Cox, William Hayter, and Thomas Haines all erecting cottages in Porrige Hill, Newbury, or Ham Common; the encroachments included 'John Matthews for encroaching a piece of land on the common called Little Marsh, the same to be thrown open by Ladyday, under penalty of 10s.'

22. The signatories were William Chafin Groves, Rev. Mr Freke, William Tinney, Edward Read, Edw Sly, Henry Matthews, John Harris, Thomas Matthews, Silas Martin, Edward Card, Robert Hixon, and John Cave.

23. DHC D/GIM N3/2.

24. D/GIM N3/1

25. For the Mere enclosures see Mere Papers no.9, *Enclosure! The changed face of Mere.*

26. DHC D/GIM/N3/2-4

27. Weinstock, M. (1953) *Studies in Dorset history,* p.66. In this village the vicar had carried out his own survey of the parish.

28. Gillingham wills in the Wiltshire and Swindon Archive, Chippenham.
29. Kerr, ibid. Tinney's lands included Higher Ham Farm.
30. Silton Women's Institute (1983), *Silton, Records of a Dorset Village.* From which we also learn that the water was sprayed or 'lecked' over the flax from long-handled oval-shaped brass bowls. The stalks were then re-bleached and beaten hard with hammers until they divided into fine, smooth fibres.
31. Baileys Western, Midland, and London Directory, 1783-4; Extracts from Universal British Directory, 1793-8.
32. Inventories in DHC.
33. National Archives inventory PRO PROB4/11901, copy in DHC; *Silton, Records etc,* ibid.
34. The principal source for the Gillingham Silk Mill is the note in *SDNQ* XIV 1915, p.289. The information was supplied by the great-grandson of Stephen Hannam.
35. Ibid.
36. Ross, M.S. in *PDNHAS* 113 (1991), and 114 (1992); Bellamy P. in *PDNHAS* 125 (2003).
37. Document of the Sun Fire Insurance company, from Dr John Shepphard.
38. Pigot's Directory of Dorset, 1823.
39. Inventories from the National Archives, transcripts in the DHC: Blacker PROB4 /3641.
40. Ibid., Nason PROB4/7792; Carrant PROB4/3357; Ellis from DHC files.
41. Pigot's Directory, ibid.
42. DHC D/GIM/A7/1/1.
43. DHC D/GIM A7/2/1.

Chapter 7: 1680 to 1820: manor, church, and parish

1. An 1895 Parish Council meeting recorded the existence of several books of parish records, including workhouse account books 1771-1813, vestry books 1799-1843, poor rate books 1779-1844, and highway books 1800-1855. None of these are known today.
2. The Gillingham Local History Society has produced a brief history of the Lock-up.
3. Cited in Biggs B.J. (1987), *The Wesleys and the Early Dorset Methodists,* p.14. Reward poster in Gillingham Museum.
4. DHC Churchwardens accounts.
5. Howe C. (1983), *Gylla's Hometown,* p.81, and (1992) *GLHS* Journal. The top of the well structure was made of bricks from the Silverthorn brick yard, the remainder of the well to a depth of 25 feet being of stone from a quarry in Pierston Lane. A bore hole was then sunk through 65 feet of clay and a further 8 to 10 feet of rock to tap the water below. The well structure was fully revealed when the Vicarage wall was moved in 1980.
6. Hutchins p. 617. All following references relating to the courts are from the Gillingham manor court books in the Dorset History Centre.
7. WSHC D27/7/3/3.
8. WSHC D27/15/2.

9. Hutchins p.647, and other sources. Edward Emily was a major benefactor to St. Nicholas' Hospital at Harnham, Salisbury. He left his property without condition to his friend Bishop Barrington, who was able to fulfil what he knew to be Emily's intentions by selling the estate and leaving the proceeds to the hospital, giving it its most important benefaction since medieval times. *Victoria County History of Wiltshire*, Vol.3, pp.343-56.

10. Biggs, op.cit, p.53.

11. Wagner A.F.H.V. (1956), *The Church of St. Mary the Virgin, Gillingham*, p.50-1; WSHC D27/15/3a and 3b.

12. The Royal Lancastrian Society was founded by Joseph Lancaster; it was noted for its use of the monitorial system of teaching. It was later renamed the British and Foreign School Society.

13. *Gillingham Sunday School Society Fifth Annual Report, 1820.*

14. WSHC Visitation book D27/13/1.

15. DHC D/GIM A1/1 Churchwardens accounts.

16. Churchwardens accounts ibid.

17. Wagner, ibid., pp.44-5.

18. WSHC Visitation book D27/13/1.

19. WSHC D27/6/4, Acts in cases of legacies.

20. Biggs p.53.

21. Biggs pp.53, 59. Lloyd D, '200 Years of Methodism in Gillingham', *GLHS Journal*, 1993. WSHC Visitation book D27/13/1.

22. DHC Shaftesbury Society minute books.

23. This account of the tithe dispute is taken from Kerr, B. (1968) *Bound to the Soil: a Social History of Dorset*, pp.173-8.

24. Kerr ibid., and WSHC D27/6/4.

25. Kerr, ibid.

26. Wagner A.F.H.V. (1958) *Gillingham Grammar School, Dorset.* p.13.

27. Wagner, ibid, pp.23-28. The feoffees reappointed in 1810 were the Rev. Weston Fullerton, Edward Hannam, Henry Martin, William Mullins, Henry Bigging, William Bell, and William Whitacker. The new feoffees were John Matthews of Milton, William Godwin, Josiah Hannam, Samuel Davis of Silton, and Morgan Dove Blandford of Swallowcliffe .

28. *Sherborne Mercury*, April 27 1737.

29. WSHC Visitation book D27/13/1; Wagner, ibid.

30. DHC D/GIM/K9/1-3.

31. DHC D/GIM/A3/3/1 The memo, of 70 handwritten pages, covers appeals, the many ways in which settlement can be claimed, removals, the operation of the poor rate, poor relief, the overseers accounts, bastardy, filiation, apprentices, and vagrants.

32. This and the following material is from the overseers' account books, DHC DIM A3/1. There are some transcriptions and notes in the Gillingham Museum.

33. Dr Thomas Tatum (1681-1757) of Mere had seven children, three of whom were also doctors. Thomas junr (1712-67) and Harry (b.1722) also practised in the town. John (b.1724) was a surgeon at Salisbury

General Infirmary. Thomas junr is commemorated by a tablet in Mere church. From Longbourne, D. (2004) *The Book of Mere*, p.26.

34. Report of the Commissioners of Inquiry Concerning Charities, 1836. (HMSO 1837). Howe, *Gylla's Hometown*, p.76.

Chapter 8: The Gillingham of John Fisher and Henry Deane

1. This account of Constable's visits to Gillingham is largely based on John Flashman's publication by the Gillingham Local History Society (2000). An earlier description of Constable's Gillingham work appeared in *Country Life,* Dec.14, 1972.
2. The Act relating to the Trust is 26 G 2 c.60; see also Good, R. (1966), *The Old Roads of Dorset*, p.125. DHC D/GIM/A7/1/1, highways account 1791, expenditure by William Bell.
3. No record has been found to indicate that the Wyke cottage was once used as a toll house.
4. Quoted in Flashman, ibid.
5. Act 1 & 2 Wm IV, c.XXX. Good, op. cit., p.137. The Wincanton Trust may already have turnpiked the route from Milton to Bourton by this time. It is thought that there may have been a gate at the Martins Lane and Slodbrook Lane junction.
6. 1822 flyer in Gillingham Museum; Pigot directories for 1823, 1830
7. Dewhurst R. (2005), *Crosstracks to Hindon*, p.62.
8. Bettey J.H. (1977), *Rural Life in Wessex, 1500-1900*, pp.117-8; Kerr, B. (1968), *Bound to the Soil: A Social History of Dorset*, p.182; Jones I. (1993) *The Stalbridge Inheritance, 1780-1854,* p.75.
9. Bettey, ibid; Kerr, ibid; Meeting notice, Gillingham Museum.
10. Meeting notice, Gillingham Museum.
11. Lloyd D, 'Poverty and Distress Part 2: The Shaftesbury Union 1835-40,' *GLHS Journal*, 2001.
12. Ibid.
13. DHC D/GIM A2/1/1 Vestry minutes.
14. Feoffees minute book.
15. Wagner A.F.H.V.(1958) *Gillingham Grammar School, Dorset*, pp.30-2.
16. Notes on the history of Gillingham Grammar School by A.H. Mumford, Gillingham Museum; Wagner, ibid.
17. Lloyd D (1993), '200 Years of Methodism in Gillingham', *GLHS* Journal.
18. Some of the early Baptists were George Way, Paul Alcock, John Webb, David Bridgeman, James Hannam, Thomas Pierce Giles, Joseph James, Samuel French, John Brit, and William Winter; DHC QDP (M): R3/38, railway proposal.
19. DHC Shaftesbury Meeting House minutes. After 1804 the Shaftesbury Friends joined with the other groups mentioned here, and meetings were held at each house in turn on a monthly basis. Edward Neave, Josiah Hannam, and other members of the Neave and Hannam families travelled regularly to these meetings at this time.
20. DHC D/GIM F6 1/1-3

21. DHC D/GIM A2/1/1 Vestry minutes Nov-Dec. 1858.
22. Flashman, ibid.
23. Ash J. (1982), *Victorian Vicar: The Story of Henry Deane*, p.17.
24. C.H. Mayo in *SDNQ* 1917 pp.25, 73.
25. Ash, ibid. Kerr, ibid. p.184.
26. Wagner, A.F.H.W. (1956) *The Church of St. Mary the Virgin, Gillingham*, pp.17-23. Historic Churches Preservation Trust, ICBS plans 01733. The new floor is the explanation for the unusual feature of steps down into the chancel.
27. Kerr, ibid., p.187. Ash, p.18. Wagner, ibid., reveals that the food consumed at thus celebratory meal included 46lb of boiled beef, 40lb of roast beef, a whole ham .... and many other items.
28. Mayo, *SDNQ* ibid. p.210.
29. Ash, ibid., p.19-20.
30. Ash, ibid., p.21.
31. Kerr, ibid. p.190-2.
32. Allman R, 'Matthews Wyke Brewery: 200 years of brewing', *GLHS* 1992. Pigot and Kelly directory entries.
33. Ash, ibid., p.26-7.

Chapter 9: Around Gillingham on the eve of the Railway Age

1. Most of this chapter is based on the Tithe Map and Schedule of 1841, the 1841 and 1851 censuses, and the several trade directories of this period. The tithe schedule was updated in 1863, and this has helped to provide some of the later information. Some of the architectural references are from the *Historical Monuments* volume produced by RCHM in 1972.
2. Chantry Cottage is the former Chantry House used for manor courts by Sherborne School (see earlier chapters). In 1841 it was occupied by Robert Candy, a saddler and harness maker.
3. The range facing the Phoenix was later occupied by the physician Dr. Theophilus Woods (Chapter 12).
4. The blacksmith at this time was Nathaniel Read. I am grateful to the present occupiers of the Old Toll House for allowing me to see the deeds of this house.
5. There has long been a gap in this range of buildings, opposite the church west door, over which the church formerly claimed a right of way.
6. Ann Lawrence died in 1852 aged 65; her memorial stone is in the Wesley Garden.
7. *GLHS* Journal, 2001, where there is more detail on this house. I am grateful to Dr John Shepphard for further information about The Barton and its history.
8. *GLHS* Journal, 2000.
9. Wagner A.F.H.V. (1958), *Gillingham Grammar School, Dorset*, p.26.
10. DHC D/GIM/K1/1-4. These include accounts of land tax, church rates, etc, paid for the Red Lion between 1739 and 1754.
11. This row of buildings is clearly shown on sales details for Barnaby's Farm, 1855 (Gillingham Museum).
12. Brickmaking references by Ross

M.S. in *PDNHAS* 113 (1991) pp.17-22, and 114 (1992) pp.263-4

Chapter 10: The Coming of the Railway

1. Nicholas J. and Reeve G. (2007), *Main Line to the West: Part 2, Salisbury to Yeovil*, pp. 175-8.
2. Gillingham Museum, sale particulars of Barnaby's Farm, 1855, occupied by John Dunn, who was also a carrier; 'and a favourable opportunity is now offered to the purchaser of continuing and increasing such trade in connection with the intended Salisbury and Yeovil Railway.'
3. Nicholas and Reeve, ibid. Ruegg L. (1878), *The History of a Railway*, p.2.
4. Kerr, B. (1968) *Bound to the Soil: A Social History of Dorset*, p.191.
5. DHC QDP (M): Misc 10
6. DHC 1836 QDP(M): R3/4; 1844 R3/10; 1851 R3/38.
7. Nicholas and Reeve, ibid. Ruegg, ibid., p.1.
8. DHC S235: A4/3/6. The company surveyor was Thomas Matthews of Gillingham.
9. DHC D/FAN Gillingham Manor Court Books.
10. Ruegg, ibid. Nicholas & Reeve, p.179-80.
11. Nicholas and Reeve, p.65.
12. Ibid. p77.
13. Ibid, pp.180, 186.
14. Carver, B. (2009), *Gillingham 2009: A brief history celebrating 150 years of the Railway*, p.15.
15. Nicholas and Reeve, pp.63-4;

16. DHC Parish Council minutes D/GIM C1/1/1.
17. Gillingham Parish Magazine, October 1879; Howe C. (1983), *Gylla's Hometown*, p.96.
18. Nicholas and Reeve, p.69.

Chapter 11: 1860 to 1914: Gillingham at work

1. DHC, Gillingham manor court books, vols. 32-34.
2. Much of what follows in this chapter is based on the entries in the Post Office, Kelly and other directories for Dorset, and on the many local trade advertisements in these directories and elsewhere. An outline of Gillingham's industrial development was given by Robin Lord's 'Industrious Gillingham' articles in the *Dorset County Magazine* nos. 30-32, 1973, and some of the detail from these articles has been drawn upon. Charles Howe's lively portrayal of Gillingham in *Gylla's Hometown* is another source of detail on the trades and businesses of this time.
3. Jefferys also opened a livestock market in Shaftesbury in 1902.
4. DHC D301/1-3.
5. DHC D301/4. William Horwood Oake (1840-89) is recorded in the 1870s as a wine merchant living in Lambeth; no record has been found of his work as a bacon curer. Evan Down (b.1849) was the son of Edwin Down, architect and surveyor of Wembdon, near Bridgwater. The technique of using ice-houses in the bacon curing

industry was patented by George Harris of Calne; other bacon producers took up this method under licence.

6. In 1894 Eden Shute advertised in the *Dorset County Chronicle* for more butter from local farmers; he would supply the necessary baskets and cloths and pay carriage from the nearest station.

7. United Dairies were later to join with Cow and Gate to become Unigate. Aplin & Barrett of Yeovil, who took over Shutes, were also later absorbed into Unigate (see later chapters).

8. Allman R, 'Matthews Wyke Brewery: 200 years of brewing', *GLHS* 1992.

9. Howe C. (1983), *Gylla's Hometown*, pp.97-101.

10. Howe, ibid., pp.106-8. Hudson & Martin 1865-1965 Centenary booklet, Gillingham Museum.

11. DHC D/GIM F8/1/5/1 Maloney coal ledgers for 1889-92; DHC D/GIM F8/1/6/1 coal journals for 1894-7.

12. DHC D/GIM F8/1/4/5 Maloney meal day book 1895-6.

13. DHC D/GIM F8/1/7/1 Maloney stores journal 1893-4.

14. The complaints continued up to the time of the factory's closure (Chapter 15). The town Medical Health Officer was once heard to say 'Bring me a corpse and I will close it in minutes', but the factory remained open.

15. Howe, ibid., p.110; Maloney factory sale agreement in Gillingham Museum.

16. Howe, ibid.

17. Howe, ibid., pp.87-92.

18. Howe, ibid.

19. Lord, 'Industrious Gillingham', 30, p.47.

20. Howe, pp.123-4.

21. Apprenticeship indentures held by the Gillingham Museum.

22. Day book of Shepphard's tailors, DHC D/GIM/F2/1

23. Crocker P. (1992), *Around Gillingham, The Second Selection*, p.108.

24. Bettey J.H. *Discover Dorset: Farming*, pp.44-6.

25. Minute books of the Gillingham and Shaftesbury Agricultural Societies. I am grateful to Sam Braddick for allowing me to see these.

26. Ibid.

27. Ibid.

Chapter 12: 1860 to 1914: The Gillingham of the Freames

1. Pike W.T. (1906, ed.) *Contemporary Biographies (of Wiltshire and Dorset)*, p.279. Freame's home, 'The Chantry' is not to be confused with the much older 'Chantry Cottage' a little further along the riverside.

2. Gillingham Museum (2003), *The Freame Diaries: Excerpts from the Diaries of Ethel Freame, 1897-1900*. Other volumes of the *Diaries* are being transcribed by members of the Gillingham Local History Society, but are not yet published. Robert Freame was eventually baptised a Catholic in 1909, towards the very end of his life.

3. DHC Parish Council minutes D/GIM C1/1/1. The first 15 councillors elected were Bertram E. Freame, Theophilis Woods, H.P. Green, Gerrard G. Matthews, Mark Churchill, W.M. Branson, Bernard D. Jupe, John H. Rose, H.J. Wadman, Henry Kaines, G.P. Hornby, Rev. S.E. Davies, J. Staddon, Thomas Tucker, and Thomas Hayter. Dr. T.Woods was elected to the Chair. Messrs Green and Staddon later stood down for Charles Mead and Joseph Shute. The subsequent history of the Parish Council can be followed in *GLHS* Journal, 1995.

4. DHC Parish Council minutes, ibid.

5. DHC Urban Committee minutes 1898-1910, D/GIM C1/6/1.

6. DHC Vestry minutes D/GIM A2/1/1; D/GIM C5/3/1.

7. DHC Parish Council minutes D/GIM C1/1/1.

8. Ibid.

9. *GLHS* Newsletter, No.4 (1981) and No.10 (1987).

10. The Ham well stood at the corner of Kings Court Road inside its own brick shelter, and had the wheatsheaf insignia of the Duke of Westminster; it is now in the Museum. At Colesbrook it was reported that there was 'a population of about 80 who were dependent on the polluted River Shreen for their water supply', while 'the whole of the tenements here have to rely on the river'; Parish Council minutes. A distinctive development in Milton was the wind-powered pump to supply the Matthews family homes, erected in 1896.

11. Parish Council minutes and *GLHS* Journal, 1992.

12. DHC Parish Council minutes C1/1/1; C1/2/1; report in *Three Shires Advertiser* 23 Aug. 1913; *GLHS* Journal 1994.

13. Map in Gillingham Museum. This map is not dated and appears to include information from several dates between around 1890 and the early 1900s.

14. DHC Vestry minutes D/GIM A2/1/1. Good R. (1966), *The Old Roads of Dorset,* Ch.6.

15. Parish Council minutes op.cit. Other similar gates, perhaps from the same time, can be found behind Waitrose and in Chantry Fields. Some of the gates bear the name of B.P. Edwards, who had a smithy in the High Street.

16. Parish Council Minutes op.cit; *GLHS* Journal 1995.

17. DHC Parish Council Minutes PC/GIL acc.8991.

18. Parish Council Minutes C1/1/1.

19. Ibid.

20. Wagner A.F.H.W (1958) *Gillingham Grammar School, Dorset,* pp.37-41.

21. Wagner, pp.41-58.

22. The first governing body was John W. Bell, Josiah Hannam, James H. Dunn, William P. Laurence, James Herridge (all Vestry); Rev. Henry Deane, Robert S. Freame, Philip W. Matthews, George Parham, Henry Kaines jr (all Feofees); Henry S. Bower (Dorchester Grammar School); Rev. Osborne W. Tancock (King's School, Sherborne).

Wagner, ibid. et seq.

23. Staff register, Gillingham School Records.

24. Wagner, ibid.

25. Wagner ibid., and governors' minutes; school prospectus. Miss Dunn's School was the building which later became the Masonic Lodge.

26. Grammar School admissions register, Gillingham School Records.

27. In January 1874 the following were elected by the Vestry as a School Board: John Williams Bell, Josiah Hannam, James Henry Dunn, James Herridge, and William Paul Laurence.

28. School log books, Gillingham School Records.

29. Kelly Directory, 1911.

30. School log books, Gillingham School Records.

31. 1871 Census and directories.

32. Ash J. (1982), *Victorian Vicar, The Story of Henry Deane*, pp. 28-30.

33. DHC Easter Vestry minutes D/ GIM A2/1/2 ; papers in Gillingham Museum.

34. Gillingham Parish Magazines, Gillingham Museum.

35. Deane's successors through this period were Edward Inman (1882-91), Sidney Davies (1891-9), William Heygate (1899-1905), and Walter Sotheby (1905-1916); In 1895 Rev. Davies' curates were Walter C.K. Sylvester and Arthur S.G. Peters; In 1905 the curates were Marshall W. Lumsden, Charles M. Gay, and John C. Blackett; Kelly Directories.

36. DHC Easter Vestry minutes D/ GIM A2/1/2.

37. Lloyd D.J. in *GLHS* Journal, 1993.

38. Others identified as Methodists with business interests are John Coombes (corn merchant), James Herridge and George Pitman (High Street grocers), Thomas Hayter (coal merchant) Mark Churchill (dairy factory manager), Edwin Stickland (High Street ironmonger), John Bracher (cabinet maker and builder), and John Harris (gasworks manager). Davis, P. (2004), *Early nineteenth-century Gillingham Wesleyans and Primitive Methodists: a comparison;* unpublished dissertation for Open University.

39. Newspaper report in Gillingham Museum.

40. From information in the Gillingham Museum, researched by Peter Crocker.

41. Ibid.

42. DHC Parish Council minutes C1/2/1.

43. Gillingham Parish Magazines, Gillingham Museum.

44. Queen Victoria's Jubilee Institute for Nurses was established by Royal Charter in 1889 with the objectives of providing the training and support for a supply of nurses to meet the needs of the sick poor. In 1911 it was suggested that the foundation of a cottage hospital would be a suitable commemoration of the coronation of George V, but was dismissed as too costly (Parish Council minutes).

45. There is a brief history of the Kings

Court Lodge in the *GLHS* Journal for 2003.

46. There had been a Catholic priest in Marnhull since at least the seventeenth century; the present church dates from 1832. Bonham chapel was at Bonham House, Stourton. The Wardour chapel is the All Saints chapel at New Wardour Castle, built for the Arundell family in 1769-76; it still has regular Sunday services. All were local centres of Recusancy. Around 1900 Thomas Matthews made a room available for Catholic worship at Pierston House in Milton.

Chapter 13: Around Gillingham at the turn of the century

1. Treves, Sir F. (1906), *Highways and Byways in Dorset*. 1906. Mates (1899), *Dorsetshire Illustrated*.
2. Auction notice in Gillingham Museum. DHC Gillingham manor court books, vol. 34, April and June 1868.
3. Gillingham manor court books, vols. 33, August 1862 and May 1865.
4. A lot of the detail in the following pages is derived from the Census Returns of 1901 and the trade directories from around this time. The many photographs of the town taken at this time have also helped with the identification of premises and occupiers. Many have been reproduced in the two volumes of *Around Gillingham* and *Around Gillingham, a Second Selection*, where some notes on the

photographers can also be found.

5. The bank manager William Green was living here in 1865. By 1871 the manager was Joseph Mullings. In 1877 he moved with the bank to the new premises in the High Street; Bell and Freame then moved into The Square from previous premises in St. Martin's Square. Mullings lived at the High Street bank until around 1895-1900 when he moved to Fairview on Wyke Road.
6. The 'Eclipse' car was made here (Chapter 14). The glove company was Southcombes.
7. Those living along this road in 1901 included Patrick Cleary, Colour Sergeant of the Volunteers, and Alfred Barnes, a builder. William Cobbett, Assistant Curate, and James Lodder, cemetery keeper and gardener, occupied the Cemetery Cottages.
8. DHC D/GIM A2/1/1 Vestry minutes May 26 1881: Burial Board to be allowed to build on their own ground a place for tools and a mortuary.
9. Ann Elizabeth Martin was also Hudson's daughter, Hudson having been in business with his son-in-law (Chapter 12). The other members of the household were Hudson's own daughter Mary Jane, seven Martin children and grandchildren, and three servants; the need for the large house seems clear. It is not known why the former chapel became known as Portland House. Further along the street the baker was Walter Collins, who came from Bognor.

10. The lower end of Turners Lane is marked 'Victoria Place' in the 1901 census. The supposed explanation for the observation 'tower' is that it allowed the owner to look across to his own land; it was once higher than it is now. In 1901 the District Nurse was Harriett Peck, who came from King's Lynn. In 1905 Arthur Edward Light was living at The Haven.

11. Some businesses recorded in Peacemarsh at this time were those of William Read, a grocer and picture framer; J. Ball, a grocer and bookbinder; William Bealing, a bookmaker; Thomas Cave, a cutler and umbrella maker; Frank and Charles Bealing, carmen and wood dealers; and Albert Hellyar, a blacksmith and farrier. The Bay Store shop of Robert Lush is also recorded.

12. Mr Freame's 'Chantry' is entirely unrelated to the chantry chapel of medieval times (Chapter 2), or to the 'Chantry House' where later courts were held (Chapters 5 and 6).

13. Folly's End seems to be the 'Wyke cottage' of the 1901 census, occupied by the retired solicitor John W. Bell; in earlier years he had lived at Sandley. Rosebank in 1901 was the home of George Godwin, the auctioneer; Mountview in 1902 of the Inland Revenue Officer Thomas A. Martin, and in 1911 of the tailor Clarence Shephard. Older pictures of Wyke House show that the frontage included a porch with columns.

14. The 1901 occupations of residents included characteristic brewery employments such as carter, cooper, cellarman, drayman, groom, and wheelwright.

15. Fernbank and the adjoining shop were acquired in 1868 by James Bond from Josiah Hannam as 'house and shop now in course of erection' (Manor court book vol.34 p.381). By the 1920s Bowles had become Peach's, a tobacconist and hairdresser. Fish's shop was later used by Hudson and Martin as a showroom; the site has since been redeveloped.

16. The Hann's shop later became Brice's butchers, which it remained until the 1950s. It is now an estate agent. In 1861 James Herridge was loaned £500 by the Gillingham General Permanent Building Society for a house with a shop and stores in Newbury formerly in the tenure of Richard Light; Manor court book vol.33 p.344.

17. From 1860 the land in the corner between Station Road and the High Street was owned by Thomas Hayter, who was a road surveyor for the parish. The Hayters operated a coal business from one of the Station Road cottages until at least the 1900s.

18. Above, and note 3; Advance of mortgage to James George and George Cave, builders, for messuages in course of erection.

19. Before 1890 this area belonged to Nathaniel Benjafield, who had an auction yard here, and to Thomas Tucker, a coal merchant who lived

at Newbury House. Maloney's expansion seems to have been very much at the expense of Tucker's land and property.

20. Manor court book vol.34 p.381, April 1868, Joseph Light to Edward Light, parcel of ground in Newbury on east side of road to station, together with a messuage divided into two dwellings now in course of erection. The field referred to was later owned by Sam Braddick for his agricultural machinery business. In 1901 Edward Light's house was the detached brick Laurel Villa.

21. James George had built the houses in Station Road described earlier; he also owned the cottages and property extending towards Lodden Farm.

22. In the 1901 census the Weare hotel had only one boarder; Harwood House was a lodging house run by Catherine Field and her sister Beatrice, and had three boarders. The association of Lanark Villas with a similarly named property in London is explored by John Pinnock in the *GLHS* Journal for 1995.

Chapter 14: Gillingham in war and peace, 1914 to 1939

1. Freame Diaries, August 1914, Gillingham Museum.

2. Ibid.

3. *History of the Dorsetshire Regiment, 1914-19. Part II: The Territorial Units.* Howe, C (1983), *Gylla's Hometown*, p.177-8.

4. Lloyd, D. (2001), 'Gillingham and the Great War Part 1', *GLHS* Journal.

5. Lloyd, D. (2002), 'Gillingham and the Great War Part 2', *GLHS* Journal. Senior boys from the Grammar School were detailed to meet the trains at Gillingham Station and escort the walking wounded to their hospitals (from Mr. A. Woodcock, aged 96 in 2000).

6. Lloyd, D. (2005), 'Gillingham at War Part 5', *GLHS* Journal.

7. Lloyd, D. (1992), '75 Years Ago – Devastating Floods in Gillingham.' *GLHS* Journal. Reported in *Western Gazette*, July 6th 1917.

8. From detail on the Gillingham Church website researched by Theresa Goatham. The three were Henry Hooper, Robert Lockett, and Henry Vincent, who died in the explosion on *HMS Bulwark* in September 1914, an incident which cost over 700 lives.

9. Ibid.

10. Lloyd, D (2001), 'Gillingham and the Great War Part 1', *GLHS* Journal.

11. The original reredos design was rejected as being too large for the church, darkening the chancel. Carlton Cross established a trust to maintain the chapel; £1250 was invested producing an income of £54 in 1931 (Museum records).

12. These were son-in-law Robert Lancaster, the father of Osbert Lancaster, the cartoonist; and a nephew, George Kitson.

13. The church in a Grade 2 listed building. The inspiration for its design is considered to be St.

Agnes, Freshwater, built 1908 by the architect Isaac Jones. Charles Manger died in 1929; his son, Lt. Col William Bourne Manger, last of the name, died in 1954.

14. Arthur 'Dinger' Bell is said to have acquired a portrait of Earl Haig for the Club; he then took it to London, where he talked his way into Earl Haig's office in order that the Field Marshal could sign it.

15. United Dairies was formed in 1917 by a merger between Wiltshire United Dairies, Metropolitan and Great Western Dairies, and the Dairy Supply Company.

16. Lloyd D. (2000), 'Registers of motor cars and cycles', *GLHS* Journal. Baker, V.N. (1993), '80 years of P.O. Baker', *GLHS* Journal. Information on Sticklands is from Crocker, P. (1992), *Around Gillingham, A Second Selection*.

17. *GLHS* Newsletter, 1988. The proprietors were G.B. Gush and Mr. Le Croisette.

18. Howe, *Gylla's Hometown*, pp.116, 137-8. Shaftesbury RDC minutes; winter (November-January) hours were shorter; the rate of pay was subsequently increased to match that of contractors.

19. Howe, ibid.

20. Green, J. 'Life on the Farm', *GLHS* Journal, 2011.

21. Gillingham Agricultural Society minutes.

22. Railway figures derived from Southern Railway, Western Division, Traffic Statistics; another 'vital' statistic was the number of lavatory pennies collected, which showed a small decline over the period. Oake, Woods information from company minutes and Chamber of Commerce handbook, Gillingham Museum; the directors at this time were Evan B. Down, H. Brown, and Harold Dale. Hudson and Martin information from Trading Accounts, Gillingham Museum.

23. The name was subsequently changed to the Gillingham Chamber of Commerce and Industry. The first officers were E.B. Down (President), J. Cole (Hon. Treasurer), Eno Nicholson (Hon. Secretary), H.C. Wyld (Hon. Solicitor). The Committee was W.E. Samways, E.J. Stickland, W.G. Hughes, S. Braddick, Miss J. Down, R.J.G Shute, E.A. Martin, R.J. Bracher, A.H. Pheby, Mrs G.J. Shephard, J.J.W. Slade, J.J. Nicholson, G. Brice, J. Case; Chamber Book of Minutes 1930-2, Gillingham Museum.

24. From information supplied by Sam Woodcock. The shops in Gillingham were in Queen Street (now the Wine Bar), and in the High Street (Cheapside House).

25. DHC DC/SYR, Minute Books, 4.7.1918 and 10.7.1924. Gillingham Museum letters, 1937.

26. From a section of Osbert Lancaster's *All Done from Memory* reprinted in the *GLHS* Journal, 2007. The baronet referred to is most likely to be Sir Harold Pelly of Thorngrove, but could also be Lord Stalbridge of Motcombe House.

27. Lancaster's childhood memory

may not have served him entirely well, for he writes that the smells were of brewing and that the station buildings were of yellow brick.

28. Most of the local government references which follow are drawn from DHC DC/SYR, Minute Books of Shaftesbury Rural District Council.

29. Water references from DHC DC/SYR. Lighting from Parish Council papers in Gillingham Museum. Gas detail from Chamber of Trade Shopping Week handbook.

30. DHC DC/SYR. Peacemarsh Terrace, a block of four cottages, may date from the early 1920s.

31. DHC DC/SYR, Lodbourne Farm housing plans, 1936-9.

32. DHC DC/SYR Shaftesbury RDC Minutes; DHC DCC A9/1/10 Dorset County Council, Minutes of General Purposes Committee. Gillingham Parish Council Report of Committee, March 1931. The other Urban Districts in Dorset were Sherborne, Wimborne, Swanage, and Portland, all with larger populations than Gillingham.

33. The enclosure was reported in the *Western Gazette*, 19 March 1925. Burial ground papers are Shaftesbury RDC DC/SYR in DHC, 1937-8. When Major Freame died in 1936 his property consisted of Chantry Farm with 54 acres (value £2500), Higherfield (£2500), the Catholic church, old Drill Hall, and 15 cottages in and around the town (Gillingham Museum).

34. Chamber of Trade handbooks, 1931-1936.

35. Ibid. The Southern National bus company was a subsidiary of the Southern Railway.

36. Wagner A.F.H.V (1958), *Gillingham Grammar School, Dorset,* pp.59-60.

37. Dorset County Council: Development Plan (Education Act, 1944). Mr. Lock had previously been headmaster of the Elementary (Board) School.

38. Lord R. 'Industrious Gillingham', (1973), *Dorset County Magazine,* no. 31. The Regal was built by Williams Bros. of Shaftesbury and designed by E. De Wilde Holding, a well known Bournemouth architect responsible for cinemas elsewhere in Dorset, Somerset, and Devon; Dyson P. *A Century of Cinema in Dorset,* p.34.

39. Chamber of Trade handbook, 1935.

Chapter 15: Gillingham in war and peace, 1939 to 1974

1. Howe, C. (1983), *Gylla's Hometown,* pp.185-6. Lloyd, D. (2006), 'Gillingham at War Part 6', *GLHS* Journal.

2. Ibid.

3. I am grateful to Mrs. Suter for her notes on life as an evacuee in Gillingham (Gillingham Museum).

4. 'Gillingham at War', Part 6.

5. Lloyd, D. (2008), 'Gillingham at War Part 8', *GLHS* Journal; and (2009), Part 9. J.E. Allbrook, Mere Museum Monograph no.6; Zeals airfield was used mainly by the USAAF from 1943.

6. Lloyd, D. 'Gillingham at War Part

7', *GLHS* Journal 2007.

7. Among the locally born were William Collis, Albert Hunt of Mere, Ernest and Reginald Sharpe, both of Hunger Hill, Leonard Gatehouse, Ronald Davies, Percy Alger, Frank Tucker, Kenneth Read, Dick E. Dear of Kington Magna, Charles Kingham, Philip Pitman of Motcombe, and Ernest Smith of Milton.

8. DHC SYR/DC Shaftesbury Rural District Council, extracts from housing committee minutes, clerk's correspondence and papers on housing tenancies.

9. Shaftesbury RDC Annual Report of Medical Officer of Health, 1952.

10. Gillingham Museum papers. Even today Milton on Stour still has no mains sewerage, gas, or street lighting. The bus shelter date is from the town website.

11. Gillingham Museum papers.

12. Carver, B. (2009), *Gillingham 2009: a brief history celebrating 150 years of the Railway.*

13. DHC S.289/1/1, DHC S.289/1/2, Minutes of the Modern School 1951-9.

14. Ibid. Also D. Lloyd (2010), '50 Years of Comprehensive Education', *GLHS* Journal, based on an interview with John Webster.

15. Minutes of Coronation Club Committee, Gillingham Museum.

16. Letters from Col. Wallis, Gillingham Museum.

17. *Dorset Life*, March 2005.

18. The first Committee of the Society included R.G.J. Shute (Chairman), J. Burtt (Secretary and Treasurer), and Lt. Col. C.R.A. Wallis (Curator). Capt. G.B. Matthews was the first President.

19. The next few paragraphs are based on the information in Lord R. (1973), 'Industrious Gillingham', *Dorset County Magazine,* pp.30-32.

20. DHC GIM C1/1 Gillingham Parish Council minutes 24.8.1970.

21. *Western Gazette* 29.11.1963 and 28.2.1964. The closure of Templecombe brought about the loss of 257 jobs. Many references to railway developments generally are to be found in Nicholas J. and Reeve G. (2007), *Main Line to the West: Part 2, Salisbury to Yeovil.*

22. Nicholas and Reeve, various references.

23. DHC PC/GIL acc. 8991 Parish Council minutes 1965-66. Report in Municipal and Public Services Management Journal, 19.8.1966.

24. *Western Gazette* 9.9.1966.

25. Gillingham Local Plan, 1971; also used as basis for the following paragraphs.

26. Local Plan, ibid. Parish Council minutes 13.8.1969.

27. Parish Council minutes 24.4.1972.

28. Ibid. 23.10.1972.

29. Ibid, various references as indicated. The Parish Council of June 1971 was made up of S.P. Hiscott (Chairman). E. Batho, M.R.R. Miles, A.R. Coombes, F.H. Evill, E.A.R. Hart, D. Kendall, S.J.F .Lockyer, S.J. Maidment, K.R. Newport, E.R. Samways, W. Sloan, R.B. Weeks, R. Whitmarsh.

Chapter 16: Expansion and change since 1974

1. The Town Council of September 1975 was A. Coombes (chair), S. Hiscott, E. Samways, J. Sheen, E. Batho, D. Dear, R. Weeks, S. Ballard, F. Evill, R. Whitmarsh, Mrs. H. Burt, Mrs. R.D. Grouchy, M. Pike, G. Jones, M. Osmond.

2. Over the years Mr. Wathen has been the winner of many contest as a crier, including overseas competitions.

3. Gillingham Local Plan (1986), North Dorset District Council. Most of the references which follow are taken from the Plan.

4. Approval for the scheme was eventually achieved by a visit to London by Gillingham councillors to present the case to the Roads Minister.

5. The 1986 Plan was reviewed by a Working Party which reported in March 1992. The North Dorset District Wide Local Plan was revised in 2003, and is still current.

6. 1991 Chamber of Commerce and Industry Directory.

7. More detail on the early history of the band can be found in the *GHLS* Journal for 2008; this had been written by Charles Howe some years earlier.

8. Gillingham Landscapes and Open Spaces Assessment Report, North Dorset District Council, February 2004.

9. Milton on Stour Village Plan, 2009.

Select Bibliography

This is a list of works which refer to Gillingham in a general way, or provide useful background information and context to the town's development. The many manuscript and secondary sources used for this study of Gillingham, including specialist articles, are fully referenced in the notes to the chapters.

Ash J. *Victorian Vicar: The Story of Henry Deane*. Gillingham, 1982.

Bayley A.R. *The Great Civil War in Dorset, 1642-1660*. Taunton, 1910.

Bettey J.H. *Discover Dorset: Farming*. Wimborne, 2000.

Biggs B.J. *The Wesleys and the Early Dorset Methodists*. Gillingham, 1987.

Carver, B. *Gillingham 2009: A brief history celebrating 150 years of the Railway*. Gillingham, 2009.

Claridge, J. *A General View of the Agriculture of the County of Dorset*. London, 1793.

Crocker P. (ed.) *Around Gillingham, The Second Selection*. Stroud, 1992.

Coker, W. *Thomas Gerard's Survey of Dorsetshire*. London, 1732.

Cunliffe, B. *Wessex to AD 1000*. London, 1993.

Dewhurst R. *Crosstracks to Hindon*. East Knoyle, 2005.

Dorset County Council: Development Plan (Education Act, 1944),1946.

Dyson P. *A Century of Cinema in Dorset*. Ferndown,1996.

Evans T.S. (ed). *The Life of Robert Frampton, Bishop of Gloucester*. London, 1876.

Good, R. *The Old Roads of Dorset*. Bournemouth, 1966.

Goodwin T. *Dorset in the Civil War, 1625-65*. Dorset Books, 1996.

Green, M. *A Landscape Revealed: 10,000 Years on a Chalkland Farm*. Stroud, 2000.

Haime, J.W. *The Haimes – A Dorset Family*. Wimborne, 1970.

Haslam J. (ed.) *Anglo-Saxon Towns in Southern England*. Chichester, 1984.

History of the Dorsetshire Regiment, 1914-19. Part II: The Territorial Units. Dorchester, 1932.

Hutchins, J. *The History and Antiquities of the County of Dorset*. London, 1861-4, repr. 1973.

Howe, C. *Gylla's Hometown*. Gillingham, 1983.

Inventory of Historical Monuments in the County of Dorset. Volume IV, North. Royal Commission on Historical Monuments. London, 1972.

Kerr, B. *Bound to the Soil: A Social History of Dorset*. London, 1968.

Lloyd, D. (ed.) *Around Gillingham*. Stroud, 1998.

Longbourne, D. *The Book of Mere*. Wellington, 2004.

Mates Illustrated Guide. *Dorsetshire Illustrated: A Complete Handbook to the County of Dorset, its History and Antiquities.* Bournemouth, 1899.

Mills A.D. *The Place-names of Dorset.* English Place-Name Society, Part III. Cambridge, 1989.

Nicholas J. and Reeve G. *Main Line to the West: Part 2, Salisbury to Yeovil.* Clophill, 2007.

Page W. (ed.) *Victoria County History of Dorset.* London, 1908.

Pike W.T. (ed.) *Contemporary Biographies (of Wiltshire and Dorset),* 1906.

Penn, K.J. *Historic Towns in Dorset.* Dorchester, 1980.

Porter, J. *Discover Dorset: Towns.* Wimborne, 2008.

Putnam, Bill. *Roman Dorset.* Stroud, 2007.

Roscoe E.H. (ed.) *The Marn'll Book.* Gillingham, 1952.

Ruegg L. *The History of a Railway,* 1878.

Ruegg L.H. Farming of Dorsetshire. Prize Report, *Journal of Royal Agric. Society,* vol.15 Part 2, 1854.

Sharp B. *In Contempt of All Authority: Rural Artisans and Riot in the West of England, 1586-1660.* Berkeley, 1980.

Skelton-Wallace J. *A Selection of Parish Churches In and Around Gillingham.* Gillingham, 2004.

Stevenson, W. *A General View of the Agriculture of the County of Dorset.* London, 1815.

The Freame Diaries: Excerpts from the Diaries of Ethel Freame, 1897-1900. Gillingham, 2003.

Treves, Sir F. *Highways and Byways in Dorset.* London, 1906.

Wagner A.F.H.V. *Gillingham Grammar School, Dorset.* Gillingham, 1958.

Wagner A.F.H.V. *The Church of St. Mary the Virgin, Gillingham.* Gillingham, 1956.

INDEX

This index contains references to the text, but not to the notes, appendices, or colour plates.